THE INTRODUCTION OF COMMUNITY SERVICE ORDERS

AN HISTORICAL INTERPRETATION

THE INTRODUCTION OF COMMUNITY SERVICE ORDERS

AN HISTORICAL INTERPRETATION

Shane Kilcommins

Barry Rose Law Publishers Limited
Chichester

Barry Rose Law Publishers Limited
Little London
Chichester

For my family

ACKNOWLEDGEMENTS

In writing this book, I owe a debt of gratitude to a number of people. Warm thanks must initially be offered to all the people who cultivated and nurtured my interest in penal history. These include John B. McLoughlin, Laurence Koffman, Christopher Harding, Craig Lind and Ritchie Ovendale. My journey has also been made easier by my academic colleagues and friends at the University of Wales, Aberystwyth, Waterford Institute of Technology, and, currently, at University College Cork. I am grateful for the advice, encouragement and insights they provided. I am also grateful to Barry Rose Law Publishers (who have had more faith in me than I merit) for offering me the opportunity to work with them. It has been a privilege.

I am especially thankful to Richard W. Ireland for his tireless assistance (mostly beyond the call of duty and not necessarily always in respect of clarifying my thinking on penal issues) over the years. I am extremely fortunate to be able to count on his long-standing friendship and academic guidance. Of all the debts of gratitude, however, perhaps the greatest is that owed to my family. My parents, John and Rena, my sisters, Mary, Emma and Tara, and my wife, Maria, and daughter, Kate, have been unflagging in their support of my academic endeavours. This book is dedicated to them. Needless to say, all faults are mine alone.

CONTENTS

INTRODUCTION

The originality of community service orders as a penal sanction has provoked a considerable amount of debate over the past three decades. Many would argue, given that work has been employed as a means of expiation for offenders throughout the ages, that there is little new about the sanction. The European Committee on Crime Problems, for example, suggested in 1976 that the concept of community service was not new: "it can be traced a long way back into penal history, in various jurisdictions" (European Committee on Crime Problems, 1976:34). Young took this notion a stage further in respect of community service orders in England and Wales. Albeit that he made no substantive attempt to examine work-based penal dispositions from the past, he suggested that work "formed an important element of the regimes of prisons and houses of correction as far back as the sixteenth century, and, in the penal sense, had earlier found expression in other practices such as slavery" (Young 1979:23). Having accepted that the lineage of community service orders could be traced back to past penal practices such as that embodied in the houses of correction, Young was rather perplexed to discover the lack of attention devoted to such an historical parallel in the literature:

"[C]uriously no direct reference was made to this [the phenomenon of utilising the labour of offenders] in the discussions leading up to the community service order.

Instead, the emphasis was placed upon the concept of voluntary service and the development of voluntary organisations" (*ibid*).

In 1980, Pease argued that because the "wages of sin" were often work, one was entitled to ask what was new about community service (Pease 1980:1). Slavery, transportation, penal servitude and houses of correction could all, he suggested, be put forward as community service's "less reputable forebears" (*ibid*). But rather than provide us with an appraisal of these various penal sanctions, he simply described the practice of impressment, which he believed had remarkable parallels when perpended with community service. From this analysis, he concluded that community service was only "in detail a novel disposal" (*ibid*: 5). His approach found approval in Van Kalmthout and Tak's book, titled *Sanction Systems in the Member States of the Council of Europe*, where it was also suggested that impressment and community service had a "remarkable similarity of purpose" (Van Kalmthout and Tak 1988:12). Thus, withstanding that community service was inimitable in that it was measured in hours worked and required the consent of the offender, its uniqueness was somewhat diminished given that the practice of utilising the labour of offenders had a long history. Community service, as Pease would have us believe, accommodated many of the same components as its "less reputable forbears", and was, in essence, merely an augmentation of them - albeit a more sophisticated and innovative augmentation.

In 1984, Vass further extended this framework for

understanding community service orders. By adopting a processual approach, he believed that we could begin "to appreciate the significance of the order and the probable reasons that led to its creation" (Vass 1984:6). After completing this processual approach - it involved a snapshot of sanctions such as bridewells, transportation, impressment, workhouses, hulks and penal servitude - Vass believed he was in a position to reveal that an affinity and continuity existed between penal work sanctions of the past and sanctions such as community service which are advocated in contemporary society: modern punishments are at variance to those in earlier periods only "in shape but not in character" (*ibid*: 9). His argument became even more explicit in 1990. Whilst discussing the lineage of community service, he suggested:

"[I]t is obvious that the enactment of penal policy does not take place in a vacuum. From the Bridewell, the workhouses, the hulks, transportation, impressment ... and beyond, the social forces behind the expansion of controls show a remarkable affinity ... Old and new penal sanctions always appear to share similar backgrounds. New models are like new models of motor cars. We look after them, care for them and polish them with some pride, and ceremonially display them for others to see and envy. When the ageing process sets in, they begin to lose their lustre ... What do we do then? We usually search for an alternative motorcar. We consider our finances. We compare options - what make, what model, to what end. The outcome of that decision-making process is always justified out of expediency ... The process remains the same, car after car. The same with the criminal justice system. Penal options come and go. In particular, "alternatives" (old with new) may coexist for a while but in the long term they join the scrapyard of the criminal justice process; and more "up-market", "innovative" and "desirable" penal measures spring up to take their place. They may look different and their mechanical (operational) layouts may have a higher degree of sophistication, but they are essentially clones of previous models" (Vass 1990: 14-15).

As such, albeit that community service was a more "up-market", "innovative" and "desirable" penal measure, it was, essentially, a "clone" of previous sanctions - such as transportation, impressment, and the hulks - and could not, accordingly, be viewed as prototypical in design.[1]

Of course, Vass would argue that whilst on the one hand

---

1. See also Hoggarth who dedicates a chapter in her book on community service orders to antecedents and cites, *inter alia*, the German tribes of AD 98 and the Inca dynasty in the period between the thirteenth century and 1582, both of which used labour as a form of punishment, together with bridewells, workhouses, the Amsterdam *Rasp-huis* and impressment (Hoggarth 1991:40-51). See also Professor Max Taylor who suggests: "The idea that criminals who prey on the community should pay something back to the community is age-old ... The origins of this response to crime go back to the very beginnings of criminal justice systems. In ancient Roman law, convicted but free criminals could be rendered slaves and bought - the purchase price going to the victim. Echoes can be heard in the Middle Ages practice of forcibly conscripting criminals and vagabonds, a sort of military community service. Indeed transportation to Australia offered a kind of public service to open up that colony" (Taylor 1999: 16).

he believes that the "expansion of controls show a remarkable affinity" and that it is only the "shape of sanctions which undergoes a metamorphosis, not their substance" (Vass 1990:14), he, on the other hand, is also cognisant of the need to avoid packaging history into "square, polished and well-labelled compartments" (*ibid*: 3). It is my contention, however, that attempts to provide a contextual analysis of community service through the utilisation of a prefatory, narrative account of the history of penal work sanctions has little purposive effect. The broad span of its processual approach, and the uncomplicated and undeviating course of progression which it adopts, is spurious in that it either distorts or discounts key forces acting consciously and subconsciously on penal work sanctions at particular moments in time. Furthermore, this method of analysis proceeds as if penal work sanctions have always been governed by the same principles and assumptions. Under this framework of understanding, community service was, in effect, a sanction always fated to appear on the statute books; all that was needed was a sufficient degree of "sophistication" and *savoir faire* to make it happen. As the fictitious Irishman replied to the lost traveller inquiring about the way to Ballynahinch: "if I were you, I would not start from here at all". In the same way, if Professor Vass is fully committed to highlighting the reasons for the introduction of community service orders in 1972, then he should not start his analysis, in my view, with the presumption (which acts as a justification) that all penal work dispositions are in some way governed by the same determinants.

In this book, I adopt a theoretical choice. This choice is founded upon the belief that the history of community service orders is something more than the simple marshalling of work-based penal dispositions of the past into a sequential order. Instead, it is premised on the understanding that the specific sanction of community service is grounded upon a particular set of penal, social, cultural, political and economic practices. Thus, whilst community service may have a long past in that sanctions have embodied work since ancient times, it has a "short history" in that it was driven by a particular and specific complex of penal strategies, agencies, representations and techniques which render anachronistic any unqualified collations between it and past penal work practices.[2] As Fuchs suggested:

"Meines Erachtens ist es jedoch ... falsch, diese historischen Beispiele bis zur heutigen community service order zurückverfolgen zu wollen. Man kann sogar sagen, dass es falsch ist, eine neue Sanktion so vorzustellen, weil eine grosse Gefahr besteht, dass die Strafe in einem völlig falschen Licht erscheint" (Fuchs 1985:137).[3]

This book, then, is an argument for the construction of a

---

2. In respect of criminology's long past but short history, see Garland (1994: 17-68).
3. "In my opinion, it is wrong to want to trace historical examples of contemporary community service. One can simply say that it is wrong to portray a new sanction in this way because there is a great danger that the penalty will appear in a totally false light."

more historical approach to the introduction of community service orders. It will provide an analysis in a broad historical form by exploring avenues of enquiry not touched upon by academics such as Vass and Pease and by developing a broad penological framework within which the introduction of community service orders can be understood.

Whiggism

One of the main problems inherent in an approach which seeks the historical antecedents of a contemporary phenomenon is that it can quite easily lend itself to a foreordained and cosmetic prognosis which eschews the polymerous nature of proper diachronic analysis. In our case, it is my contention that tracing continuities and affinities over time between various penal work sanctions, in order to highlight the lineage of community service, is ahistorical in that it distorts the contemporary significance and character of community service whilst also obscuring the contextual significance and usage of past penal work practices. One of the most useful polemics on the deficiencies in such a teleological approach to history was published in 1931 by Butterfield in a book, titled, *The Whig Interpretation of History*.[4] Attacking Protestant whiggery (on the grounds that it attempted to write the history of politics

---

4. See also, in respect of relativism, Becker (1932: 221-236) and Beard (1934: 219-229).

in terms of the triumph of the Enlightenment and ignored the problems of historiographic anachronism) Butterfield was keen to draw attention to the "relativist character of historical interpretation" and to the "dangers of projecting modern ways of thinking backwards in time and to discount those aspects of past experience which are alien to modern ideas" (Elton 1984:729-743; Tosh 1991:120). Essentially Butterfield's critique was directed against all those who plundered the past in order to explain a contemporary phenomenon:

"The study of the past with one eye, so to speak, upon the present is the source of all sins and sophistries in history, starting with the simplest of them, the anachronism" (Butterfield 1963:31-32).

He went on to suggest:

"The whig historian stands on the summit of the 20th century, and organises his scheme of history from the point of view of his own day; and he is a subtle man to overturn from his mountain-top where he can fortify himself with plausible argument ...The fallacy lies in the fact that if the historian working on the 16th century keeps the 20th century in his mind, he makes direct reference across all the intervening period between Luther or the Popes and the world of our day. And this immediate juxtaposition of past and present, though it makes everything easy and makes some inferences perilously obvious, is bound to lead to an over-simplification of the relations between events and a complete misapprehension of the relations between past and present" (*ibid*: 14).

As such, apart from the fallacy of anachronism, whiggism, through the principle of exclusion, compartmentalises the historical process into a neat linear package of progress with little or no attention devoted to dissociation or resistance - what Butterfield would term the "crooked and perverse ways of progress" (*ibid*: 23). Moreover, such an interpretation presents history as an "unfolding logic" (*ibid*: 42): for our purposes, community service is portrayed as an eschatological point in the history of penal labour sanctions which gravitated ever closer to the introduction of the sanction in 1972 as "sophistication", "innovation" and the "up-market" nature of the late 1960s and the early 1970s permitted. Finally, according to Butterfield, whig historians who view the past with too direct a reference to the present in mind subdue their original telos which was to draw upon the past to illuminate the present: "if we seize upon those things in the 16th century which are most analogous to what we know in the 20th, the upshot of all our history is only to send us back finally to the place where we began, and to ratify whatever conceptions we originally had in regard to our own time" (*ibid*: 62).[5] There is, in effect, a circularity of argument: in order to highlight a phenomenon in the

5.   It has been suggested, however, that Butterfield's book, *The Englishman and his history*, written in 1944, reversed the content of *Whig Interpretation* and was, in fact, quite presentist (Hall 1983: 45). See also Ashplant and Wilson who suggest that the "whig fallacy is but one species of the larger genus of present-centredness", an issue not touched upon by Butterfield (Ashplant and Wilson 1988: 253-274).

present, the whig historian makes certain assumptions about the past which, in turn, find expression in any conclusions being made about the phenomenon being explained. In respect of community service orders, such assumptions result in the "loss of a chance of discovering where in the stream of the centuries", its "ideas" and "prejudices" stand (Butterfield 1963:63) - this will manifest itself most palpably, as we shall see, in respect of the cultural determinant of leisure and its shaping of the sanction. Accordingly, Butterfield called for the need to be mindful, when we are attempting to abridge history, that the paths we take cut across a panoply of labyrinth interactions which will not fit neatly into any linear present-oriented vista of under-standing (*ibid*: 16).[6]

---

6. Nietzsche has made a similar point on what he would regard as Hegelian historical optimism which measures the course of history according to the idea of temporal progress towards an eschatological fulfilment at the end of time. Such a philosophy, in Nietzsche's view, fosters a very dangerous trend: "I believe that there has been no dangerous vacillation or crisis of German culture this century that has not been rendered more dangerous by the enormous and still continuing influence of this philosophy, the Hegelian. The belief that one is a latecomer of the ages is, in any case, paralysing and depressing: but it must appear dreadful and devastating when such a belief one day by a bold inversion raises this latecomer to godhood as the true meaning and goal of all previous events, when his miserable condition is equated with a completion of world-history. Such a point of view has accustomed the Germans to talk of this world process ... Here and there one goes further, into cynicism, and justifies the course of his history, indeed the entire evolution of the world, in a manner especially adapted to the use of the modern man, according to the cynical canon: as things are they had to be, as men now are they had to become, none may resist this inevitability" (Nietzsche 1874: 104-107). Thus, for Nietzsche, instead of furthering the creative mind - through questioning and scepticism - linear, presentist history encourages an uncontested acceptance of the

Not surprisingly, historical syntheses quickly began to exhibit a more heightened awareness of relativist interpretation. Such an outlook manifested itself most distinctly among historians of political thought. Pocock's work in 1957, for example, *The Ancient Constitution and Feudal Law*, urged academics engaged in the history of ideas to appreciate that major political philosophers of the past could only be understood against an historically specific backdrop; in Pocock's case, this involved the illumination of the common law interpretation of English legal history, which he believed was the "predecessor and to a large extent parent of the more famous *Whig Interpretation*" (Pocock 1957:46; Pocock 1971). Skinner's critique on the history of ideas in 1969 also focused on the problem of present-centredness and the absurdities of interpretation in which it can result. In criticising such an approach, he cogently argued that there were no "timeless elements" in the form of "universal ideas", or "dateless wisdom" with "universal application", to which all classic thinkers of political thought addressed themselves (Skinner 1969:4; Skinner 1974:277-303). In addition to falling into the trap of anachronism, Skinner believed that present-centredness as a methodology in political thinking was ahistorical in that

---

fulfilment and inevitability of history. For example, in *Thus spoke Zarathustra*, Nietzsche gives a portrait of the results of such an evolutionary interpretation of history - *der letzte Mensch* (to be contrasted with the Übermensch), a particularly contented bourgeoisie man who is thoroughly happy with his life and says with a smile and a wink, "we have invented happiness" (Nietzsche 1969).

it accredited classic writers with anticipating later doctrines[7] thus resulting in a *mythology of coherence*. On the nature of the approach to the history of ideas, he claimed:

"[A]ny attempt to justify the study of the subject in terms of the "perennial problems" and "universal truths" to be learned from the classic texts must amount to the purchase of justification at the expense of making the subject itself foolishly and needlessly naive. Any statement, as I have sought to show, is inescapably the embodiment of a particular intention, on a particular occasion, addressed to the solution of a particular problem, and thus specific to its situation in a way that it can only be naive to transcend ... The classic texts, especially in social, ethical and political thought, help to reveal - if we let them - not the essential sameness, but the essential variety of viable moral assumptions and political commitments. It is in this, moreover, that their essential philosophical, even moral, value can be seen to lie. There is a tendency ... to suppose that the best, not merely the inescapable, point of vantage from which to survey the history of ideas of the past must be that of our present situation, because it is by definition the most highly evolved. Such a claim cannot survive a recognition of the fact that historical differences over fundamental issues

---

7.   "[S]o Marsilius is notable for his 'remarkable anticipation' of Machiavelli; Machiavelli is notable because he 'lays the foundations' for Marx; Locke's theory of signs is notable as an 'anticipation' of Berkeley's metaphysics; ... Shaftesbury's treatment of the theodicy problem is notable because it 'in a certain sense' anticipated' Kant" (Skinner 1969: 11).

may reflect differences of intention and convention rather than anything like a competition over a community of values, let alone anything like an evolving perception of the Absolute" (*ibid*: 52-53).

Thus the meaning of any text was to be derived from the complex intention of the political thinker in question; the aim of the historian of ideas, therefore, was to reconstruct the particular complex intentions (which arose in a specific environment) of that political thinker so as to give effect to proper historical analysis. Much of what has been discussed centres around the subject of historical time. Some of the best studies on historical tempos have been carried out by academics such as Fernand Braudel and other historians from the *Annales* School. Rather than systematising history as a course simply determined by temporal progress, the *Annalistes* were keen to demonstrate a clear awareness of the plurality of time spans in history. For example, in 1949 Braudel published his influential work, titled *La Mediterranée et le Monde Mediterranéen á l'Époque de Phillipe II*. His inquiry centred on a three tiered analysis of time, all of which were interdependent. The first historical duration, *la longue durée*, "is the endless inexhaustible history of structures and groups of structures"; the second, *une historie lentement ryhthmée*, is the history of gentle rhythms, and; the third, *l'historie événementielle*, is a "history of brief, rapid, nervous fluctuations, by definition ultra-sensitive, the least tremor sets all of its antennae quivering" (Braudel 1980:3; Marwick

1989:121-139).[8] Braudel defined the three types of historical duration as geographical, social and individual time respectively.

This attention to relativity and time boundness in all histories was picked up by Foucault. Influenced by Nietzsche and the *Annales* School[9] - particularly the development of the history of mentalities as witnessed in Ariés' 1962 study of the sense of childhood (Ariés: 1962) - Foucault was keen to avoid the foibles of viewing history as a teleological structure from which growing perfection and evolution in reason, consciousness and thought naturally unfolded:[10]

8.　Gramsci was also very aware of the rudiments of historical time. Albeit that his interests were - contrary to the *Annales* School - primarily political, he did note in respect of historical methodology: "[I]n studying a structure, it is necessary to distinguish organic movements (relatively permanent) from movements which may be termed *conjunctural* (and which appear as occasional, immediate, almost accidental)" (Hoare and Smith 1971: 177; Bates 1975: 351-366).

9.　Like the *Annales* School of history, Foucault placed more emphasis on *practices* rather than *institutions, great events or individuals* - what Nietzsche would describe as "monumental histories". These practices included a focus on ideas such as "milieu", "mentalités", "genres de vie", "civilisations", and "mechanisms of power in its strategies" (Gordon 1991: 4; Foucault 1980: 37).

10.　But see Habermas who suggests that Foucault's attempt to "leave behind modernity's presentist consciousness of time" is in fact presentist because it is a history that "is narcissistically oriented towards the standpoint of the historian and instrumentalises the contemplation of the past for the needs of the present" (Habermas 1987: 248-278). In Foucault's defence, however, his *wirkliche* history is a history which is purposefully designed to enrich the present through, in part, the employment of structural discontinuity to reject humanist rationalism. This adherence to structuralist discontinuity acts, to some extent, as a counterpoint to such an unqualified criticism being levelled at him. Indeed Foucault would undoubtedly accept that he is a prisoner of his own age. Aware of this limitation, however, he proceeded

"The old questions of the traditional analysis (What link should be made between disparate events? How can a causal succession be established between them? What continuity or overall significance do they possess? Is it possible to define a totality, or must one be content with reconstituting connections?) are now being replaced by questions of another type: *Which strata should be isolated from others? What type of series should be established? What criteria of periodisation should be adapted for each of them? What system of relations (hierarchy, dominance, stratification, univocal determination, circular causality) may be established between them? What series of series may be established? And in what large-scale chronological table may distinct series of events be determined*" (Foucault 1972: 3-4) (my italics).

He went on to suggest:

"Beneath the great continuities of thought, beneath the solid, homogeneous manifestations of a single mind or of a collective mentality, beneath the stubborn development of a science striving to exist and to reach completion at the very outset, beneath the persistence of a particular genre, form, discipline, or theoretical activity, one is now trying to detect the incidence of interruptions" (*ibid*: 4).

---

with an attempt to highlight, through epistemic jumps, deficiencies in progressivist analyses which obfuscated the contemporary significance of particular institutions and conventions. Of course, he too was engaging in a re/construction of generative processes (as problématiques rather than solutions) but he did so in a manner designed not to impose on them a "positivity or valorisation" (Foucault 1980: 50).

In order to demonstrate that our present practices and institutions are by no means eternal and immutable, Foucault, through *epistemes* (the "historical *a priori*" which enable certain forms of knowledge and ideas to become possible) attempted to write histories not of "growing perfection" but of their "conditions of possibility" (Foucault 1970:xxii). In other words, he attempted to draw up the rules of formation which govern particular forms of knowledge and which demonstrate the epistemological caesuras that represent the transformation from one *episteme* to another. The need to deny the importance of progress-based perspectives and to highlight discontinuities can be seen quite clearly in *Historie de la folie a l'âge classique*, first published in 1961. Here, Foucault was keen to demonstrate how the "consciousness of madness" had transformed from the 1400s where the mad were not interned but expelled from the limits of towns and cities to lead a wandering existence in the country (symbolised in *Stulifera Navis*); to the classical period beginning in the mid-seventeenth century when exclusion was replaced by confinement (as symbolised in the *Hóspitaux Généraux* of France, the Houses of Correction of England and Wales, and the Zuchthaüsern of Germany) when social undesirables and the animality of the mad began to be perceived as a threat to bourgeois sensibilities; to Pinel's releasing of inmates in 1794 in Bicêtre which represented the supposed beginning of the new age of the asylum and the more humane treatment of the insane (Foucault 1997). But for Foucault, this transformation did not represent the ineluctable progress of humanity or scientific objectivity: "it did not evolve in the context of a humanitarian movement that gradually related it more closely to the madman's human reality, to his most affecting and most intimate aspect; nor did it evolve under the pressure of scientific need that made it more attentive, more faithful to, what madness might have to say for itself" (*ibid*: 224). Rather, the modern conception of madness was constructed both from the very nature of confinement itself which continued to impose bourgeois values on the inmates (*ibid*), and from the inversion of madness perceived as animality to madness perceived as a natural phenomenon which was repressed by human society.

Notions of discontinuity[11] and the "incidence of interruptions" are very much in evidence in Foucault's book, titled, *Discipline and Punish*, where he set out to write a "history of the present" of prisons, mindful of the need to avoid "writing of the past in terms of the present" (Foucault 1991b: 31). In order to demonstrate the discontinuous nature of penal history, Foucault began by contrasting the execution of Damiens in 1757 with the rules drawn up by Léon Faucher 80 years later for the House of Young Prisoners in Paris. For Foucault, the dissimilar nature of

---

11. It is important to note, however, that Foucault does, in some instances, recognise long range continuities in social and cultural practices. As he noted: "My problem was not at all to say, '*Voilá* long live discontinuity, we are in the discontinuous and a good thing too', but to pose the question, 'How is it that at certain moments in time and in certain orders of knowledge, there are these sudden take-offs, these hastenings of evolution, these transformations which fail to correspond to the calm, continuist image that is normally accredited'" (Foucault 1991: 54). He is, for example, a continuist in that he recognises the true/false dichotomy that history always produces.

both sanctions represented a distribution in the "entire economy of punishment" (*ibid*): it denoted the movement from "being an art of unbearable sensations" to an "economy of suspended rights" (*ibid*: 11), the latter of which was composed of "a whole new system of truth and a mass of roles hitherto unknown in the exercise of criminal justice" (*ibid*: 23). It was only in this latter penal system that we could begin to understand the "present scientifico-legal complex" with its particularistic "corpus of knowledge", "techniques" and "scientific discourses" (*ibid*); accordingly, it is within this framework of understanding that we must operate if we are to avoid the dangers of present-centredness.

Perhaps the most brilliant illustration of such an approach in recent times has been undertaken by Garland in respect of British criminology. Taking criminology to be a specific "genre of discourse" which burgeoned out of the convergence of two quite distinct programmes - the "Government project" (the long series of government inquiries into the administration of justice since the eighteenth century) and the "Lombrosian project" (an etiological scientific approach to the criminal which manifested itself in the late nineteenth century) - Garland sought to provide a diachronic analysis which was sensitive to "context and contingency" and which did not treat the subject as the "gradual unfolding of a science which was always destined to appear" (Garland 1994: 18-19). As such, he denounced the manner in which criminology's history was often condensed into the prefaces of textbooks. These prefaces - which compartmentalised the historical process of criminology into a neat, linear, progressivist package - outlined the writings of criminal law reformers of the eighteenth century such as Becarria, Bentham, Romilly and Howard, followed by the positive school in the late nineteenth century involving individuals such as Lombroso and Garafalo (*ibid*: 21). Garland noted that under such an approach: "criminology's history becomes the history of everything that has ever been said or thought or done in relation to law breakers"; the meaning of earlier writers is contorted; and it gives the impression that criminology is "our modern response to a timeless and unchanging set of questions which previous thinkers have also pondered over, though with notably less success" (*ibid*: 24). Instead, he argued that the phenomenon to be explained was a present day one - the statements of earlier writers such as Bentham are "structured by assumptions and objectives ('not to mention institutional contexts and cultural commitments') which are quite different from modern criminology" (*ibid*: 23), albeit that the current arrangements have been constructed, in some respects, out of events which manifested themselves at earlier points in time. In this sense, Garland was also concerned with highlighting interruption in an effort, as Foucault would put it, to "direct historical analysis away from the search for silent beginnings and the never ending tracing-back to original precursors", in order to show that "the history of a concept is not wholly and entirely that of its progressive refinement" (Foucault 1972: 4).

The purpose of this book, then, is to demonstrate the way in which academics such as Vass and Pease have misrepresented the links between the past and present in order to accentuate the continuities and affinities which they believe exist over time between various penal work sanctions. It will be argued that their approach to community service orders is anachronistic; employs the "principle of exclusion" by gathering information which supposedly supports their cause whilst ignoring that which does not; leads to a "mythology of coherence" in that a sanction such as impressment is credited with having a "remarkable similarity of purpose" with community service orders - it will be demonstrated that such an arrangement amounts to the "purchase of justification" at the expense of proper historical analysis;[12] and gives the impression that penal authorities faced the same "perennial questions" in the 1500s as they did in the late twentieth century - albeit with a lesser degree of success given that houses of correction, transportation, penal servitude and impressment were viewed as community service's "less reputable forebears".

Mindful of the complex and interactive criteria which apply to understanding the history of penal work sanctions, I will proceed with a methodology which attempts to discover where the actual germs of community service lie, so as to give proper effect to its "ideas" and "prejudices". Such a framework, it is hoped, will assist in avoiding

---

12. As Garland noted in respect of the prefatory history approach to criminology: "The telling and retelling of the standard historical tale is the most effective way of persuading the discipline's recruits that whatever else may be contested, this much, at least, can be taken for granted" (Garland 1994: 20).

fallacies such as anachronistic assumptions, incongruous periodisations and the distortion of the complexities of the past so as to make them conform with perceptions of the present. By being sensitive to context and by using discontinuity as an instrument of analysis which will aid in providing a proper periodisation framework, I hope to write a more emendated historical account of the emergence of community service orders. This task has been made easier in recent years given the number of revisionist scholars who have all highlighted the "incidence of interruptions" in order to write histories of the present in respect of the penal complex.

Revisionism

Attempts have increasingly been made since the 1960s to develop a more coherent and historical understanding of penality which would aid in delineating the strategies and indeed resistances that have gone into forming either the modern penal complex (or elements thereof) or the penal complex of earlier times (or elements thereof). This movement, loosely termed "revisionism", has attempted, as one of its primary leitmotivs, to highlight the deficiencies associated with a teleological narrative view of criminal justice history which portrayed penal phenomena as moving in a continuous and unopposed fashion towards their "proper modern end"(Philips 1983: 51). Brought about as a result of a more heightened critical awareness of notions of reform, a desire to provide proper, social, ideological, economic and political contexts to any criminal justice period being described, and scepticism and disillusionment that emerged as a consequence of the penal crisis that manifested itself in the late 1960s and early 1970s (how could a progressivist, presentist analysis, account, for example, for the decline of rehabilitation, for the growth in prison overcrowding, for increases in crime, and the decline in consensus policing?), revisionists sought to demonstrate how criminal justice history had become "an ahistorical discipline" (Pisciotta 1981: 109), how it was based, for the most part, "on a single-minded idealist view of history" (Cohen 1994: 15) and, how its history was often portrayed as a "narrative of reform" which emphasised "conscience" as the "motor of institutional change" (Ignatieff 1983: 75), whilst eschewing proper analysis of context, power relations, real intentions and actual consequences. At a general level, revisionist analysis has evidenced itself, *inter alia*, in the rejection of simple Whiggish analysis of police history (Silver 1967: 1-24; Storch 1975: 61-90), in respect of the history of prosecution (Hay 1984: 1-29), and in respect of the history of women's imprisonment (Dobash *et al* 1986).[13] For the purposes of this book, however, revisionism will only be examined in respect of its attempt at constructing master strategies of social control through highlighting the "incidence of interruptions" in the criminal justice history process. It is hoped that by examining revisionist analysis from this perspective that we will be able to begin

---

13. For an excellent review of revisionism in respect of the police, courts, capital punishment, prisons and transportation, see Rawlings (1990: 62-112).

constructing a history of the present of community service which will aid in our interpretation of the probable reasons that led to its introduction in the early 1970s.

First, there has been a return to Rusche and Kirchheimer's 1939 text, titled, *Punishment and Social Control*, which was reissued in 1968. Dissatisfied with an approach which viewed punishment as being "eternal and immutable" (Rusche and Kirchheimer 1968: 4), they sought to show that there was a need to "strip from the social institutions of punishment its ideological veils and juristic appearance and to describe it in its real relationships" (*ibid*: 5). These "real relationships", according to Rusche and Kirchheimer, would reveal that "punishment as such does not exist; only concrete systems of punishment and specific criminal practices exist" (*ibid*). Beginning their broad historical account in the Middle Ages, they argued that the system of punishment to be found therein was grounded upon a law of feud and penance which viewed criminal wrongdoing as a matter of private vengeance (*ibid*: 8).[14] However, by the fourteenth and fifteenth centuries, with the rise to prominence of the disciplinary function of the feudal lords, the emergence of central powers and the increased emphasis placed on "fiscal interest", the private constitution of punishment began to be transformed into an "instrument of domination" (*ibid*: 10). At the same time, the increase in population, the exhaustion of the soil and the decreasing

14. Such a view of criminal law, according to Rusche and Kirchheimer, was possible in an era "which assumed the existence of sufficient land to meet the requirements of a continually increasing population without lowering their standards of living" (*ibid*).

yield, the movement from agriculture to grazing and the rise of the pasturage system did much to increase the number of propertyless people roaming the countryside (*ibid*: 11). This displacement of a vast population of peasants, and the threat it posed to order, consequenced itself in the creation of a harsh criminal law directed by a bourgeoisie anxious to protect its property. Increases in the use of physical and capital punishment became commonplace in the period concerned (72,000 major and minor thieves were hanged during the reign of Henry VIII according to Rusche and Kirchheimer) (*ibid*: 19), and new methods were continually devised to heighten the pains of imprisonment - these included physical punishments such as the cutting off of hands, tongues, eyes and ears, and castration, and execution by axe, knife, plank, plough, or being burned alive, bled or starved to death (*ibid*). Such a scant regard for human life in the period in question was, for Rusche and Kirchheimer, very much a product of the conditions of a social structure which had an over supply of labour resources.

By the end of the sixteenth century, the possibility of utilising the labour of offenders underwent a review. Such a review was not founded upon any humanitarian considerations but manifested itself as a result of increasing urbanisation, the extension of markets, the importation of precious metals, the conquest of colonies, and the reduction of population growth. All of these phenomena resulted in an increased emphasis on the commodity of labour in the market place (*ibid*: 26). Not surprisingly, the system of punishment adapted to such changes in the market place by introducing sanctions such as galley slavery, transportation and penal servitude at hard labour, all of which also placed an increased emphasis on the values of life and the utilisation of labour power (*ibid*: 24). The late mercantilist period also witnessed the emergence of the modern prison (when the exploitation of labour was still valued as a clear objective). But no sooner had it emerged than the nature of punishment began to be redefined in accordance with a mode of production which witnessed a decline in the demand for labour power as a result of massive increases in population and the introduction of industrial machinery (ie, spinning machines). By the early nineteenth century, such a transformation, according to Rusche and Kirchheimer, had resulted in massive increases in crime and violence (*ibid*: 97-98). In such an environment, it was the prison, with its ability to be utilised for strictly deterrent and repressive purposes, that took centre stage. Solitary confinement, strict rules of discipline, unproductive labour in the form of carrying stones, working pumps where the water flowed back to its sources, or treadwheels which simply ground the air, were some of the techniques embodied in a concrete system of punishment which emphasised the elements of terror and intimidation, albeit that these techniques were disguised beneath a rhetoric of reform: "solitary confinement, without work or with purely punitive labour, is symptomatic of a mentality which, as a result of surplus population, abandons the attempt to find a rational policy of rehabilitation and conceals this fact with a moral theology" (*ibid*: 137). Finally, the late nineteenth and early twentieth century, also manifested itself in another shift in the system of punishment. This shift, according to Rusche and

Kirchheimer, was brought about by improvements in the standard of living, mass production, mass consumption, the rise in wages, lower birth rates and better transportation facilities (*ibid*: 138-140), and resulted in a period in which the bourgeoisie no longer felt the need to engage in a "spirit of violence" against the proletariat. In such an environment:

> "[T]he problem of penal methods was no longer viewed as a problem of maintaining a just proportion between crime and punishment; it was examined from the viewpoint of the criminal's future, the expectation of rehabilitation, and the precautions which it was worth taking" (*ibid*: 143).

The prison, as a purely punishing machine, was replaced as a result of this "greater tendency towards leniency" by both internal means (decreases in the length and severity of prison sentences, the construction of new prisons with better living conditions, the improvement of diet and health, the decline in the use of chains and other forms of physical restraint, and the provision of educational facilities) and external means (more extensive use of fines, after-care, probation, and by prolonged attempts at improving the social conditions of the poor so as to reduce crime) (*ibid*: 145-150). For Rusche and Kirchheimer, then, there are a series of interruptions in the criminal justice history process, all of which are related to the mode of production. These interruptions, which enabled the break-up of concrete systems of punishment and which were directly attributable to changes in productivity relations in the market place, included: the shift from a system grounded upon private vengeance in the Middle Ages to a system in the fifteenth century which was more willing, in a period symptomised by scant regard for human life, to inflict corporal punishment; to a system in the seventeenth century which was more appreciative of the benefits of an offender's labour power; to a system in the nineteenth century which harnessed the potential of prison's deterrent and repressive functions as the demand for the commodity of labour power diminished; to a system in the late nineteenth and early twentieth centuries which, in accordance with the advance of industrialisation and the decline in population, enabled a "more rational and humane praxis" (*ibid*: 163) to develop in respect of penal measures, but which could still result in a "policy of repression" under certain economic conditions as occurred in Fascist States such as Italy and Germany (*ibid*: 177-192).

Rusche and Kirchheimer's book has, to some extent, become a starting point for other Marxist debate on punishment. For example, Melossi and Pavarini, in *The Prison and the Factory*, also attempt to show that the system of social control is premised upon changing relations of production. But rather than focusing on the history of all penal measures, their book focuses specifically on the "connection between the genealogy of capitalism and the genealogy of the penal institution" (Melossi and Pavarini 1981: 21). For them, corrective institutions in the seventeenth and eighteenth centuries - a period they believed was marked by a relative scarcity of labour - acted as a place for "teaching the discipline of production" (*ibid*). Following increases in the population in the eighteenth century, together with the introduction of industrial machinery and the movement towards a factory system of production (and the growth of crime, poverty and disorder which such a transformation caused), Melossi and Pavarini argue that prison became an increasingly dominant acquisition of "bourgeois punitive practice" (*ibid*: 47) in which the "principle of discipline *tout court* prevailed over that of productive factory discipline" (*ibid*: 58). By the late nineteenth century, however, and as a result of profound changes in the "socio-economic framework" in respect of the composition of capital, labour organisation, trade union movement, class composition and the role of the State, Melossi and Pavarini suggest - it did not form an intrinsic part of their text, but was included on the grounds that it may assist future research *vis-à-vis* prisons - that a new strategy of social control focusing on dispersal became apparent:

> "Individuals are no longer locked-up; they are got at where they are normally locked-up: outside the factory, in society as a whole. Propaganda, the mass media, a new and more efficient network of police and social assistance, these are the bearers of a new kind of social control" (*ibid*: 2).

Thus, broadly speaking, we have witnessed a movement from a conception of punishment in pre-capitalist society which embodied elements of *retributio* (the law of an eye for an eye and a tooth for a tooth) and *espatio* (divine chastisement), which "explain the significant absence of prison punishment from feudal society" (*ibid*: 2); to a system of correctional institutions in the seventeenth and eighteenth centuries which aimed at disciplinary training for capitalist production through productive work practices; to a system in the nineteenth century which increasingly utilised the prison as a means of strict discipline rather than as a means of productive factory discipline; to a system in the twentieth century which concentrated more on dispersal as industrialisation advanced.

Foucault's work, *Discipline and Punish*, also recognised, like Rusche and Kirchheimer, the need to analyse "concrete systems of punishment" and to "study them as social phenomena that cannot be accounted for by the juridical structure of society alone" (Foucault 1991b: 24). He attempted to put forward his own history "of the modern soul and a new power to judge" by studying "the metamorphosis of punitive methods on the basis of a political technology of the body" (*ibid*: 23-24). Unlike Rusche and Kirchheimer, however, Foucault attempted to view discontinuities from the perspective of power/knowledge and governance relations that focus on the internal mechanics of the penal system.[15]

Torture, amputation, exposure, execution and dismemberment were, according to Foucault, the characteristics of the old, theatrical, public spectacle order of punishment. The

---

15. But see Garland who suggests that although Foucault's investigations adopt a level of analysis which is quite different from that commonly used by Marxists, "his findings have sometimes been used to extend Marxist accounts rather than to contest them" (Garland 1990: 132).

body of the condemned under such a system of punishment functioned as a locus for the ritual display of vengeance and terror - a terror and vengeance which confirmed to the public the omnipotent and unrestricted power of the sovereign. Such a penal system made the body "of the condemned man the place where the vengeance of the sovereign was applied, the anchoring point for a manifestation of power, an opportunity of affirming a dissymmetry of forces" (Foucault 1991b: 55). But this form of punishment could not simply be understood in terms of its "internal organisation"; rather it had to be seen as part of a social system which held a "contempt" for the body in a period of diseases, hunger, epidemics, formidable child mortality rates, and precarious "bio-economic" balances (*ibid*).

But between the late eighteenth and mid-nineteenth century, Foucault detected a shift from the corporal master system of punishment to a more solitary, discreet mode of punishment with the prison as its fulcrum (albeit that notions of a juridical system were toyed with before the carceral modality of punishment came to dominate). Given the excesses of power, logic of atrocity, and ambiguous rituals which corporal punishment drew upon, the authorities came to realise that such a system of control ran the risk of "being rejected by the very people to whom it was addressed" (*ibid*: 63). This risk evidenced itself in the numerous "centres of illegality" which burgeoned on execution day (work stopped, taverns were full, fights broke out, and the authorities were abused), and the challenge that punishment of this kind threw down (tyranny is drawn ever closer into confrontation with rebellion in a regime of punishment that embodies excessive violence). Under such conditions, a new modality of punishment was required which would focus more on a rationality and economy of power that would function to make punishment more discreet and hidden, where its effectiveness would be seen "as resulting from its inevitability, not from its visible intensity" (*ibid:* 9).

It was with the emergence of the modern prison that a new technology of domination - centred upon disciplinary techniques that view the body as an object and target of power - began to take effect. Discipline, according to Foucault, was the cornerstone of this technology of domination: "it is the specific technique of power that regards individuals both as objects and instruments of its exercise" (*ibid*: 170; Owen 1994: 175). An art - which can be viewed as a "political tactic" - of distributing individuals in space through enclosure and partition (of spaces which were both functional and hierarchical) came to prominence in the seventeenth and eighteenth century. Such a phenomenon, according to Foucault, was supported by a series of techniques which attempted to control activities in these spaces. These included: *timetables* ("which help to establish rhythms, impose particular occupations, regulate the cycles of repetition"); *the temporal elaboration of the act* which breaks down an act into a series of constituent elements (ie, the way in which troops march); the correlation of the body and the gesture which "imposes the best relation between a gesture and the overall position of the body, which is its condition of efficiency and speed" (good handwriting, according to

Foucault, demands a rigorous bodily code from the position of the feet to the tip of the index finger); the *body-object* articulation which consists of a "breakdown of the total gesture into two parallel series: that of the parts of the body to be used ... and that of parts of the object manipulated" (ie, the raising, aiming, firing and lowering of a rifle in the army); and, *exhaustive use* which sought maximum efficiency and speed (Foucault 1991b: 141-154). Techniques of this nature quickly found expression in the army, to begin with, but also in schools, workshops, factories, hospitals and prisons. It marked a shift from the body being perceived with contempt to the body being perceived as susceptible to a series of operations, capable of being "manipulated by authority rather than imbued with animal spirits" (*ibid*:155).

The emergence of this disciplinary power marked the reversal in what may be termed the *axis of individualisation*. In pre-panoptic society, such as in feudal society, *individualisation* existed but only in ascending form. By this, Foucault meant that the less power one possessed, the less one could be marked as an individual. Accordingly, it was only those who possessed power, who were immortalised in "literary accounts" and "ceremonies", and who were given allegiance and suzerainty, that were *individualised* (*ibid*: 192-193). In panoptic or disciplinary society, on the other hand, individualisation was *descending*: "as power becomes more anonymous and more functional, those on whom it is exercised tend to be more strongly individualised; it is exercised by surveillance rather than ceremonies, by observation rather than commemorative accounts, by comparative measures that have the *norm* as reference rather than genealo/gies giving ancestors as points of reference" (*ibid*). Essentially, according to Foucault, individualisation changed from being a process which turned inwards on those who possessed power to a process turned outwards (by those in power) so that it would act as a means of domination and observation on those without power. As such, and as a result of the extension of disciplinary mechanisms in the eighteenth century, punishment began to embody more individualised normalising methods which were capable of operating everywhere. Of course, in such a homogenised and rationalised environment, it became much more difficult to view criminal justice in terms of localised relations or as an exercise in "common peace" (Herrup: 1987).

Moreover, the exercise of disciplinary power under this new modality of punishment was founded upon principles of power/knowledge in that it acts as a means of observing individuals in space and their ability to attain and maintain a desired standard of conduct. For example, the "geometry" of the military camp - which acted as an "ideal model" for other observatories such as hospitals, asylums, prisons, factories and schools - made surveillance and, as a consequence, "detailed and articulate control", possible (1991b: 171-172). For Foucault, the embodiment of these power/knowledge principles in punitive terms was perfectly illustrated in the Panopticon which arranged spatial unities so that it "was possible to see constantly and to recognise immediately" (*ibid:* 200).[16] But observation, in addition to producing "homogenous effects of power", also acts as a "laboratory", as a means to carry out experiments and alter behaviour through a method of sanctioning termed "disciplinary normalisation" (*ibid:* 203). Soon, according to Foucault, the value of these panoptic, disciplinary principles became more palpable and they proliferated across the entire social body. In penal terms, the transformation witnessed a shift in concrete systems of punishment from a corporal to a carceral modality of control aimed at the soul of the offender through the utilisation of disciplinary techniques that were founded upon inevitability rather than intensity of effect.

Similarly Ignatieff attempted to account for a shift in concrete systems of punishment between 1775 and 1840 by concerning himself with "the modern norms governing the exercise of power within prisons" (Ignatieff 1978: xiii). Dismissive of economic determinism and anxious, unlike Foucault, to highlight the religious, philosophical and philanthropic impulses behind the shift, Ignatieff proceeded by analysing the unproductive, discretionary, independently controlled, and communal nature of workhouses, houses of correction and gaols prior to the late eighteenth century. Such a modality of punishment, in his view, was tolerated in a period where the public ritual rather than confinement formed the bedrock of the system

---

16. "In short, it reverses the principle of the dungeon; or rather of its three functions - to enclose, to deprive of light and to hide - it preserves only the first and eliminates the other two" (*ibid*).

of punishment (*ibid*: 42). By the late eighteenth century, however, a series of interruptions had combined to create a new order. These interruptions included, *inter alia*, the increasing focus of medical practice on hygienic conditions in confined settings; a growing loss of confidence by reformers in the deterrent effects of ritual punishments and the belief that the public was increasingly perturbed by the excessive violence inherent in such punishments; the proposals for prison reform derived largely from Howard's visits to the *Rasp-huis* of Amsterdam and Rotterdam and the *Maison de Force* in Flanders; the increasing number of "sites of crisis" after 1815, such as the rural crisis that took place in the South-East, the Anti-Corn riots, Spa Field disturbances and rising rates of juvenile crime in London, and the decline of labour market relations in northern towns; and the introduction of mechanisation, fines, bells, rules, and extended divisions of labour by new industrialists in the period concerned (*ibid:* 44-91; Ignatieff 1983: 88). All of these resulted in a shift towards a new modality of prison punishment which substituted the "pains of intention" for the "pains of neglect", distanced the criminal from the outside world, and subjected him or her to a "disciplinary ideology" in the form of an "authority of rules" (1978: 113). This system succeeded, according to Ignatieff, because it convinced the offender "to accept the benevolent intention behind institutional deprivations" (what may be termed "symbolic persuasion" as opposed to what Foucault would call "disciplinary routinisation") (Ignatieff 1983: 88).

For Garland, any genealogy of the modern system of punishment must begin in the years between the Gladstone

Committee Report of 1895 and the start of the First World War. It was in this period, in his view, that the "basic structures of modern penality were first assembled in a distinctive pattern which is discontinuous with the Victorian system, while being continuous with that of the present day" (Garland 1985: 5). Garland's approach, then, attempted to illuminate the present penal complex by juxtaposing it with a Victorian system of penal practice which operated under a different set of objectives, techniques, political forces and discourses. In the Victorian epoch, the favoured political ideology of economic liberalism also found support in the penal domain. Market discipline notions of "individual responsibility" and "presumed rationality" were indispensable components of perceptions of offending, and punishment, accordingly, embodied a policy of deterrence and retribution, "the former to deny the utility of crime, the latter to reconstitute the social contract after its breach" (Garland 1981: 29-45). It was, in effect, a system which recognised "individuals" but not "individuality". This is aptly demonstrated in respect of the Victorian prison system which subjected all offenders to a homogenised system of prison discipline without having any regard to the idiosyncratic attributes specific to each individual offender.

But in the late nineteenth century, a new form of penality began to emerge which was founded upon the logic of "welfare/control" and was brought about, *inter alia*, as a consequence of the concentration of industry and finance, economic decline, concerns about levels of efficiency, trade unionism, changing perceptions of social problems, the eugenics movement, and working-class militancy (Garland

1981: 35). All of these phenomena, according to Garland, resulted in a shift towards a "form of sociality constructed around mass democracy, monopoly capital and an interventionist State" *(ibid)*. In penal terms, this resulted in the decline in dominance of the prison and the rise to prominence of a whole panoply of sanctions, agencies and institutions, which radically transformed the modality of punishment. This extended network of sanctions included the introduction of probation, borstals, preventive detention, detention in inebriate reformatories, detention in institutions for the morally defective, supervised fines, the reorganisation of licensed supervision, and the introduction of juvenile courts throughout the country *(ibid: 19-25)*. It also resulted in the abandonment of certain sanctions such as the abolition of penal servitude in respect of children and young persons, and the restricted use of imprisonment to young persons between the ages of 14 and 16 whose characters were deemed to be so unruly or depraved that detention in a reformatory was not considered appropriate *(ibid: 21)*.

Moreover, penality increasingly dissociated itself from the *type abstrait* of classical jurisprudence - which embodied the belief that legal subjects were born free and equal and therefore could be punished in accordance with a homogenised system of prison discipline *(ibid: 25-26)* - and became, albeit in a dilatory manner, a more knowledgeable form of social control that required a series of inquiries and investigations before a penal disposal could be given to an offender *(ibid: 30)*. As such, the transformation for Garland represented, as we shall see in more detail as we proceed through the book, the movement from a *"calibrated, hierarchical structure"* to *"an extended grid of non-equivalent and diverse dispositions" (ibid:* 28). It was this extended grid:

> "that marked the formation of a reformulated strategy of control which functioned through new means and according to new rules (the welfare sanction, administrative segregation, the normalisation of characters, the policing of families) producing in its wake new forms of social division (citizen/client, adequate/ inadequate, responsible/irresponsible etc.). Moreover, it was a strategy with a future - one which would later become generated in the functioning of the post-war welfare complex" *(ibid:* 42).

On the other hand, penal commentators, such as Scull, have proposed that efforts to de-institutionalise deviant populations through community treatment from the mid 1960s onwards have amounted, in part, to a reversal of Foucault's "great transformation" from a corporal to a carceral modality of punishment. But rather than attempting to account for this transformation in terms of the progress of medical technology and social scientific understanding, Scull, in 1977, attempted to locate the decarceration movement in the "context of deep-seated changes in the social organisation of advanced capitalist societies" (Scull 1977: 152; Scull 1983: 142-165). In brief, he argued that as a result of massive expansion in welfare provisions in the 1950s and 1960s, there was a growing need - given the budgetary impact as a result of such expansion - to restrict the costs involved in prevailing segregative methods of social control. This would enable expenditure on welfare provisions to continue. The fiscal crisis which demanded such a change was augmented by increases in state aid to private industry, improvements in economic infrastructure, the need to curtail a situation where the costs of state social service were rising faster than average price level, the expansion of dependent populations and the absence of competition pressure (Scull 1977: 135-138).

Cohen, however, suggests that rather than there being a reversal of Foucault's transformation, community treatment must be seen as a continuation of the same disciplinary project in that it represents the spread of state control ever more deeply into the social network. The extension of Foucauldian disciplinary mechanisms can be evidenced from the fact that non-custodial sanctions: (a) *widen the net* of social control by increasing rather than decreasing the amount of intervention directed at many groups of offenders and by increasing "the total number of offenders who get into the system in the first place"; (b) *thin the mesh* by increasing the level of intervention with the result that "new populations are brought into the system who would otherwise not have been processed at all, or would have been placed on traditional options like probation"; (c) *blur the boundaries* of the social control apparatus so that "it is by no means easy to know where the prison ends, and the community begins" (Cohen 1979a: 609-611); and (d) *penetrate* more deeply into the informal networks of society (Cohen 1994: 85). Thus, instead of any destructuring movement, there is in fact an expansion of penal control which is consistent with original Foucauldian transformations:

"[T]he original structures have become stronger; far from any decrease, the reach and intensity of state control have been increased; centralisation and bureaucracy remain; professions and experts are proliferating dramatically and society is more dependent on them; information has not made the legal system less formal or more just; treatment has changed its form but certainly has not died. Unevenly to be sure, and in some parts of the system much more clearly than others, there has been an intensification, complication and extension of these early nineteenth century master patterns, not their reversal. Those original patterns - rationalisation, centralisation, segregation, classification - were not born fully grown. They were trends which are still going on and the more recent changes are also trends yet uncompleted. But it was as if the destructuring impulse revealed how deep were those original structures" (*ibid*: 37).

Convinced by such an argument, Scull, in a second edition of his 1977 book, modified his economism and functionalism, and his assumption that the "language of radical, non-intervention closely coincided with everyday practice", so as to accommodate phenomena such as the "substantial growth of the criminal control apparatus", "heightened control", and the "widening of the network of social control" (Scull 1984: 177-79). Similarly Mathiesen recognised that the control system "as a totality may expand rather than shrink" (Mathiesen 1983: 132). In this sense, he recognises that Foucauldian disciplinary mechanisms have been extended into the modern penal complex. But

1

Mathiesen also argued that in the "great transformation", disciplinary mechanisms - which were open in that they could be clearly recognised by the offender - took the form of a disciplining of individuals (*ibid:* 140). Such an outlook, according to Mathiesen, has largely been abandoned in the modern penal complex where a societal understanding of crime prevails:

> "[T]he large mass of traditional crime - the thefts - may no longer as easily be explained as understandable materially oriented acts, committed by individuals against the background of their total material situation. To be sure, the sociologist may still argue that theft, especially in the recidivist form, is associated with a lack of material resources and with material need. But in the light of general material growth, it is politically very difficult to uphold such a lack and such a need as a basic causal principle" (*ibid*: 134).

In his view, under this new societal understanding, crime is perceived as a consequence of weakened social control This has resulted in: (a) crime been given a definition which is explicable in rational terms; (b) the strengthening of social control; and c) the movement away from the disciplining of individuals to the control of *whole groups and categories* - which is a more *hidden* form of discipline in that it is either outside the individual's "range of vision" or "less visible" than control forms under Foucault's modality of punishment (*ibid*: 135-139).

All of these revisionists, as we have seen, have attempted

to highlight the "incidence of interruptions" in the criminal justice history process. These respective interruptions have been highlighted by focusing: on modes of production and systems of punishment; on power/knowledge and governance mechanisms; on the extension of such mechanisms into the penal complex of the late twentieth century; on religious, philosophical and philanthropic impulses; on the emergence of the logic of "welfare/control"; on the fiscal crisis that manifested itself in advanced capitalist societies; and on the emergence of a societal understanding of crime as a result of general material growth. Albeit that the points of interruption around which they construct their respective parameters of punishment are very different, all revisionists are united in their attempts to dissociate themselves from progressivist, presentist analysis. Instead, by using discontinuity as a tool of analysis, they endeavour to put forward more conceptual frameworks (concrete systems) which seek to avoid ahistorical analysis. This book, then, will draw upon these respective approaches so as to construct a history of the present of community service orders which is more sensitive to diachronic analysis than that espoused by academics such as Vass and Pease. There is, however, a clear danger in simply relying upon revisionist analysis. It is that, in attempting to highlight interruptions, revisionists often over schematise the complex historical processes involved and are too reductionist in stance. Thus, whilst whiggish analysis views history from a linear, one-dimensional perspective, revisionist analysis, in its attempt to highlight the fallacies inherent in such an approach, is also too schematic in methodology. Let us focus more closely on this criticism by examining Foucault's hypothesis concerning the change from a corporal to a carceral master strategy of punishment.

Foucault and the Revision of Revisionism

Foucault's thesis is excellent in that it highlights the inner and discontinuous nature of the workings of the penal system in a manner much more complex than that espoused by whiggish historians. There are, however, a number of complications which prevent it from being wholly adopted as a framework for understanding penality. To begin with, it can be argued that it is over schematic to view pre-capitalistic punishment as being characterised, in part, by the absence of carceral constituents.[17] Secondly, the level of capital punishment inflicted in Britain was far milder than that conceded by Foucault. In reality, legislation of the eighteenth century almost always defined offences in a very narrow way and often mentioned a particular institution or piece of property only.[18] Moreover, it can be argued the

---

17. R.W. Ireland, for example, has cogently argued that medieval imprisonment was far more common than generally perceived (Ireland 1987: 56-67).
18. Destroying Westminster Bridge, for example, was a similar offence to destroying Fulham Bridge, yet each offence had its own capital statute (McLynn 1989: xv). See also Mowery Andrews who suggests that even in France under the "Old Regime", "the most prevalent confiscation of criminal bodies was not on executionary scaffolds". It was by galleys, *bagnes, and hospitaux* for periods of three to nine years (Mowery Andrews 1994: 409).

Foucault's "dyssymetry of forces" perception of punishment prior to the carceral model is very one-dimensional in outlook given that it proceeds in a manner founded upon the uncontested power of the sovereign and the intrinsic verdancy and pusillanimity of plebeian society. Albeit that they were not referring to Foucault, Brewer and Styles, for example, noted:

> "The question of the relationship between the legal system, authority and state power in seventeenth and eighteenth century England is one of quite extraordinary complexity. On the one hand, the courts were powerful regulatory mechanisms, dealing not only with crime but numerous aspects of social and economic life. It is no exaggeration to argue that the long arm of the law was the strongest limb of the body politic. But, on the other hand, law enforcement varied in its intensity and efficiency: some areas were virtually lawless zones; the practice of local courts deviated considerably from the letter of the law as enacted or interpreted in Westminster; and most legal officials were rank amateurs who were as much concerned with the preservation of local harmony as they were with the (often divisive) business of litigation. In sum, there were considerable institutional constraints on the exercise of authority through law" (Brewer and Styles 1980: 12-13; Thompson 1971: 76-136; Fletcher and Stevenson 1985: 17-31).

In this sense, whilst the concept of order may have been pervasive under the corporal modality of punishment, it certainly was not monolithic as Foucault would have us believe.

There are two further points - they also highlight the more equalised set of relations that existed between the governing classes and plebeian society - which prevent Foucault's hypothesis from being wholly adopted as a framework for understanding the Bloody Code. The first issue concerns the whole process of pardoning. In many cases, in the eighteenth century, a judge would provide an offender with a free or conditional pardon on the grounds, *inter alia*, that the offence was minor, that the offender was of tender years or good character, or because it acceded to the petitions of the victim or local gentry, or propitiated the "winds of public opinion" (Stone 1987: 244; Kilcommins 2000). Less known, however, is the fact that judges would also recommend pardons for individuals who had been wrongfully convicted by juries acting out of prejudice or as a result of misconstruing the evidence before them; judges were also disposed to pardoning in cases where offenders appeared to have been convicted on insufficient evidence to sustain the charge (Beattie 1986: 409).

The crucial point that interests us here is that the ceremony of punishment in eighteenth century Britain was not, as Foucault would have us believe, just an "exercise in terror" that made "everyone aware, through the body of the criminal, of the unrestricted power of the sovereign". Rather hegemony was maintained both by the use of theatre (and the exemplary display of terror inherent therein) and the flexible employment of concessions through judicial discretion and executive clemency. Bifurcation of this nature, of course, must be viewed against a historically specific background of social relations and social control. As Hay noted, the great majority of petitions for mercy in the eighteenth century were written by gentlemen on behalf of labourers (Hay 1975: 42-43). Concessions, then, ensured, to some extent, that a good many offenders left the courtroom indebted to the local gentry and convinced of the impartial nature of justice. In this way, the penal complex attempted to instil compliance through examples of brute terror (but not so many as to destroy the perception of justice or rupture the bonds of paternalism - this was particularly axiomatic in an epoch where tight social control in the form of policing was anathematical) but also, in a much more subtle fashion, through examples of mercy and objective justice. In Gramscian terms, whilst Foucault highlights *domino* (associated with the threat or use of force by "political society" as a means of coercion), he excludes *egemonia* (notions of equilibrium, persuasion and consent which help to consolidate acceptance of the socio-political order) (Gramsci 1971: 56-61; Williams 1960: 586-599). It was, however, the combination of both (albeit a dynamic combination) in seventeenth and eighteenth century England and Wales that enabled the ruling class to legitimise its position and ensure that its beliefs were propagated and maintained. In this regard, what is called for is a more syncretic analysis of social control which will highlight the syntheses and unions - both coercive and consensual - of the period in question.

Secondly, it is submitted that Foucault's corporal modality of punishment is too schematic in that he fails to appreciate that formalistic procedure in respect of framing indictments in the seventeenth and eighteenth century ensured that some element of parity existed between the Crown and the accused in the courtroom. For example, in the decision in *Long's* case (1605) it was declared that "indictments of felony, which are as counts and declarations for the King against the parties for their lives, ought to have certainty expressed in the record of indictment ... for if the counts between party and party for land or chattels ought to have two things, *scil.* truth and certainty ... because the counts are the foundations of the suits, to which the party shall answer, and on which the Judges shall adjudge; *a fortiori* indictments, especially those which concern the life of a man, and which are the King's counts, to which the party shall answer, and on which the Court shall adjudge for his life, ought to have full and precise certainty." Formalities of this nature have been described by Sir William Holdsworth as "this extraordinary and irrational set of rules which have grown up around the wording of indictments" (Holdsworth 1908: 618-619).[19]

What should be apparent from this synopsis is that the exercise of established authority for most of the seventeenth and eighteenth century Britain was subtle and complex; it was governed not only by a myriad of local contingencies but also by a penal hegemony which operated in a protean manner (from full exposure to the Code to the employment

---

19. See also Hale who suggested in 1736: "That in favour of life, great strictness's have been in all times required in points of indictments, and the truth is, that it has grown to be a blemish and inconvenience in the law and the administration thereof" (Hale 1971: 193).

of pardons and strict adherence to formalistic procedure) in order to maintain the *status quo*. On the one side there is the history of terror; on the other, the history of pardoning and evidentiary rules. Although history in relation to the latter is, in many instances, far less exhilarating than elucidating the history of terror, it is just as pivotal to our understanding of the penal complex because it enables us to close the gap between transitional penal discourse and actual penal practice.

Much of the same argument can also be made in respect of Foucault's carceral modality of punishment. It can be argued, for example, that there are a number of forces which are diametrically opposed to the deterministic perception of individualised normalising methods proceeding in an uncontested fashion both inside and outside the penal complex. These forces, in my view, prevent Foucault's disciplinary power interpretation of modern punishment from being wholly adopted as a framework for understanding penality. As shall become more apparent in chapters 2 and 3, there was, for example, immense resistance to the extension and rationalisation of the State control apparatus which included, *inter alia*, a lack of financial resources necessary to implement intended changes and a general anathema to government interference right up to the 1870s.[20]

---

20. See, for example, Patricia O'Brien who noted in respect of French imprisonment: "[C]ertain formal aspects of old regime punishments, ... survived in the carceral world of the nineteenth century. Most striking was the physical continuity of the very buildings, few new structures were actually built; instead, old buildings were converted to new needs. The

Less apparent are the forces of resistance which emanated from those upon whom power was intended to be imposed. It is my contention that any attempt to write a history of the implementation of individualised normative methods must also recognise that such methods had, for the greater part of the eighteenth and indeed nineteenth century, to exist side by side with a dynamic criminal culture that demonstrated a remarkable durability over time. In particular, it can be argued that Foucault's study of individualised normative methods in the late eighteenth and nineteenth century was founded upon a very "functionalist logic" that viewed penal history from the "top down" and allowed little for the possibility that the criminal classes themselves had their own habits, customs, techniques and beliefs which aided their survival and impeded the progress of the "panoptic society" perception of penality - the simple situation of an offender screwing up his or her face to confound the process of keeping a record of him or her by way of a photograph causes a breakdown in the view of uncontested disciplinary progress (Kilcommins 2000; Valier 1998: 88-105; Thompson 1981: 189-208).[21]

---

central prison of Nîmes, for example, was a converted citadel that held its first prisoners during the Terror. It also served as a *dépôt de mendicité* for the poor during the Napoleonic regime. Other prisons were built in the shells of seminaries, convents and retreat houses ... [N]either architecture nor penal practice in the nineteenth century reflected an immediate or sharp rupture with old-regime practices, the transformation extended over a longer period of time than has been commonly supposed" (O'Brien 1982: 15-17).

21. See also Dobash *et al* who argue that revisionists such as Foucault fail to consider the extent to which "gender based assumptions" impacted upon the development of the modern prison: "[I]t is clear that patriarchal and

Finally, although physical punishments (focusing on publicity and the infliction of physical suffering) were in evidence in the 1700s, Foucault's study of their replacement by the rise of a rationalised, carceral modality of punishment is also too deterministic in argument. It is my contention that the transition was much more dilatory and intractable than that depicted in *Discipline and Punish*. For example, Foucault fails to appreciate that the hulks, transportation, public floggings, and public ceremonies of execution, all continued well into the 1800s, or that prisoners treading the wheel or engaged in shot-drill in the 1870s and 1880s would undoubtedly have regarded their incarceration as being directed as much against their bodies as their souls.

At this juncture, only Foucault's critique has been questioned.[22] But it should already be clear that a much lower level of analysis - in the sense of getting one's hands dirty with *micro* history - is required so as to account for resistances, disparities, various ideological and cultural forces, internal debate, and the dilatory nature of change, all of which impede or shape the nature of criminal justice reformulations. Too often, the historical caesuras that

---

paternalist conceptions played a crucial role in the responses to women right from the beginning of the modern prison. The work provided for women was always predicated on assumptions about their natural skills and limitations, and the surveillance and regulation was always closer and more omnipresent than that usually directed at men" (Dobash *et al* 1986: 61).

22. I have chosen Foucault's account of the birth of the prison - and the phenomenological account of penal relations as power relations inherent therein - as an example because his work has become a central reference point for much revisionist discourse (including the works of Melossi and Pavarini and Cohen) on the technologies of penal power.

Foucault seeks to highlight lead to what Gramsci might term as "an excess of doctrinaire pedantry" with insufficient attention being paid to the "correct relation between what is organic and what is conjunctural" (Gramsci 1971: 178).[23] Much of the same argument will also be used in respect of other revisionist critiques.

This is not to deny what may be regarded as the *Nutzen* of revisionist analysis. Revisionists have undoubtedly advanced debate on the penal complex by demonstrating a more heightened critical awareness of notions of reform and emphasising the need to associate penal developments with prevailing conditions in the broader social structure. However, by also being aware of the *Nachteil*, it is hoped that the analysis that follows will not fall into the trap of adopting any form of totalising or mechanical determination in seeking to highlight the "incidence of interruptions" in the historical penal process. Instead, any endeavour to capture the essence of a particular penal epoch will be prepared, where possible, to integrate the central with the local, the élite with the criminal, the durable with the

---

23. For example, Gramsci would argue, in respect of the periodisation of the French Revolution, that it was only in 1870-71 that "all the germs of 1789 were finally historically exhausted". For Gramsci, it was only by studying the entire period between 1789 and 1871 that the proper "dialectical nexus" between organic and conjunctural could be achieved because: "It was only then that the new bourgeois class struggling for power defeated not only the representatives of the old society unwilling to admit that it had been definitively superseded, but also the still newer groups who maintained that the new structure created by the 1789 revolution was itself already outdated; by this victory the bourgeoisie demonstrated its vitality *vis-à-vis* both the old and the very new" (*ibid*: 179; Sassoon 1980).

transient, and the intended with the actual.[24]

This book will proceed then by attempting to highlight the anachronistic, prefatory history approach adopted by most commentators in relation to the introduction of community service orders. Part I of the book will commence with a rough outline of the history of leisure as a concept in order to determine whether it has remained constant throughout history. The reason for focusing on the cultural phenomenon of leisure is that it forms the punitive element of community service in that an offender is deprived of it in order to carry out suitable work tasks. It will be argued that it was only in the period after the Second World War that leisure was sufficiently formulated as a concept so as to allow policy makers to deprive an offender of it as a suitable means of punishment.

Part II will then go on to highlight the discontinuous nature of the penal process by highlighting transformations in perceptions of offenders, state control and the application of reformative practices in order to create a broad historical framework within which community service orders can be understood. It will then proceed to examine more specific aspects of criminal justice thinking which have had a direct impact on the introduction of community service. Such an analysis will examine issues such as the emergence of the

---

24. For a similar call in respect of the way in which women impede the construction of gender, see Carol Smart who suggests: "[M]ore needs to be done in tracing how women have resisted and negotiated constructions of gender, since we should not slip into a new form of determinism which suggests that, because power constructs, it produces women in some predetermined, calculated, powerless form" (Smart 1995: 198).

"therapeutic community" as a suitable means of social control, the utilisation of labour as a means of deterring and rehabilitating offenders, and the emergence of international rights concerning the use of forced labour. The practical implications of the theoretical choice being adopted in Parts I and II of the book will then be applied to the specific sanction of impressment in order to illuminate the ahistorical approach adopted by Pease and his cohorts and their attempts to draw linear lines of comparison between a sanction from the seventeenth and eighteenth centuries and a contemporary sanction. The book moves on in Part III to examine more positive and genuine claims of relevance in respect of the germs of community service by examining enthusiasm for the ideal in the 1950s and 1960s in the voluntary sector, in prisons, in borstals and detention centres, in the establishment of intermediate treatment programmes, and through international penal experiences. It will be argued that it is in these phenomena that the historical conditions of emergence of community service can be traced. Having examined more positive and historical claims of relevance in respect of the community service order ideal, the book will conclude by providing a pluralistic framework in which to understand the manner in which those germs were moulded together by considering a whole plethora of determinants such as, *inter alia*, rising crime rates, the sensitisation of moral panics, the politicisation of law and order, and the declining influence of the rehabilitative ethos.

There are, however, a number of preliminary observations which must be made with regard to the way in which the genealogy of community service orders will be considered. First, in attempting to define the "roots of the modern system", I am, as Harding and Ireland put it, "acutely aware of the danger of removing a practice from its original context and forcing it into a theoretical framework that does not accommodate such problems as comparative analysis" (Harding and Ireland 1989: 17). In this sense, I will attempt to adopt some form of middle ground between *macro* and *micro* approaches to the criminal justice history process in order to maintain a balance between historical actuality and a wider conceptual framework. As Ignatieff noted:

"The real challenge is to find a model of historical explanation which accounts for historical change without imputing conspiratorial rationality to a ruling class, without reducing institutional developments to a formless ad hoc adjustment to contingent crisis, and without assuming a hyper-idealist, all triumphant humanitarian crusade" (Ignatieff 1983: 77).

Implicit in my methodology, therefore, is the need to take account of the "total context of conditions" (cultural, political, ideological, economic, and technological) (Pisciotta 1981: 120) when mapping the contours of modern penality rather than adopting an over deterministic approach (i.e. viewing penality purely in economic or disciplinary terms) as is sometimes the case with revisionist analysis. As such, I hope to embody a methodology which illuminates the complex and tortuous nature of the penal process in my search for the broad contours of the modern penal complex in which the genealogy of community service can be traced. I am, therefore, aware that there can be no "perfect synchrony" in terms of capturing the essence of the modern modality of punishment. It is, as Braudel suggests, "conceivable only in terms of a *multiplicity of descents*, following the innumerable rivers of time" (Braudel 1980: 39). Moreover, by employing discontinuity as a tool of analysis, I do not wish to maintain that modern penality has resulted in a complete break with past penality; rather I simply wish to argue that elements of old penality had to be incorporated into a new modality of punishment which "displayed a distinctive pattern of sanctions, strategies and representations which ranged across an altered and extended domain" (Garland 1985: 5). As Foucault suggested:

"To say one ... formation is substituted for another is not to say that a whole world of absolutely new objects, enunciations, concepts, and theoretical choices emerges fully armed and fully organised ... [I]t is to say that a general transformation has occurred, but that does not necessarily alter all the elements; it is to say that statements are governed by new rules of formation, it is not to say that all objects or concepts, all enunciations or theoretical choices disappear" (Foucault 1972: 173).

Thirdly, in recent years there have been analyses which argue that a paradigm shift is currently taking place from modern to post-modern penality and policing. In contemporary society, post-modernism - which is viewed as a condition rather than an ideology - tends to imply the end of Enlightenment thought, and the rise of plural rationalities, eclecticism and fragmentation (Lyon 1994; Lyotard 1984). In the field of penality and policing, it is argued that these post-modern phenomena have manifested themselves through the emergence of actuarial and technocratic managerial styles, privatisation, incapacitation, control of groups of offenders, the regulation of rational choice offenders (consumers), and the demise of normalising individual offenders (Steptycki 1998: 485-503; Simon and Feeley 1995: 147-180; Nelken 1994; Ericson and Heggarty 1997). Such analysis does not form any element of my book since it only extends to the introduction of community service orders in 1972, but, for what it is worth, I, like Garland, would argue that such developments as are affecting "contemporary penality are occurring *within* the contours of modernity and modernism (albeit high modernity and modernism), rather than representing some kind of break with them" (Garland 1995: 192; Lucken 1998: 106-123). Fourthly, in criticising progressivist interpretations of penal history, I do not wish to advocate an entire loss of belief in progress. Progress of one kind of another is indeed possible. Progress, however, is not always eternally valid and simultaneous for all; it cannot always advance in a linear and continuous manner, and "it should not be taken as an uncontested foundation, historical law, or abstract standard in interpreting history" (Carr 1986: 103-127).

Furthermore, it is important to bear in mind that the construction of modern penality that is being proffered in this book provides only rough parameters for analysis. I do not wish to suggest that once modern penality has been defined that penal phenomena have remained static and subject to no further change. Of course they continue to change, but it is submitted that the changes that have manifested themselves since modern penality first emerged have not resulted in a reformulation of the kind witnessed in the late nineteenth and early twentieth centuries. So although the late 1960s and early 1970s witnessed, for example, the decline in rehabilitation and the emergence of containment as a policy goal, such a change, in the greater scheme of things, does not amount to a radical transformation and can, for the most part, still be understood in terms of a broad conceptual framework, titled "the modern penal complex".[25]

Two final points can be made. This work only focuses on the genealogy of community service and no attempt is made to investigate the contemporary operation of the sanction. Indeed, in this regard, the author accepts that academics

---

25. What, in effect, is of concern here is *levels of analysis*. At a *macro* level of historical analysis, the decline in rehabilitation and the subsequent rise of containment does not constitute any radical shift in the modality of punishment. At a *micro* level of analysis, however, it can be argued that such developments do constitute a shift in policy terms, albeit that it would be wrong to view such a shift as constituting a new concrete system of punishment. This issue has been touched upon by Foucault in an interview with Gerard Raulet: "The solemnity with which everyone who engages in philosophical discourse reflects on his own time strikes me as a flaw ... I think we should have the modesty to say to ourselves that, on the one hand, the time we live in is not the unique or fundamental or irruptive point in history where everything is completed and begun again. We must also have the modesty to say, on the other hand, that - even without this solemnity - the time we live in is very interesting; it needs to be analysed and broken down, and that we would do well to ask ourselves, 'What is the nature of our present?'" (Kritzman, L.D. 1990: 35-36).

such as Pease and Vass have been some of the leading commentators on the operation of community service orders over the last 25 years, particularly in respect of its position in the range of sentencing alternatives, its employment by the courts, the selection of offenders, the nature of work tasks, and the reconviction rates of offenders ordered to perform community service. Secondly, the analysis that follows is contentious and polemical in that historical interpretation necessarily involves a "multiplicity of truth" and the "possibility of choice". As the relativist E.H. Carr noted:

"The world of the historian ... is not a photographic copy of the real world, but rather a working model which enables him more or less effectively to understand it and to master it. The historian distils from the experience of the past as is accessible to him, that part which he recognises as amenable to rational explanation and interpretation, and from it draws conclusions which may serve as a guide to action" (Carr 1986: 97-98).

This is supported by David Lowenthal who noted in his influential work, *The Past is a Foreign Country*, that "historical narrative is not a portrait of *what happened*, but a story *about* what happened" and "no process of verification can totally satisfy us that we know the truth about the past" (Lowenthal 1985: 215). Thus, rather than adopting a Rankean model of historical interpretation (*wie es eigentlich gewesen*), the purpose of the book is to establish credibility or verisimilitude rather than truth or certaintist claims in historical terms: what is meant by credibility or verisimilitude in historical terms is "not that it actually happened, but that it is as close to what actually happened as we can learn from a critical examination of the best available sources" (Gottschalk 1969: 35).[26]

With these provisos and qualifications in mind, let us begin our analysis of the claim that community service is only in detail a novel disposal (because of the perceived affinities and continuities that exist over time between various penal work sanctions) by examining the cultural determinant of leisure and its influence on the shaping of community service. By focusing on the cultural determinant of leisure - the deprivation of leisure time is considered to be the punitive aspect of community service orders - I hope to

---

26. Karl Popper's notion of truth in respect of scientific knowledge is very similar. For Popper, all generalisations are conclusively falsifiable although they are not conclusively verifiable: "[I]f we are rational we shall always base our decisions and expectations on the best of our knowledge ... and provisionally assume the truth of that knowledge for practical purposes, because it is the least insecure foundation available; but we shall never lose sight of the fact that at any time experience may show it to be wrong and require us to reverse it." For example: "All measurement, whether of time or space, can only be within a certain degree of accuracy. If you order a piece of steel six millimetres long, you can have it made accurately to within the finest margin of which the very best instruments are capable, which is now fractions of a millionth of a millimetre. But where, within that margin, the *exact* point of six millimetres lies is something which, in the nature of things, we do not know ... All you know is that the length is accurate to within such and such a fraction of a millimetre, and that it is nearer the desired length than anything measurably longer or shorter. With the next improvement in machine tools you may be able to get a piece of steel whose accuracy you can be sure of within an even closer margin ... But the notion "exactly six millimetres" ... is not something that can ever be met with in experience" (Magee 1973: 27).

move away from the internalism of previous studies and to open up new possibilities for understanding the conditions of emergence of community service orders.

PART I

A CULTURAL PERSPECTIVE

CHAPTER 1

LEISURE AS A CULTURAL DETERMINANT OF PENAL PRACTICE

The functioning of community service is clearly dependent on the cultural phenomenon of leisure in that it compels an offender (who has consented to the order) to spend a fixed period of leisure time (calculated in hours) undertaking constructive work in the community. The purpose of this chapter is to illustrate that this cultural phenomenon of leisure has not remained invariable throughout history but has undergone and continues to undergo a metamorphosis which has not only altered its shape but also its substance. Penal policy initiatives are more often than not founded upon accepted societal attitudes and sensibilities. These attitudes unconsciously set parameters to a policy maker's ambit. But they have not remained rigid; rather they demonstrate a protean nature and expand and constrict with the changing cultural climate. In this chapter it will be shown that it was only in the mid- to late-twentieth century that depriving an offender of his or her leisure time could be condoned as a civilised mode of punishment. It was only in this epoch that the policy maker's ambit was sufficiently formulated *vis-à-vis* leisure to allow for the introduction of such a sanction.

One must be careful, however, not to isolate leisure as a distinct subject when studying its transformations; to do so would provide too schematic an interpretation of its history.

1

For this reason, the chapter describes prevailing attitudes to leisure by placing them in the context of prevailing attitudes to labour. By presenting leisure in terms of its inter-relationship with labour, it is possible, in the author's view, to demonstrate most palpably how work centrality in industrialised society - with its emphasis on clock time sentience, labour differentiation, and spatial and disciplinary rationalisation - shaped significantly not only our conception of leisure but also the activities which comprise, in part, our culture of leisure. As Haywood *et al* noted about the process of urbanisation and industrialisation in Britain between 1750-1900:

> "Work came to dominate people's lives during this time, not simply in the sheer amount of time demanded by the new processes and practices of industrial labour, but much more powerfully because of changes in the nature of work. This demanded a new way of seeing the world ... Pleasure came a poor second in this scenario, and the modern view of leisure emerging against this background reflects this conception: leisure is dependent on work for its time and justification. Leisure though 'separate', paradoxically comes in many ways to resemble work, such is the predominance of the work-centred view of the world" (Haywood *et al* 1995: 22).[1]

---

1. For further justification, see Stedman Jones: "The necessity to obtain work, to remain fit enough for work and to make ends meet is far more important than any packaged consumerist ideology which succeeds in intruding upon the worker's weekly or nightly period of rest and recuperation. Leisure time is clearly constricted by type and hours of work. To study leisure on its own

Of course, in prioritising labour's significance on the development of leisure, I have overstated the importance of the conjunction at the expense of a whole series of other powerful variables such as non-employed (Martin and Mason 1992: XI, 81-86), gender (Deem 1982: I, 29-46; Deem 1986; Green *et al* 1990), and individual experiences, all of which undoubtedly impinge upon opportunities and indeed perceptions of leisure. However, the work-leisure conjunction adopted here is the most convenient means, in the author's view, of demonstrating the context dependent and mutable nature of leisure: in different economic, industrial, social and political contexts in Britain, the conception of leisure has had different significations, constructions, domains, and temporal and spatial features. In this regard, the reader should bear in mind that my purpose is to illustrate how leisure as a concept is not static; how it has undergone a considerable metamorphosis in the transition from pre-modern to modern society; and, ultimately, how our conception of leisure has had an impact on the introduction of community service orders - an impact not touched upon in the prefatory history accounts of the introduction of the sanction. Accordingly, the perspective posited here is not to be embraced as a balanced or inclusive history of leisure *per se* - there are a whole host of social historians more disposed and adept at writing such histories. Rather, the purpose of this chapter is less grandiose in design; its intention is merely to demonstrate, as already outlined, that our conceptions of leisure have in

is dangerous" (1985: 49).

part shaped the sanction of community service and that these conceptions do not fit neatly with any progressive or continuous analyses. To this end, the adoption of a labour-leisure conjunction can serve a useful purpose as long as the reader understands that it is not being employed to convey some total reality.

Moreover, in order to delineate the transformations which have occurred, it has been necessary to divide history into various crude stages - that sacrifice precision for breadth - which act more as rudimentary demarcations than rigid and distinct transitional points in time. There is a tendency when compartmentalising history under various labels to simplify the notions of transition from one period to another. Whilst labels assist in identifying pertinent and powerful transformations, they can conceal the process of change which is often more multifarious and complex. Changes did not occur systematically or simultaneously and there were marked variations in the patterns of work and leisure to be found in different regions. Yet the purpose of this chapter is not so much concerned with the intricacy, reflexivity and contested nature of change as it is with substantiating the macro thesis that change did in fact occur. Apropos of this macro thesis, three periodisations - 1500 to 1750, 1750 to 1850, and 1850 to 1970 - have been adopted as conceptual devices which will assist in highlighting the interruptions, discontinuities and mutations which have manifested themselves in the history of leisure. Let us begin, then, by providing a backdrop to the first of these periodisations.

In the Middle Ages, agrarian rhythms dictated a society very much relaxed in nature and undemanding in relation to production. Self-sufficiency and self-reliance, combined with terms of shared assistance, were the predominant features of the way of life. Work was regulated essentially by the cycle of the farming year. Seasonal variations magnified or diminished the workload accordingly. Holy days and Saints' days, which more often than not involved periods of wild saturnalia, marked the onset of new seasons. Work formed an indispensable component of community and family life and was typically carried out in or around the vicinity of the household. Money, whilst gradually growing in importance, still had a secondary role to play as people normally produced the necessities of life themselves. Social mobility was limited and most people were born, lived and died in the same locality. Divisions of labour were not as conspicuous as in late industrial society.

The unit of labour time in rural medieval society was the day (Le Goff 1984: 44). The sequence of tasks which governed this day were dictated by the natural rhythms of the seasons. The specificity of time was of less concern. People were not equipped to monitor passages of time: hourglasses were rare; sundials were inadequate, particularly when the skies clouded over (Bloch 1978: I, 73). As such, time was dominated in the main by natural events such as sunrise and sunset. The calendar for the year was demarcated by a procession of agrarian undertakings - harvesting period, lambing period, ploughing period, sowing period, shearing period and so on. The system of time which arises in such contexts has been described as "task orientated time" (Thompson 1967: No. 38, p.60). Distinctions between work and leisure were minimal. Social pleasure and leisure were interwoven and carried out in tandem with work throughout the day. The focus of past agrarian civilisation to the task in hand may seem mystifying in a modern world dominated by rigidly defined periods of time. Office hours, factory hours, timetables, calendars and diaries constrain and circumscribe our lives and agendas. Pre-industrial society was not so limited by temporal restraints. All kinds of non-work activities shamelessly punctuated the workday and no distinct boundary existed between work and leisure.[2]

Leisure was not, accordingly, a demarcated and separate segment of an individual's daily routine. It co-existed and interspersed with the labour rhythms of the day. Work was ordinarily performed around the family home or within the home itself. Recreational activities and festivals frequently interfered with and disrupted the process. It was only after work was enclosed in restricted spaces, to be carried out at scheduled times and under specialised conditions, that leisure came to be seen as a right (Parker 1976: 20-21). This is not however to imply that society was unaware of leisure prior to industrialisation. To allege that people could not distinguish between work and leisure is, as Cunningham proposed, "sheer romanticism" (1980: 57). Although leisure was fastened to labour, people were still capable of discerning that certain activities constituted leisure.

---

2.   It would be a fallacy, however, to over-aggrandise the *Gemeinschaft* type of existence that endured in pre-industrial times. As Robertson correctly infers, the majority of individuals were more impoverished and poverty-stricken than their counterparts in contemporary society and their lives were shorter and less secure (Robertson 1985: 28).

Opportunities for pastimes found expression in communal celebrations which were both religious and secular. All evince a traditional appreciation of time and were organised at relaxed stages of the agrarian year. Certain recreations were distinctly related to war - archery, riding and wrestling, tilting and sword play (Thomas 1964: no.29: 53-54; Bailey 1994: 167-168) Others such as football - Shrovetide football melees were notorious - were supposedly more harmless in orientation, though they often descended into "licensed mayhem" (Birley 1993: 59-61). Others again reflected the web of kinship associated with medieval life. This was noticeable in the many convivial weddings and funerals which were attended by the majority of the community.

It is also true to say, however, that the Middle Ages was a period which witnessed developments which would have important ramifications for generations to come. It was, for example, an epoch when ecclesiastical and secular philosophies on asceticism and just price were being rejected in favour of the quest for prosperity and success. Moreover, life in urban areas was becoming more regimented and the period witnessed the introduction of mechanical clocks - which replaced church bells that were often determined by imprecise sundials and water clocks - into more urbanised areas such as Northern Italy, Catalonia, Southern England, Flanders and parts of Germany (Le Goff 1980: pp. 36-49). It is, however, necessary to refrain from oversimplifying these changes. For most people living in the Age, and indeed for numerous generations to come, the day was still primarily regulated by agrarian enterprise and natural occurrences. How time conscious could they have been in an era where, as Landes points out, no uniformity of measurement existed? Units of distance were linked to physical characteristics (the English *foot,* for example) while weights were often converted to volume standards (*a bushel* of grain, for example) that perpetually varied from one location to another (1983: 72). Accordingly, the Middle Ages, in terms of the masses, can still be classified as a period when the rotations of the agrarian year prescribed the patterns of working life and where leisure did not exist as a separate and autarchic conception but punctuated and interspersed work periods.

1500 to 1750

Notwithstanding that life in the sixteenth and seventeenth centuries was still predominately pre-industrialised and pre-mechanised in nature, it is still possible to uncover evidence of transformations. In particular the expansion of trade, both in domestic and international markets, and the conglomeration of resources and capital instigated and encouraged the development of enterprise. Such development was supported by the Church which no longer regarded profit making as an immoral activity (Coulton 1930: 140-145).

With the passage of time the increasing use of money operated as a stimulus to emerging economic and commercial activities. Merchants drafts, letters of credit and bills of exchange became more and more acceptable and the quantity of credit transactions grew in number (Minchinton 1974: 103). Wages rose in prominence and came to be regarded as an autonomous factor of production. Yet there was a hesitancy about bestowing high wages on the labouring population. The commercial classes were of the impression that the State could only prosper in an increasingly competitive market when wages were kept to a minimum. Moreover, it was also assumed that high wages encouraged idleness and inertia.

This growth in commerce was also accompanied by the pressing need for a more complete range of professional services as lawyers, bankers and brokers found themselves in considerable demand. The metamorphosis from medieval to quasi-modern was also represented by a proliferation in the amount of people residing in towns and cities. Urbanisation was becoming more prevalent despite the fact that the majority of the population continued to live in the countryside.

The transformation in religious beliefs fashioned by the Protestant revolution cemented this new attitude to trade and commerce by depicting labour as a vocation and the most obtrusive means of obtaining God's benefaction. By pursuing a calling and by performing work to the best of one's ability, each individual could unlock the door to the kingdom of heaven. Calvin elaborated upon these ideas with his concept of predestination: the chosen people - the elect - were guaranteed salvation, whilst the remainder were anathematised, never to receive God's grace. Hence in order to obviate any consternation as to whether or not one was a member of the favoured few, the believer could assure his or her troubled conscience by engaging in good work and maintaining high moral standards, thereby providing proof of his or her salvation (McGrath 1990: 240).

Puritanism evolved out of the doctrine of Calvinism. It emphasised and exhorted the dignity of labour and cherished it as a solemn and social obligation to be discharged through secular assignments. The duty to work was a form of ascetic discipline; time lost to nugatory exertions and idleness were fateful sins punishable by God on judgement day. Engagement in profit-making exercises was not iniquitous provided participants took cognisance of the fact that it was God's will. Protestantism, and more particularly Puritanism, were endearing to small employers and self-employed men for whom parsimony and toil might make all the difference between prosperity and poverty in the age of nascent industrialisation (Hill 1986: 134).[3] Indeed it may also be proposed that it was equally advantageous to wealthier traders and merchants who were now free to immerse themselves in business enterprise with the concurrence of the Church, provided they acknowledged that it was their vocation and agreed to abstain from vivacious and idle living.

Religious opinion also began to place less emphasis on the obligation of charity than upon the duty of work. Industry was desirable and commendable and would result in God's blessing. Poverty, on the other hand, was deemed a result of

---

3.   The accumulation of wealth, then, was only immoral in that it was a temptation to idleness, and its acquisition was only unethical if it was for the purpose of later living a life without work (Weber 1976: 163).

idleness and wickedness. To simply indulge in alms giving would exacerbate such idleness despite its attempt to allay it. Accordingly the most suitable charity was not to succour the impoverished with futile relief but rather to reform their characters and dispositions so that the requirement of relief would become superfluous (Tawney 1987: 238-264).

Vagrants and beggars could be supported in feudal society as a number of customary arrangements were set in place to cater for such groups. These arrangements were conventionally informal in nature and beggary was not regarded as a threat to social order. As the sixteenth century wore on, however, vagabondage was experienced on a new scale causing grave concern among the authorities. Beggars now appeared as a positive terror to ordinary society. New forms of relief were required to attend to the mass of unemployed beggars, vagrants and paupers who flocked to the towns and cities as a result of the turmoil and disorder that emerged during the protracted transition from feudalism to capitalism.

There are a variety of reasons put forward for the increase in poverty in Tudor times. It has been suggested that the emergence of increasing numbers of "masterless men" on the streets and in the countryside was as a result of the dissolution of the monasteries which had been considered a traditional source of poor relief (Ignatieff 1978: 11-12). The inflationary movement brought about by the increase in the supply of precious metal and by the debasement of coins is also considered to be a contributory factor to the economic distress of the era (Van der Slice 1991: 32). Moreover, as a consequence of the declining mortality rates in the fifteenth century, the pressure of population growth resulted in a proliferation of poverty. The population of England rose from about 2.3 million in 1524 to a peak of 5.3 million in 1656 (Slack 1988: 43-44). Furthermore, as the wool industry developed in England, it began to redefine the economic and social arrangements governing agriculture (Piven and Cloward 1972: 12). As sheep rearing became more lucrative, large tracts of land were converted from tillage to pasture. Many peasant farmers were displaced by an entrepreneurial gentry anxious to profit from such business. As a consequence, the agricultural labouring class, deprived of a means of support on the land and unable to gain employment in nascent manufacture, were compelled to seek out philanthropy.

With the rise in the number of vagrants, the authorities became increasingly conversant with the perception that indiscriminate charity was menacing; coercive measures were needed to stave off any intimation of insurgency. In turn, such measures would assist in inculcating a proper work ethic among the lower orders. A distinction had to be made between the impotent and deserving poor who could not work through no failing of their own and the able-bodied who could work but were simply too indolent or too untoward to find it. The latter category was to be obliged to labour for any relief provided. Hobbes acknowledged this when he suggested that although:

> "[M]any men, ... became unable to maintain themselves by their labour; they ought not to be left to the charity of private persons; but to be provided for, as far forth as the

12

necessities of nature require, by the laws of the commonwealth ... But for such as have strong bodies, the case is otherwise: they are to be forced to work; and to avoid the excuse of not finding employment, there ought to be such laws, as may encourage all manner of arts; as navigation, agriculture, fishing, and all manner of manufacture that requires labour" (1839: III, 334-335).

Similarly, Thomas More recommended in 1516 that thieves should not be executed as their labour was more advantageous than their death. He postulated that instead of such a punishment it would be far more beneficial to provide them with a means of livelihood. In order to do this, he suggested that the wealthy had to be prevented from cornering markets and establishing monopolies. If the agriculture and wool industries could be revived, useful work could be provided for the unemployed and consequentially reduce idleness (1967 repr: 44-49).

By the sixteenth century, then, the authorities began to differentiate between the poor who were entitled to donations and those who were not. Institutions such as the house of correction, the workhouse and the poorhouse were devised as a means of exerting control over the latter group of individuals. Indeed these institutions were regarded as an excellent solution to the vagrancy problem as "the occasion of giving vitally needed assistance can easily become the occasion of inculcating the work ethic, for example, and of enforcing work itself, for those who resist risk withdrawal of that assistance" (Piven and Cloward 1972: 22). The first of these houses of correction was founded in the former royal palace of Bridewell (from which the popular name has been derived). It was originally granted by Edward VI in 1553 and it was handed over to the corporation of London in 1556 (O'Donoghue 1923: I, 5). By the 1560s Gloucester and Norwich had founded similar institutions and they proliferated after an Act of 1576 ordered their establishment in every county (Innes 1987: 62; Beier 1985: 164-165). Similarly the Corporation for the Poor established in London in 1649 may be treated as the forerunner to the workhouse movement of the late seventeenth century (Pearl 1978: 210). An Act of 1670 outlined the status of workhouses, appointed officers to collect taxes which would permit their functioning and authorised Justices of the Peace to control their administration (22 and 23 Car II, c. 18). It was not, however, until a workhouse was established in Bristol in 1696 under the guidance of William Cary that the idea began to gain credence. Cary suggested that the aims of his institution were "to put to work a great number of people, many of which had been habited to laziness and beggary; to civilise such as had been bred up in all vices that want of education could expose them to, and to clothe, lodge, and feed them well" (Cary 1700: 4; Marshall 1926: 127). The example was soon to find other imitators in Crediton, Tiverton, Exeter, Hereford, Colchester and Hull in 1698, and King's Lynn and Sudbury in 1700 (Oxley 1974: 81). These then were some of the more important measures devised to control vagrancy, instil a work ethic among the poor and deter potential malefactors. But as we shall see in the next chapter, these aspirations could not all possibly be achieved within the confines of one institution.

Labour for the greater number of the population toiling outside such an institution was not yet imposed upon by the constraints and restrictions of the factory or the office but by the demands of routine and the rhythms of the agrarian year. The attributes and characteristics of labour sustained this process. Although regular and unchanging employment was not as commonplace as it is in the present-day, workers contended with such difficulties by engaging in assorted occupational tasks concomitantly. Agricultural work was in many instances mixed with the "putting out" system where, for example, families would contract with middlemen to perform a number of tasks such as spinning and weaving by a prescribed date. These assignments were carried out in the household and supplemented the seasonal nature of agricultural work. Despite the fact that people worked long hours, they were masters of their own time and they dictated when work should begin and cease or when and for how long breaks should be.

As work was still very much task related, time could be set aside for domestic and leisurely activities as the worker deemed appropriate. Indeed some days, "Saint Monday" being an example, were customarily designated as non-work days, particularly in urbanised areas. Many trades appear to have practised this custom: shoemakers, tailors, colliers, printing workers, potters and weavers, to name but a few (Thompson 1967: no. 38, p. 73; Kumar 1988: 47). Workers therefore would only graft to the extent required to provide adequately for the household. Once this had been achieved, it was more desirable to partake in leisurely activities than to exert oneself for additional economic gain. This attitude to labour is often referred to as being consistent with the "backward sloping supply curve": labourers toil during the week to earn an intended sum of money, once this has been attained no further work is undertaken until the following week. So, whilst workers might preserve Monday as a day of rest, by Thursday and Friday they would be labouring intensively to reach their requisite quotas. Although such an approach to labour is one of the key features of a pre-industrialised economy, care should be taken to appreciate that variations and exceptions did exist. As has already been noted, many individuals wanted to better themselves and build up a reserve for times of scarcity. Accordingly, merely providing enough to survive was not sufficient. Nor is it possible to precisely discern when such attitudes no longer held sway.[4] But certainly by the early 1800s, due mainly to the discipline of the factory and the increased emphasis on time management, a more ordered and regimented outlook began to take hold.

In the sixteenth and seventeenth centuries work and leisure were still, by and large, integrated. Leisure in an agrarian society is dominated by the cyclical nature of the seasons and the tasks on hand. Recreation, therefore, forms part of the daily routine as opposed to a segregated

---

4. Adam Smith suggested that the transformation had already taken place by 1776: "some workmen, indeed, when they can earn in four days what will maintain them through the week, will be idle the other three. This, however, is by no means the case with the greater part. Workmen, on the contrary, when they are liberally paid by the piece, are very apt to over-work themselves, and to ruin their health and constitution in a few years" (1930 repr: I, 83-84).

component of it. As the majority of the population still dwelled on the land, it was these notions of labour and leisure which prevailed. Nor were the boundaries more discernible in towns and villages. Drinking, gossiping, and singing all formed an intrinsic part of the diurnal work routine. Labourers had become habituated to toiling at their own momentum and sojourning for playful interludes as they pleased. Levels of work could intensify or diminish as was necessitated. The point to bear in mind, then, is that although people were undoubtedly aware that the performance of certain tasks constituted work, labour and leisure were not compartmentalised or disjoined to the same degree as they are in modern society. It was only when urbanisation and industrialisation combined together to condense and isolate leisure that a process of differentiation and compartmentalisation was set in motion. This is supported by Jonathan Barry, who, after studying popular culture in seventeenth century Bristol, stated:

"[W]ork was ... all-encompassing, stretching in theory from dawn to dusk, rather than according to the clock, and punctuated only by Sundays and public holidays. In practice, leisure was probably available in the interstices of the working day, since few were yet involved in capitalised industries where time literally meant money" (1985: 79).

But by the late 1600s the different forms of recreation pursued by the masses were increasingly coming under attack. Protestants exhalted the Sabbath and beheld it as a day for ascetic worship. They condemned the copious amounts of festivals and other recreational activities which had until now been a part of everyday life. Religious preachers, employers and the authorities combined together to instil in the commonalty a proper work ethic. In 1655, for example, Cromwell ordered his Major-Generals to suppress dissolute behaviour - including drunkenness, blasphemy, gambling, frequenting brothels, music in alehouses, and non-observance of Sabbath day laws - and unlawful assemblies gathered for recreations such as bear-baiting, cock-fighting, and horse racing were outlawed (Birley 1993: 86). An Act in 1670 disqualified all except the landed classes from game hunting (22 and 23 Car II: c. 25). A similar Act in 1692 declared that because "great mischiefs do ensue by inferior tradesmen, apprentices, and other dissolute persons neglecting their trades and employments who follow hunting, fishing, and other game, to the ruin of themselves and damage of their neighbours", such activities were to be declared illegal (4 and 5 Gul. And Mar.: c. 23). Although in reality the celebration of holidays demonstrated an impressive durability over time, by the end of the seventeenth century the majority of workers took very few holidays. The alehouse, which had long played an important role as a site for popular recreation, particularly in Winter and at night, became more significant as criticisms of leisure grew in momentum. They were central to the promotion of pastimes, in some parishes providing the only location for festivity, in others protecting popular recreation from the furore of official disapproval (Wrightson 1981: 9-10).

The oppression of recreational activities occurred simultaneously with the heightened demand for the synchronisation of labour. Commercial advancement involved extracting additional output from work and increased utility from time. The length of a sea crossing or of a journey by land from one place to another, the predicament of prices which rose or fell in the course of a commercial transaction and the need to produce quickly in an expanding market, all induced merchants and traders to devote more attention to the explicit regulation of time (Le Goff 1986: 34-35). The incongruity between time-free workers and time-bound employers gave rise to growing hostility and apprehension. The requirement of a strict measurement of time, which would determine economic and social rhythms, was still extraneous to the masses. Their unwillingness to engage in disciplined and sedulous work routines agitated employers anxious to maximise profits (Landes 1983: 72).

By the beginning of the eighteenth century, the days of a task orientated independent labour force had become numbered as the conjunction between time and money grew ever closer. The preparation for the labour patterns of an industrial society was facilitated by the Church's antipathy to time wastage. The Puritan conscience regarded the squandering of time as a deadly sin. Each person hoping to receive God's salvation had to demonstrate their righteousness, and this was best exhibited through exertion at work. Thus, although manufacturing industry still remained on a domestic or small scale, the alliance of religious doctrine and commercial spirit assisted in augmenting the transformation of work attitudes (and as a consequence leisure attitudes) which accelerated during the industrial revolution and contributed, *inter alia*, to the establishment of Britain as the "workshop of the world".

It may be important, at this juncture, to reiterate the main leitmotiv of this chapter. It attempts to provide a very loose narrative of the history of leisure in order to demonstrate how it has not remained constant and continuous over time. This task is undertaken in order to illustrate how the cultural phenomenon of leisure had an impact on the introduction of community service orders and how this impact was subject to the phenomenon existing as a separate and autarchial right of society. By highlighting its emergence as a separate and autarchial right, I intend to highlight the deficiencies in Whiggish analysis which simply views the introduction of community service orders as being a product of linear developments and progress in the domain of penal work sanctions. To date, we have seen that leisure was, for the most part, not a separate and distinct element from work but punctuated work periods which were dictated, in the main, by agrarian and seasonal rhythms. By the late 1600s and early 1700s, however, and as a result of a growing emphasis on temporal precision and the dignity of labour (as witnessed, for example, in institutions such as the workhouse and house of correction), leisure activities and festivals which interrupted daily work routines came under increasing attack.

1750 to 1850

The dawning of industrial capitalism in the eighteenth and nineteenth centuries effectuated great change. Albeit by no means a unitary process, it was brought about, *inter alia*, by an enclosure movement - together with the decline of the common field system of cultivation and the amalgamation of small farms into large - which affected seven million acres of land between 1760 and 1815 and resulted in 1,800 parliamentary acts (Toynbee 1908: 68);[5] by the philosophy of political economy espoused by thinkers such as Adam Smith, particularly his "invisible hand" thesis, which could "salve the conscience of landowners, tycoons, rakish sprigs of aristocracy, 'money grabbing' Dissenters, pious distillers, Quaker plantation owners, sanctimonious bankers, owners of gambling dens, brothel keepers and all who pandered to human frailty for profit" (Birley 1993: 129); and by a common law disposed to economic growth and development, by the substantial wealth accumulated particularly as a result of colonial expansion and the excellent inventory of cheap natural resources available. It was also supported and maintained by technical innovations such as Hargreaves' jenny, Crompton's mule, Arkwright's waterframe, Cort's puddling and rolling processes and Watt's steam engine; by the entrepreneurial enthusiasm and endeavour[6] of individuals such as Josiah Wedgwood at

---

5. Exodus from the land into urban areas was a somewhat more protracted process than is sometimes portrayed in the literature (Phyllis 1988: 147).
6. It was often an over imposing enthusiasm and endeavour that resulted in the cruel exploitation of their labourers.

Etruria, Mathew Boulton at Soho, Abraham Darby and his successors at Coalbrookdale, Richard Arkwright in his spinning factories, and Jedediah Strutt in his cotton factories; and by improvements in transportation - particularly the network of canals constructed in 1759 and the advancement of the railways in the 1820s and 1830s (Briggs 1979: 8-74).

Work was now to be concentrated in specialised institutions, known as factories and mills, where it became increasingly regulated by temporal constraints. Labourers, alienated from their households and customary habits, found themselves restrained by a new set of precepts which demanded more of their attention and endeavour as working hours became longer and more organised. Time related as opposed to task related toil became the order of the day. Workers were no longer at liberty to absent themselves from the task in hand as and when they desired. The machine regimented and governed their working lives and mechanical bells signalled when interludes from work were to be taken and for what duration. Such labour rhythms were wholly incompatible with the outlook and perceptions of the majority of the labouring classes. Alongside the transformation in the nature of the work, this period may also be characterised by very harsh conditions of dislocation, the manipulation of women and child workers, the centralisation of population in urban communities and the advent of a diffident class of industrial labourers (Anthony 1977: 65).

Factories had existed in England as far back as the 1500s. Yet by reason of their atavistic technology and the high levels of capital required to establish them, the "putting out" system remained in the ascendancy. Water-driven factories were forced to locate in isolated rural areas on the banks of streams or rivers. Thus an employer was faced with the constant struggle of unearthing sufficient labour to operate them. Many were compelled to provide housing and other services, to compensate with high wages and to persist in employing the labour force in times of recession to deter them from drifting to other areas (Deane 1979: 147). Seasonal interruptions continued to fracture the operation of these institutions so long as they were reliant upon water-power. But the use of new gas-illuminated steam-driven mills and factories entirely reconstructed the association between workers and proprietors. Gas-illumination enabled factories to remain open perpetually and consequently removed the restrictions placed on levels of output by climatic and seasonal variations. Steam-power facilitated the erection of plants in towns and cities, where pools of labour were immense in relation to the desideratum of the factories. The paternalistic nature of water-powered factories succumbed to a more detached form of industrial relations as industrialisation advanced and became more urbanised. Employers were now in a position to callously jettison workers as profit margins tightened. The necessity of providing housing and other incentives were no longer matters with which they concerned themselves (*ibid*: 134-148). Thus the wheel had turned full circle: it was the labourers who were now utterly vulnerable and reliant upon emerging omnipotent capitalists, spoilt for choice as to who they might employ. Order, compliance, productivity and consistency were inculcated into a new time conscious workday where labour was sold in units and bought in wages.

No employer in the late eighteenth or early nineteenth century could ignore the fact that ill-discipline could project the whole process of industrialisation into disorder. Factory labour necessitated factory diligence. Hence it was inevitable that the traditional impulses of the labour force would be supplanted by a new sense of individual and collective work discipline[7] with an increased emphasis on assiduity and commitment. Workers were now convened by the factory bell; their routines were dictated by factory hours; their work was closely supervised and monitored by overseers; there was, in effect, a complete loss of liberty to a machine or engine which performed without fatigue or the need for intermissions (Hammond and Hammond 1917: 19). Failure to adhere to the regulations set by a particular factory could result in a penalty. Bad time-keeping, for instance, was punished by fines totally disproportionate to the value of time lost, or else those guilty of being a few minutes late were locked outside the gates and forced to forfeit a whole shift's pay (Rule 1986: 137; Fitton and Wadsworth 1958: 233). Contemporary society has grown accustomed to the image of order and regulation in the workplace. But much of society in the late 1700s was still partial to abandoning and resuming work as they pleased.

The process of conditioning peasants and rural labourers

---

7. On the extension of the need for discipline into other aspects of life, see Thompson (1988: 442).

to work in a factory was fraught with difficulty. Workers regarded such institutions as an abnormal and abhorrent physical restraint on their personal well-being and rebelled against the notion of week after week of regulated toil. For the employers it was like "pulling a molar barehanded" to get labourers to co-operate (de Grazia 1974: 74). One of the most frequent expressions of workers' disdain for the new discipline was their reluctance to commence work punctually, much to the annoyance of their time conscious employers. This form of action was even carried out in the face of threats to dock wages. The destruction of machines and other property of employers, as characterised by the Luddite riots of the early 1800s, was another approach employed by workers. Such deeds were undertaken in two different instances, though it should perhaps be noted that they were for the most part localised in nature - as opposed to representing some form of sweeping riposte to mechanisation - occurring predominantly in areas of Lancashire, Yorkshire, Nottinghamshire and Cheshire (Mathias 1983: 333). First, it was carried out as a demonstration of working class hostility to the unusual environment in which they found themselves. Secondly, it was practised by labourers who depended, in the main, on the sale of their labour to entrepreneurs. Whenever they were involved in a dispute - an increase in wages for example - the threat to inflict damage on factory equipment could be used as a coercive influence on the bargaining process (Hobsbawm 1952: no. 1, 59-60). It is not surprising, then, that employers were very willing to employ children in their establishments. They did not have the same desire to absent themselves from their work. Nor, for the most part, were they so insidious as to contemplate wrecking the machines. Although they too required training, it was not first of all necessary to extirpate existing work habits as it was with adults.[8]

The performance of work in a growing industrial economy was, on the whole, carried out by a proletarian labour force which increasingly found itself confined to a more impersonal way of life as urbanisation accelerated. In modern society the vast majority of people residing in towns and cities readily accept that their work duties will be discharged at a location far removed from their homes. This was, however, not such an established norm for much of the population existing in the early nineteenth century. It was something which they had to acclimatise and grow accustomed to. In 1750 there had been two cities in Britain with more than 50,000 inhabitants - London and Edinburgh; in 1801 there were eight and by 1851 there were 29 including nine with a population exceeding 100,000 (Hobsbawm 1968: 67). Moreover, workers became reliant on a means of support derived from one particular duty only. This reciprocal arrangement took the form of a cash wage which labourers received as a result of the products of their work.

---

8. See also Plumb who noted: "The children of the poor had always worked as soon as they could walk, but now their work was exceptionally valuable to factory owners. Children are tractable and easy to discipline; for simple repetitive operations they were ideal, and they were cheap. Naturally they had none of the ingrained antipathy to factory work common among adult offenders" (Plumb 1971: 87-88).

So far as the daily hours of work were concerned in the period between 1750 and 1850, a normal workday generally consisted of 10 to 12 hours of employment. There were a number of exceptions which deviated from the norm. Indeed the difficulty in making generalisations about the quantity of hours worked is that it fails to appreciate numerous regional variations and the nature of the work at issue. Mayhew, for example, informs us that coopers in the mid-1800s usually worked 14 hours a day from six in the morning until eight o' clock at night (1971: 442; Bienefeld 1972: 72). Moreover, whilst work was restricted to a 10-hour day in most of the large industries, even in these a propensity towards longer hours manifested itself in the form of a widespread reduction in the number of hours set aside for meals (Bienefeld 1972: 49). Aside from such quandaries, generalisations do assist in outlining an overview, albeit unsophisticated, of working life in the nineteenth century. A week's work normally consisted of six full days, although in Scotland an early Saturday was common. By the mid-1800s this custom had also commenced in a number of larger centres in England (*ibid*). The period in question also witnessed a heightened desire on the part of policy makers to monitor the hours of employment. In 1833 the authorities considered it necessary, having regard to the education and health of children and young persons, to regulate the hours of their labour. It was specified that persons under the age of 18 were prohibited, except in limited circumstances, from working at night in factories or mills. In addition they were not permitted to toil for more than 12 hours in any one day with at least an hour and a half for meal breaks, nor more than 69 hours in any one week. Again, with certain exceptions, children under the age of nine were entirely prevented from work whilst those under the age of 13 could be employed, but for no longer than eight hours in any given day (1833: 3 and 4 Gul IV, c. 103). Eleven years later an Act was ratified which outlawed the employment of women save for the same duration and in the same manner as young persons (1844: 7 and 8 Vict, c. 15). By 1847 the hours of work for young persons and women had been curtailed to 10 hours in any day and not more than 58 hours in any week (10 and 11 Vict: c. 29).

Work in a pre-industrialised society was, as has already been delineated, interspersed with the recreational and social pastimes of the people and little or no demarcations existed between them. In a developing industrial economy on the other hand, as a result of being carried out in a confined space for a scheduled period of time, work became segregated into an unequivocal compartment of daily life. Although leisure had, to some extent, been overwhelmed by the mounting criticism of the 1700s, it re-emerged after the advent of industrialisation. The difference now though was that work and leisure no longer existed in an intermingled and fused form. Work time and free time now existed as separate entities.

Yet recreational pastimes were still viewed in a hostile manner by employers, legislators and clergymen. Their desire for a competent and disciplined labour force militated against the expansion of working class leisure activities. By regaling themselves with entertainments and games, workers' attention was diverted away from the more pressing need of orderly production. Thus it continued to remain subdued while such an antagonistic outlook prevailed. The suppression of popular culture was supported by a series of Acts.[9] For instance, an Act of 1835 declared that any person who managed a premises for the purpose of fighting or baiting of bears, cock-fighting, baiting or fighting of badgers or other animals, could be imprisoned for any period not exceeding two months (5 and 6 Gul. IV: c. 59). A similar Act prohibited the playing of football or any other game, the pitching of tents, stalls or booths by hawkers, higglers, gypsies; or the baiting of bulls on public highways (1835: 5 and 6 Gul. IV, c. 50). In effect, the rural,

---

9. See Judd who noted the following about the early nineteenth century: "A wide variety of forces were reshaping the nature of popular culture. The increasing provision of education to all levels of society raised literacy rates and coupled with major technological advances in the printing industry served to undermine the primitive beliefs sustained by the oral tradition; the rise of Methodism and the reforming zeal of Evangelicals (led by Wilberforce and Hannah More), promoted the principles of sobriety, respectability and self-discipline and laid the ideological foundation for the attack on the violent animal sports and other unruly forms of leisure by such groups as the Society for the Suppression of Vice and the R.S.P.C.A., founded in 1802 and 1824 respectively. The building of the railways bridged the gulf between town and country and by facilitating population mobility eroded that identification with the community which lay at the heart of local customary observances. The rise of industrial capitalism demanded new labouring habits: as the working day became increasingly regulated by the factory clock, so the fairs, wakes and religious holidays - adapted to the seasonal rhythms of agricultural work - came under pressure. Above all the process of urbanisation, fuelled by a population explosion and immigration from the countryside and Ireland, alienated the new generation of city dwellers from the pre-industrial village traditions without immediately providing an alternative urban culture other than that centred on the alehouse" (Judd 1983: 12-13).

agrarian genre of leisure, so exemplified in pre-industrial society, was no longer appropriate in an urban, industrial milieu - rowdy mass football games, the unregulated control of beer houses, animal blood sports and wild saturnalia at fairs all threatened the maintenance of factory discipline and thus necessitated more ordering and control. Space which heretofore was regarded as a common right of the public was now being dominated and manipulated by the upper and middle classes. Land prices in the new urban environment were exorbitant as much of the space available was required for housing and buildings. This shortage of open spaces did as much as anything else to deprive plebeian society of its recreations (Walvin 1978: 3). Moreover, popular culture was also coming under attack from the middle classes on the ground that it was not in the interests of the labouring classes to engage in such activities.[10] Moral reforming bodies believed that free time should not be spent in wild saturnalia and the pursuit of primitive pastimes but on the advancement of each individual and society as a whole.[11] This is commonly referred to as "rational recreation". Books, music and

---

10. See also Haywood *et al* who noted: "The other concern of both the aristocracy and the new industrial interests was social order. The American and French Revolutions provided evidence of the potential for insurrection. The establishment was, therefore, understandably nervous about gatherings of large, rowdy crowds among the lower orders for fairs, wakes, public hangings and other popular pastimes, seeing them as potential seedbeds for expressions of dissatisfaction with the existing order" (1995: 169).
11. For example, the London City Mission, the Ragged Schools Union, Model Dwelling Companies and the Christian Socialists were all active in "civilising the poor of the Metropolis" in the mid-nineteenth century (Judd 1983: 13).

museums were advocated as excellent methods of spending leisure time. The Museums Act of 1845 (8 and 9 Vict: c. 43) and the Libraries Act of 1850 (13 and 14 Vict: c. 65), whilst not making an immediate impact, paved the way for future generations. Similarly, the Y.M.C.A. was founded in 1844 and focused on promoting friendships and developing social skills (Argyle 1996: 24); Sunday School recreation programmes were introduced by the Church of England to promote day trips and educational visits (Henry 1993: 10); the "muscular christianity" movement encouraged regulated games of football and rugby, as we shall see, on the grounds that they promoted health, teamwork and discipline;[12] and Working Men's Clubs were originally recommended on the basis, *inter alia*, that working class pastimes should be promoted in environments that were alcohol free (Haywood *et al* 1995: 170).

The period also witnessed a contraction in the number of holidays taken by workers. The Bank of England, for example, closed on 47 days in 1761; by 1825 this had been reduced to 40 days; in 1830 to 18 and finally in 1834 bank officials had to settle for four rest days - Good Friday, Christmas Day, and the first of May and November (Dept of Labour 1938: Cmd 5724, 11). Similarly the six to 14-day drunken celebration of Whitsun was gradually reduced to the ordered one day bank holiday of the 1900s. A number of reasons for this rapid decline has been proposed: first, the magical allotment of Old Whitsun was undermined by more

---

12. Football clubs initiated as a result of this impetus included Everton, Aston Villa and Barnsley (Haywood *et al* 1995: 170).

scientific methods of farming; secondly, the landed class, increasingly aware of the impact of the "reformation of manners" refused to support such violent holidays and encouraged rational recreation instead; and finally, the Evangelical and Methodist movements created a new consciousness among the laity concerning their spiritual and moral improvement (Howkins 1981: 204-205). Drunken revelry and prolonged absenteeism from work were no longer appropriate. Employers were reluctant to acknowledge any requests for holidays as they merely punctuated the work routine and, accordingly, affected profit margins. Hence a downward trend in the number of holidays taken by people occurred. Monday to Saturday was devoted to toil with Sunday acting as a lacuna between intensive stints of work.

The late 1700s and early 1800s may be characterised as an era in which work came to be concentrated at a central location with increased emphasis on effective use of time. Regulation and order displaced the traditional impulses of the work force. Differentiation and specialisation of labour replaced the more "holistic" form usually found in pre-industrial society (Haywood *et al* 1995: 24).[13] The process of

---

13. See also Thompson who noted: "It is clear that between 1780 and 1830 important changes took place. The 'average' English working man became more disciplined, more subject to the productive tempo of the clock, more reserved and methodical, less violent and spontaneous." He went on to note: "While many contemporary writers, from Cobbett to Engels, lamented the passing of old English customs, it is foolish to see the matter only in idyllic terms. These customs were not all harmless or quaint. The unmarried mother, punished in a Bridewell and perhaps repudiated by the parish in which she was entitled to relief, had little reason to admire 'merrie

urbanisation and industrialisation brought about a marked disjunction between work and the free time of the people. But although clearer demarcations existed, the pursuit of recreational activities by the masses was still very much disapproved of. Toil and graft were ennobled as being essential for the prosperity of the nation. Leisure was still very much constrained by the environment and by the attitudes of the middle classes and upper classes who regarded ill-disciplined and boisterous popular culture as a threat to the work ethic which they sought to inculcate. However, rational recreation, a middle class creation, was acceptable as it was something which implied both order and control. Thus although work and recreation were no longer fused, leisure was, nonetheless, not yet regarded as a social right of the work force.

1850 to 1970

The following section attempts to illustrate the developments in labour and leisure which occurred in the late nineteenth and twentieth centuries. To begin with, the demarcations between work time and free time became more palpable; what individuals determined to do during their spare time was now, within reason, a matter to be decided by themselves. Moreover, the period in question witnessed a substantial reduction in the hours of work and

England'. The passing of Gin Lane, Tyburn Fair, orgiastic drunkenness, animal sexuality, and mortal combat for prize money in iron-studded clogs, calls for no lament" (1988: 450-451).

a growth in the range of recreational pastimes as leisure became less restricted and confined. The pursuit of such activities was no longer perceived as posing a danger to society but rather as a right and compensation for hard graft and toil. This evolution of leisure accelerated in the 1950s and 1960s as the national economy developed. Increased standards of living and urbanisation enabled a growth in consumer spending - the purchase of cars, radios, and televisions all assisted in shaping and transforming the concept of leisure to such an extent that it was hardly comparable with its pre-industrial form. The cause of this increase in real spending was brought about by the rise in real wages after 1850. But the earning capacity of workers was not the only process to undergo a transformation. There were also notable non-monetary improvements in living standards. Significant advancements were made in health and education, in safety at the workplace, in child welfare and the provision of old age pensions and insurance against unemployment and illness.

Modern societies where industrialisation has occurred may be defined as employment societies. The commodity of work is bought and sold on the labour market for a remuneration. It is only a privileged few who can work for themselves or the pleasure to be derived from it: for the majority, however, work becomes a means to an end closely associated with paid employment; non-market activities such as child rearing and cooking are thus debased and reduced to the status of non-work activities. One of the outstanding features of employment society is the issue of unemployment. In the years after 1870, and particularly as a consequence of the great depression of the 1930s, dilemmas regarding the provision of work became a matter of contention with which governments increasingly concerned themselves. It was anticipated that full employment would be attainable with the progression of industrialisation. This was, in part, achieved in the ensuing decades after the Second World War as growth and profitability stimulated a golden age of employment. In 1949 the percentage of individuals wholly unemployed excluding school leavers was fixed at 1.5 per cent, 10 years later it had risen slowly to a figure of 2 per cent and by 1968 it stood at 2.3 per cent of the population (Dept of Employment 1971: 316). In 1970, the year which heralded the introduction of the Wootton Report, unemployment remained moderate at 2.5 per cent of the population (Dept of Employment 1973: 194). Nobody at this juncture could have envisaged the onset of unprecedented levels of unemployment which have so characterised the last 25 years of British history.

Welfarist considerations dictated that much amelioration was required as regards the nature of work. Prior to 1908, most workers persisted in toiling until their physical or mental capabilities dictated otherwise. When work was no longer feasible due to infirmity, they became dependent on their families, benevolent charity or poor relief. The concept of a pension was unheard of in most instances. The late nineteenth and early twentieth centuries, however, witnessed growing "disillusionment with the methods and pauperisation of the Poor Law, vested interests of friendly societies, insurance companies and trade unions" (Freeden

1978: 200). In 1908 the Old Age Pension Act was enacted.[14] The aged were no longer reliant on support but now earned it as a practical right. Furthermore it permitted them to display a certain amount of independence and plan their retirements. In the same spirit the Education Acts of 1870,[15] 1876,[16] 1880,[17] 1893,[18] and 1899,[19] which introduced compulsory education, did much to restrict the employment of children in factories and mills. Employers also observed that long hours of graft in the workplace were a source of danger both to the workers and to the public. Continuous toil brought about fatigue and inattention frequently culminating in accidents - such observations spread with the advance of Taylorism in the twentieth century. Significant advancement was also made in upgrading the physical environment of workers. The Employers Liability Act, for example, was enacted in 1880 (43 and 44 Vict: ch. 42). This was regarded by trade unionists not only as a symbolic gesture but also as "a move towards obtaining equal rights with the rest of British society" (Bartrip and Burman 1983: 157). The Act, however, contained a number of specific

14. The chief beneficiaries of pension schemes prior to 1908 were civil servants, white collar workers and servicemen (Hunt 1981: 8).
15. (33 and 34 Vict: ch. 75). Section 74 stated that every school board may make by-laws requiring children of not less than five or more than 13 to attend school.
16. (39 and 40 Vict: ch. 79). Section 5 stated that no person shall take into his employment any child under the age of ten who has not obtained a certificate of education or previously attended school.
17. (43 and 44 Vict: ch. 23).
18. (56 and 57 Vict: ch. 51). Section 1 raised the age from which a child could obtain total or partial exemption from the obligation to attend school to 11.
19. (62 and 63 Vict: ch. 13).

limitations on the right of employees to claim and employers could still absolve themselves from liability by relying upon two legal defences - the principles that either negligence on the part of the plaintiff or his or her consent to undertake a risk prevented any claim or compensation (Wiener 1990: 206). It was only in the late 1800s that judicial opinion began to shift more towards restricting defences founded upon the employee's implied consent. In *Yarmouth v. France*, Lord Esher, M. R., expressing the majority view of the Divisional Court and rejecting the defendant employer's claim that the employee had assented to the risk, stated:

> "[T]o say that a master owes no duty to a servant who knows that there is a defect in machinery, and, having pointed it out to one in authority, goes on using it [is] ... cruel and unusual, and in my view utterly abominable" (1887: 19 Q.B.D. 647 at 653).[20]

Thus began the "judicial emasculation"of the defence by employers that the fact that an employee continued to work while knowing of a danger was proof of his or her consent to that danger (Bartrip and Burman 1983: 183-184). It was not, however, until the 1891 decision in *Smith v. Baker and Sons* that the doctrine of implied consent was decisively rejected. In that case, the plaintiff was employed by railway contractors to drill holes in a rock cutting near a crane. The crane lifted stone and at times swung over the plaintiff's head without warning. The plaintiff was fully aware of the

---

20. See also *Thrussel v. Handyside and Co.* (1888) 20 Q.B.D. 359.

danger to which he was exposed. After a stone had fallen from the crane and injured the plaintiff, he sued his employers. The majority in the Court of Appeal held that the mere fact that the plaintiff undertook and continued in the employment with full knowledge of the dangers did not preclude him from recovery. Lord Herschell stated:

"It was suggested in the course of the argument that the employed might, on account of special risk in his employment, receive higher wages, and that it would be unjust that in such a case that he should seek to make the employer liable for the result of the accident. I think that this might be so. If the employed agreed, in consideration of special remuneration, or otherwise, to work under conditions in which the care which the employer ought to bestow, by providing proper machinery or otherwise, to secure the safety of the employed, was wanting, and to take the risk of their absence, he would no doubt be held to his contract, and this whether such contract was made at the inception of the service or during its continuance. But no such case is in question here. There is no evidence that any such contract was entered into at the time when the plaintiff was first engaged, and the fact that he continued work notwithstanding the employer's breach of duty affords no evidence of special contract as that suggested ... I must say, for my part, that in any case in which it was alleged that such a special contract as that suggested had been entered into I should require to have it clearly shown that the employed had brought home to his mind the nature of the risk he was undertaking and that the accident to him arose from a danger both foreseen and appreciated" ([1891] A.C. 325 at 362-363).

Accordingly an employment contract would no longer be simply construed as an implied acceptance by the worker of liability for most industrial accidents. Employment rights also took on a new significance in the period concerned: the right to employment, to safe work conditions, to join trade unions and engage in strikes, to fair wages and equal pay, to equal opportunity, to reduced hours, to compensation for wrongful dismissal and to a right against forced labour all assisted in improving the work life of a worker. These rights were very much a twentieth century innovation. Neither the 1787 Constitution of the United States of America or the French Declaration of the Rights of Man and of Citizen of 1789 ever made any reference to such rights. French law only enshrined such rights after 1945.[21] Similarly the American Constitution offered very little protection to workers and judicial interpretation tended to support a *laissez faire* philosophy in the workplace. The willingness of the judiciary to uphold contracts entered into by employers

---

21. The Preamble of the French Constitution of 1946 stated: "[that] ... [E]veryone has the duty to work and the right to obtain employment. No one may suffer in his work or his employment because of his origins, his opinions or beliefs. Every man may defend his rights and his interests by trade union action and may join the union of his choice. The right to strike may be exercised within the framework of the laws that govern it. Every worker, through his delegates, may participate in collective bargaining to determine working conditions, as well in the management of business ... It guarantees to all, and particularly to the child, the mother and the aged workers, health protection, material security, rest and leisure" (Bermann *et al* 1994: s 2-6).

and employees is also evident from the *Lochner* decision 1905 in which the State of New York adopted a statute forbidding employers to require or allow employees to work more than 10 hours a day or 60 hours during the week. Lochner, a bakery shop owner, was indicted for employing his workers for more than 60 hours a week. In defence, he challenged the constitutionality of the statute. On appeal to the Supreme Court, Justice Peckham, delivering the opinion of the court, declared that:

> "[T]he freedom of master and employee to contract with each other in relation to their employment, and in defining the same, cannot be prohibited or interfered with, without violating the Federal Constitution" (1905 198 U.S. 45 at 944-945).

Thus the State of New York had unreasonably and arbitrarily interfered with the contracting process by passing a law limiting the number of hours a baker could work in a bakery. The courts, however, gradually relaxed this principle and allowed for government intervention to address the dilemmas of workers.[22] The regulation of employer/employee relationships and the protection of workers gathered momentum as the 1900s progressed. In 1948, the United Nations Universal Declaration of Human Rights, of which Great Britain is a signatory, stated that:

---

22. See, for example, *Muller v. Oregon* (1908 208 U.S. 412). See also Steinburg (1981).

(1) Everyone has a right to work, to free choice of employment, to just and favourable conditions of work and to protection against unemployment.

(2) Everyone, without any discrimination, has the right to equal pay for equal work.

(3) Everyone who works has the right to just and favourable remuneration ensuring for himself and his family an existence worthy of human dignity, and supplemented, if necessary, by other means of social protection.

(4) Everyone has the right to form and join trade unions for the protection of his interests.[23]

The last one hundred years, and since 1945 in particular, have accordingly witnessed wholesale changes in employment rights and working conditions. The balance of power, which for most of the 1700s, 1800s and early 1900s weighed heavily in favour of industrialists, has shifted to

---

23. Article 23. Similarly Article 7 of Part III of the International Covenant on Economic, Social and Cultural Rights of 1966 declared that: "[T]he State parties to the present Covenant recognise the right of everyone to the enjoyment of just and favourable conditions of work which ensure, in particular: (a) remuneration which provides all workers, as a minimum with: (I) fair wages and equal remuneration for work of equal value without distinction of any kind, in particular women being guaranteed conditions of work not inferior to those enjoyed by men, with equal pay for equal work; (ii) a decent living for themselves and their families in accordance with the provisions of the present Covenant; (b) safe and healthy working conditions; (c) equal opportunity for everyone to be promoted in his employment to an appropriate higher level, subject to no consideration other than those of seniority and competence; (d) rest, leisure and reasonable limitation of working hours and periodic holidays with pay, as well as remuneration for public holidays."

some extent to incorporate and recognise the demands and requirements of the labour force.

One example of this shift is the substantial reduction in the number of hours worked. From 1850 to 1970 changes in the duration of the working week may be compartmentalised into four main phases: the early 1870s; 1919-20; 1946-49 and 1960-66. The years from 1871 to 1874 effectuated widespread reorganisation of the working week as trade unions grew stronger and a nine hour day became the norm for the majority of workers.[24] From 1919-20 onwards a 48 hour week became standard. There was little alteration for the remainder of the 1920s and 1930s, but between 1945 and 1950 normal weekly hours of work diminished from 47.1 to 44.6 and in 1968 most employees toiled for 40.5 hours a week (*ibid*: 160). One must note, however, that although work hours may have diminished throughout the era, there was a tendency towards a correlative increase in overtime. Nonetheless, it is still fair to assume that the majority of society in the 1950s and 1960s had much more potential and scope for the enjoyment of leisure than their predecessors.

Paralleling the movement for reduced hours of work was the campaign for paid holidays. Prior to 1919, extended paid leave for wage earners was uncommon. Even the three days' holidays allotted to such workers - Christmas Day, Easter and Whit Monday - were normally not remunerated. Salaried employees, on the other hand, have customarily

---

24. For instance the weekly hours of work for cabinetmakers in 1871 was 59.5 hours but by 1880 this had been reduced to 54. Similarly the normal weekly hours of work for fitters and turners diminished from 57.5 hours in 1871 to 54 by 1880 (Dept of Employment 1971: 28-36).

enjoyed the benefit of holidays with pay since the 1870s. It was with the Holidays Act of 1871, however, that the growing national urge for compensated days off began to advance (34 Vict: ch 71).[25] Although somewhat restricted, its extension in 1875 to cover docks, custom houses, inland revenue offices and bonding warehouses made it much more probable that such legislative interference would be accepted and observed by the majority of employers and employees alike (38 Vict: c. 13). Paid holidays spread slowly after the First World War but gathered momentum in the 1930s, as the number of collective and individual agreements increased. Yet they were still not required by statute save in one instance. The Shops (Hours of Closing) Act of 1928 declared that when shops in a holiday or sea fishing town remained open after the hours fixed for compulsory closing, any shop assistants employed for additional hours had to be compensated by holidays with full pay after the season had ended (18 and 19 Geo. V: ch. 33). In April 1938, however, the Amulree Committee recommended, *inter alia*, that an annual holiday with pay should be established, to consist of as many days as were in the working week, and these were, as far as was practicable, to be taken consecutively (Dept of Labour 1938: Cmd 5724, 60). The government welcomed the recommendations and announced its desire to implement them. In the same year,

---

25. The days allotted were to be Easter Monday, the Monday in Whitsun week, the first Monday in August and the twenty-sixth day of December, if a week day in England, Ireland and Wales. In Scotland the days were New Year's Day, Christmas Day, Good Friday, the first Monday of May and the first Monday of August.

the Holidays with Pay Act empowered all statutory wage regulation authorities to give directions providing holidays with pay for the workers for whom they prescribed minimum wages or fixed their statutory remuneration in addition to any other holidays or half holidays to which such workers might be entitled under any other enactment (1938: 1 and 2 Geo. VI, c. 700). After the Second World War, holidays became one of the favourite spare time activities of the British. The five to 10 working days' holiday extended to 15 or 20 days in the affluence and boom years of the fifties and sixties. They were no longer centred around religious celebrations or communal fairs. Holidays perform a whole plethora of functions in the contemporary world: they relieve fatigued individuals from the rigours of both market and non-market work, they enable the pursuit of sporting activities, social fraternising, relaxation and education. In addition they are not now so spatially restricted and often involve travel overseas.

It is generally accepted that the period around 1850 marked a turning point in the history of leisure. To begin with, policy makers became more responsive to society's essential requirement for recreation to counterpoise intensive employment in the workplace. Improved technology in the form of railways and motor transport also made a dramatic impact on the leisure habits of people. Moreover, the influence of the clergy with regard to popular recreation and the conduct of the masses waned considerably. Individuals were normally now at liberty to choose pastimes of their preference without moral reprimand from the Church. Leisure thus expanded to fill the vacuum left by the reduction in the weekly hours and annual days of work. The majority of the population now resided in towns and cities and brought home better earnings than ever before. As a consequence, leisure became even more differentiated from work as a concept but more rigidly associated with it as a recompense for hard graft. One had to exert oneself in the labour market in order to enjoy fully the increasingly commercialised nature of leisure. Indeed, the sustained economic growth between 1945 and the early 1970s - it has sometimes been referred to as the "30 glorious years" - enabled the continued expansion of people's commercial leisure opportunities (ie, holidays away from home, television viewing, driving) (Roberts 1999: 39-41). Moreover, the change to a more disciplined work routine was paralleled by a similar change in the domain of leisure, as it became increasingly shaped by the dictates and needs of industrialisation. Recreational pursuits underwent a metamorphosis to accommodate the peculiarity of mechanised society. As Haywood *et al* noted:

"Football, for example, developed from a formless scrimmage for the ball in which all players pursued undifferentiated roles, into a formulated attack and defence. Play was thus divided; formations developed; and efficiency in the achievement of goals became of heightened importance. Other leisure forms exhibited similar tendencies; for example the old multi-purpose fairs which combined commerce and entertainment gradually gave way to specialisation as commerce was separated into more specific occupations and the funfair (exploiting the new mechanical wonders) became an entity in its own right" (Haywood *et al* 1995: 24).[26]

To sum up, then, leisure in its new disciplined form became legitimate as it was no longer perceived as a danger to the economic, political and religious hegemony of the period.[27] As work became less of an encumbrance and better remunerated, a host of leisure industries sprung up to cater for the needs of consumers. The notion of leisure as a defined right and social necessity was acknowledged and accepted in most industrial countries by 1970. Article 24 of the Declaration of Human Rights, for example, stated that "everyone has a right to rest and leisure including reasonable limitation of working hours and periodic holidays with pay". Similarly the American Declaration of

---

26. See also Walvin who suggested that: it was "no accident that the recreations spawned by industrial society were to be disciplined, controlled and orderly, regimented by rules and timing, characterised by a greater degree of orderliness among the spectators and encouraged by men of substance and local position. It was, for example, symptomatic that the brand of football which emerged in its new disciplined form from the public schools in the 1860s was as disciplined as its pre-industrial forebear had been lawless, and was played and encouraged in the first instance, by men of superior social station (1978: 10)."
27. Godbey succinctly puts forward a number of factors which influenced the nature of leisure as it was understood in the late 1960s in industrial Britain. They are: the increased production of material goods through the application of technology; the use of labour saving devices for household duties; the declining role of the Church; transformations in attitudes to pleasure; increased educational levels; the reduced levels of fatigue associated with many forms of work and the increase in discretionary income (1978: 10-12).

the Rights and Duties of Man states that "every person has the right to leisure time, to wholesome recreation, and to opportunity for advantageous use of his free time to his spiritual, cultural and physical benefit" (Article XV). In 1964, in the House of Commons, Mr Denis Howell stated:

"I put the provision for leisure alongside health, education and welfare as one of the aspects of life for which it is the government's job to provide" (Hansard, 1964: 697, 85).[28]

Precise time schedules and express divisions between labour and leisure are fundamental features of modern life. Intervals of time are no longer dictated by natural phenomenon such as the sun, moon, stars and seasons but in hours, minutes and seconds. This propensity towards exactitude has become more pronounced as the industrial mode of work has evolved. Individuals must now have the ability to co-ordinate their work routines around the constraints of a clock dominated environment. Rationalisation of time is increasingly required to combat

---

28. In 1959, Labour and the Conservatives produced two consensus documents, *Leisure for Living* and *The Challenge of Leisure* respectively, which advocated greater State involvement in leisure policy - this was, in part, a response to a growing affluent culture, particularly youth culture - and the establishment of a Sports Advisory Council. The Wilson government of 1964-1970 was also very active in the leisure domain. As Henry noted: "Harold Wilson had declared the theme of his government to be that of modernisation in his 'white heat of technology' speech, and leisure was the most 'modern' of public service areas in which to promote opportunities" (Henry 1993: 18).

the hurried and demanding nature of life. Clocking on and off, complying with measured interludes or breaks, working to formulated deadlines and the duration of journeys to and from the workplace are all symptomatic of labour for the majority of workers in twentieth century industrial society.

Labour and leisure now exist as entirely distinct compartments of people's lives. But as this separation grows ever wider, their symbiotic relationship grows ever stronger. To revel in and appreciate many of the recreational pastimes and newfangled technology of the modern world - it may be referred to as the "increased monetarization and commodification of leisure in consumer society" (Roberts 1999: 171-172) - necessitates a greater disposable income. This is acquired by most of humankind through longer toil. Thus as industrial society has advanced and consumer demand has intensified in the seventies, eighties and nineties, the progressive reduction of work time has been eclipsed. Optimistic notions of a four or five hour workday have not materialised.[29]

Conclusion

The peculiarities of transition from pre-industrialised to industrial society is invariably more complex than has been

---

29. In the House of Commons, in 1964, Mr Driberg stated: "But I believe that in a relatively short time - perhaps by the end of the century, when many of us, except the youngest among us, will not be sitting here - it may well be that the majority of people will only have to work 10 or 15 hours a week." (Hansard 1964: 697, 65-66).

captured in the trajectory delineated here. Yet this crude historical trip through time still enables us to make some generalised statements about the nature of work and leisure. Work in the past was dictated by the seasons, climatic conditions, the hours of daylight and darkness, and was more often than not undertaken in or around the household. It was not so identified with earning a living or with temporal restraints as it is today. Agrarian labour rhythms - the rhythms which prevailed for the majority of society - focused on the tasks in hand and leisure punctuated such rhythms in a disorderly manner. The advent of industrialisation, however, brought about powerful transformations. Work was increasingly located in confined spaces with more emphasis on time and discipline. The cash nexus between employers and employees became more pronounced as the task related nature of work was displaced by a more efficient time oriented labour process. People's lives were, thus, increasingly dominated by clock time sentinence and a growing divide manifested itself between free time and work time.

The twentieth century, and in particular the period following the Second World War, has witnessed a widespread reduction in work schedules from one averaging 60 hours a week in the early 1900s to one averaging 40 hours a week by 1970. Furthermore these years may also be characterised as a period when the rationalisation of people's time intensified further and the distinct boundaries between work time and free time grew ever stronger. These factors facilitated the establishment of the leisure industry as one of the largest employers of the twentieth century. Easier access to gymnasiums, heated swimming pools, outdoor adventure centres, indoor saunas, steam rooms, package holidays, theme parks, televisions and early retirement, together with an increase in disposable income and consumer spending, all added to its appeal. As one commentator noted:

"Leisure in its modern sense - as a sphere of positive non-work activity enjoyed by the mass of the working people - is thus a *modern phenomenon and a product of modern industry*. Crucial to its development is not only the reduction in hours of work but also the development of needs and capacities for leisure activities. It is these which give modern leisure its distinctive character, and make it not simply a time of passivity and idleness, but a sphere of activity and creativity" (Sayers 1989: 46) (my italics).

This is supported by Mr Quintin Hogg, the Secretary of State for Education and Science in the mid 1960s:

"We are in the presence of a very greatly intensified use of leisure - and this goes across the whole spectrum of recreational activity, from dancing to Bach to physical sports. The people of this country, far from suffering from 'spectatoritis', are year by year spending their leisure hours with far greater intensity and far greater intelligence, though, of course, at a good deal more expense, in a whole variety of new and more exciting ways" (Hansard 697: 94).

It is only within this modern framework that leisure became established as an enshrined right and internalised social norm. It was brought about, as we have seen, through the increasing emphasis on clock time sentience, through the way in which free time was won from working time, through the processes of urbanisation and industrialisation, through the reduction in working life, through increases in holidays (particularly holidays with pay), through the recognition of leisure as a right, and through the establishment of a leisure industry. Of course it would be over schematic to propose that this shift can be incorporated into a meta-theory; undoubtedly a wide range of forces (at an individual and local level) deviate from the general review delineated in this chapter. Nonetheless it is hoped that what has been described is sufficient to sketch a broad framework which enables us to appreciate that leisure has established itself, particularly since the Second World War, as a distinct and separate component within the structure of society.

It is, accordingly, difficult to envisage how a work based sanction of the early 1970s - which embodies the deprivation of leisure time as one of its defining characteristics and which is calculated so precisely in work hours - can take its roots from other work based sanctions prior to the industrial revolution. It is respectfully submitted that it was only with the creation of a particular leisure environment, as existed after 1945 when leisure was established as an actual right of each individual, that the authorities could justify depriving offenders of it as a means of punishing them for their wrongdoings.

Thus the supposition proposed by Vass and Pease that a continuity and affinity exists between community service and various other penal sanctions is tenuous in that it fails to appreciate that the particular cultural determinant of leisure - which has unconsciously exerted an influence on the shaping of community service - has changed over time. As Garland has noted:

"Penal practices are shaped by the symbolic grammar of cultural forms as well as by the more instrumental dynamics of social action, so that, in analysing punishment, we should look for cultural expression as well as for logics of material interest or social control" (1990: 199).

The crucial point to be derived from this approach is that penal policy initiatives, in addition to being driven by their penal context, are also determined by external cultural forces which often only exist within a specific context.[30] Yet

---

30. See Garland who noted: "Things such as prison building and bread and water diets, cranks and tread-wheels and picking oakum, lock-step marching and the gallows procession, scaffolds and pillories and electric chairs - not to mention inmate subcultures and the languages, roles, and relations they create - however much they owe to external forces, are, in the first place, artefacts, which were created within the penal realm and which embody penal culture. Each specific item which has been developed for penological use will have been shaped, first of all, by the needs and meanings of its penal context and by the usages of penal actors and authorities. Contained in the concrete details of each penal fact is a story of penal place and penal purpose and of the penological culture from which it derives. But precisely because penal institutions never exist in a vacuum, these specific forms and meanings can also be traced out, beyond the penal

Vass and Pease completely overlook the possibility that sanctions, to some extent, are shaped and changed by the types of cultural situation within which they exist. Moreover, notwithstanding that leisure has always existed in some form or other, Vass and Pease also fail to appreciate that it was only in the period after the Second World War that it could have acted as a determining force on the introduction of community service. In this sense, community service is not only "in detail" a novel disposal. As Roberts notes:

"Leisure as it is experienced today is really a product of industrial society. It is not just that the productive power of industrialism has given to the population time and money to cultivate leisure interests on an unprecedented scale, but that it has also created a new cultural awareness of leisure that was previously impossible. Industrialisation has created not only the spare-time and surplus income that is available for discretionary spending: it has also instituted a rhythm of life in which set hours are devoted to work after which man's time is free. Social obligations, centred upon an individual's occupation, are compressed in terms of time, and people are left with a part of their lives to use purely in

---

sphere, to reveal the linkages which tie penal culture into the frameworks and categories of the world outside. The analysis of penalty's meanings - like the cultural analysis of any other form of life - will thus be a matter of tacking back and forth between a detailed ethnographic description of the specific meanings which clothe penal practice, and a more generalised conception of those mentalities which are dominant elsewhere in social life (1990: 211)."

accordance with their own inclinations and interests. As a consequence of this, institutions have developed to cater for people's leisure needs, and leisure thereby has become a differentiated element within the structure of society. But apart from this structural separation of leisure the population has been made aware that certain activities are leisure activities and that certain occasions are leisure time. *The population has been made consciously aware of leisure as a distinct element in its rhythm of life, and particular pursuits can now be valued purely for their worth as leisure activities. Leisure values, in this way, are incorporated into society's culture, and people are able to think about and experience leisure in a way that was formerly impossible"* (Roberts 1970: 89-90) (my italics).

Herein lies the crucial point. It was only when the population had been made consciously aware of leisure as a "distinct element in its rhythm of life" that the authorities could begin to deprive an individual of it as a means of social control. As Garland noted:

"Penal laws and institutions are always proposed, discussed, legislated, and operated within *definite cultural codes*. They are framed in languages, discourses, and sign systems which embody *specific cultural meanings, distinctions and sentiments*, and which must be interpreted and understood if the social meaning and motivations are to become intelligible. ... Punishment, then, can be viewed as a complex cultural artefact, encoding the signs and symbols of the wider culture in its own practices. As such it forms one local element within the interlocking circuits of meaning which compose a society's cultural framework and can be analysed to trace its patterns of cultural expression" (1990: 198-199) (my italics).

We have now seen how the cultural meaning and code of leisure, to take one example, has effected both the shape and substance of community service. We have also seen that this determinant of leisure cannot be viewed as an unchanging constituent in the structure of society throughout history. Accordingly, and as has been described, leisure in industrial society can broadly be understood - bearing in mind the purpose of this chapter - against a background of increased non-work time and disjunction from labour, greater political involvement, shorter working weeks (particularly with the five day week and free weekends) and working lives, and increased commercialisation. Of course it is also important to recognise that experiences and conceptions of leisure have continued to mutate since the early 1970s. In particular, the last 25 years have witnessed a growing shift away from manufacturing industry to service production, increased levels of unemployment, changing perceptions of the role of the State in respect of the provision of leisure services which increasingly exhibit "a market based discourse rather than one of social welfare" (Haywood *et al* 1995: 257), the "destandardisation of working time", the growth of "night-time economies" (Hewitt 1993: 13), the extension of weekly hours of work (Martin and Mason 1992: 81-86), the increased "feminisation" of paid employment, improved understandings of women's leisure experiences, and more individualised leisure demands. The implications that these alterations to leisure conceptions will have for a sanction that seeks to punish by depriving offenders of their leisure time - if we can assume that the punitive aspect of the sanction is taken seriously and noting that the sanction will also be driven by its own internal penal dynamic - remains to be charted, particularly in respect of the decision to sentence,[31] the tasks to be undertaken,[32] by whom and when.[33]

It is now necessary to examine community service from other perspectives in order to better appreciate its introduction in the early 1970s. As such, the ensuing chapters will build on this theme, where possible, by viewing penal phenomena from social as well as penal perspectives. Much of my argument will concentrate on historical transformations in the penal system in order to highlight the modern penal complex within which community service must be understood. And again, it will be argued that Vass and Pease's one-dimensional progressivist approach to history is unable to contend with

---

31. The proportionate lack of women sentenced to community service may be accounted for, in part, by the still dominant "malestream" interpretation of leisure and the criminal justice system's inability to reckon with women's leisure experiences and opportunities. See, in particular, McIvor (1998: 280-290).

32. Although there are more women in paid employment today, employment symmetry between the sexes has by no means been reached. This is particularly palpable in respect of community service orders where women appear to have fewer choices in terms of place allocation (McIvor 1992; McIvor 1998: 280-290).

33. I am referring here to the growing trend of "destandardisation" of predictable work cycles.

issues such as the decline of the moral consciousness concept of punishment, the emergence of more factual and inductive strategies towards offending, and the rise of a centrally controlled State apparatus, to name but a few, all of which shaped to some extent the sanction of community service.

PART II

CRIMINAL JUSTICE HISTORY PERSPECTIVE

CHAPTER 2

HISTORICAL SPECIFICITY AND GENERAL TRANSFORMATIONS

Having demonstrated in the last chapter that leisure only emerged as a cultural determinant on penal policy after the Second World War, the purpose of the following section is to establish that historical penal work sanctions themselves do not, in many instances, provide a satisfactory explication for the germs of the community service order ideal since they have been exposed to fundamental transformations and reformulations which have either changed the nature of their operation or resulted in their abandonment. In the course of our analysis it will be necessary to examine general criminal justice characteristics - such as the individualisation of treatment of offenders, the emergence of a uniform State control apparatus, and the application of reformatory practices - as well as more specific community service order characteristics including the use of penal labour, our attitudes to forced labour and the rise of the "therapeutic community" as a panacea for reoffending. Part II will end with a detailed and thorough examination of the claim that the practice of impressment is a legitimate germ of community service orders.

The underlying argument contained in these chapters is that one should refrain from viewing and writing about the past, as Vass and Pease have done, with the present very much in mind. Their approach, focusing as it does on continuities over time, reads, in my view, as a progressivist, presentist narrative which depicts community service as a sanction that was always fated to appear in the statute books. Historiography of this nature, however, eschews the complicated terrain that is criminal justice history. It disfigures the aims, objectives and practices of earlier sanctions but also the historical context in which they must be construed. Moreover, the search for continuities between the past and the present tends to portray the introduction of community service in the 1970s as a reaction to a "timeless and unchanging set of questions" which previous policy makers had also deliberated over, but with a much lesser degree of success.[1] In this sense it validates the commencement of community service as an apogee in the history of progress which little by little edged ever closer to the enactment of the Criminal Justice Act of 1972 and which would, thereafter, make headway under the same programme of progression.

Foucault, Ignatieff and Garland have all reacted against such Whiggish interpretations of history and developed instead hypotheses which focus attention on fundamental shifts in penal policy. There is much to commend in their respective approaches, particularly Garland's, but, as we shall see, they have in some instances over exaggerated and over qualified what are in essence tortuous historical transformations. As Wiener noted:

---

1.   For a criticism of Whiggish interpretations of history in respect of criminology, see Garland (1994a: 24).

"If earlier generations were too complacent about the progressivist nature of British history, revisionists have surely succumbed to the opposite vice; their picture of an onward march of surveillance and control embodies an unconvincingly gloomy photographic negative of Whiggism" (Wiener 1990: 8).

With this in mind, then, an attempt will be made to provide a thorough appraisal of any transformations delineated. No endeavour is made, however, to fasten onto any particular transformation and adjudge it to be the hiatus between old and new penalty; indeed it may be argued that a number of different transformations are tenable. In many instances, where an individual deems new penalty to commence will depend on the perspective from which he or she views criminal justice history.[2] In this chapter the transformations are viewed from the general perspective of government control, individualisation of treatment and the application of reformatory practices. All three perspectives elucidate different transitional points. As such the emphasis in this chapter lies very much in illustrating that transformations have occurred rather than attempting to locate one fixed transitional point between old and new penalty. It is argued

---

2. For example, and as we have seen, modern penalty has been located by Foucault at the beginning of industrialised society with the movement from a corporal to carceral archipelago; Garland argues that its formation came together in the period between 1895 and 1914; Marxist writers such as Melossi and Pavarini place the origins of modern penalty in the emergence of a more capitalist mode of production, and; commentators such as Scull, would argue that modern penalty commenced with the development of community corrections in the 1960s.

that it is the sum of these transitional points that constitutes new penalty and enables us to appreciate the *general* framework within which the introduction of community service must be understood.

Before embarking on our investigation in this chapter of the transformations that have manifested themselves, it is necessary to qualify, to some extent, the approach being adopted. First, it is not being implied that any changes in penal policy culminated in an absolute break with the past. It would be a fallacy to propose that old penalty was completely supplanted by new penalty. Rather what is being argued is that these transformations eventuated themselves in a new general stratagem of penal sanctioning within which characteristics of old penalty had to function. Thus, for example, the concept of "less eligibility" - which has existed since punishment itself - has had to operate in the modern penal process in a domain where new techniques, attitudes, discourses and institutions all displaced the moral consciousness concept of offending with a more welfarist, scientific and individualised approach. Secondly, in delineating the transformations that have occurred, it has been necessary to focus on the administrative aspects concerning strategies of punishment; little attempt has been made to incorporate fully popular views of crime and punishment as it is considered to be beyond the scope of this thesis - between 300 and 500 years of criminal justice history from an administrative perspective is daunting enough in itself!

The Rise of a Centrally Administered State Control Apparatus

The concept of centralised policy was anathema to Georgian reasoning on administration. Political conjecture concerning government was dominated by supporters of Locke. He considered society to be composed of an aggregation of individuals who were bequeathed with a number of natural rights. The power of the government was confined to ensuring that these natural rights - which were essentially conditions of equality - were respected and upheld. He suggested that all people were in "a state of perfect freedom to order their actions, and dispose of their possessions and persons as they think fit, within the bounds of the laws of Nature, without asking leave or depending upon the will of any other man" (Locke 1989: 118-119). But although it was a state of liberty, no one had the right to harm another, "in his life, health, liberty, or possessions" (*ibid*; Ashcraft 1994: 226-251). Political power, then, was the right to make laws which would govern these rights and protect the commonwealth from "foreign injury". In this sense, what legitimised political authority for Locke was the functional ministrations it could confer upon its subjects; the right to command was justified by the services that could be proffered rather than by the relation of owner over his or her subjects. In the late 1700s and for most of the 1800s, political developments were dominated, in the main, by two strands of political thought: the "classic economics" school, associated with Adam Smith, Malthus, James Mill, Ricardo and John Stuart Mill; and Benthamite utilitarianism, associated with Jeremy Bentham and his coterie. Although comprising two different bodies of thought, it has been suggested that "in their methodology, and, to some degree in their substance, as well as in the *dramatis personae* of the period"(Atiyah 1979: 292), classical economics and utilitarianism were closely associated:

> "They both shared a belief in individualism, as a value and as a social mechanism; they believed in freedom of contract as a general principle; they accepted as their starting point that individuals generally knew their own interests best; both were concerned primarily with maximising - the one wealth and the other happiness - without unduly worrying about how the resulting wealth or happiness was distributed" (*ibid:* 234).

Thus the State was still merely regarded as having safeguarding duties and was very weak in its functioning. This belief is articulately and expressively represented by David Roberts in the following statement:

> "By continental standards England's central government seemed absurdly small. A French Minister of the Interior, accustomed to extensive powers and a staff of 200,000 employees throughout France, would have been humiliated to sit at England's Home Office with its limited power and 29 officials. The same economy and paucity of powers characterised all the departments of government, with the exception of the Courts, the Treasury, and the Army and Navy. England's central

administration did little in 1833 besides administer justice, collect taxes, and defend the realm. It rarely touched the life of the ordinary individual and showed little concern for his well-being. It failed even to supervise those local authorities and voluntary institutions that did concern themselves with the individual's welfare" (Roberts 1969: 12-13).

English society, according to Atiyah, advocated the notion of weak central government for three reasons: it kept taxes to a minimum; increases in bureaucracy and control would, it was thought, result in increased corruption and jobbery; and, it was generally assumed that local government was more democratic and essential for the maintenance of civil liberties (Atiyah 1979: 246).[3] A brief exposition of the forms of administration which pertained for most of the seventeenth and eighteenth centuries will better illuminate the insignificant extent of state intervention.

For example, most prisons were administered by staff, who after fulfilling their obligation to confine offenders, were left - safe in the knowledge that State supervision was practically negligible - to discharge their duties in whatever manner they deemed appropriate. Houses of correction were also in effect operated as private ventures (Webb and

---

3.   Even as late as 1865, Mr Podsnap in *Our Mutual Friend* stated: "But I see what you are driving at, I knew it from the first. Centralisation. No. Never with my consent. Not English" (Dickens 1982: 131, as quoted in Scull 1984: 15).

Webb 1922: 14-15).[4] Similarly the Webbs noted that the administration of workhouses during the 1700s was defective with few or no trained officers, poor auditing and account-keeping, the practice of fraud in almost all of the institutions and the general lack of central direction (Webb and Webb 1927: I, 298). Transportation too was inconsistent and arbitrary in its application and erratic in its administration. Felons transported to America were put up for auction on arrival and sold to the highest bidder. A corresponding lack of predictability was evident in Australia, particularly with regard to the assignment system which enabled convicts to be leased out to free settlers. It was not until assignment was abolished in 1838 that the entire process became more consistent and measured, and even then it was much maligned.[5] The functions of the police were also embedded in local administration and offered little in the way of a uniform or regular degree of security. It is perhaps even anachronistic, as Rock suggests,

---

4. Corruption and inertia appeared to be widespread. Coke stated that as long as "Justices of the Peace and other officers were diligent and industrious, there was not a rogue to be seen in any part of England, but when Justices and other officers became tepidi or trepidi, rogues and so swarmed again" (Coke 1797: 729).

5. Assignment was succeeded by a progressive-stage system. One interesting method of penal administration adopted on Norfolk Island by Captain Machonochie was the "Marks System". It enabled an offender to earn marks as wages, a certain number of which were required in order to earn a discharge. If offenders misbehaved, marks were deducted in relation to the seriousness of their misconduct. In this way, it was hoped that they would learn self-denial and self-discipline. Unfortunately, the Home Office became uneasy about Machonochie's relaxed system of punishment and he was relieved of his duties in 1844. See Barry (1960: 77).

to describe attempts at social control as "policing", as there was during that epoch no correlative to any contemporary agency (Rock 1983: 192).[6] Nor prior to 1805 was there any sustained effort to compile national crime figures (Emsley 1996: 21).[7]

The governing class was undoubtedly confronted with many perplexities as the Industrial Revolution advanced. Former communal methods of social control were inefficacious as the majority of the population began to concentrate in the larger towns and cities. To maintain order, the governing class began to assume, albeit hesitantly, a more functionary and proficient design. This metamorphosis meant:

"in place of parish constables, police forces; in place of lay Justices, stipendiary magistrates; in place of local gaols and houses of correction, a system of penitentiary prisons, ultimately under national Home Office control" (Philips 1983: 65).

The nation gradually transformed itself from a rural economy founded upon a parochial administrative structure to an industrialised and urbanised society centred upon

---

6. Indeed it was only when the city of Dublin established a full-time professional police in 1786 that the word "police" was officially used for the first time (Wegg-Prosser 1986: 4).
7. In 1791, however, annual registers, which included the name of the offender, a physical description, place of birth, a summary of the crime, the place where he or she was committed and by whom, the sentence of the court and the date of discharge, began to be collected in the county of Middlesex (Hawkings 1992: 35).

greater bureaucratic uniformity. Yet such a transformation did not occur in a unilinear and uncontested fashion and immense struggles were encountered in the establishment of the new administrative apparatus. Indeed resistance to centralisation and uniformity was apparent across the entire social spectrum. The intention of the following section is to investigate the upheaval which occurred in the area of criminal justice from the perspective of State control and social thinking.

Individualism, as has already been noted, was ascendant as an ideology right up to the late 1800s. Each rational citizen was considered to be capable of practising self-help and self-reliance. As the word "individualism" implies, it is founded upon a social structure which is detached and impersonal in nature. The government did not, on the whole, concern itself with the welfare of individuals and considered that it should not assume any undertakings which could be carried out by ordinary citizens. As John Stuart Mill, who argued that members of a civilised community had a right to a sphere of individual liberty which authorised most actions that did not harm others, stated:

"There is a circle around every individual human being, which no government, be it that of one, of a few, or of the many, ought to be permitted to overstep: there is a part of the life of every person who has come to years of discretion, within which the individuality of that person ought to reign uncontrolled either by any other individual or by the public collectively" (Mill 1878: 569; Thomis 1976:

93-133).

This *laissez-faire* philosophy manifested itself distinctly in relation to the function of the judiciary. In contract law, for instance, it was generally accepted that individuals should be accountable for their own commercial dealings and the role of the judiciary was simply to enforce actual agreements once *consensus ad idem* became apparent. Thus "freedom of contract" and "sanctity of contract" formed cornerstones of judicial perceptions on the formation and interpretation of agreements (Atiyah 1989: 8-9). Sir George Jessel, even in the late nineteenth century, declared that:

"if there is one thing which more than another public policy requires it is that men of full age and competent understanding shall have the utmost liberty of contracting, and that their contracts when entered into freely and voluntarily shall be held sacred and shall be enforced by Courts of Justice. Therefore, you have this paramount public policy to consider - that you are not lightly to interfere with this freedom of contract. Now, there is no doubt that public policy may say that a contract to commit a crime, or a contract to give a reward to commit a crime, is necessarily void. The decisions have gone further, and contracts to commit an immoral offence, or to give money or rewards to another to commit an immoral offence, or to induce another to do something against the general rules of morality, though far more indefinite than the previous class, have always been held to be void. I should be sorry to extend the doctrine much further" ((1875) LR 19 Eq. 462 at 465).

Yet it would be a fallacy to propose that the State completely eschewed any form of intervention. Administrative interference of one kind or another is a prerequisite for any society, particularly for one which undergoes industrialisation. The establishment of Millbank penitentiary in 1816, the Prison Acts of 1823 and 1835, the Factory Acts of 1833 and 1844, and the Poor Law of 1834 are a testimony to such interference. Nonetheless the degree of intervention was conspicuously circumscribed. When it did occur, it was designed to accommodate and maintain the spirit of individualism and every citizen was still, for the most part, the creator of his or her own destiny. One may cite as an example the Poor Law of 1834. Although it organised relief along more uniform lines, it did so in a manner designed to ensure that characteristics such as self-reliance and self-responsibility remained crucial. By ensuring that the conditions in all workhouses were more repulsive than the normal conditions suffered by independent able-bodied labourers, the Poor Law encouraged most able-bodied paupers to support themselves. This is supported by John Stuart Mill who suggested that whilst "the great majority of things are worse done by the intervention of government than individuals most interested in the matter would do them", intervention was justifiable in the areas such as the Poor Law - "which leaves to everyone a strong motive to do without it" - because it promoted uniformity and was essential for the common good (Mill 1878: 571-585).

Gradually however a change of direction was effectuated with regard to beliefs concerning government intervention. It would be futile at this juncture to comprehensively account for the vast array of influences and determinants which engineered such a transformation. Nevertheless a scant synopsis is essential if we are to better appreciate the alterations which occurred in punitive thinking. Slowly the notion emerged that economic and social prosperity could not adequately be attained by pursuance of an individualist ideology. From the 1870s onwards, political theorists, such as Thomas Hill Green, began to perceive the State as a positive agency whose *raison d'être* was to guarantee the collective welfare of the population. In order to promote general well-being, he argued that it was necessary for the government to ensure that minimum standards of welfare were realised and maintained. Thus uniform national policies on issues such as work, education and general health were required (Sabine 1963: 676). Similarly the Fabians, adopting a form of liberal socialism, advocated the greater employment of the legislative authority of the State so as to effect greater economic and social order (*ibid*: 677). But what were the phenomena which encouraged the development of such philosophies? In very general terms, the events which motivated the rejection of old liberalism were as follows: the unprecedented development of monopoly groups and cartels together with the increasing centralisation of finance, which by seeking to control markets rejected the whole concept of *laissez-faire* individualism (Garland 1981: 34-35); the intensity of the social problems created by industrialisation (MacDonagh

1960: 17-37); the steady advance of the "professional ideal" which augmented the movement towards central administration by promoting confidence in the government offices (Perkin 1989: 16); the realisation that England's hegemony in world industry and trade and the ascendancy of economic liberalism no longer prevailed as America, Germany and Japan caught up and the period of the Great Depression (1873-1896) set in on the domestic front (Hobsbawm 1974: xiii-xiv); the startling growth of New Unionism between 1888 and 1893 as railwaymen, transport workers and miners took giant strides forward in attempts to better their positions (*ibid*: 71-114); the growing awareness of the problems posed by "externalities" - an externality is an indirect consequence of free exchange such as the external costs of pollution and disease which are inflicted on society by industry - which often profited private individuals but proved detrimental to the public interest (Atiyah 1979: 22-23); and, a deepening consciousness of the need to protect by law the defenceless and vulnerable from an increasingly unsatisfactory and unjust system (*ibid*) - we have already witnessed part of this movement in the last chapter through the enactment of the Employers Liability Act of 1880 and the Old Age Pension Act of 1908, through restrictions on the doctrine of employees' implied consent, and through the establishment of a nine hour workday.

Most of these phenomena were highlighted by the diffusion of information on a scale which was not previously available. The 1880s was an era in which the incessant insistence on facts and statistics "widened circle after circle of social awareness" and illuminated the defective ideology of individualism and *laissez-faire* liberalism (Lynd 1968: 413-419). All of these processes, which occurred in a fractionalised and disunited fashion, converged in the late nineteenth century to produce one outcome - the extension of the power of the central government to intervene in the regulation of the market and the provision of welfare. Thus the idea of individualism declined as collectivism emerged, based as it was on the ideology that benefit could be derived from governmental interference and guidance. Legislation such as the Conspiracy and Protection of Property Act of 1875 (38 and 39 Vict: ch. 86), the Public Health Act of 1875 (38 and 39 Vict: ch 55), the Education Acts of 1870, 1876, 1880, 1893, and 1899, the Workmen's Compensation Act of 1897 (60 and 61 Vict: ch 37), the Trade Disputes Act of 1906 (6 Edw VII: ch 47), the Old Age Pension Act of 1908 (8 Edw VII: c 40), the Finance Act of 1910 (10 Edw VII: ch 8) and the National Insurance Act of 1911(1 and 2 Geo. V: ch. 55) may all be cited as examples of this increased willingness to extend the authority of the State. Moreover, from about 1870 onwards, the belief in the unlimited power of the freedom of contract gradually began to decline as a more extensive range of principles and circumstances were created by the judiciary to alleviate consensual obligation. Atiyah argues that three factors in particular brought about this decline: the emergence of standard form contracts; the weakening of the significance of self-reliance and self-responsibility with regard to free choice and intention, and; the materialisation of the consumer as a contracting party (Atiyah 1979: 18-30). All of these factors resulted in a restriction in the ways in which a contract could be made and performed. Coinciding with such a process was the expansion of tort law. As the values of self-reliance and private initiative began to diminish before the demands for social protectionism, tort law also witnessed, *inter alia*, the development of strict liability which made an individual responsible, in certain circumstances, irrespective of fault or negligence on his or her part (Fleming 1985: 1-18; Manchester 1980: 301). The fragmented growth of central authority will become readily apparent in our discussion of the centralisation of the penal system. It is to this discursive shift in penal thinking that we must now focus our attention.

Increased disquiet manifested itself over the dearth of cogent administration in the prisons in the late 1700s. John Howard's diligent exposition on the conditions of English and Welsh prisons and houses of correction publicised the consummate lack of any uniform system of management and the extent of desolation which pertained in many of the institutions which he surveyed. In addition, the authorities found themselves confronted with a crisis with the cessation of transportation to America as a result of the outbreak of the American War of Independence. The hulks were introduced as a stop-gap measure to alleviate overcrowding in the prisons. It was anticipated that when the war was resolved, transportation to the colonies would resume. The decision to use the hulks was embodied in an Act of 1776 and shortly thereafter two floating prisons, the *Justitia* and *Censor*, were moored on the Thames (16 Geo III: c. 43). In the early years of the sanction's development, an overseer could contract with the authorities for the convicts at so much per head, appoint his or her own wardens and organise the prisoners' accommodation. However by 1802, as criticism mounted about the conditions on board the hulks, Aaron Graham was appointed as "Inspector of Vessels". Shortly afterwards, on Graham's advice, the government instituted a scheme at Portsmouth for managing its own service and this marked the beginning of a complete Home Department take-over. The overseers were now to be employed as chief administrative officers on the various ships, which were supplied, equipped and staffed by the government (Playfair 1971: 43). Nonetheless it should be borne in mind that although the government had assumed responsibility for the prisoners on the hulks, it did so on the assumption that it was merely providing a temporary form of incarceration.

Yet the 1700s did to some extent witness the attempted initiation of some protracted involvement by the government in criminal justice. The 1779 Penitentiary Act, embodying many of the ideas of Howard, Blackstone and Eden, authorised the establishment of two penitentiaries which were to be managed by a committee of supervisors. It also endeavoured to determine the salaries of prison officers without reversion to the appropriation of gaol fees (19 Geo III: c. 74). Such encroachment met with approbation on the grounds that it was for the common good in that it would promote a more rationalised system of incarceration and it would also provide a much needed alternative after transportation had been suspended. Moreover, it was also permissible on the grounds that it did not usurp the power of local justices, and prison administration remained, for the most part, a county and borough matter. The enterprise was abandoned however. To begin with, the Commissioners assigned with the task of selecting an appropriate site could not form a consensus on any one location. Furthermore, the government appeared reluctant to make itself accountable for such a massive capital outlay, favouring instead the temporary makeshift stratagem of the hulks. Finally, much of the momentum was lost with the enactment of a new Transportation Act in 1784 (24 Geo III: c. 56). But the renewal of transportation did not purge the system of all its difficulties. Indeed one look at the overcrowded and decrepit state of the hulks was sufficient confirmation of the exigency for a more befitting regime of incarceration at home. Aware of such deficiencies the government elected to establish Millbank penitentiary in 1816 as a reformatory training institution for convicts prior to transportation to Australia. In doing so, it assumed a more perennial role in the functioning and administration of prisons. Furthermore its establishment marked the onset of a partitioned prison system:

(a) the central service which was composed of the hulks, Millbank and the subsequent establishment of numerous convict prisons such as Parkhurst (1839), Pentonville (1842), Portland (1849) and Dartmoor (1850), all of which acted as antecedents to the upsurge in government prison building which ensued after the foundation of a Board of Directors of Convict Prisons in 1850 (13 and 14 Vict: c. 39; Rose 1961: 3-4). Impetus for the increasing use of convict prisons was provided by the cessation of transportation to Australia and by the diminished employment of the hulks.[8] These sanctions were largely replaced in 1853 with the introduction of penal servitude.[9]

(b) the local service which was composed of prisons and houses of correction managed by local justices. It is to this system that we now turn our attention.

The earliest legislation to prescribe rules for all prisons in England and Wales was the 1791 Gaols Act. It obliged Justices of the Peace to examine "the state of the buildings, the behaviour and conduct of the respective officers, and the treatment and condition of the prisoners, the amount of their earnings and the expenses attending such prisons" (31 Geo III; c. 46). The Act, however, created no mechanism by which the legislation could be enforced and there was little or no attempt to comply with it by the majority of local authorities "who, for economy's sake, preferred to stick to their bad old ways"(Playfair 1971: 73). From a penological perspective, the Gaol Fees Abolition Act of 1815 was more far reaching in its attempt to promote uniformity of practice.

---

8.   The *Defence,* the last of the hulks to be used on home waters was destroyed by fire on July 14, 1857. The Bermuda and Gibraltar establishments closed on March 31, 1863 and May 30, 1875 respectively. (McConville 1981: I, 201). However this was by no means the last time that prisoners found themselves detained on board ships around British waters. In 1915 nine ships were moored on the Thames for Germans awaiting repatriation and from 1922 to 1925 the government of Northern Ireland confined many of its political prisoners on board the *Argenta* in Belfast Lough (Branch-Johnson 1957: 1). In 1997, a ship, *The Resolution*, was purchased by the British government and used off Portland as a prison ship (The Guardian 1997: 1).
9.   The Home Office still however retained the right to transport convicts. It was only in 1867 that the entire operation ceased (Tomlinson 1981: 133).

Fee-taking had long been the mainspring of defective prison administration. The Act prohibited the payment of fees or gratuities by any prisoner to a gaoler for entrance, commitment or discharge to or from a prison. In lieu thereof, the gaoler was to receive a salary or compensation from the Justices in Quarter Sessions. Any gaoler who exacted a fee from a prisoner would lose his or her office and would also be liable to a fine or imprisonment (55 Geo III: c. 50).[10]

The next notable enactment was Peel's Gaol Act of 1823. Other than consolidating the entire statutory law on prison administration, the Act also stipulated, *inter alia*, that Justices undertake standardised inspection tours of the prisons, that gaolers, chaplains and surgeons submit reports at Quarter Sessions and that all private trading by gaolers be abolished (4 Geo IV: c. 64; Blom-Cooper 1978: 66; Playfair 1971: 76). The Act was, however, ineffectual in actuating the homogeneity which Peel desired. It failed to commission the use of government inspectors who would have ensured that the legislation was adhered to. It also, as the Webbs pointed out, proved a disappointment in that no provision was made for coercing contumacious local authorities into complying with the provisions (Webb and Webb 1922: 73-75). Moreover, it also contained an alarming oversight in that it only pertained to county gaols and those of a few specified towns. As such, about 140 gaols - "the filthiest and

---

10. Nonetheless Harding *et al* inform us that fee-taking continued unabated in respect of debtors until the 1840s, even if it was disguised "in the form of hiring out furniture and so forth" (1985: 163).

most abominable in the kingdom" (they included the London debtors' prison and a large number of borough prisons) - accommodating circa 8,000 inmates were excluded from its jurisdiction (Clay 1861: 98). Even in prisons where the actual Act was in operation, it appears only to have been properly complied with in very few instances (*ibid:* 164). With such inadequacies, the Act was predominantly sterile in its endeavour to secure a more consistent and reliable prison system. In this respect, it further demonstrates the autonomy of local and corporate jurisdictions and the indifference with which they attended to attempts at government interference. Indeed this aversion and apathy was so great with respect to penal administration that it culminated in the otiose operation of the aforementioned Act in many localities.

Nevertheless, although advancements in the penal sphere were dilatory and considerable diversity remained in the management of local prisons, the need for uniformity and the analogous reduction of personal and local discretion was becoming more entrenched. The 1835 Prison Act, in its attempt to promote uniformity, provided that the rules for the government of prisons had to be submitted for approval to the Secretary of State and it also made it lawful for the Secretary to appoint a number of inspectors, not exceeding five, to visit every prison, house of correction and penitentiary (5 and 6 Gul IV: c. 38). The intention of the Act was to leave the day to day running of the prisons in the care of the local authorities, but impress upon them the need for uniformity by requesting the submission of their regulations concerning management and by appointing a number of inspectors who would oversee the effectual discharge of their various duties. But the creation of this prison inspectorate was not, as Thomas incorrectly suggests, "a further major step to centralisation" (1972: 15).[11] As shall become more evident later on in this section, there has been a tendency to construe the Prison Acts of 1823, 1835, and 1865 simply as stepping stones on the ongoing march towards centralisation. It is my contention, however, that such a standpoint is chimerical when compared with the mood and outlook of early nineteenth century society which still perpetuated its belief in notions such as individualism and limited government interference. These Acts, in my view, must be understood not only in the light of the desire towards a more rationalised system of punishment, but also in the light of the need to promote such a desire in an environment where a general anathema towards government interference prevailed. For example, the 1835 Act attempted nothing more than to foster uniformity by appointing a number of inspectors to oversee the management of prisons, houses of correction and penitentiaries. Yet the power and authority of these inspectors - in keeping with local authority ascendancy - was severely restricted. If their annual report on a particular prison was disparaging, the Home Office could only reprimand the offending local authority and disclose its maladministration to the public. Sir George Grey, acting as

---

11. McGowan has similarly argued that central government control of Irish prisons "can be said to have begun as far back as 1786 when the Lord Lieutenant was empowered to appoint an Inspector General for all prisons" (1978: 496).

Home Secretary, was rather circumspect about even granting this incapacious extension to the state control apparatus. He convinced Parliament that the inspectors' right of reporting was minimal and that:

> "the duty of these inspectors was defined by law; it was their duty to inquire into facts, rather than to report opinions or make recommendations. They might undoubtedly make recommendations to the Secretary of State for the consideration of the government, but it was out of their province to make recommendations to the county magistrates" (House of Commons 1850: CXIII, col. 274).

David Roberts provides further support for the argument that the 1835 Prison Act was merely a limited encroachment on the dominion of the local authorities. He suggested:

> "The magistracy of England did not mind surrendering irksome duties and co-operating with central inspectors - they had made such sacrifices in the Factory Act and Poor Law Amendment Act - but they jealously guarded their control over the county rate" (1969: 47).

Accordingly the dominant power after the Act remained vested in the local authorities.

This antagonism and resistance to government interference was also palpable in relation to civil order. In 1822 a Select Committee on the Police of the Metropolis, whilst discussing the merits and demerits of a more uniform system of policing, stated:

"It is difficult to reconcile an effective system of police, with that perfect freedom of action and exemption from interference, which are the great privileges and blessings of society in this country, and your Committee think that forfeiture or curtailment of such advantage would be too great a sacrifice for improvements in police, or facilities in detection of crime, however desirable in themselves if abstractly considered" (1822: IV, 11).

Nonetheless by 1828 the authorities, alarmed by the widespread escalation of offences against property and the disunited and impotent system of policing which prevailed in London, recommended "that an Office of Police acting under the immediate directions of the Secretary of State for the Home Department" should be established for the London area, but excluding the city itself (Report from the Select Committee on the Police of the Metropolis 1828: VI, 30). An Act for improving the police was duly passed in 1829 in which the Metropolitan Police, consisting of 3000 men, replaced the old Bow Street patrols who had been found "inadequate for the prevention and detection of crime, by reason of the frequent unfitness of the individuals employed, the insufficiency of their number, the limited sphere of their authority, and their want of connection and co-operation with each other" (10 Geo. IV: c. 44). The concept of an improved police quickly proliferated into the county boroughs. In 1833, the Lighting and Watching Act enabled all the parishes of England and Wales to assemble their own police forces, if they so desired, independent of local justices (3 and 4 Gul IV: c. 90). The 1835 Municipal Corporations Act required boroughs to establish Watch Committees which, in turn, were to appoint within three weeks of their formation a "sufficient number of fit men...having jurisdiction within the borough to act as constables for preserving the peace by day and by night, and preventing robberies and other felonies, and apprehending offenders against the peace" (5 and 6 Gul IV: c. 76). In 1839 Justices of the Peace were permitted, at their discretion, to appoint full-time constables in their respective counties up to a maximum of one per 1000 of the population (2 and 3 Vict: c. 93).

Hence a number of legislative enactments had resulted in a plethora of police organisations.[12] Yet the new police - displaying a concordance with other spheres of administration - met with widespread condemnation. The London parishes denounced "Peel's bloody gang" as an affront to freedom and it was rumoured among many that they were a collection of spies or that they were assembled in order to secure the throne for the Duke of Wellington (Critchley 1967: 54). Moreover, many boroughs were disinclined to fulfil their statutory obligations under the Municipal Corporations Act of 1835. Of the 178 boroughs referred to in the legislation, approximately only 100 had established police forces by 1838; of those that had, it often entailed the town functionaries, such as the sword bearer,

---

12. For a comprehensive account of all the Police Acts of this period, see Radzinowicz (1968: 252-302).

the beadle and the watch, donning uniforms and declaring themselves to be policemen (Emsley 1996: 225-226). Similarly by 1856, only half of the counties had adopted the 1839 County Police Act, and some of those that had only operated the Act in part of their counties (Wegg-Prosser 1986: 7). In truth, local administrators did not have the inclination or resolution to formulate competent units of local administration. Nor was there any likelihood of national uniformity whilst they remained dominant. In this regard, the fundamental unit of policing under the 1835 and 1839 Police Acts continued to endure under local imperium and whilst this remained the case, an efficient police force could not be established on a nation-wide basis.

The County and Borough Police Act was passed in 1856. Its objective was to raise the level of efficiency of the police by employing an element of coercion within the traditional structure of local government. It was motivated, in part, by the departure of troops from Britain to the Crimean War which signified a substantial weakening of the military at the disposal of local government for the suppression of riots, and, the virtual cessation of transportation in 1853, with the consequence that offenders had to be catered for at home (Emsley 1991: 51). Although the existing relationship between the watch committees and borough forces established under the 1835 Act remained unaltered after the 1856 Act, it did make the creation of county forces compulsory. In addition, it made it lawful for the Crown, excepting the Metropolitan Police District, to appoint three inspectors to visit and inquire into the efficiency of the police and to report annually to the Secretary of State. If it was established that the police of any counties or boroughs had maintained their police in a proper state of efficiency, they would become eligible to receive an Exchequer grant amounting to one-quarter of the cost of pay and clothing. This provision did not apply however to forces serving a population of less than 5000 (19 and 20 Vict: c. 69). This grant scheme was clearly an attempt to entice smaller forces to accede to consolidation agreements. In introducing the Act, the authorities found themselves walking a tightrope between the usurpation of local authority rights and the desire for an organised and unvarying system of policing. It was, in the end, a compromise. Although the 1856 Act failed to wrestle control of the police forces from the local authorities and thus fell short of providing a more uniform police structure, it did institute a form of central administration by authorising the use of inspectors and by linking their reports to the payment of Exchequer grants. Nonetheless this idea of central inspection was greeted with disdain:

"This was expressed in the familiar radical rhetoric of the threat it posed to 'individual liberty'. Such liberty reposed in that most English of institutions, 'local self-government', and was to be contrasted with tyranny which resided in that most un-English of government institutions, the 'continental spy' system" (Jefferson and Grimshaw 1984: 32).

During this period the local prisons still continued to remain in a very unsatisfactory condition. The legislative reforms, as outlined earlier, did not have the desired effect and chronic deficiencies and anomalies were still very much in evidence. In 1862, out of 193 prisons in England and Wales, there were 63 which gave admittance to less than 25 prisoners; and of these there were 22 prisons which incarcerated between 11 and 25 prisoners; 14 prisons which incarcerated less than 11, and more than six; and 27 which received less than six prisoners or were, in some cases, absolutely tenantless (Carnarvon Committee Report 1863: IX, xv). In 1863 the Report from the Select Committee on Prison Discipline was published. It stated:

> "that many and wide differences, as regards construction, labour, diet and general discipline, exist in the various gaols and houses of correction in England and Wales, leading to an inequality, uncertainty and inefficiency of punishment, productive of the most prejudicial results" (*ibid*: iii).

Furthermore the Committee formed the view that the inspection of prisons provided for under the Prison Act of 1835 had been downgraded in many instances to a mere formality both as a means of supervision and the subsequent use made of that supervision by the Secretary of State and the local authorities in counties and boroughs. Accordingly, it recommended a tightening-up of the entire inspectorate process (*ibid*: xiv). As a consequence of its findings, the Committee regarded it as desirable to establish without delay a system based, as far as was practicable, upon uniformity of practice. Yet in 1863, establishing uniformity of practice still did not entail centralisation. How best then could it be achieved, given the fact that antecedent Prison Acts had all foundered upon the rock of local government? The answer was quite simple. Homogeneity, it was felt, could be ensured by adopting similar means to those employed in policing, and in particular the 1856 County and Borough Police Act. Since local authorities were amenable to acceding to Exchequer grants for complying with uniformity in respect of policing, there was no reason to doubt that it would not work in respect of prisons. Such a course of proceeding was in harmony with the principle that government donations were contingent upon local action. Moreover, it could be argued, as McConville does, that attempting to establish uniformity through government payments did not amount to direct control since, at least in theory, the magistrates could determine to disregard the specified rules and regulations, forfeiting thereby the grant, or part of the grant, for prison maintenance (McConville 1995: 123). Thus the Carnarvon Committee also sought the middle ground in attempting to promote uniformity by withdrawing the Treasury grant from recaltricant authorities. These authorities would, in turn, have to explain to local ratepayers, out of whose pockets the penalty would be paid, why the grant was forfeited. In this sense, the local authorities were by and large coerced into complying without feeling that their power was being usurped by the Home Secretary. This is in direct contrast to the view of rationalisation proposed by Garland. He suggested:

"By 1865, the organisation and control of Britain's prison

institutions had been subjected to a process of centralisation and rationalisation, brought about through the mechanisms of state inspection, regulation, and financial subvention" (Garland 1985: 9).

To illustrate the point that uniformity of practice did not entail centralisation, it is necessary to provide a closer analysis of the 1865 Prison Act.

This Act implemented for the most part the proposals of the Carnarvon Committee. In attempting to promote uniformity, it established a code of rules binding on all prison authorities. These rules were incorporated into the first Schedule of the Act under the title, "Regulations for the Government of Prisons". Justices in Sessions were however entitled to make rules in addition to the regulations outlined in the schedule. Power was also given to the Secretary of State to issue a certificate of non-compliance to the Treasury where a prison had failed to comply with the requisitions of the Act in respect of the separation of prisoners, or of the enforcement of hard labour, or of providing a chapel. Upon receipt of such a certificate, the Treasury was compelled to refuse to make any contributions towards the upkeep of the said prison until the Home Secretary, having been satisfied that the prison had begun to comply with the requisitions of the Act, revoked the certificate. In addition, if it became apparent that a prison had failed to comply for four consecutive years, the Home Secretary could give notice to the gaoler of such a prison to bring it into conformity with the stipulated rules within six months. If the gaoler still failed to comply after the six month period had lapsed, the

Home Secretary could order the prison to be closed (28 and 29 Vict: c.126). Yet the attainment of absolute uniformity would always remain unachievable, so long as the system of local administration exerted some degree of control. Sir George Grey was at pains to point this detail out in the House of Commons:

"... the opinion of the [Carnarvon] Committee, as distinctly expressed in the second paragraph of their Report, was that it is desirable to establish without delay a system approaching as nearly as may be practicable to an uniformity of labour, diet, and treatment. Now, in that general object, I must express my entire assent, but I believe it is impossible to obtain absolute uniformity in these respects unless you subvert the existing system of local administration, which I, for one, should be sorry to see superseded in regard to borough and county prisons. If you are to retain the management of those gaols in the hands of local gentlemen not all agreeing in their views, but acting in accordance with certain general rules, with a certain margin for the exercise of their own opinion, you must be prepared to sacrifice something of that absolute uniformity which it may be desirable to attain. For instance, we should all doubtless be glad to see established a system of uniformity in respect of the punishments awarded to crimes of equal magnitude; but when you have your criminal law administered by 15 Judges as well as by the Courts of Quarter Sessions and by Recorders, you must submit to some inequalities and anomalies, and some variety both in the punishments awarded and the mode in which they are carried into effect" (House of Commons Parliamentary Debates 1864: CLXXV, 2046).

Moreover, the 1865 Prison Act itself was not entirely successful in promoting uniformity. To begin with, even if the Home Office closed an inefficient prison under section 36 of the Act, it was still faced with a dilemma, given that other prisons were not under a specific obligation to accept inmates from a discontinued institution, but rather had to express a willingness to do so. Not surprisingly, as McConville noted, "this nullified the power of closure under the 1865 Act" (McConville 1995: 192). Secondly, although the Act stipulated that prison authorities could contract with each other regarding an amalgamation (28 and 29 Vict: c. 126), no obligation was placed on the parties to reach an agreement. More often than not, justices in different localities did not wish to contract with each other given their rivalry and their dislike of interference. Accordingly, the clause was, in effect, a "dead letter" (McConville 1995: 192). Thus it is fallacious to propose that rationalisation was complete by 1865. But Garland's statement also begs the question: why was a further Act necessitated in 1877 if the system had been substantially rationalised and centralised, as he maintains, by 1865? Two reasons in particular can be put forward if, and only if, it is borne in mind that the rationalising process was by no means complete by 1865. First, a Conservative government found itself back in power in 1874. It was committed to reducing the rates and considered the centralisation of the prison system as one of the ways in which this policy initiative could be attained (Blom-Cooper 1978: 67-71). Secondly, an appreciable number of local prisons, which were incapable through want of prisoners and financial resources of complying with the 1865 Prison Act, remained in operation. It was thought therefore that it would be more beneficial, both from the perspective of uniform penal policy and the burden placed on local rates, to transfer en bloc the local administration of prisons over to the Home Secretary. With regard to the rates, Sir Massey Lopes alluded to the fact that £667,000 was contributed by the counties and boroughs towards the upkeep of prisons in 1870. In the same year, the government supported their operation with a grant of £118,000, of which £107,000 was for the maintenance of convicted prisoners. Lopes regarded it as "a most galling anomaly" that the Home Secretary and his inspectors sought to promote uniformity within the prison system and yet only provided something in the region of 17.6 per cent to its total upkeep, the largest contribution being made by the local ratepayers (House of Commons Parliamentary Debates 1872: CCX, 134). It was of little surprise that county and borough prison administrators were unable to comply with the various Prison Acts given this financial arrangement and given the fact that new legislation such as the Habitual Criminal Act of 1869 (32 and 33 Vict: c. 99) and the Prevention of Crime Act of 1871 (34 and 35 Vict: ch 112) placed more expense on them by providing that expenses incurred in the completion of registers for the newly established criminal register were to be defrayed locally. Indeed the 1871 Act increased this expense by stipulating that they also had to include photographs on these returns. With regard to uniformity of practice, a deputation from the Social Science Association visited the then Home Secretary, Sir Assheton Cross, in 1874. They indicated that, although the 1865 Prison Act had done much to enhance the discipline and management of the local prison system, there was still a "great want of uniformity of discipline in the prisons throughout the country, a great want of efficiency in many of those prisons, and a great amount of unnecessary expense, owing to the excessive number of our prisons" (House of Commons Parliamentary Debates 1876: CCXXIX, 1537). This absence of homogeneity can best be illustrated by examining the distribution of prison accommodation in England and Wales in the 1870s. In Rutlandshire, there was one gaol for every 20,000 inhabitants; in Lincolnshire there were seven gaols, or one for every 48,000; Worcestershire had one gaol for every 338,000 individuals; Lancashire, one for 469,000; Middlesex, one for 507,000; and Stafford, one for 858,000 individuals (*ibid*: 1538). It was now obvious that absolute uniformity could only be attained if the system of local administration was entirely subverted by central government. The insurmountable difficulties that met any attempt at promoting a rationalised system of punishment around local autonomies was noted by Du Cane. In calling for a complete government take-over of the prison system, he suggested:

"It can hardly be doubted that the effect would be to raise the badly-managed prisons at least to a higher degree of efficiency, and it may fairly be assumed that the first aim of punishment, viz., the decrease of crime, would be more effectually served if the Prison Service was reorganised as proposed" (as quoted in McConville 1995: 193).

As such, the 1877 Prison Act had two cardinal motives: to promote uniformity in the management of prisons and to relieve the burden of local rates. It ventured to realise these aspirations by vesting the ownership of all local prisons together with the furniture and effects belonging thereto in the Home Secretary from 1 April, 1878. All expenses incurred in respect of the maintenance of such prisons were, from that date forth, to be defrayed out of money provided by Parliament. Prison Commissioners were to be appointed (not exceeding five) to assist the Secretary of State in carrying into effect the provisions of the Act and these in turn were to be aided in the performance of their duties by inspectors, storekeepers, accountants, and other officers and servants as may with the sanction of the Treasury as to number, be determined by the Secretary of State. Visiting Committees consisting of Justices of the Peace were to be annually appointed for every prison to hear the complaints of prisoners, to report on any abuses or any repairs which may be urgently required, and to take cognisance of any other matters of pressing necessity (40 and 41 Vict: ch 21).[13]

---

13. The convict prisons continued under a separate Board of Directors until 1898. But since the chairman of this Board was Sir Edmund du Cane who was also the first chairman of the Prison Commissioners under the 1877 Prison Act, the two bodies were, for all intents and purposes, merged together following the 1877 Act (Harding *et al* 1985: 192). For the effect of central control on the Home Office, see Pellew (1982: 33-64).

The Prison Commissioners promptly asserted absolute dominance over the local prison system. Out of 113 local prisons assigned to them, 38 were immediately closed on the day of transfer and in the ensuing decade a further 19 were discontinued. By 1894 only 56 former local prisons remained in operation (Webb and Webb 1922: 201-203).[14] One of the results of such a shift in policy and practice towards a hierarchical bureaucracy was that the prison system became enveloped in a fog of official secrecy. Investigative individuals would no longer be permitted to engage in fact-finding missions after 1877 and were actually adjudged to be a needless impedance (Blom-Cooper 1978: 72-73). Similarly, voluntary bodies were forced to play a more subordinate role in penal activities, particularly in respect of prisons (Webb and Webb 1922: 233-241).[15]

At this juncture it may be appropriate, in the interest of lucidity, to restate the more important developments which occurred in respect of local prisons. The State hesitantly assumed a more important role following a protracted struggle with local and corporate jurisdictions to enforce a greater degree of uniformity. Pertinacious and moderate attempts to rectify the system - such as the abolition of gaol fees in 1815, the stipulation that gaolers, chaplains and

---

14. In Ireland, full central control of the prisons was authorised by the General Prisons (Ireland) Act of 1877 (40 and 41 Vict: c. 45). As a result, 64 of Ireland's 95 bridewells were shut immediately and 14 of the 38 local prisons were reclassified as remand prisons (McGowan 1978: 501).
15. I say "in respect of prisons" because the development of probation had for a good many years, as one of its defining characteristics, an entirely different stance in relation to voluntary agencies.

surgeons submit reports at Quarter Sessions in 1823, the establishment of an inspectorate in 1835, and the attempt to create a more uniform system of management by incorporating a code of rules into a statute in 1865 and by offering the inducement of the exchequer grant for compliance with its conditions - were all ineffectual in actuating the degree of homogeneity considered essential by the authorities. By the mid 1870s it was an indubitable fact that if this sought-after degree of uniformity was to be attained, the government would have to pursue it alone. Moreover such a pursuit would necessitate the total usurpation of the power of local authorities and the analogous rise of a more functional system under government control. It is in this context that the Prison Act of 1877 must be understood.

The process of rationalisation following the 1877 Act was a complete success in terms of creating a uniformed, disciplined and more economic regime. But what were the objects of this highly organised and administrative network? From the outset it appears that this drive towards rationalisation, focusing as it did on order, finance, homogeneity and logistics, attempted to subject all offenders to one uniform and severe method of penal discipline. Although inmates were categorised according to age, sex, conviction and sentence length, the Victorian penal system did not acknowledge the idiosyncratic attributes specific to each individual offender. Punishment was administered to all individuals in the most precisely measured and impersonal fashion. But this rationalised system of certainty and severity of punishment, embodying as it did the concepts of self-reliance and self-responsibility, quickly found itself subject to disparagement on the grounds of its rigid and austere qualities. As has already been noted, the *process of intervening to rationalise* (the 1823, 1835 and 1865 Prison Acts) culminated ultimately in the 1877 Prison Act. Although the need for *rationalisation* was rendered nugatory after 1877 given that the entire prison system was nationalised, the *capacity to intervene* remained operative. It could now be turned to other purposes. Essentially the point being made is that if you could adopt a process of intervention to *rationalise* (a process which developed in intensity), you could also adopt the same process of intervention to *individualise* - particularly so after 1877 when intervention amounted to a totality in that it resulted in nationalisation. Prior to 1877, critics of the prison system did not, on the whole, question the use of imprisonment as a punitive technique. Rather the focus of individuals such as John Howard, William Crawford, Rev. Whitworth Russell, Elizabeth Fry and the Rev. Sidney Smith was directed at prison conditions, prison design, disciplinary techniques and the urgent need for uniformity. After 1877, however, when the prison system was, by and large, *distributed in homogenous circuits* (Foucault 1991b: 80), the effectiveness of the prison as a punitive technique began to be called into doubt. Indeed the rationalising process itself had thrown up a whole host of misfits which did not fit into a homogenised prison apparatus. As Wiener noted:

"[T]he utilitarian drive towards rationalisation ultimately worked against its own universalist principles. The very drive to subject all criminals to uniform discipline made prisoners, who, for whatever reason, did not fit the criminal stereotype for which that discipline had been devised, into a problem requiring new and special measures; ironically, a more lax, less single-minded regime, such as had existed before Victorian reform, would not have revealed these problems. Thus hardly had the aims of underlining personal responsibility and promoting self-discipline by penal methods of certainty, uniformity, and severity been established than they began to be qualified, as the very aim of uniform treatment implanted in the system by prison acts from 1835 to 1865 increasingly drew the attention of administrators to prisoners who did not fit, to exceptional cases" (Wiener 1990: 308-309).

Across a broad social spectrum, increased calls for intervention began to be voiced as the belief emerged that individualist ideology could not secure minimum standards of welfare. A more welfarist mode of operation was required. From a penological standpoint this approach manifested itself in the decline in the social contract philosophy of punishment, based as it was on repression, and the corresponding rise of a more positive and constructive attempt at reformation, centred as it was on individualisation. In this environment it became more difficult to argue that all individuals, such as the inebriate, the weak-minded and the young offender, should be deemed fully accountable for their conduct and treated in the same manner as other common criminals. This reduction in expectation with regard to an individual's ability to be both reliable and responsible also evidenced itself in other spheres and includes, as we have already noted, the restriction of the ways in which a contract could be enforced and the expansion of tort law.

The Youthful Offenders Act of 1854 provided the first institutional alternative to prison for young offenders by enabling the courts to sentence individuals under the age of 16 for two to five years in a reformatory school after a minimum of 14 days imprisonment (17 and 18 Vict: c. 86). Mid-century legislation of this kind however, as Wiener correctly points out, did not attempt to disaffirm the assumption of personal responsibility or the consequential liability to punishment of these offenders for reckless and irresponsible behaviour (Wiener 1990: 135). Indeed the precondition of a minimum period of imprisonment evinces the sternly held belief in rationality and the importance of taking responsibility for the consequences of one's own actions. But as England's hegemony in world trade declined, and the sciences, such as psychiatry and genetics, began to enunciate a greater profundity on the polymerous nature of society, the Victorian concept of individual responsibility and self-reliance was undermined. A new archetype of punishment was beginning to materialise which although continuing to reprimand individuals, did so in a manner more susceptible to the complexities of human nature. A regard for this "diminished power of individual will" may be seen in the Habitual Drunkards Act of 1879 which enabled the establishment of retreats to facilitate the control and cure of habitual drunkards (42 and 43 Vict: ch 19); the

Summary Jurisdiction Act of 1879 which encouraged a lowering of penalties for first offenders, limited children's liability to trial for offences that did not involve homicide, and categorised juveniles between 12 and 16 apart from adults for indictable offences, if the court thought it expedient to do so having regard to the character and antecedents of the offender (42 and 43 Vict: ch 49); the Criminal Lunatics Act of 1884 which gave the Home Secretary power to make, revoke or vary regulations for persons sentenced to penal servitude or imprisonment who appeared to be "from imbecility of mind either unfit for penal discipline or unfit for the same penal discipline as other prisoners", and (47 and 48 Vict: ch 64); the Probation of Offenders Act of 1887 which provided that an individual who was convicted of his or her first offence which was punishable by imprisonment up to two years, could at the court's discretion be released on his or her entering into a recognisance, with or without sureties (50 and 51 Vict: ch 25).[16] Thus a gradual picture emerges of individuals of diminished responsibility such as the inebriate, the imbecile, the first-time offender, and the child no longer being considered as strict legal personalities but rather as subjects in need of state protection.

Yet such a phenomenon was not just confined to offenders. The Factory and Workshop Act of 1878, for example, regulated the period of employment, length of

---

16. Factors which a judge could use in making a decision included the offender's youth, character, antecedents, the nature of the offence and any other extenuating circumstances. For an application of the aforementioned Act, see Bochel (1976: pp. 14-15).

continuous employment and allocation of holidays for children, young persons and women (41 Vict: ch 16). Social protectionism was in addition discernible in the Criminal Law Amendment Act of 1885 which raised the age of consent to 16 and also made it a misdemeanour to have unlawful carnal knowledge of any "female idiot or imbecile" (48 and 49 Vict: ch 69); in the Married Women (Maintenance in the case of Desertion) Act of 1886 which enabled a married woman, deserted by her husband, to have him summoned before two petty justices or a stipendiary magistrate and ordered to maintain her for a weekly sum not exceeding £2, if he was in a position to do so (49 and 50 Vict: ch 52); in the Intoxicating Liquors (Sale to Children) Act of 1886 which in order to "protect young children against the immoral consequence from their being permitted to purchase intoxicating liquors" provided that it was an offence for a licence holder to knowingly sell, or allow any person to sell alcohol to any person under 13 for consumption on the premises (49 and 50 Vict: ch 56); in the Employment of Young Persons in Shops Acts of 1892 which, anxious to preserve the health of many young persons, restricted their employment to 74 hours including mealtimes in any one week; and (55 and 56 Vict: ch 62) in the Prevention of Cruelty to Children Act of 1899 which sought through the imposition of criminal penalties to discourage mistreatment of children (52 and 53 Vict: ch 44).

Increasing disquiet about the efficacy of the prison administrative system and the continuing reappraisal of the State's responsibility pertaining to the punishment of individuals at the beginning of the 1890s prompted the creation of a Departmental Committee of Inquiry to re-examine the principles which governed the entire penal realm. Published in 1895, the Gladstone Committee stated that one of the cardinal objects of the criminal justice system was to humanise offenders and to counteract their presumptions that the State merely incarcerated them without caring for their personal welfare or well-being. This reformation principle was to be placed, along with deterrence, as the primary and concurrent objects of the entire penal apparatus. It could be attained through classification according to individual character and physical development. Thus first offenders, young offenders, habitual criminals, habitual drunkards, weak minded prisoners, and female prisoners with children should be separated in order to aid their treatment.

As Foucault has noted, and as we shall see more readily in the next section of this chapter in our discussion of individualisation:

"By now a quite different question of truth is inscribed in the course of the penal judgement: The question is no longer simply: Has the Act been established and is it punishable? But also: What is this Act , what is this act of violence or this murder? To what level or to what field of reality does it belong? Is it a fantasy, a psychotic reaction, a delusional episode, a perverse action? It is no longer simply: Who committed it?: But: How can we assign the causal process that produced it? Where did it originate in the author himself? Instinct, unconscious, environment, heredity? It is no longer simply: What law punishes this offence? But: What would be the most appropriate measure to take? How do we see the future development of the offender? What would be the best way of rehabilitating him? A whole set of assessing, diagnostic, prognostic, normative judgements concerning the criminal have become lodged in the framework of penal judgement" (Foucault 1991b: 19).

The Gladstone Report, then, which espoused individualisation as one of the foremost objectives of punishment, took account of and supported what was to the forefront in penal policy and social policy thinking. Examples of increased state interference after 1895 include: the Inebriates Act of 1898, which permitted the courts when dealing with habitual inebriates to order their incarceration in a state inebriate reformatory; the Reformatory Schools Amendment Act of 1899, which abrogated the normal 14 day period of imprisonment which was a precondition for the committal of a young offender to a reformatory school; the 1907 Probation of Offenders Act, which made it lawful for judges to make probation orders having had regard to the character, antecedents, age, health, or mental condition of the offender; the Prevention of Crime Act of 1908, which made it lawful for a court in lieu of passing a sentence of imprisonment on a young offender to pass a sentence of detention in a borstal institution; the same Act which also established preventive detention for habitual criminals; the Children's Act of 1908, which restricted the use of imprisonment for children and created juvenile courts for offenders under the age of 16; the Mental Deficiency Act of

1913, which gave the courts power to sentence "idiots, imbeciles, feeble-minded persons and moral imbeciles" in an institution for defectives or have them placed under guardianship; and, the Criminal Justice Administration Act of 1914, which established supervision licences in circumstances where an offender either in a borstal or under a sentence of preventive detention was likely to refrain from crime and lead a useful and industrious life.[17] This new moral duty of the State to intervene in order to rectify dysfunction and degeneracy or simply to quarantine for the protection of society culminated in the displacement of the prison from its deployment as the keystone of the criminal justice system to one sanction among many in an expanded network of penalties. Of course it continued to be an essential punishment. But it was now utilised in the main for a distinct stratum of the criminal population and "often as a back-up sanction for other institutions rather than the place of first resort"(Garland 1985: 23).

In conclusion, one may suggest that the seventeenth and eighteenth centuries were characterised by localised and disparate penal arrangements. There was widespread antipathy towards homogeneity and centralisation. Individualism, regarded as it was as sacred from

---

17. Again, the dilatory nature of this transformation must be emphasised. With regard to probation for example, a reluctance to finance the system was evident among a number of local authorities for a number of years after the legislation had been enacted. Moreover, many of the officers employed to supervise probation were agents of voluntary societies as opposed to full time probation officers. The establishment of a more bureaucratic probation machinery only became apparent after the enactments of the Criminal Justice Administration Act of 1925 and the Criminal Justice Amendment Act of 1926 (Bochel 1976: 45-72; Newburn 1995: 86).

authoritative intrusion, was the prevailing ideology of the era. When it was necessary for the State to intrude, it did so in a manner structured to facilitate the spirit of individualism. A change of direction was, however, moderately engineered in relation to beliefs concerning government interference. Yet this transformation was dilatory in nature and one should bear in mind that even for the greater part of the 1800s a striking hostility and antagonism was evident in relation to government attempts at promoting uniformity. The authorities often found themselves engaged in a balancing act, mindful on the one hand of the local authorities' animosity towards usurpation of their power, and on the other of the general dearth of homogeneity and concordance in penal practice throughout the country. It was apparent that absolute uniformity and consistency could only be effectuated through the total appropriation of the power of local jurisdictions. After 1877, following the centralisation of the local prison system, a new archetype of punishment began to emerge under state control. This period witnessed - albeit in a dilatory manner - not only the flowering of a highly, rationalised, professionalised and bureaucratic penal apparatus, but also one which was more capable of accommodating the multifarious complexities and intricacies associated with human behaviour. Subsequent developments mirrored this approach for the greater part of the twentieth century.

Modern penalty, then, is no longer based on local and disparate arrangements but is founded, instead, upon a new archetype of punishment centred upon homogeneity of penal practice and the employment of more "diagnostic, prognostic, normative judgements" in respect of offending. Vass and Pease, however, in their attempts to construct continuities through history, completely neglect the issue of homogeneity and centralisation of penal practice.[18] Such an issue, as we have seen, has radically altered the process of penal practice and, whilst not immediately apparent from any anaemic appraisal of continuities over time, fundamentally effects both the shape and functioning of community service. The remainder of this chapter will continue to highlight fundamental flaws in their approach

---

18. Moreover, an understanding of centralisation may have important ramifications for those engaged in the study of contemporary penal practice. In recent years, it has been argued that there has been a decline in the perception of the state as "primary protector", coupled with a palpable hardening in punitive responses. Increases in the incidence of crime, the politicisation of law and order, growing attacks on rehabilitation as a legitimate policy goal, and the rise of containment as a principal policy goal in criminal justice thinking all have resulted, as Garland suggests, in a crisis of penal modernism that has "begun to erode one of the foundational myths of modern society: namely, the myth that the sovereign state is capable of providing security, law and order, and crime control within its territorial boundaries" (Garland 1996: 448; Garland 1997: 180-199). In its place a new mode of crime control is beginning to emerge in which the UK Government is trying to "devolve responsibility for crime prevention on to the agencies, organisations and individuals which are quite outside the State" (Garland 1996: 445-471). What is interesting about such an argument is that a Nietzschean critique of such a penal phenomenon would no doubt note: "[W]henever a community gains in power and pride, its penal code becomes more lenient, while the moment it is weakened or endangered the harsher methods of the past are revived. The humanity of creditors has always increased with their wealth; until finally the degree to which a creditor can tolerate impairment becomes the measure of his wealth. It is possible to imagine a society flushed with such a sense of power that it could afford to let its offenders go unpunished" (Nietzsche 1956: 205).

to understanding the sanction from an historical perspective.

Distinguishing Between Various Types of Offenders

In the last section it was noted that an appreciation of the diminished capabilities of a whole variety of offenders culminated in more interventionist State action in respect of offenders. But rather than viewing this transformation from the perspective of state control and social thinking, the purpose of this section is to examine it from the standpoint of scientific reasoning on human behaviour, and, in particular, from the standpoint of penal reasoning on miscreant behaviour. Although recognising that forms of classification did exist prior to the nineteenth century (ie, according to sex, age and types of offence), it will be argued that little or no attempt was made to focus on the individual characters of offenders or the etiological causes of crime. This section will also endeavour to describe the gradual emergence of a more deterministic approach to offending - occurring as it did in the late nineteenth century when science was highlighting ever more thoroughly the web of connections that nature is composed of - and the extension of the range of penal sanctions to respond to such a movement.

Penology prior to the late 1800s paid little attention to the various characteristics and attributes of offenders. Specific modes of treatment for individual offenders was unfamiliar and, by and large, unregarded by the makers of criminal justice policy. This system of justice advocated the notion of proportionate punishments for various crimes, without acknowledging the particular situations of individual offenders or the specific circumstances in which offences were committed. Accordingly, there was no obligation to require a knowledge of offenders, other than that of the offences they committed. But this inattention to individualisation did not obviate the employment of certain forms of classification. Prisoners were, as Garland accurately points out, to some extent categorised and separated according to sex, sentence length and type of offence for administrative and segregational purposes (1985: 14). This may be seen quite clearly with regard to houses of correction.

Although intended primarily for three distinct classes (those being children, the sick and vagabonds), they in fact provided for a much more far-reaching range of inmates. Children, the infirm, elderly, insane and indigent were all attended to within the spatial constraints of these institutions. In truth, by the 1700s it was difficult to determine any difference between gaols and houses of correction, whether in administration, discipline or the character of inmates. An Act of 1719 made it lawful for Justices of the Peace, within their respective jurisdictions, to commit such "vagrants and other criminals, offenders and persons charged with small offences" either to the common gaol or house of correction, "as they in their judgment shall think proper" (6 Geo. I: c. 19).[19] The practice of sentencing offenders to either institution soon ran into difficulties. The authorities realised that it caused great inconvenience in relation to the segregation of inmates. As a result, it was decided that houses of correction should be the only place of confinement for all "idle and disorderly persons, rogues, vagabonds, incorrigible rogues and other vagrants" (4 Geo IV: c. 64). Nonetheless the cardinal principle to be derived from such a sanction was that offenders were still assessed in the main according to their offences, rather than their characters, antecedents and specific factors which led them to commit crimes. A corresponding indifference evidenced itself in workhouses. It was hoped that through the inculcation of habits of discipline, hygiene and work, the whole amalgam of inmates (which included the young, aged, infirm, able-bodied, feeble-minded and insane) could be reformed to live dependent-free lives.

As regards the type of offenders sentenced to hard labour on board the hulks - where segregation was almost impossible - one witness informed Parliament that they were "notorious felons, who are everyday expected to break prison, some of them have already made attempts to do so, and are a class of people too dangerous to remain in this country" (Journals of the House of Commons 26 Geo. III: 40,

---

19. John Howard warned against such a merger when he advised that every county and town should be careful to ensure that each bridewell was suitable for its intended purpose: "In many places the county gaol is also a bridewell. But the prison ought to be quite separate from the bridewell; at least not within the same walls; nor should even the courtyard be common to both" (Howard 1977: 68-69; Webb and Webb 1922: 16-17).

955).[20] Not all offenders, however, detained on these ships could be classed as dangerous criminals. It was noted in 1778 that the 1776 Act which introduced the hulks and was intended for the most "dangerous and daring offenders" had been extended to several criminals, "who from their bodily infirmities, from their extreme youth, or their advanced age, and also from the nature of their crimes, might have been more properly subjected to some other mode of punishment" (Journals of the House of Commons 20 Geo. III: 37, 313).[21] It is not surprising then that the Committee on the Laws relating to Penitentiary Houses in 1812, having taken note of such like evidence, suggested that the hulks were obviously ill-calculated for the reception of any offenders but those whose age and bodily strength would admit of their being employed in laborious occupations. Except for a few elderly men who could be

---

20. Jeremy Bentham similarly noted that the hulks were designed for only the worst type of offenders (Bentham 1962: 4, 15).
21. This is supported by a witness who reported that there were several boys of about 13 or 14 on board the hulks, "not strong enough to wheel a barrow, several under the age of 16, and many lame and unfit for labour" (*ibid*: 309). Abell informs us that a number of French prisoners of war were also confined on the hulks (1914: 38). Finally a number of gentleman convicts also appear to have been sentenced to periods of imprisonment on the hulks. David Brown Dignum was convicted of fraudulently pretending to sell the office of Clerk of the Minutes to his Majesty's Custom House in Dublin and of fraudulently appointing another individual as a writer in *The London Gazette*. Being a wealthy individual, and having notions of gentility, he arrived at the hulks in Woolwich with his servant, expecting that his money would procure every indulgence in his favour. He was badly mistaken. The supervisors of the hulks would not permit his servant on board, and Dignum was immediately put to hard labour (Wilkinson 1963: 112-113).

employed on ship's duty or as attendants upon the sick, as well as some shoemakers and tailors, all other offenders not having the aforementioned characteristics or skillswere to be confined elsewhere (1812: III, 145). A similar lack of attention prevailed in relation to the types of offenders in prisons. In 1840 there were 10,000 children aged 16 or less in prison; three quarters had been committed by courts of summary jurisdiction. By 1857 the number had escalated to 12,500, 1,900 of them being under 12 years of age. Altogether it was estimated that children and young persons (under the age of 16) made up 10 per cent of all committals to prison during the 1840s and 1850s (Radzinowicz and Hood 1986: 5, 624).

With the advance of the 1800s, a growing disquiet about the efficacy of methods employed in the penal system became palpable. Could children, for instance, not be deprived of their liberty without having to be cast among serious offenders? The focus of attention came gradually to bear, albeit in a fragmented and piecemeal fashion, on the characters of offenders rather than on their exploits. New policies emerged intent on isolating juvenile criminals from adult offenders in order to preserve them from corruption. The Youthful Offenders Act of 1854, for example, made it lawful for any person under the age of 16 convicted of an offence punishable by law, either upon an indictment or on summary conviction, to be sent after a minimum of 14 days of imprisonment to a reformatory school for a period not less than two or exceeding five years (17 and 18 Vict: c. 86; Wiener 1990: 131-141). But as has already been delineated, if this Act conceded somewhat to the special nature of juvenile crime, it did so in a manner designed to uphold what may be regarded as Victorian moralism. As Wiener noted, the dominant position in the movement until late in the nineteenth century still supported the need to first subject juvenile offenders to a term of penal imprisonment before placing them in reformatories, thus maintaining the "presumption of personal responsibility and consequent liability to punishment of these offenders" (*ibid*: 135).

Nevertheless, individualisation of treatment did become more prominent in the latter decades of the nineteenth century. For example, the physiological and psychological differences between male and female offenders was noted and a network of semi-penal institutions for wayward and criminal women was established to augment and, in part, supplant the use of prisons (*ibid:* 130).[22] Likewise the treatment of insane felons began to undergo change. In the 1700s the natural repository for lunatics who had committed unlawful acts was the local gaol or house of correction, where they were deemed an ineluctable inconvenience. As the 1800s progressed, however, the concept of mental deficiency began to create more interest among alienists, psychologists, educationalists, eugenicists and administrators. By the close of the nineteenth century, considerable numbers of felons were being certified as insane and transferred to more specialised institutions where professional treatment could be administered (Walker and McCabe 1973: 93-112). A new image of

---

22. For a good account of the changes in the use of imprisonment for women, see Dobash *et al* (1986).

drunkards also emerged as inebriety came to be regarded as a disease. An Act of 1879 allowed for the voluntary commitment of persons defined as habitual drunkards to newly created retreats wherein they would undergo a course of treatment to facilitate their control and cure (42 and 43 Vict: ch 19).[23] It was for each individual to decide that they sought assistance and the criteria for admission were dangerousness or incapacity. The perpetration of a criminal offence did not, however, constitute grounds for admittance. The increased attention paid to habitual drunkards also reiterated itself with regard to the problem of habitual criminals as increased consideration was given to the distinction between wilfully cruel and remorseless offenders, and other cases of habitual offenders who demanded and required different modes of treatment (32 and 33 Vict: ch 99; 34 and 35 Vict: ch 112).

This recognition of the various characteristics of individuals in the mid- to late-1800s was motivated by the advances being made by the natural sciences on human behaviour. Seventeenth and eighteenth century accounts of the causes of crime lacked any developed awareness of diacritical etiology and often made recourse to theological impositions such as sin, destiny, predestination or divine will. When in the last few decades of the nineteenth century, a new scientific approach to crime materialised, it immediately repudiated all forms of spiritual and

---

23. This Act came into force at a time when measures for the disposal of drunken offenders were confined to imprisonment, fines and occasionally binding over for good behaviour (Harding and Wilkin 1988a: 191).

conjectural reasoning on the characters of malefactors. As John H. Wigmore *et al* noted in 1911 in the general introduction to Cesare Lombroso's book - *Crime: Its causes and remedies:*

"Two centuries ago, while modern medical science was still young, medical practitioners proceeded upon two general assumptions: one as to the cause of disease, the other as to its treatment. As to the cause of disease, - disease was sent by the inscrutable will of God. No man could fathom that will, nor its arbitrary operation. As to the treatment of disease, there were believed to be a few remedial agents of universal efficacy. Calomel and blood-letting, for example, were two of the principal ones. A larger or smaller dose of calomel, a greater or less quantity of blood letting, - this blindly indiscriminate mode of treatment was regarded as orthodox for all common varieties of ailment ... Nowadays, all this is past in medical science. As to the causes of disease, we know that they are facts of nature, - various, but distinguishable by diagnosis and research, and more or less capable of prevention or control or counteraction. As to the treatment, we now know that there are various specific modes of treatment for specific causes or symptoms, and the treatment must be adapted to the cause. In short, the individualisation of disease, in causes and in treatment, is the dominant truth of modern medical science (1911: vi)."

Wigmore *et al* go on to suggest:

"The same truth is known about crime; but the understanding and the application of it are just opening upon us. The old and still dominant thought is, as to cause, that a crime is caused by the inscrutable moral free will of the human being, doing or not doing the crime, just as it pleases; absolutely free in advance, at any moment of time, to choose or not to choose the criminal act, and therefore in itself the sole and ultimate cause of crime. As to treatment, there still are just two traditional measures, used in varying doses for all kinds of crime and all kinds of persons, - jail, or a fine (for death is now employed in rare cases only). But modern science, here as in medicine, recognises that crime also (like disease) has natural causes. It need not be asserted for one moment that crime is a disease. But it does have natural causes, - that is, circumstances which work to produce it in a given case. And as to treatment, modern science recognises that penal or remedial treatment cannot possibly be indiscriminate and machine-like, but must be adapted to the causes, and to the man as affected by those causes. Common sense and logic alike require, inevitably, that the moment we predicate a specific cause for an undesirable effect, the remedial treatment must be specifically adapted to that cause. Thus the great truth of the present and the future, for criminal science, is the individualisation of penal treatment, for that man, and for the cause of that man's crime (*ibid*: vi-vii)."

Crime was as a result of delinquent personalities and should only be treated by positive State regulated techniques of intervention and human transformation. This was, as has previously been mentioned, greatly aided by the advancement in sciences particularly in the fields of anthropology, psychiatry, sociology and genetics. What occurred, then, was a gradual development away from a moral attempt to account for crime to one based on a more deterministic approach. Miscreants were no longer simply adjudged to be incorrigible or immoral persons but rather as individuals whose fundamental character defects were congenital or as a consequence of their social environment. This is supported by Wiener who stated:

"As both the practicality and humanity of insisting upon an individual's responsibility for his fate came into question, the once-dominant policy outlook of moralism - the distribution of benefits and penalties according to the moral deserts of the people involved in a situation - was losing its formal consensual force. In its place was emerging a new outlook we might entitle *causilism*. Bypassing the questions of blame central to moralism, causilism aimed to minimise overall harm and suffering regardless of the moral status or past behaviour of the parties involved. If moralism was associated with the Victorian State, causalism came to be associated with the more expansive, but less punitive twentieth century State (1990: 338)."[24]

---

24. The vast majority of Victorians were still, however, of the opinion that although poor social conditions may, for instance, affect people's abilities to determine what the right course of action should be, amelioration of these conditions could not in itself result in a diminution of crime (Radzinowicz

Evidence of causilism with regard to behaviour in both criminological and non-criminological spheres can be detected as far back as the early 1800s with the emergence of the phrenological and physiognomist movements. The former believed that behaviour was associated with prenatally determined and differing sized areas of the brain (Forsythe 1991: 9) whilst the latter related the antisocial impulses of the criminal to the peculiarities in his or her external features (Radzinowicz 1966: 46). It was not, however, until the publication of Darwin's doctrine of genetically conveyed characteristics and defects in 1859 in *Origin of the Species* that evolutionist hypothesising began to make a breakthrough. In considering the embryological structure of humans, he suggested that:

"[W]ith mankind some of the worst dispositions, which occasionally without any assignable cause make their appearance in families, may perhaps be reversions to a savage state, from which we are not removed by very many generations. This view seems indeed recognised in the common expression that such men are the black sheep of the family (1871: I, 173)."[25]

Thus the criminal, the lunatic, the mentally defective, the vagrant and the pauper were the black sheep whose

---

and Hood 1986: 49).
25. His views were greatly resisted by individuals such as Samuel Wilberforce, Bishop of London, and, to begin with, by scientific journals which believed his doctrine to be an attack on established religion. See Oldroyd (1980: 193-201).

deficiencies in the struggle for existence could lead, as a result of the laws of natural selection, to their obsolescence provided they were prevented from breeding at a greater rate than those with unblemished characteristics.

But why was it only in the mid- to late-nineteenth century that causilism emerged to challenge the dominance of moralism? To start with, it was only in the middle decades of that century that scientism came of age (Knight 1986: 3). In these years British science took on a more organised, purposeful and permanent role. In the 1840s, for example, laboratory training was greatly expanded by the establishment of the Royal College of Chemistry, the Putney Engineering College and the Pharmaceutical Society (Cardwell 1972: 106). The ensuing decades witnessed the incorporation of science modules into the examination syllabuses of universities, the introduction of the London Science degree and the beginning of state aid to science through the agency of the new Science and Art Department (*ibid*). Accordingly the sciences became more specialised and subjects such as physiology, embryology, biology, evolutionary biology, chemistry, biochemistry and bacteriology all began to establish and define themselves as specialist designations.

This maturing in the sciences, particularly the biological sciences, had a profound effect on the belief that each specific species was as a result of God's endeavour. The human being was increasingly viewed as a product of natural phenomena as opposed to the sacrosanct will of God. As Coleman noted:

"The most salient feature of the rapidly advancing nineteenth century studies regarding man was their general presumption that he, too, was or must soon become a proper object of scientific investigation. Science was reaching out to seize the supreme product of creation. With science came the assurance that its admired qualities - certain knowledge grounded always in facts, experimental control over phenomena, and rigorous logical systematisation, the whole giving promise of predictive power - might extend from the inorganic realm to plants and animals and, ultimately, to man and human society (1977: 116)."

Francis Galton, for example, inspired by his cousin Charles Darwin, proposed in *Hereditary Genius* that if we could observe humans as we observed animals, and measure their abilities, we could, by a process of natural selection, produce a highly gifted body of people. This natural selection process could be carried out by judicious marriages during several consecutive generations (Galton 1962: 45). Such a belief was taken one stage further in the ensuing decades by eugenicists. The term eugenics was defined as the study of agencies under social control, that may improve or impair the racial qualities of future generations, either physically or mentally (Pearson 1912: 1-6). Motivated by a fear of the decline in influence of Britain as a world power and the emergence of nations such as Germany, Japan and the United States, they argued for a more scientific analysis of the features relating to race development. In particular they wished to create a strong, efficient and competitive society by adapting and accelerating the purifying force of natural selection (*ibid*). One means of ensuring a more purified race was to sterilise all insane, mentally defective, criminal, tuberculous, blind, deaf and diseased. Thus it became an artificial and purely scientific process of intervention as opposed to a simple natural one. In this way it was hoped that Britain could discard many of its socially inferior groups and would, accordingly, emulate and better other powerful nations in all forms of competition.

Viewed in this context, it is not difficult to comprehend that the criminal justice system would aim towards a more deterministic analysis and individualistic approach to the treatment of criminal behaviour. Henry Mayhew, for example, was influenced by evolutionist hypothesising. This can be discerned from the following statement in 1862:

"The subject of juvenile crime, however, helps to strip the matter of a considerable proportion of its difficulty. It is no longer hard to tell how the *predatory maggot* got within the *social nut*, for here we detect the *criminal ovum* lying in the very blossom of the *plant*; and as in certain processes of the body we can discover, microscopically, the new tissue in the course of being secreted from the blood, and see little spiculae of bone thrown down, one after another, from the same mysterious fluid, in the wondrous and beautiful efforts of nature to repair a limb - *in like manner can we behold, with the enlarged vision of experience, how the young criminal tends to renovate the wasted ranks of the old offenders* (1862: 381)" (my italics).

Mayhew was also anxious to dispel myths about the moral plague of crime. He tested, or attempted to test, some of the popular causes of crime - such as density of population, poverty, vagrancy, the non-observance of the Sabbath, and the fall of man - by collating the statistics associated with each cause. He found that "none of the received explanations would bear the searching test of figures" (*ibid*). In his view, theories of crime had to explain the causes of crime all over the world and not merely that "little clique among society which we happen to call our own State" (*ibid*: 383). Thus the causes of crime must apply equally to the "songuas and bushmen of the Hottenots, the fingoes of the Kaffirs, as well as to the pickpockets, vagrants and burglars of England and Wales" (*ibid*). Similarly, the psychologist, Henry Maudsley, rejecting moral discourse on crime, suggested in 1874:

> "It is certain ... that lunatics and criminals are as much manufactured articles as are steam engines and calico-printing machines, only the processes of the organic manufactory are so complex that we are not able to follow them. They are neither accidents nor anomalies in the universe, but come by law to testify to causality; and it is the business of science to find out what the causes are and by what laws they work (1874: 24)."

Scientific approaches to the study of crime became more pronounced in 1876 with the publication of the first major criminological work, titled *L'Uome Delinquente*, by Cesare Lombroso. Having accumulated knowledge from the fields of anthropology, physiology, biology, physiognomy, phrenology and psychiatry, his hypothesis - by applying an inductive method of science to human and social phenomena - suggested that offenders could be distinguished on the basis of a number of physical abnormalities which were a result of an atavistic or degenerative lineage. This concept of atavism was closely associated with Darwin's "reversion to a savage state" theory. Thus he believed that the characteristics presented by savage races were very often found among born criminals. These included:

"the slight development of the pilar system; low cranial capacity; retreating forehead; highly developed frontal sinuses; great frequency of Wormian bones ... To these we may add the lemurine appendix; anomalies of the ear; dental diastemata; great agility; relative insensibility to pain; dullness of the sense of touch; great visual acuteness ... Besides these there is a great vanity; a passion for gambling and alcoholic drinks; violent but fleeting passions; superstition; extraordinary sensitiveness with regard to one's own personality; and a special conception of God and morality (1911: 365-366)."

Nor did he believe that this concept of atavism was a fitful or isolated phenomenon. He cited the common oak as an example in nature of atavism. It would develop characteristics of the Quaternary period under certain unfavourable conditions, such as in severe weather or poor soil. Similarly a stray dog left to run wild in the forest would revert in a few generations to the type of his wolf-like progenitor, and the cultivated garden rose when neglected would demonstrate a tendency to reassume the form of the original dog rose (Lombroso Ferrero 1911: 135-136). The special conditions which could force human beings to alter, according to Lombroso, included "hunger, syphilis, trauma, and, still more frequently, morbid conditions inherited from insane, criminal, or diseased progenitors, or the abuse of nerve poisons, such as alcohol, tobacco, or morphine cause various alterations, of which criminality - that is, a return to the characteristics peculiar to primitive savages - is in reality the least serious, because it represents a less advanced stage than other forms of cerebral alteration" (*ibid*).[26]

Thus by the late 1800s human beings were increasingly viewed as a product of natural phenomena and subjected to scientific investigation. Criminal justice was also influenced by such deterministic modes of understanding human nature. As mentioned in the last section, a new archetype of punishment was emerging which although continuing to

---

26. For a clear rejection of Lombrosco's hypothesis, see the writings of Charles Goring. He suggested, in the early 1900s, that Lombroso's findings were dominated by unfounded beliefs and was, in effect, "superstitious criminology". As evidence for this, he stated: "Lombroso's ingenuity in abstracting positive results even from recalcitrant measurements is illustrated by the following passage ... Seeking to establish the inferior cranial capacity of criminals, he has to record that "arithmetically speaking the average capacity of criminals (1322cc) is higher than the average shown by normals (1310cc)"; but, the author adds, "in only 11 per cent of normals was the capacity below 1200cc, whereas, among criminals, 20 per cent fell below this figure: a result which establishes the inferiority of criminals" (Goring 1913: 18).

punish individuals for wrongdoings did so in a manner more receptive to the intricacies of human nature and human fallibility. The Summary Jurisdiction Act of 1879, the Criminal Lunacy Act of 1888, the Probation of Offenders Act of 1887, the Criminal Law Amendment Act of 1885 and the Prevention of Cruelty to Children Act of 1889 all elucidate and signpost this increased concern for individual offenders.[27]

In 1895, the Gladstone Committee presented its findings on the prison system to the Home Secretary. It condemned the uniformity of treatment which was championed by Edmund du Cane (Chairman of the English Prison Commission) and practised in prisons. It urged instead the use of a system of classification which would make it possible to deal with prisoners collectively by reason of their circumstances being of like nature. It stated that "the system should be made more elastic, more capable of being adapted to the special cases of individual prisoners; that prison discipline and treatment should be more effectively designed to maintain, stimulate, or awaken the higher susceptibilities of prisoners, to develop their moral instincts, to train them in orderly and industrial habits, and whenever possible to turn them out of prison better men and women, both morally and physically,

27. British intellectuals and penal officials, although interested in the idea of individualisation of treatment, played very little part in the early development of the actual criminological movement. Most of the relevant research and publication took place in Italy, France and Germany, and the British were notable absentees at the international congresses held to debate the claims and counter claims of the various schools (Garland 1994a: 42).

than when they came in" (1895: LVI, 8). Moreover, it was also suggested that within the "orderly equality" advocated by Du Cane, there existed the most striking inequalities. What was a temporary inconvenience to an adult criminal may have been regarded as a bitter disgrace to a young offender from which he or she would never recover (*ibid*). Uniformity was no longer to be looked upon as a cardinal aim of penal practice. As a result, Du Cane, unable to contend with such an assault on his administration, resigned within three days of the publication of the report. The Gladstone Report itself, however, did not instigate immediate action and it was three years before any legislation was enacted.[28]

The significance of individualisation within the criminal justice system grew even more in stature after 1898 as the attributes and dispositions of offenders came under closer scrutiny. Prisoners were differentiated with the intention of administering a more suitable form of treatment and efforts were also made to deflect some of them to more appropriate institutions. These specialised institutions were designed to cater for specific categories of offenders and their regimes were adapted accordingly. Their advance accelerated the decline of the common amalgamated prisons of the Victorian period. The insane, inebriate, juvenile and first time offenders no longer formed an important component of the prison populations composition as it assumed a role

---

28. The 1898 Prisons Act segregated young inmates from older ones and first offenders from recidivists (61 and 62 Vict: ch. 61).

which focused to an increasing extent on a more constricted segment of the criminal community. This is favourably illustrated by the number of distinctive sanctions, ranging across an extended domain, which became available to the criminal courts after the Gladstone Report. This diffusion and diversification in penal sanctions included the following new sentences: borstal training; preventive detention; corrective detention; detention in an inebriate reformatory; detention in an institution for the mentally defective; probation; various forms of licensed supervision; supervised fines; absolute and conditional release and suspended sentences.

The Inebriates Act of 1898, for example, allowed the courts when dealing with habitual inebriates to order their detention for a term not exceeding three years in any State inebriate reformatory in addition to or in lieu of any other sentence (61 and 62 Vict: ch. 60). Moreover, the imposition of the sanction was determined by the character and antecedents of the accused as opposed to the actual offence which had led to his or her committal. A number of State reformatories were established under this legislation and private reformatories validated and approved by the Home Office could also be employed (*ibid*). In a similar fashion, the Mental Deficiency Act of 1913 also attempted to divert "idiots, imbeciles, feeble-minded persons and moral imbeciles" from the penal system. The Act gave the courts authority to sentence any mentally deficient person found guilty of a criminal offence to an institution for defectives or be placed under guardianship. An order made under this Act was to be for one year in the first instance, thereafter renewable for successive periods of five years by the Board of Control after considering a special report as to the mental and bodily condition of the defective and a certificate by a medical practitioner stating that the defective was still a proper person to be detained in an institution or under guardianship (3 and 4 Geo. V: ch. 28).

The Gladstone Committee itself had manifested an express concern in the 16 to 21 age group (ubiquitously referred to in contemporary nomenclature as young adult offenders). In 1895, 2,226 prisoners between the ages of 16 and 20 were still contained within the prison system (Gladstone Committee Report 1895: LVI, 29). The Committee, referring to the "headsprings of recidivism", stated that the most fatal years were 17, 18 and 19 and a "more determined effort should be made to lay hold of these incipient criminals and to prevent them by strong restraint and rational treatment from recruiting into the habitual class". Indeed they found it quite remarkable "that previous inquiries have almost altogether overlooked this all important matter" (*ibid*). Because it was felt that young offenders came out of prison as bad or worse than when they went in, the establishment of penal reformatories were recommended. They were to act as half-way houses between prisons and reformatories, to be situated in rural settings with both penal and coercive characteristics which could be applied according to the merits and demerits of individual cases. They were to be "amply provided with a staff capable of giving sound education, training the inmates in various kinds of industrial work, and qualified generally to exercise the best and healthiest kind of moral influence" (*ibid*: 30-31).

The 1908 Prevention of Crime Act, acting upon these recommendations, made it lawful for a court in *lieu* of passing a sentence of penal servitude or imprisonment to pass a sentence of detention under penal discipline in a borstal institution for a term of not less than one year nor more than three years on any person not less than 16 nor more than 21 years of age (8 Edw. VII: ch. 59; Fox 1952: 335).

The same Act also dealt with "habitual criminals" by way of a new sanction of preventive detention. These were offenders who were dedicated to a life of crime and remained ostensibly unconcerned by any sentence the penal system could contrive to deter them. The Gladstone Committee proposed that:

"[A] new form of sentence should be placed at the disposal of judges by which these offenders might be segregated for long periods of detention during which they would not be treated with the severity of first-class hard labour or penal servitude, but would be forced to work under less onerous conditions. As loss of liberty would to them prove eventually the chief deterrent, so by their being removed from the opportunity of doing wrong the community would gain" (Gladstone Committee Report 1895: LVI, 31).

Section 10 of the 1908 Act accordingly provided that where an offender was convicted on indictment of a crime and was found to be an habitual criminal, the court could, after passing a sentence of penal servitude, pass a further sentence ordering that on the conclusion of the penal servitude the offender be detained for such a period not exceeding 10 nor less than five years, provided that the criminal, since the age of 16, had been convicted at least three times previously of a crime and was found to be "leading persistently a dishonest and criminal life" (8 Edw. VII: ch. 59).[29] Thus the Prevention of Crime Act sought to make a two-pronged attack on the normal prison system - by removing young people under the age of 21 who ought not to be subject to it and by removing, in addition, habitual criminals who were neither reformed nor deterred by it.

Although specialisation converged in the main around the different institutional regimes which were developed to cater for the persistent criminal, the mentally disordered, the habitual drunkard and the young offender, other non-institutional responses also emerged to attend to certain types of offenders. There was, for example, the formalisation of probation as a result of the 1907 Probation of Offenders Act. It constituted a revolutionary change in the sanctions of the criminal law by transforming the hitherto *ad hoc* practice of notables and evangelical missionaries into a statutory provision which made it lawful for the courts to make probation orders, having had regard to the character, antecedents, age, health, or mental condition of the offenders or the nature of the offences (7 Edw. VII: ch. 17). It also made it lawful for the local authorities to appoint professional probation officers to advise, assist and befriend offenders and report to the courts on their behaviour *(ibid)*.

---

29. For the failure of the 1908 Act in relation to the habitual criminal, see Fox (1952: 298-324).

The court by which the probation order was made was bound to furnish the offender with notice in writing stating the conditions that he or she was required to observe. They could include a recognisance prohibiting the offender from associating with thieves and other undesirable persons, or from frequenting other undesirable places, or to abstain from intoxicating liquor, or generally for securing that the offender lead an honest and industrious life (*ibid*). The Criminal Justice Administration Act of 1914 extended the range of these conditions to include specific directions as to residence and "any other matters, as the court may, having regard to the particular circumstances of the case, consider necessary for preventing a repetition of the same offence or the commission of other offences" (4 and 5 Geo. V: ch. 58).

Supervision licences, although not autonomous sanctions, were also salient addendums to borstal or preventive detention sentences. Section 5 of the 1908 Prevention of Crime Act authorised Prison Commissioners, if satisfied that there was a reasonable probability that certain offenders would abstain from crime and lead useful and industrious lives, to permit such offenders to be discharged from borstals on the condition that they be placed under the supervision of any Society or person named in the licence who was willing to take responsibility (8 Edw. VII: ch. 59). Likewise section 14 of the said Act authorised the Secretary of State to take into consideration the condition, history and circumstances of a person detained in custody under a sentence of preventive detention with a view to determining whether he or she would be better placed on licence (*ibid*). And finally, a number of provisions of the Criminal Justice

Administration Act of 1914 attempted to restrict the imprisonment of fine defaulters by requiring magistrates to allow time for the payment of fines. Moreover, where a person was allowed such time to pay a fine and was not less than 16 or more than 21 years of age, the court could, if it thought fit, order that person to be placed under supervision until the sum adjudged to be paid was paid (4 and 5 Geo. V: ch. 58).

Besides the inauguration of new forms of punishment for offenders, this epoch also witnessed the casting aside of certain antiquated ones together with the refinement of some others. Section 102 of the Children's Act of 1908 restricted a child from being sentenced to imprisonment for any offence, or committed to prison in default of payment of a fine, damages or costs. It similarly restricted a young person from being sentenced to penal servitude for any offence but such an individual could be sentenced to imprisonment if the court certified that he or she was of so unruly a character as to be unfit for any other form of detention (8 Edw. VII: ch. 67). Section 103 prohibited the pronouncement of a sentence of death on any child or young person (*ibid*). The Act additionally established juvenile courts for offenders under the age of 16, in which no person other than members and officers of the court and the parties to the case, their solicitors and counsel, and other persons directly concerned were allowed to attend and it also endorsed and clarified the law with regard to the use of the reformatory and industrial school network for individuals under the said age (*ibid*).[30] By the same token, one may also allude to the Reformatory Schools Amendment Act of 1899 which nullified the customary fourteen day period of imprisonment that formerly preceded a reformatory school committal (62 and 63 Vict: ch 12) and the Penal Servitude Act of 1891 which shortened the minimum sentence of penal servitude from five to three years as being further illustrations of the abandonment or modification of some of the older punishments with regard to offenders (54 and 55 Vict: ch 69).

A similar process of individualisation occurred in relation to workhouses. Established as an unspecialised institution, the workhouse began to decline as professional knowledge was applied to social problems such as unemployment, old-age, illness and insanity. In 1909 the Report of the Royal Commission on the Poor Laws and Relief of Distress denounced workhouses and suggested the use of specialised institutions instead. They argued that the workhouse had ceased to be a true test of destitution. They attributed this, in part:

"to the great size to which some of these institutions have grown which makes it impossible to deal with *all classes of inmates* in a suitable way. But the difficulty mainly arises

---

30. In 1854 the first Reformatory Schools Act was enacted and it enabled the courts to commit offenders under the age of 16 to a reformatory, after not less than 14 days of imprisonment, for periods of not less than two or more than five years (17 and 18 Vict: c. 86). The first legislative Act to give legal status to industrial schools was in 1857 and it regarded them primarily as training schools for children under the age of 14 and above the age of seven (20 and 21 Vict: c. 48).

out of the attempt to deal in one institution, under one master, with people requiring such *very different treatment* as the infirm or the able-bodied, the old and the young, the feeble-minded, epileptic, insane, and those of bad character. The difficulty can only be met by setting apart *special institutions* for special classes (1909: 135)" (my italics).

In 1929 the powers of the Board of Guardians were transferred to a much smaller number of county and county borough councils (19 Geo V: ch. 17; Townsend 1962: 23-29).

Hence the criminal justice system witnessed a gradual movement away from moral discourse on crime and its causes to a more scientific approach founded upon increased individualisation and categorisation of criminal types, and from *homo penalis*, the individual who has infringed the social contract, to *homo criminalis*, a waste product of social organisation around "which penal theory will construct its special savoir" (Pasquino 1991: 235-250). This trend towards individualised treatment of offenders extended in conjunction with the heightened generic appreciation of the intricacy of societal disorders, whether palpable in relation to criminal deviancy or other perceived constructions of misanthropic behaviour. As such, personality disorders were no longer simply regarded as congenital and this progressively began to influence penal thinking. Punishment was to an increasing extent administered according to the diagnosis of each individual's condition and his or her likely response to it as compared with it being apportioned with reference to the offence committed only. Such a response to anti-social behaviour became more pronounced with the advance of the twentieth century as the increasingly specialised and diversified penal system endeavoured more and more to cater for discrepant categories of offenders (such as the young, habitual, petty, first time, inebriate and insane) under different regimes where genuine attempts could be made at reform.

The growing impact of specialisation became even more pronounced after the First World War. Perhaps one of the greatest changes of all has been the broadening of categories of mental disorder which could qualify for deliberation by the courts for treatment in hospitals instead of sentence. The Mental Deficiency Act of 1927 extended the definition of mental defectiveness to include a larger class. According to section 1(2) of the said Act, mental defectiveness meant "a condition of arrested or incomplete development of mind existing before the age of eighteen years, whether arising from inherent causes or induced by disease or injury" (17 and 18 Geo V: ch. 33). In 1932 the Departmental Committee on Persistent Offenders suggested that the mental condition of offenders was a matter for careful attention. Indeed they considered that a certain number of patients might benefit by attending under probation approved mental hospitals or out-patient clinics (1932: Cmnd 4090, 67). Section 4 of the Criminal Justice Act of 1948 incorporated this recommendation by enabling the court to make probation orders on the evidence of a medical practitioner that the offender was such as may require treatment but was not such as to justify being certified a lunatic or defective. Provided that proper treatment was available and the offender was willing to undergo it, the court could make an order with the condition that the offender attend for such treatment (11 and 12 Geo. VI: ch. 58). The Mental Health Act of 1959 provided a new schema for dealing with mentally disordered persons by classifying them into four groups: the mentally ill, the severely subnormal, the subnormal and the psychopathic. Section 60 empowered the courts, having had regard to the nature of the offence and the character and antecedents of the offender, to authorise the compulsory admission or guardianship of patients convicted of criminal offences (11 and 12 Geo. VI: ch. 58). Where it was felt that a patient convicted of an offence presented a risk of committing further offences if set at large, the court could order that the offender be subject to special restrictions, if it was necessary for the protection of the public to do so. During the period of a restriction order, the patient could not be discharged, given leave of absence or transferred to another hospital without the consent of the Home Secretary (7 and 8 Eliz II: ch 72). The prison system itself also acquired some treatment functions, despite the intention of the legislation of 1913 and 1959 to redirect the mentally disordered to more suitable institutions. The period after the Second World War saw the employment of prison staff with psychiatric experience and centres for psychiatric treatment were established in some prisons, notably Wakefield and Wormwood Scrubs. For inmates with more psychiatric difficulties, a special prison was founded in Grendon in September, 1962 (McClean and Wood 1969: 264-281; Havard 1961: 296-308).

With regard to inebriates, the Advisory Council on the

Treatment of Offenders in 1957 suggested that, *prima facie*, imprisonment was unsuitable for chronic alcoholics (Home Office 1957: 4). By 1965 special efforts were being made to help prisoners who were alcoholics. Branches of Alcoholics Anonymous were established in many prisons, and special units for the treatment of alcoholism had to be set up at Wandsworth, Pentonville, Wormwood Scrubs, Wakefield and Holloway. It was also decided to use the open prison at Spring Hill to house men who had hitherto served short-term sentences for drunkenness in Pentonville and Wandsworth prisons. Spring Hill was chosen as it was adjacent to the psychiatric prison at Grendon and its medical resources would be made available to any new inmates suffering with alcohol related illnesses (Home Office 1965: Cmnd 2852, 8). Moreover, section 34 of the 1972 Criminal Justice Act enabled constables to arrest drunken offenders and take them to treatment centres for alcoholics where they would be deemed to be in lawful custody (1972: c. 71).

Developments also occurred with regard to limiting the use of imprisonment for young offenders. The Children and Young Persons Act of 1932 established juvenile courts specially adapted for the purpose of dealing with children and young persons in which only specially qualified justices could sit in order to determine the welfare of the juveniles as well as prescribing appropriate treatment for them (22 and 23 Geo V: ch. 46; Morris and Giller 1987: 69). The Criminal Justice Act of 1948 increased the range of penalties available for dealing with delinquents in the hope that it would further reduce the need to imprison young offenders.

It abolished the use of imprisonment for those under the age of 17 who came before the courts of summary jurisdiction and those under 15 who were dealt with by the courts of assize or quarter sessions. It also stated that no court could impose a sentence of imprisonment on any person under the age of 21, unless having considered a full report, the court was of the opinion that there was no other appropriate method of dealing with the offender (11 and 12 Geo. VI: ch 58).[31] The Act also introduced two new dispositions: detention centres (for juveniles between 14 and 17) and attendance centres (for juveniles between 8 and 17). Attendance centres evinced the trend set by probation in employing non-institutional forms of treatment. Detention centres, on the other hand, demonstrated that when institutions were employed, they were increasingly aimed at a specific class of offenders. In 1965 the Labour Government's White paper, titled *The Child, the Family and the Young Offender*, was published. It suggested that the arrangement for the trial and treatment of young persons in the 16 to 21 age group should be divorced as far as possible from the ordinary criminal courts and from the penal system as it applied to adults (Home Office 1965: Cmnd 2742, 12). An attempt at incorporating some of the White Paper's recommendations - albeit in a more limited form - was made in the Children and Young Persons Act of 1969. The spirit of the Act and some of the allied procedures, advocated, as far as was conceivable, the diversion, care and treatment of

---

31. The prohibition of imprisonment on young persons was made absolute in 1961 (9 and 10 Eliz. II: ch. 39).

young offenders outside the criminal justice system (1969: ch 54; Parker *et al* 1981: 3).

It appears, however, that whatever measures have been taken with regard to the special class of criminals known as persistent offenders have been doomed to fail. As Sir Lionel Fox remarked:

"Throughout this century the penal systems of Europe and America have sought, with little enough success hitherto, the answers to many questions arising from the central problem of penal law, the habitual criminal ... (1952: 297)."

The Report of the Departmental Committee on Persistent Offenders noted as far back as 1932 that it was essential for first time offenders to be dealt with in a manner best calculated to prevent them becoming habitual criminals. As such, they stressed the importance of borstals and probation. But they were of the opinion that the methods in existence for treating the "persistent class" were neither reformative nor deterrent. Of the 39,000 sentences of imprisonment imposed in 1930, 28,000 were for persons previously found guilty of offences. Of these, 20,384 were offenders who had previously been sentenced to a term in prison. Thus it was recognised that a substantial part of the prison population was made up of a "stage army" of individuals who passed through the prisons again and again. In order to combat this dilemma, the Committee recommended that new forms of detention be instituted (1932: 2-3). As a result, section 21(2) of the 1948 Criminal Justice Act made it lawful for a court, where a person was not less than 30 years of age and was convicted of an offence punishable with imprisonment for a term of two years or more, and had been convicted on at least three occasions since he or she had attained the age of 17, to order a sentence of preventive detention for a term not less than five years nor more than 14 years (11 and 12 Geo VI: ch. 58). In addition it made it lawful for a court, where a person had attained the age of 21 and was convicted on indictment of an offence punishable with imprisonment for two years or more and had been convicted on at least two previous occasions since reaching the age of 17, to pass a sentence of corrective training for not less than two or more than four years having been satisfied that it was expedient for the offender's reformation and the prevention of crime.

However the Act also proved to be a disappointment with regard to persistent offenders. It became difficult to distinguish preventive detention and corrective training from the ordinary prison regime and many prisoners so sentenced were more of a nuisance involved in petty crime than an obvious threat to society. In 1965 the White Paper on the *Adult Offender* submitted that the special sentences of corrective training and preventive detention should be abolished. In *lieu* thereof, it proposed that the courts be given jurisdiction to impose longer sentences on persons adjudged to be persistent offenders. It also appended a proviso to the effect that it was essential that the term persistent offender:

"be defined in such a way as to apply only to delinquents whose character and record of offences put it beyond all doubt that they are a real menace to society, and to exclude the petty criminal who commits a series of lesser offences. He is certainly a nuisance but not the menace against whom special protection is necessary" (Home Office 1965: Cmnd 2852, 5).

Accordingly the Criminal Justice Act of 1967 abolished preventive detention and corrective training and provided instead for an "extended term" of imprisonment, in cases where the need for public protection was felt to necessitate a longer than normal sentence of imprisonment and where it was satisfactory by reason of the offender's previous conduct and the likelihood of his or her reoffending (1967: ch 80). The object was to place offenders under control for a substantial time, by means of a period in custody followed by supervision under licence, in order to re-establish them in the community on termination of the sentence.

Various endeavours have also been made since 1945 to classify and segregate other types of offenders. Attempts have been made, for example, to curtail the imprisonment of debt defaulters. In the past committal orders or the threat of imprisonment were regarded as the most effective and potent means of inducing debtors to pay their debts. But by 1965 the pressure which such debtors imposed on an already congested prison system prompted the creation of the Payne Committee to consider what changes were desirable in the law in relation to the recovery of debts. They recommended that "the imprisonment of maintenance defaulters or of civil debtors is morally capricious, economically wasteful, socially harmful, administratively burdensome and juridically wrong" (1969: Cmnd 3909, 286). The 1970 Administration of Justice Act accordingly restricted the power of the courts to commit debt defaulters to prison (1970: c. 31). Similar measures have been taken to restrict the imprisonment of first time offenders by the magistrates' court (6 and 7 Eliz II: ch. 31). Finally, institutions emerged to cope with individuals, such as the old, vagrants and unemployed who had been previously been confined in workhouses. The National Assistance Act of 1948, for example, placed a duty on local authorities to provide "re-establishment centres" for those who lacked a regular occupation and "reception centres" for those without a settled way of living (1948: ch. 29).[32]

The process of specialisation and classification has been greatly succoured by the courts' readiness to consider the peculiarities of specific offenders. Sentencers have, as the twentieth century in particular has advanced, devoted increased attention to the needs of offenders and their culpability relative to their social and domestic backgrounds. As the range of sentences with their own characteristic regimes expanded, the use of information about the nature of punishment and the offenders likely response to it began to take on a more essential role. As Baron Raffaele Garofalo noted in his book, titled *Criminology*, in 1914:

---

32. For women offenders, see Hall-Williams (1970: 240-250); for sex offenders, see West (1980).

"What we are aiming at is not to fix the quantum of suffering occasioned by the offence, on the basis of the value of what has been stolen, but to designate the repressive means which shall be exactly appropriate, that is to say, the obstacle capable of averting the danger. The problem then can be formulated in but one way. By what means are we to determine the offender's degree of constant perversity and the degree of sociability which he still retains? ... For this purpose we ought to know the previous history of the offender, and it will therefore become necessary to investigate as closely as possible his family and social relationships. The age of the criminal will be a most important circumstance. Inquiry must also be made as to the education which he has received, his occupations, and his general aim of life" (1914: 299-300).[33]

Hence there was a gradual movement towards more formalised and perspicacious levels of knowledge with regard to offenders. Relevant and comprehensive reports which were essentially diagnostic in constitution began to be compiled in order to assist the judiciary in sentencing.

---

33. This is supported by E. Ray Stephens, a judge of the Ninth Judicial Circuit in Wisconsin, who wrote the introduction to Garofalo's book. He stated: "We have given too much consideration to the offense, too little to the offender. We must give consideration to the individual, less to the chapter and verse of the written law that declares the punishment for each offense. If the offense be burglary, we have been prone to impose the same punishment whether the defendant be a recidivist or first offender. We have given altogether too little consideration to the personal history of the individual in determining what shall be done to protect society against future harm" (*ibid*: xix).

Section 1 of the Probation of Offenders Act of 1907 required the court to have "regard to the character, antecedents, age, health or mental condition of the person charged" (7 Edw VII: ch. 17). Most of these reports were presented to the courts by Police Court Missionaries. Section 35(2) of the Children and Young Persons Act of 1933 required a local authority, which received notification or charged any child or young person itself with any offence, or brought any child or young person before a juvenile court as being in need of care or protection, to make such information as to the home surroundings, school record, health or character of the child or young person available to the court (23 Geo. V: ch. 12). The 1948 Criminal Justice Act similarly extended the duties of probation officers to cover the home surroundings of the offenders in relation to probation (11 and 12 Geo. VI: ch. 58). The Streatfield Report in 1961 stated that although a report should not follow a stereotyped form, it should in most instances include: details of the offender's home and family background; attitudes to family and their response to him or her; school and work record; attitudes to employment and present and previous offences; detailed histories about relevant physical and mental conditions; and, an assessment of personality and character (1961: Cmnd 1289, 95; Bean 1976: 100-101). Section 57 of the Criminal Justice Act of 1967 enabled the Secretary of State to require a court to consider a social inquiry report before passing sentence (1967: ch. 80). By the early 1970s these reports were an inherent feature of the functions of the probation service.

It may be appropriate at this juncture to provide a

compendium of what has being postulated with respect to the evolution in penology as it applied to offenders. Criminal justice prior to the nineteenth century was, by and large, indifferent to the specific characteristics of offenders and to the manner in which offences were committed. An etiological approach to the causes of crime was still, for the most part, unheard of. The 1800s, on the other hand, witnessed the increased employment of proportionality and uniformity as the prison system established itself as the nucleus of the penal system. Punishment was meted out in precisely the same manner to all offenders. It was not open to administrators to treat some prisoners differently because of their specific attributes as this would in effect constitute a form of re-sentencing. The late 1800s witnessed the gradual decline in the pursuit of uniformity of treatment (it was, by and large, effectuated by 1877) and the emergence of new techniques which concentrated more on specialisation. This new emphasis on individualisation took place initially in adapted institutions fitted for the needs of specific offenders but later evinced itself in a plethora of non-institutional sanctions which materialised throughout the 1900s. They included probation, absolute and conditional discharge, new methods of fine enforcement, attendance centres and suspended sentences. Moreover, there was also a shift in the judiciary's thinking away from merely attempting to assess the penalty most befitting the crime to a system directed more at a treatment befitting the offender. They achieved this by paying closer attention to the inherent attributes of the particular offence committed. No two cases were ever indistinguishable and the courts assumed the role of taking into account the circumstances and significance of each offence. In addition they began (with the assistance of prepared reports) to give more deliberation to the health, age and likelihood of reoffending of each individual offender when determining the appropriate sentence.[34] As one commentator noted:

"In this sense, penality changes from being a blind, repressive discipline to being a more perspicacious, knowledgeable form of regulation" (Garland 1985: 30).

It is my contention that it was only after the transformation to "a more knowledgeable and perspicacious form of regulation" that the sentencing of offenders to community service can be understood.[35] And this more "knowledgeable form of regulation" is in evidence in the shaping and substance of community service. For example, a court, prior to sentencing an offender to community service, would have to satisfy itself that the offender was reasonably likely to co-operate; the probation service was to be employed to provide information to the courts on the suitability of offenders; a number of eligibility criteria were established in deciding who was or was not a suitable candidate for the sanction; and, a number of suitability criteria were drawn

---

34. In France, the late nineteenth century also witnessed the introduction of the suspended sentence for first time offenders, as well as other dispositions such as the placement of minors in homes and the introduction of a parole system (O'Brien 1982: 4).
35. It will be argued, however, in chapter 6 that the Wootton Committee did not utilise this more "knowledgable form of regulation", particularly in criminological terms, to its full extent.

up by the Kent probation service for use among probation officers in writing their social inquiry reports. Let us examine these issues in more detail.

In 1966 the Home Secretary petitioned the Advisory Council on the Penal System to consider what variations and annexations might be made to the existing range of non-custodial penalties. Its appointment may be regarded as the first all-embracing investigation into the adequacy of the existing powers of the courts to sentence offenders without recourse to the use of custody. In general it suggested that imprisonment was both harmful and expensive and should be employed only as a punishment of last resort. Moreover, it was of the opinion that there was a broad scope for the development of sanctions within the criminal justice system which would act as alternatives to deprivation of liberty. Although no attempt was made to precisely categorise the type of offenders for whom community service might be appropriate, the report did recommend that it was ill-suited for trivial offences and was aimed at "some cases of theft, for unauthorised taking of vehicles, for some of the more serious traffic offences, some cases of malicious damage and minor assaults" (Home Office 1970: 13).[36] They also recognised that community service might be particularly beneficial with regard to the treatment of young offenders, especially in view of the association which was envisaged with the voluntary sector (*ibid:* 14).

---

36. See Roger Hood, however, who stated that the Wootton Committee made no attempt to justify the introduction of community service "in terms of a coherent analysis of crime, criminal behaviour or the effects of penalities" (Hood 1974: 380).

From the outset it was hoped that community service would prove to be a less sterile treatment than imprisonment. This was highlighted by the Home Secretary who stated:

"I was attracted from the start to the idea that people who have committed minor offences would be better occupied doing a service to their fellow citizens than sitting alongside others in crowded gaols" (House of Commons Parliamentary Debates: 826, 972).

Before making an order for community service, the court had to satisfy itself that the offender was capable of undertaking such service and was reasonably likely to co-operate. There was some debate as to which organisation would assist the courts in providing information about offenders. The voluntary agencies themselves could not be expected to provide the courts with all the services that would be required, and it was therefore necessary to establish some intermediate organisation whose functions would include reporting to the courts before sentence was passed on the merits or demerits of each individual offender for community service. The prison service, although it may have been well placed to allocate offenders to particular projects, to receive them from the courts and to supervise them, was disregarded because it was felt that prisons would in principle be unsuitable as reporting centres. Furthermore, prisons were, in a geographic sense, poorly distributed and their use for community service may have involved serious issues of security. Similarly local authorities were dismissed on the ground that it was impractical under the prevailing circumstances for such a body to undertake the tasks. The probation service, on the other hand, was locally based with an extensive network of offices. It existed to serve the courts and carried out a wide range of duties connected with the treatment of offenders in the community. For these reasons, it was decided that this service would be the most fitting organisation to administer the sanction (Home Office 1970: 17). Community service was intended primarily as a process for dispensing with individuals who might otherwise be sentenced to short terms of incarceration. When determining the appropriateness of offenders, the aspect of risk to the community and beneficiaries was of crucial importance. Those who were violent, addicted to alcohol or drugs, mentally ill or convicted of sexual offences were not deemed suitable because of the threat they posed and also because it was felt that they would not correspond appropriately. Thus before an offender could commence an order there were a number of eligibility and suitability criteria which had to be fulfilled. The eligibility criteria were:

(a) The offender had to be convicted of an offence punishable with imprisonment.
(b) The offender must have attained the age of 17.
(c) The offender must have consented to the order.
(d) The court must be satisfied having considered a report by the probation officer that the offender was a suitable individual to perform work under community service.

(e) That provision could be made for the offender to perform the work ordered in the petty sessions area in which he or she resides (1973: c. 62).[37]

(f) The offender must have sufficient leisure time to complete the order within 12 months, without interfering with his or her work, religion or education (1973: c. 62).

Some of the suitability criteria which could be noted by probation officers in their social inquiry reports (now called pre-sentence reports) were mentioned in an interim report undertaken by the Kent probation service. Personalities that could profit most in their opinion from community service included the following:

(a) The one who is purposeless and may have had little opportunity for making a positive contribution to society.

(b) The person who functions below potential and may be helped and encouraged by working group situations.

(c) The isolated and withdrawn person who does not relate well in a case-work setting.

(d) The person who is at variance with a particular law rather than lawbreaking in general, whose offence might reflect certain attitudes toward society and be

---

37. The 1982 Criminal Justice Act reduced the age of an offender who could be so sentenced to 16 but they could only perform 120 hours of work (1982: c. 48). The number of hours for 16 year olds was increased to 240 in 1991(1991: c. 53).

seen more as a community problem than a psychological problem; e.g. cannabis smoking.

(e) Those who need to work out a sense of guilt (Kent Probation and After-Care Service 1975: 10-11; Sussex 1974: 18).

This detailed analysis of individualisation was thought necessary to demonstrate the locus of community service in the penal domain. It cannot simply be regarded as continuous with other penal work sanctions from the 1500s, 1600s, 1700s and the greater part of the 1800s because such anatomisations are unable to take account of the broader more specialised penal network that manifested itself in the late nineteenth century; this is precisely the criticism that can be levelled at Whiggish historians such as Vass and Pease. By collecting that which supposedly supports their claim in respect of community service's genealogy ("that", for the most part being other penal labour sanctions), they ignore and indeed trample over other concepts and movements which do not support their claim. That which they ignore in this instance is the whole process of individualisation of treatment which forms such an integral component of the penal system. It is my contention that it is only having taken on board this "more perspicacious knowledgeable form of regulation" that we can begin to appreciate the introduction of community service orders. At this general level, we should already be cognisant of the fact that many of the sanction's characteristics - such as its non-custodial element, its employment of social enquiry reports, its screening of the unsuitable; in short, its adoption

of a whole set of "diagnostic, prognostic normative judg-
ments concerning the criminal" - have both consciously and
unconsciously altered the shape and substance of the
sanction. Having examined the emergence of a state control
apparatus, and the adoption of a more knowledgeable form
of regulation, this chapter will conclude by examining
another general component of the penal system, that of
reformative practices.

Reformative Practices: Rationalisation and Individualisation Processes

The desire to reform offenders has always formed a
constituent element in the penal process. Given its longevity
in historical terms, it should fit neatly into Vass and Pease's
hypothesis on "continuities and affinities" over time in the
penal domain. Yet it will be argued in this section that the
process of reformation has not remained on one single and
undeviating course of progression. Rather it has been
influenced by a variety of different determinants (scientific,
social, economic, political, and pragmatic) which have
affected the way it operates, and consequently affected the
manner in which sanctions function. The purpose of the
following section, then, is to describe the fundamental
transformations that have occurred with regard to the
employment of reformative techniques in the penal domain.
It will begin by demonstrating that prior to the late 1700s,
reformation, although an objective in gaols, houses of
correction, workhouses and transportation, was often

impeded by a lack of endeavour, intention and homogeneity of practice. In the late 1700s, however, a more rationalised and uniform system of punishment began to be advocated, one which would be directed at reforming the soul of the offender in an enclosed environment focused on *encellulement*, regulation, surveillance and religious instruction. Moreover, it will be shown that out of such a rationalising process emerged a more fundamental change in respect of reformation; as we have already seen in the last section, this utilitarian drive towards rationalisation threw up all kinds of social misfits in the late nineteenth century who could not properly be incorporated into a fully systematised prison apparatus. New modes of reformation were to be embodied under a new archetype of punishment which demonstrated an increased willingness to eschew algebraic formula perceptions of offending and adopt more diverse dispositions founded more on the individuality of each offender and the most appropriate means of reforming him or her.

Implicit, too, throughout this section is the need to refrain from universalising the effects of transformations that have occurred. Whilst revisionist historiographies, such as those espoused by Foucault, Garland and Ignatieff, are excellent in highlighting discontinuities within penal history; like Vass and Pease's Whiggish outlook, they are too linear in approach (albeit for different and more complex reasons) in that they simply view the changes delineated as a triumph without accounting for dissociation (by dissociation, I mean resistance, indifference and incapability) at grass roots level. Thus, the following section attempts to account for discontinuities in reformative practices - thereby high-lighting the ahistorical nature of Vass and Pease' approach - without overgeneralising the effects of such discontinuities.

The gaols which existed before Howard's time have been described as dustbins of demoralisation from which all kinds of evil sprang (Ives 1914: 171).[38] Many were derived from former feudal gaols, gate-houses, underground cells or disused chapels and were not designed for the proper exercise of control or reformation. Religious teaching did not form an integral component of the prison establishment: it was regarded as the "mere casting of pearls before swine; the drunkenness and promiscuous intercourse among the prisoners would have thwarted the most zealous chaplain" (Clay 1861: 17). Andrew Griffiths has suggested that these institutions acted as hot-beds for the growth of crime in which practices of the most "objectionable" kind, such as cards, dice, skittle, missipi, fives, tennis, billiards, portobello and drunkenness, flourished (Griffiths 1875: I, 5). Moreover, although gaols made some attempts at segregation - Newgate, for example, had separate wards for males and females - it is important to realise that financial constraints circumscribed the performance of such practices. The outstanding feature of eighteenth century prison administration was private profit. As such, as Evans notes, "rules were less in evidence than tables of fees, and where written rules were to be found, they regulated the domestic routine of the wards rather than personal behaviour"(1982:

---

38. For the particularistic, discretionary and personalistic nature of sentencing practice during the period, see Wiener (1990: 57-59).

23).[39] Not surprisingly, any attempts or hopes at reform were often chimerical. As Howard noted:

"[P]etty offenders who are committed to Bridewell for a year or two, and spend that time, not in hard labour, but in idleness and wicked company, or are sent for that time to County Gaols, generally grow desperate, and come out fitted, for the perpetration of any villainy. How directly contrary this to the intention of our laws with regard to these offenders; which certainly is to correct and reform them! Instead of which, their confinement doth notoriously promote and increase the very vices it was designed to suppress. Multitudes of young creatures, committed for some trifling offence, are totally ruined there. I make no scruple to affirm, that if it were the wish and aim of Magistrates to effect the destruction present and future of young delinquents, they could not devise a more effectual method, than to confine them so long in our prisons, those sects and seminaries (as they have been properly called) of idleness and every vice" (1977:

---

39.   See also Harding *et al* who suggest: "Little attempt was made to regulate the day to day life of prisoners at this time, partly because imprisonment was seen as fulfilling only a very limited function, and also because of the need to provide prison staff with access to an income. For those with funds most things were possible. Food could often be purchased from outside the gaol whilst beer and spirits were available through the prison tap run by the gaoler... Gaolers were always happy to allow prostitutes in for a fee and might keep separate rooms available for their use" (1985: 91-92; Hughes 1996: 38).

20-21).[40]

The house of correction ideal did contain a reformatory element. As has already been noted in the first chapter, the Elizabethan period witnessed vagrancy on a new scale. It was brought on, in part, by the dissolution of the monasteries, inflationary movements, pressures of population growth and the enclosure movement. Such a large increase in the numbers of "masterless men" posed a threat to the established order. To begin with, the authorities provided that vagrants should be whipped and returned to their parishes of origin. From the 1530s onwards, however, "we see the gradual evolution in the idea of enforced labour" (Harding *et al* 1985: 65-67), and the emergence of houses of correction. The authorities anticipated that these institutions would destroy the inmates' habits of idleness by replacing them with habits of industry more conducive to an honest livelihood. Lord Coke noted their reformative influence when distinguishing between them and gaols:

"Few or none are committed to the common gaol amongst so many malefactors but they come out worse than they went in. And few are committed to the House of

---

40. It would be wrong however to exaggerate the horrors of pre-Howardian prison life. The communal nature of prisons undoubtedly had its drawbacks, as De Lacy points out, but it also had many compensations which were not evident in mid nineteenth century prisons. These included the sale of alcohol, the ability to share common rooms and to indulge in banquets and celebrations at night, the support from the community outside with the provision of charity and the unsupervised visits of their families and friends (1986: 30-33; Ives 1914: 171).

Correction or Working House, but they come out better" (1797: 734).

However, rather like gaols, the buildings were not suitably designed to enable proper control or reformation. The first house of correction was set up in a former royal palace and later ones were established in barns, alehouses and outbuildings (1978: 12). In addition, as the enthusiasm of the public waned, the funds necessary to maintain these institutions also began to dwindle. Moreover, after 1609, houses of correction could be built alongside gaols. They soon lost their reforming role as they became incorporated into the general administration of prisons (Harding *et al* 1985: 69-73). By the mid- to late-seventeenth century they were "no longer required for the many purposes for which they had originally been intended and were simply permitted to be appropriated to the cheap custodial punishment of minor offenders and financed and administered accordingly" (McConville 1981: I, 48). Not surprisingly, when Howard visited many of the houses of correction throughout England and Wales in the 1770s, he remarked:

"[T]here are few bridewells in which any work is done, or can be done. The prisoners have neither tools, nor materials of any kind, but spend their time in sloth, profaness and debauchery, to a degree which in some of the houses which I have visited is extremely shocking" (1977: 8).

When William Cary established a workhouse in 1696, he suggested that the aims of the institution were "to put to work a great number of people, many of which had been habited to laziness and beggary, to civilise such as had been bred up in all vices that want of education could expose them to, and to clothe, lodge and feed them well" (Cary 1700: 4). The discipline of regular work was thus viewed by the authorities as an economic and moral necessity which had to be taught to paupers so they could rid themselves of their habits of laziness and vice, and, at the same time maintain themselves through the profits of their own productivity (MacFarlane 1986: 263). Workhouses in the eighteenth century, however, never produced an output "which even repaid the purchase of raw materials, nor did they meet the vaunted secondary objective of training the poor in habits of industry" (Rule 1992: 128). As shall become more evident in chapter three, it proved impossible to provide the inmates with sufficient labour, thus making any attempt at reformation impossible. This difficulty was brought about by the unpromising and inefficient nature of the inmate work force, the corrupt and the indifferent nature of workhouse administration, and the fact that workhouses, in many instances, sought to compete on the open market against the most competitive industries. In February, 1832, a Poor Law Commission was established to examine the operation of workhouses. Commissioners were dispatched to various parts of England and Wales to gather local information and investigate misdeeds with regard to the Poor Law. Their findings indicated that in "by far the greatest number of cases they had investigated, the workhouse was a large almshouse, where the young were trained in idleness and vice, the able-bodied maintained in sluggish indolence, the aged and more respectable exposed to all the misery that is associated with dwelling in such a society, without government or classification" (Copy of the Report made in 1834 for inquiring into the administration and practical operation of the Poor Laws 1905: 53-54).[41]

In relation to transportation to America, the Beauchamp Committee believed that it "answered every good purpose which could be expected from it - that it tended to directly reclaim the objects on which it was inflicted, and to render them good citizens" (Journals of the House of Commons 26 Geo III: 40, 1161). Comments of this nature, however, were to be expected from the Beauchamp Committee, especially when it is considered that it was established to recommend new locations for the creation of a colony of convicts following the cessation of transportation to America. In truth, transportation had a variety of salient purposes and motives, but reformation itself cannot be construed as one of its more obvious attractions. To begin with, America provided the authorities with a means of ridding Britain of its dangerous classes without hanging them (Ekirch 1987: 3) - the opportunity which this provided must be understood in terms of the erratic and capricious nature of the methods of identification, detection and policing employed in eighteenth century England. Transportation also provided

---

41. See also the Webbs who suggested that the "overcrowding, insanitation, filth and gross indecency of workhouse life during the whole of the eighteenth century, and even for the first 30 or 40 years of the nineteenth century, are simply indescribable" (Webb and Webb 1922: 248).

proof of the "King's care for his people and frequent demonstrations of his exercising his proper role by tempering justice with mercy" (Beattie 1986: 473). In addition, it supplied colonial British America with a large labour force which could be utilised in performing menial tasks for the benefit of the early British settlements in the New World (Hughes 1996: 40; Galenson 1981; Emerson-Smith 1934: 232-249). These then were the primary attractions of transportation to the authorities. Ekirch, however, has also proposed that "subjecting prisoners to hard labour, in prisons at home, though considered a possible means of reformation and though widely used on the continent, smacked to many of slavery" (Ekirch 1987: 20). Thus, "for a country threatened by mounting crime but dedicated to protecting popular freedoms, no other punishment could promise so much" (*ibid*: 21). Now it is accepted that English sentiments on liberty restricted, in part, a Bill of 1752 to introduce public chain gang labour as a punishment for criminals on the grounds that it was degrading (Hughes 1996: 40). Having said this, Ekirch's critique fails to appreciate that confinement with hard labour had already formed as a policy issue - I say policy issue because it has already been described how difficult it was to provide sufficient labour - an integral component of the house of correction system (Harding *et al* 1985: 65-73). The danger with Ekirch's viewpoint is that he gives the impression that enforced labour was not utilised within the confines of penal institutions in England and Wales prior to the decline of transportation to America. This is not to deny that voices were raised at the idea of public chain gangs in mid-eighteenth century England; it merely attempts to illustrate that Ekirch's rationale for the introduction of transportation is over simplistic in that it fails to recognise that other penal practices embodied forced work at home during the period in question.

Although reformation has been cited as a secondary advantage of transportation, it appears, on the whole, that America provided scant opportunity for such a purpose. From the outset, the sanction was governed by private enterprise and merchants treated convicts as they would any other merchandise. As a consequence, penal effectiveness played a subsidiary role to pecuniary gain; merchants such as Duncan Campbell were far more interested in the money to be derived from the sale of a convict to a settler, than in the opportunity it afforded the convict to transform his or her life. Moreover, Rawling's detailed and illuminating account of the lives of offenders such as James Dalton, Mary Young and John Poulter - in *Drunks, Whores and Idle Apprentices* - implicitly raises doubts about the reformative effects of transportation and the ability of the authorities to contain convicts on the colonies. Consider, for example, the life and times of James Dalton. Having been discovered a few months after assisting in a mutiny on a ship bound with convicts for America (of whom he was one), Dalton received a sentence of death, "under which sentence I lay six weeks, and was then reprieved, and order'd for Transportation for fourteen years" (1992: 96). A few months after his sentence, he arrived in Virginia and was sold to a Mr Fardle, "who not agreeing with my Temper, I run away from him; but he soon took me again" (*ibid*). Having remained with the settler for a brief period, he again escaped by "running away with a long-boat that lay in the river" (*ibid*). He returned to London, but was convicted of a further offence and sentenced once more to transportation. "In a few days after our Arrival I was sold for £14 but my mind not being fixed to stay, I made an agreement with two more to run away from our masters which we did" (*ibid*: 97). They were returned again to their masters after being discovered in North Carolina. "I beghan aftyer this to be very obstinate; and my master bid me to go to work, I told him work was intended for horses and not for Christians; adding, that if I had a mind to work I had no occasion to have left England; and sometimes pretending myself to be drunk, pulled out my knife and asked him how long I was to be his servant, which put him into such consternations, that he never afterwards asked me to go to work" (*ibid*). Although Dalton's endeavours - he was hanged in May 1730 for stealing in London - could by no means be taken as an indicator of all convicts' lives, it does illustrate the haphazard and inefficacious nature of transportation from a reformative perspective.

Thus from a brief perusal of gaols, houses of correction, transportation and workhouses in the seventeenth and eighteenth centuries, it should be apparent that reformation was not always a serious matter for consideration. When it was a deliberate objective, proper management, organisation or support were not often in place to result in any continuous and sustained endeavour. By the end of the 1700s, however, a reformulation and reorganisation of reformative techniques began to manifest itself. It was thought that a more rationalised, uniform and objective system of punishment would stimulate and promote greater reform among offenders. The essence of this new cause, as Beattie points out, "was not to attack the prisoner's body, but his mind and soul" as "punishment ceased to be mounted with an eye to those who watched, and was concentrated single-mindedly on the prisoner in order to reform and rehabilitate him and send him back to the world a new man" (Beattie 1986: 614-616). This process of rationalisation was to be directed at the prison as it was considered the most apposite medium through which new techniques of reformation could be advanced: in addition to being viewed as an acceptable alternative to transportation a term of imprisonment could also be calculated with "arithmetical precision", the conditions under which it would be endured could be subjected to precise measurement and calculation, and it could become a "school of moral discipline, that is, a training ground for, and a social representation of, the overcoming of immediate impulses and passions and the reconstruction of character" (Wiener 1990: 102-103). As such, and as shall become more evident, the late eighteenth century witnessed the emergence of a science of penology; this science would aim at promoting reformation within an institutional environment by enclosing prisoners, separating them, regulating their movements, monitoring their progress and subjecting them to religious instruction.

It is necessary, before setting out in search of this science, to delineate the specific factors which engendered the desire to rationalise the criminal justice system. To begin with, transportation to America was beginning to be regarded as weak and ineffectual both by the authorities and the public. It was widely assumed that people committed crimes in order to be transported and it was also argued that the severity of transportation was contingent upon the "convict's accomplishments" - if the life of a convict agreed with an individual he or she might even regard transportation as a stroke of good fortune in that his or her employment and opportunities for prosperity were often far better than in England (Harding *et al* 1985: 110-111). In addition, local authorities voiced their discontent with transportation on the grounds that it consigned them to provide for the families of the convicts (Beattie 1986: 540). By the 1750s and 1760s concerns about depopulation added another argument against transporting young men to the New World when they might be profitably employed at home. As Richard Price noted in 1769:

"Everyone knows that the strength of the State consists in the number of people. The encouragement of population, therefore, ought to be one of the first objects of policy in every state" (1769: 89-125).

More importantly, the outbreak of the American War of Independence in 1776 now compelled the authorities to house transportees either on converted ships in the Thames or in local prisons. The hulks were merely viewed as a temporary expedient. Local prisons, on the other hand, were acknowledged as a permanent feature of the system. Their inability to contend with transportees made it obvious to the authorities that they were not designed to ensure the proper incarceration or reformation of dangerous offenders. At the same time, the inefficacious nature of these prisons was being highlighted by individuals such as Dr William Dodd and John Howard. The latter, more than anybody else, ensured that imprisonment became a serious matter for discussion. With his systematic observation of the state of the prisons, and his indictment of the morals, hygiene, diet and practices of the gaolers and chaplains to be found therein, as well as his annotations on the disciplinary regulations and strict separation of inmates to be observed in institutions such as La Maison de Force in Ghent - as a result of which "I (Howard) was sometimes put to the blush for my native country" (1977: 145) - Howard, in addition to simply becoming "the symbol of the philanthropic vocation, canonised by the middle classes seeking representations of its best virtues" (Ignatieff 1978: 57), also put forward an argument for the potentiality of imprisonment as a sanction comparable with execution or transportation.

Moreover, by the mid-eighteenth century there was a growing consciousness of the need to combat disease. Typhoid fevers, dysentery, plague, smallpox, influenza, respiratory infections and measles posed a constant threat to society in the eighteenth century (Dobson 1987: 17). Overcrowding, undernourishment, filth, dirty clothes, badly ventilated houses and bad drainage systems all contributed to the spread of such diseases (Howe 1972: 147) . Contagion theory proposed that in order to alleviate the threat of the spread of such diseases, a strict regime of quarantine had to be pursued both to isolate victims from society but also from each other. It was most evident in connection with military medicine[42] - a point missed by many in relation to the ideological origins of the science of penology - in the late eighteenth century where a great premium was placed on the treatment of disease faced by troops and seamen given the specialised environment of ships, camps and hospitals in which they had to exist and the ease with which disease could spread in such an environment (Mathias 1979: 275). In addition to simply preventing the spread of contagion in the army and naval services, increases in the scale of warfare, colonial expansion and naval strategy which demanded that ships remained at sea for a longer duration, all dictated that such services should remain as disease free as possible for the good of the empire (*ibid*: 268).[43] Preventive measures devised to alleviate the threat posed by disease in the services included a greater emphasis on isolation, ventilation, fumigation, strict rules regarding the removal of dirt and excrement and the isolation of water supplies from

---

42. Apart from the military, Foucault believed that doctors themselves were among the first specialists of space: "They posed four fundamental problems. That of local conditions (regional climates, soil, humidity and dryness ...); that of co-existences (either between men, questions of density and proximity, ... the question of water, sewerage, ventilation ...); that of residences (the environment, urban problems); that of displacements (the migration of men, the propogation of diseases)" (Foucault 1980b: 148).

43. Lord Anson's navigation of the globe between 1740-1744 had resulted in the deaths of 1,051 out of 1,995 seamen, predominantly as a result of scurvy. From an economic as well as military perspective, it was axiomatic, therefore, for the authorities to curb the threat of such diseases in the mid- to late-eighteenth century (*ibid*; Blane 1965: 151).

pollution (*ibid:* 276).[44] In order to promote cleanliness itself, the practices of "stripping and washing the new recruits who may be suspected of importing infection; also by cutting of their hair, clothing them in new clothes, and destroying the old, before they are allowed to mix with the ship's company in which they are to enter" were to be encouraged (Blane 1965: 155). Dr James Lind, in 1779, also proposed:

"A point of great importance, upon which the recovery of the sick and the preservation of the whole, will in a great measure depend, is having a well-aired hospital or sick Berth, as it is commonly called on ships, appropriated for the *perfect separation* of the diseased from the healthy; between whom *no common intercourse* ought to be permitted" (1779: 69) (my italics).

On a wider national scale, quarantine systems also began to be established to contain infectious diseases. Indeed, architectural forms aided greatly in the problems posed by urbanism and disease at the end of the eighteenth century. As Foucault noted:

"Previously, the art of building corresponded to the need to make power, divinity and might manifest. The palace

---

44. Much of the success of the measures advocated, as Mathias notes, "depended upon an authoritarian regime required to enforce them: very precise instructions laid down for all controllers of hospital wards; regular inspections and systems of reports to ensure compliance; general orders imposed upon all subordinate commanders and like measures" (*ibid:* 280).

and the church were the great architectural forms, along with the stronghold. Architecture manifested might, the Sovereign, God. Its development was for long centred on these requirements. Then, late in the eighteenth century, new problems emerge: it becomes a question of using the disposition of space for economico-political ends" (1980b: 148).

For example, from the 1770s and 1780s onwards, fever patients were completely separated from other patients in fever wards and in 1802 a fever hospital was established in London. Delousing, whitewashing of walls, dispensaries, and medical inspections all formed part of this new hygienic regimen (Woodward 1974: 64-65; Porter 1987). These movements also had a profound impact on the criminal justice system. Justices believed that the conditions of prisons not only threatened their own lives - this is not surprising given that two diseased prisoners from Newgate infected the Old Bailey courtroom in April, 1750, killing at least 50 people (Ignatieff 1978: 44) - but also endangered the lives of the general public; "one means of averting the danger was the construction of new prisons which would protect prisoners from themselves and protect the outside world from prisoners" (De Lacy 1986: 93). As Ignatieff notes:

"Like the hospital, the penitentiary was created to enforce a quarantine both moral and medical. Behind its walls, the contagion of criminality would be isolated from the healthy, moral population outside. Within the prison itself the separate confinement of each offender in a cell would prevent the bacillus of vice from spreading from the hardened to the uninitiated" (1978: 61-62).

A more rationalised system of punishment was also motivated, in part, by the first generation of industrialists in the 1760s and 1770s and their attempts to discipline their workers and systematise production. Josiah Wedgwood, for example, introduced the bell, fines, a primitive clocking-in system, as well as strict rules concerning punctuality, constant attendance, fixed hours and standards of cleanliness (McKendrick 1961: 40-42). In addition, he imposed more general rules: thus, "any workman striking or otherwise abusing an overlooker [was] to lose his or her there place", "any workman conveying ale or liquor into the manufactory in working hours forfeits for every offence 2s 6d" (*ibid*: 44). As McKendrick notes:

"Although the discipline he imposed in his factory was a severe one *it was born of the desire to improve his workmen's lot*. For Wedgwood was no mere Gradgrind. He moved in a society of liberal reformers - men who read and gave him to read the works of Priestley, Price, Paine, Rousseau, Cartwright, Howard and Malthus. From there he formed his decided views of society. He saw it as it was - crude, filthy, incompetent and wasteful - and he wanted to reform it. He saw men as improvable - even perfectable. Liberal but unsophisticated in his ideals he felt that his workmen should be disciplined for their own good, and offered security in return for obedience" (*ibid:* 50) (my italics).

Nor was he the only one: individuals such as Brindley, Watt and Arkwright were doing much the same thing with other common labourers - attempting to wean them away from a task-orientated approach to labour to a time-orientated one, whilst at the same time improving them morally (Ashton 1948: 57-59).[45]

Finally, by the late eighteenth century, it was commonly believed that punishments had become too extreme and abounded with anomalies. Opponents of the Bloody Code argued that it had become a lottery of justice, given the anxiety of the courts in many instances to save offenders from being hanged and given the 200 or so capital offences which had been created in a sporadic manner to contend with individual crimes as they materialised (Emsley 1987: 202; Potter 1993: 6). As Wiener noted:

"Public violence, corporal or capital ... was increasingly perceived to be working against the civilising process, worsening popular character by legitimising the open expression of dangerous passions. Whatever the public view of the recipient of such punishment, its effect was deleterious: if hostile, the punishment roused deep

---

45. The development of a rationalised prison system was also aided by the Quakers and Nonconformists such as William Allen, Elizabeth Fry and Thomas Percival, and through the establishment of organisations such as the Society for the Improvement of Prison Discipline, established in 1816, which attempted, among other things, to have an input into the architectural plans for prisons. For a comprehensive account of the Quaker influence on penality in the late eighteenth and early nineteenth centuries, see Ignatieff (1981: 40) and McGowan (1995: 95-97).

feelings of gratification at the sufferings of others; if sympathetic, it weakened the moral authority of the law and encouraged popular desires for revenge (1990: 93)."

In respect of the latter effect, reformers of the late 1700s saw the need "to represent the suffering of punishment in such a way that those who watched its infliction conserved their moral respect for those who inflicted it" (Ignatieff 1978: 72). Accordingly, a new emphasis on scientific reasoning was beginning to manifest itself. Moral respect would be maintained if punishment only involved the infliction of so much pain as was necessary to carry out the aim of reform and was certain, quick and reliable as opposed to austere and barbaric (McGowen 1981: 66).

In 1764, Cesare Beccaria published the first methodical analysis of punishment titled, *Dei Delitti e delle Pene*. He contended that there ought to be a fixed proportion between crimes and punishment. The ultimate object of punishment was, in his view, to prevent the criminal from committing further offences and to restrain others from committing like offences. Punishment, therefore, and the mode of inflicting it, should be selected with the intention of making the greatest impact on the minds of others, with the least torment to the body of the criminal (Beccaria 1963: 131). This theory of punishment gave important direction to reformers in England. Increased pressure and agitation for law reform was taken up by Jeremy Bentham who condemned inefficacious punishments because they supported the wholesale evasion of the laws and promoted crime rather than diminished it. He believed that in the following cases punishment ought never to be inflicted:

1. Where it was groundless - where there is no mischief for it to prevent.
2. Where it must be inefficacious - where it cannot act so as to prevent the mischief.
3. Where it is unprofitable, or too expensive - where the mischief it would produce would be greater than what it prevented.
4. Where it is needless - where the mischief may be prevented or cease of itself without it (Bentham 1970: 158-164).

Bentham viewed "idleness, intemperance and vicious connections" as the three principle causes of corruption among the poor. In relation to reformation, therefore, he stated:

"When habits of this nature have become to such a degree inveterate, as to surmount the tutelary motives, and to lead to the commission of crimes, no hope of reformation can be entertained but by a *new course* of education - an education that shall place the patient in a situation in which he will find it impossible to gratify his vicious propensities, and where every surrounding object will tend to give birth to habits and inclinations of a nature altogether opposite. The principal instrument which can be employed on this occasion is *perpetual superintendence*. Delinquents are a peculiar race of beings, who require unremitted inspection. Their weakness consists in yielding to the seductions of the passing moment. Their minds are weak and disordered, and though their disease is neither so clearly marked nor so incurable as that of idiots and lunatics, like these they require to be kept under restraints, and they cannot, without danger, be left to themselves" (Bentham 1962: I, 499) (my italics).

It was thought that reformation through perpetual supervision could best be carried out by the separate confinement of offenders. As Paley noted in 1787:

"Of the *reforming* punishments which have not yet been tried, none promises so much success as that of *solitary imprisonment*, or the confinement of prisoners in separate apartments. This improvement would augment the terror of the punishment; would seclude the criminal from the society of his fellow prisoners, in which society the worse are sure to corrupt the better; would wean him from the knowledge of his companions, and from the love of that turbulent, precarious life in which his vices engaged him; would raise up in him reflections on the folly of his choice, and dispose his mind to such bitter and continued penitence, as might produce a lasting alteration in the principles of his conduct" (1787, II: 291).

Thus, the weak and ineffectual nature of transportation to America, the inability of the hulks and local prisons to combine proper reformation with imprisonment, the haphazard and extreme practices of the Bloody Code, the writings of individuals such as Beccaria, Bentham and

Howard, the rise of preventive measures for contagion in both a military and social setting, and the emergence of disciplinary regimes in the factories of the first industrialists, all contributed to a new process of rationalisation within the penal system in which new techniques of reformation were to be applied. This transformation has been succinctly summed up as follows:

"Throughout the eighteenth century, inside and outside the legal apparatus, in both everyday penal practice and the criticism of institutions, one sees the emergence of a new strategy for the exercise of the power to punish ... with its primary objectives: to make of the punishment and repression of illegalities a regular function, coextensive with society; not to punish less, but to punish better; to punish with an attenuated severity perhaps, but in order to punish with more universiality and necessity; to insert the power to punish more deeply into the social body" (Foucault 1986: 81-82).

But how was this new penal strategy to be exercised in respect of the reformation of offenders? To begin with, the authorities resorted to classification in order to combat the demoralising and disruptive characteristics of many punitive sanctions. This necessity for classification found expression in the Penitentiary Act of 1779. It provided that offenders sent to the penitentiaries were to be divided into three classes: the confinement and labour of offenders in the first class was to be the most severe; the confinement and labour of the second class was to be more moderate; and the third class was to be the most relaxed (19 Geo. III: c. 74). This search for new means of lessening the disarray of prison life gave rise, in part, to a new accentuation on architecture. It was anticipated that the proper fabrication of institutional structures would aid the perfection of techniques such as classification. Thus physical design, together with proper regulation and staffing, would separate reformation from sentimentality and its distrusted personal elements and come instead to be viewed as "a rational and calm process of strict moral education" (Wiener 1990: 110-111; Evans 1982: 1).

This attention to classification may also be discerned from the Gaol Act of 1823. The aims of the Act were to adopt such measures as would not only provide for the safe custody of offenders but would also tend to improve more effectively the morals of the offenders confined in prisons and houses of correction. These aims were to be achieved by "due classification, inspection, regular labour and employment, and religious and moral instruction". In order to secure uniformity of practice in all the prisons to which the Act applied, a number of rules and regulations were provided which were to be observed and carried into effect. Rule six stated that male and female prisoners were to be confined in separate buildings or parts of the prison, so as to prevent them from seeing, conversing, or holding any intercourse with each other. In addition, the Act provided that prisoners of each sex were to be divided into distinct classes, care being taken to provide that prisoners of the following classes did not intermix:

In Prisons	In Houses of Correction
1. Debtors and persons confined for contempt of court.	1. Prisoners convicted of felony.
2. Prisoners convicted of felony.	2. Prisoners convicted of misdemeanours.
3. Prisoners convicted of misdemeanours.	3. Prisoners committed on charge or suspicion of felony.
4. Prisoners committed on charge or suspicion of felony.	4. Prisoners committed on charge or suspicion of misdemeanours.
5. Prisoners committed on charge or suspicion of misdemeanours, or for want of sureties (4 Geo. IV: c. 64).	

The 1835 Prison Act went further along the lines of promoting uniformity by providing for inspectors to inspect the prisons and by providing that all rules and regulations made for the government of prisons were to be submitted to one of His Majesty's Secretaries of State for approval. It was made lawful for such a Secretary, if he thought fit, to alter such rules or to append further rules thereto (5 and 6 Gul IV: c. 38).

Similarly, workhouses established after 1834 were deliberately organised to allow for internal classification, with wards for women and men, a separate ward for the infirmary and quarters for children. Once paupers entered the workhouse, their clothes and possessions were taken from them; they were bathed, issued with a standard uniform and were not allowed to leave the institution without permission. As such, the workhouse displayed many similarities with the prison system, except, of course, that the pauper could discharge himself or herself whenever it was felt appropriate. No facilities were provided to enable married couples to live together. Even if, by chance, they ate near each other in the dining-halls, they were prohibited from speaking (Crowther 1981: 42; Henriques 1979: 49; Chesney 1970: 25). Poor Law Commissioners responded to criticism regarding separation of married couples by suggesting that it was impossible to manage a workhouse consistently without separation of the sexes (Poor Law Commissioners 1835: 34-35). Moreover, they argued that if all married couples were given one joint room to live in, it would result in a total lack of decency and lead to common and promiscuous intercourse (*ibid*). In effect, therefore, the Poor Law Commissioners hoped that the spatial separation of inmates would operate in at least three ways: as a basis for proper treatment; as a deterrent; and, as a barrier against contagion, both moral as well as physical (Driver 1993: 65).

One of the perceived problems associated with prisons prior to the late 1700s was that they enabled unimpeded communication between offenders. This, it was thought, promoted corruption and contagion. One technique adopted to remedy such iniquity was cellular confinement. A period of solitude would prevent an offender from being tainted by others, which was in keeping with the rise of contagion theory as has already been described, but it would also have the added benefit of forcing an offender to reflect upon past wrongs. The use of solitude first found expression in the preamble of the Penitentiary Act of 1779 where it was stated that its employment, together with well-regulated labour, and religious instruction would be a means of not only deterring the commission of crimes, but also of reforming individuals (19 Geo III: c. 74). Gilbert's Act of 1782 also adopted this technique and provided that justices of the peace, in drawing up or adjusting plans for houses of correction, were to provide separate apartments for all persons committed upon charges of felony, or convicted of any theft or larceny, and for all women committed to any such institution (22 Geo. III: c. 64). In 1785, Sir George Onesiphorous Paul began work on a penitentiary in Gloucester. He also sought the reformation of offenders by the adoption of cellular techniques of confinement. At this institution, the principle of seclusion was to be brought to bear on the offender for the duration of his or her sentence - it was not total, however, and association was permissible for attendance at chapel or exercise. Unlike the Penitentiary Act of 1779, the work to be given to an offender was not to be of the hardest and most servile kind. Instead it was to be considered as an occupation for his or her mind (Report from the Committee on the Laws relating to Penitentiary Houses 1810-1811: III, 17-20).[46] Methods and approaches to confinement differed. At Southwell House of Correction, a less strict regime of seclusion was followed. Separation was enforced at night but the prisoners worked together during the day. Total solitude was only resorted to as a punishment for misbehaviour (*ibid*: 18-20).[47] The Holford Committee of 1810 - whilst recognising the "meritorious exertions" given over to correction in both institutions - suggested that because offenders from London and surrounding areas were

---

46. This experiment lasted until 1809, when it was overwhelmed by increasing numbers of committals to the penitentiary (Henriques 1972: 61-93).
47. Harding *et al* have suggested that this approach was adopted at Southwell because it was a house of correction, and inmates generally served shorter sentences (1985: 133-134).

more depraved in character than those from Southwell, plans for the creation of a penitentiary in London or Middlesex were not to be founded upon the Southwell model, unless it was combined with another regime of discipline at least as stringent to begin with as that which operated in Gloucester (*ibid*: 20).

It was only in the 1830s, however, that the separate system burgeoned. At the beginning of that decade, the Government commissioned William Crawford to enquire into the different techniques adopted in American prisons. He found two different approaches to prison discipline, both of which sought reformation: the silent system adopted at Auburn and Sing Sing prisons under which offenders worked in association but complete silence; the separate system employed at Walnut Street Jail in Philadelphia which instituted a regime of solitary confinement in the hope that prisoners would contemplate over their misdeeds and listen to the "inner light" (Henriques 1972: 72-73; Jones 1962: 157; McGowen 1995: 100; Rothman 1995: 118-119). It was the latter technique which most impressed Crawford. In 1835, a House of Lords Committee came out in favour of the separate system. It recommended "that entire separation, except during the hours of labour and of religious worship and instruction, is absolutely necessary for preventing contamination, and for securing a proper system of prison discipline"(1835: XI, iv). As a result, the period following the report saw a more determined attempt to reformulate the prison along separist lines.

Many of the outlined transformations manifested themselves at a local level. It is true that the government did

176

endeavour to make some form of extended commitment by the enactment of the Penitentiary Act of 1779, but, as has been pointed out earlier, this enterprise was abandoned as a result of the inability of the commissioners to agree upon any site and the resumption of transportation. Nonetheless the government was still intent on assuming a more perennial role in respect of a penitentiary prison and entered into protracted negotiations with Bentham concerning the establishment of a panopticon. This scheme of Bentham's was centred upon a circular or polygonal configuration which was designed to promote perpetual surveillance by enabling the governor to see all the prisoners in their cells, without being seen. As Bentham noted:

"Under this system of continual inspection, a greater degree of liberty and ease can be allowed - that chains and shackles may be suppressed - that the prisoners may be allowed to associate in small companies - that all quarrels, tumults, and noise, bitter sources of vexation, will be prevented - that the prisoners will be protected against the caprices of the gaolers, and the brutality of their companions; whilst those frequent and cruel instances of neglect which have occurred, will be prevented by the facility of appeal which will be afforded to the principal authority" (1962: I, 498).[48]

---

48. The rationality underpinning Bentham's thinking on the panopticon can be discerned from his plans to prevent escapes. See Second Report from the Committee on the Laws relating to Penitentiary Houses (1811: III, 126-127).

Yet it appears that the panopticon ideal had one fundamental flaw. It was to be managed on a contract basis with the contractor receiving a certain allowance for the care of each offender. In addition, the contractor was to be permitted three fourths of the profit from the labour of offenders, the remainder being appropriated for their own use either during their confinement or on discharge (Report from the Committee on Laws relating to Penitentiary Houses 1811: III, 12). The Holford Committee considered that the application of reformative practice would suffer under a regime in which pecuniary gain was made such a permanent object of attention. Accordingly Bentham's panopticon was discarded with the recommendation that he be paid a liberal remuneration for his trouble and disappointment (*ibid*). In addition, the Committee went on to state that offenders could be reclaimed by means of seclusion, labour and instruction within a penitentiary. In 1816 Millbank penitentiary, constructed in the form of six pentagons, was opened as a reformative training institution for convicts. It attempted to adopt the best features from penal developments of that era. Prisoners were divided into two classes: in the first class, they were subjected to the methods employed at Gloucester; when they progressed from the first class to the second class, the regime became less severe and the Southwell methods of reformation were fostered (McConville 1981: I, 140). This endeavour to formulate a perfectly rational mode of Government-administered incarceration climaxed in the construction of Pentonville penitentiary in 1842. Inmates in this institution were confined in solitary cells, masks were worn to preserve anonymity and even for church gatherings offenders were distanced from each other by the use of cubicles:[49]

"Everything about it had been conceived with forethought, care and precision for the purpose of amending the criminal mind, a process referred to as reformation of character. On the one hand walls were raised of ever greater solidity, at an ever increasing frequency and with ever more cunning to compartmentalise and separate inmates; the cell became all important. On the other hand great tunnels of space lined with a dense network of sophisticated services were stretched throughout the prison to give all 520 cells an exactly equal status, to maintain their solitude and to reunify them under the gaze of the government who occupied the very centre ... This vast institution, with its centrifugal vistas, its overwhelming repetition of units, its gadgets and machinery, contained no accidents. Everything was arranged to prevent the genesis and spread of vice" (Evans 1982: 3-4).

Techniques which removed the offender from the disturbance of association were also heavily reliant upon eliminating moral defectiveness by spiritual vivification. Priestley has suggested that the entire organisation of the early Victorian prison was peppered with the expectation of

---

49. Methods adopted by prisoners to combat the denial of communication included boring holes through cell walls, scratching messages on meal tins, and, in some instances, the creation of friendships with spiders, flies, mosquitoes, blackbirds, rats and mice (Priestley 1985: 46-49).

repentance and reform: religious literature was left in cells; prisoners were subjected to continual visits from chaplains; and, there was divine service to attend daily (Priestley 1985: 99). If all of these failed, the offender was still, of course, left with ample time to reflect upon any wrongdoings within the confines of his or her own cell. With regard to solitude, the Chaplain of Pentonville, Joseph Kingsmill, suggested that it had the following effect on the prisoners:

"Their condition resembles that of a drunkard after the night's debauch, when his frame is subject to a pitiful depression. Men, before inconsiderate, reckless, and self-willed to an amazing degree, are now driven to reflection not for a few hours or days, but for months together: while their hitherto dormant or untaught conscience is aroused and enlightened by the word of God" (Kingsmill 1854: 115).

In this way the influence of religion had an important part to play in many of the new corrective strategies. The "classic mechanics" of the employment of religion as a reformatory technique is evident from Henry Newlake's account of imprisonment:

"I had for years refused to attend the means of grace; but God in his tender mercy and compassion for my soul, brought me into prison, and compelled me there to listen to his threats to the wicked and obstinate, and his promises to the penitent sinner. The precise time when God began the renewing of my soul, I do not know; but in a few months after entering prison, I began to listen with attention to the ministers; more especially to the young minister who preached on the love and mercy of Jesus to poor sinners" (1858: 16).

Other techniques which also embodied reformation as an essential element may also be cited. In 1837 the Molesworth Committee published its findings on transportation:

"It appears to Your Committee that it would be to maintain a position, contrary to the experience of all nations in the *science of punishment*, for anyone to assert, that the compulsory labour of a number of offenders, whether in the private establishments of settlers or on public works, under the system hitherto pursued, can have any tendency to produce their moral reformation ... It is evident, that it must be the object of a master of convicts to get as much work out of his assigned servants as possible; for this purpose the process of moral reformation will generally be considered too long a one; the chance of success, even under the most perfect system yet discovered, is too uncertain, and the advantage, therefore, too remote, to render it the apparent interest of a master, to adopt such a process, when his object can be obtained by the readier and simpler means of punishment, or by various indulgences, or when these fail, by returning the refractory convict to Government, and by obtaining another in his stead" (1837-38: XXII, xxi) (my italics).

In 1838 assignment was abolished. A progressive stage system aimed more at the reformation of offenders took its place. To begin with, this regime subjected each offender to two years labour on a public work gang; once this stage was successfully completed, convicts emerged with a pass which permitted them to seek private paid service. For this second stage, they were divided into three classes: in the first class a convict had to receive government authorisation for his work and his employer only paid him half his wages - the remainder was lodged in a bank until he received his ticket-of-leave; in the second class, the regime was less stringent and an offender was entitled to two-thirds of his wages; in the third class he received the full amount of his wages. Following the successful completion of this stage, the convict was given his ticket-of-leave (O'Neill 1977: 25-26).

In addition, Captain Alexander Machonochie devised a "marks system" at Norfolk Island. This technique (or "apparatus" as he described it) attempted to provide a convict with a genuine incentive for reform by enabling him to reduce his own sentence by self-help and self-discipline. Machonochie replaced a time sentence with a labour sentence and allotted 10 marks a day as a reward for each offender's toil; for every 10 marks a convict collected his sentence was reduced by one day. If offenders misbehaved, marks were deducted according to the seriousness of the offence. Each convict's sentence was divided into three distinct phases. In the first, the penal phase, convicts were subjected to a very strict disciplinary regime. Next they entered the social phase where they were grouped into companies of six - they were now responsible for each others' actions and accumulated and forfeited marks collectively. Before discharge, they were again divided and made to work individually. They were given their own huts and gardens and encouraged to farm plots of land (Barry 1960: 77-78). In this way Machonochie's technique attempted to reform offenders by teaching them the importance of their own endeavours and by inculcating in them a respect for the rights and property of others. Certain features of this system appeared again in a number of English prisons and it was also modified for use in the Irish convict system under the guidance of Sir Walter Crofton (Forsythe 1987: 83). The progressive stage system developed by Crofton was comprised of four stages: solitary confinement at Mountjoy prison in Dublin; hard labour on public works at Spike Island in Cork; trade training at Smithfield Institution and agricultural employment at Lusk in County Dublin; and, finally, conditional release.[50]

Furthermore, as the demise of transportation began in Australia, more and more significance was given to the length of prison sentencing and the employment of staged systems at home. Penal servitude was first provided for in 1853 (16 and 17 Vict: c. 19). Again this enabled the first period of an offender's sentence to be spent in separate

---

50. The system was highly commended on the Continent (by individuals such as Count Cavour in Italy, Bonneville de Marsagny in France, Professor Holtzendorff in Germany and Van der Brugghen, the Minister for Justice, in Holland) and in the United States (by Gaylord Hubbell, the Warden of Sing Sing Prison, and in the Declaration of Principles at the Cincinnati Congress). See Hinde (1977a: I, 115-147; 1977b: II, 295-337).

confinement where he would be set to hard labour. According to Du Cane, during the first phase the offender:

"cannot fail to feel, that however agreeable may have been his previous life, probably one of idleness and excitement, he pays dearly for it by the dull monotony and hard work, scanty fare and above all, the absence of freedom and constant supervision which is his present condition and which form his prospect for some years to come. During this time he becomes open to lessons of admonition and warning, religious influences have full opportunity of obtaining access to him; he is put in that condition where he is likely to feel sorrow for the past and welcome the words of those who show him how to avoid evil for the future" (1872: 13).

Following this, the prisoners are set to associated but silent labour quarrying stone or building breakwaters at one of the public works prisons. In this stage, the offender passes through four classes by means of a system of marks "earned for exemplary industry and lost by bad conduct" (Harding *et al* 1985: 206). Finally, prison authorities had the discretionary power to determine when the prisoner was fit for discharge on licence. Misconduct could result in remission of that licence *(ibid)*.

By the 1850s, then, the reformation of offenders was believed to be proceeding in an organised, scientific manner. *La Science Penitentaire* - with its embracement of more systematic techniques such as *encellulement*, institutional asceticism, continuous inspection, inscribed architecture,

184

staged systems and regimentation along quasi-military lines such as the wearing of uniforms and the employment of prisoner numbers rather than names - resulted in a more rationalised discourse on penology. It also marked the emergence of prisons as total communities where prisoners operated in a controlled environment organised to specific ends. One should guard, however, against the tendency to over compartmentalise or over idealise what is a complex and tortuous history. Revisionists such as Foucault and Ignatieff hypothesised on the revolution in punitive thinking by viewing the transformations from the particularistic pre-Howardian era to the more rationalised Pentonville era from the perspective of the strategy of power and humanitarian and ideological impulses respectively. Undoubtedly these histories are excellent in that they provide a more eclectic interpretation of changes and they highlight the difficulties of writing criminal justice history as a progressivist narrative. Nonetheless, in doing so, they have provided too schematic an account of the transformations which occurred, and have failed to appreciate that historical actuality is often comprised of not only a composite number of revolutionary ideas but is also composed of a complex number of impediments to the advancement of these ideas. Essentially what is being argued here is that one must attempt a historiography which accounts for fundamental changes without universalising their effects or underestimating continuities. As the new discourse and new techniques which emerged regarding the practice of reformation has been described, it is now necessary to place these techniques in the context of their efficacy in respect of reformation by examining the criminal justice system as a whole.

So where can we identify dissociation from transformations in reformatory practices between 1770 and 1850? One may begin at a national level by examining the hulks. As the Select Committee on the Laws relating to Penitentiary Houses noted in 1812:

"It appears that from the time at which the convicts are locked down within their several decks in the evening, until the hatches are opened in the morning (a period which in winter includes nearly two-thirds of the 24 hours) they are left entirely to themselves, without any other control over their conduct" (1812: II: 138).

Nor by 1835 were there any great improvements. In that year William Crawford stated to a House of Lords' Committee:

"Parties released from the hulks ... have generally turned out the very worst characters" (1835: XI, 14).

Similarly, as has already been described, the pursuit of a science of punishment found no place in the sentence of transportation prior to 1838 and the sanction had little or no tendency to encourage the reformation of offenders. Moreover, even after 1838 the practice of transportation remained arbitrary and uncertain in application. Overcrowding, lack of segregation, poor general discipline, excessive use of flogging, brutal administration such as that adopted by John Giles Price at Norfolk Island in the 1840s, the "demoralising fiasco" of Lord Stanley's probation system, and the corrupt governorship of J. S. Hampton of Western Australia between 1862 and 1867 all impeded the rationalisation of techniques of reformation (Hughes 1996: 536-580). Furthermore, in respect of the Bloody Code, the gentry, in particular, greatly resisted reformers' attempts to abolish hanging; instead they believed that it reaffirmed the state's authority and acted as a salutary lesson to the masses. Nor should such resistance be underestimated; there remained a strong belief, in a period still without a centralised police force, that the temptation to commit crime could only be countered by a will to command and a display of terror (McGowen 1986: 313-317). Indeed public executions, though smaller in number in the nineteenth century, became "ever grander in scale" until their eventual abolition in 1868 (Laquer 1989: 308).

It is at a parochial level, however, that dissociation is most palpable. It has already been noted elsewhere that the Prisons Acts of 1823 and 1835 were only properly complied with in a few instances and that disparate practices characterised prison administration at a localised level.[51] Attempts at rationalisation, as has already been delineated, were restricted by a lack of financial resources necessary to

---

51. Similarly, in respect of policing, much of the mood and outlook of nineteenth century society still perpetuated a belief in notions such as individualism and limited government interference, thus preventing the adoption of any synergetic civilising inevitability perspective on new police initiatives. Indeed, Gatrell went as far as to suggest that the "parochial principle still remained more than merely cosmetic in 1914" in respect of policing (1990: 262). See also Hobbs (1992: 17-46).

implement many of the changes - for the most part, expenses to be incurred in respect of the process of rationalisation in prisons was defrayed to the local authorities who often lacked the necessary financial muscle to make the stipulated changes, by a general anathema to government interference during the period, and by the reluctance of central government to impose its will unequivocally on the local authorities. Even by 1863, Henry Voules, referring to local prisons, spoke of his desire "to level many of them to the ground and rebuild them" as they were unsuitable, in many instances, for the operation of reformatory or disciplinary techniques (Carnarvon Committee Report 1863: IX, 184).[52] Accordingly one should refrain from interpreting the adoption of both reformation and deterrent practices alike as a symmetrical and linear process. This is not to deny that transformations occurred - they undoubtedly did; rather the purpose of the last two paragraphs was merely to emphasise the danger in overschematising the actual nature of transformations described by revisionists such as Foucault and Ignatieff.

Besides dissociation at a local level, a general cynicism emerged as the promised mass reformation of offenders had not evidenced itself. Misgivings about reformatory techniques were aggravated in the early 1860s by the London garrotting panic. The primary cause of this scare was as a result of an incident on 17 July 1862 in which a

---

52. Similarly, O'Brien has noted in respect of France: "neither architecture nor penal practice reflected an immediate or sharp rupture with old-regime practices, the transformation extended over a longer period of time than has been commonly supposed" (O'Brien 1982: 17).

Member of Parliament, Hugh Pilkington, was robbed in Pall Mall as he returned home from a late sitting in the House of Commons. Succeeding incidents, which might have gone unnoticed but for the Pilkington incident, created an impression of widespread disorder in the city (McConville 1981: I, 64; Davis 1980: 190-213). Motivated by the fear of such lawlessness, the Carnarvon Committee reported that the reformation of offenders was "frequently doubtful". They called instead for the total separation of offenders - primarily as a means of deterrence - accompanied with penal labour such as the treadwheel, crank, and shot-drill which would move "into higher and less irksome stages of industrial occupation and prison employments" as an offender progressed through his or her sentence (1863: IX, xi). This demotion of reformation to a subsidiary purpose of penal discipline was also suggested by Lord Cockburn:

"[I]t is necessary to bear in mind what are the purposes for which the punishment of offenders takes place. The purposes are twofold: the first, that of deterring others exposed to similar temptations from the commission of crime; the second, the reformation of the criminal himself. The first is the primary and more important object: for though society has, doubtless, a strong interest in the reformation of the criminal, and his consequent indisposition to crime, yet the result is here confined to the individual offender; while the effect of punishment as deterring from crime, extends, not only to the party suffering the punishment, but to all who may be in the habit of committing crime, or who may be tempted to fall into it. Moreover, the reformation of the offender is in the highest degree speculative and uncertain, and its permanency in the face of renewed temptation exceedingly precarious. On the other hand, the impression produced by suffering inflicted as the punishment of crime, and the fear of its repetition, are far more likely to be lasting, and much more likely to counteract the tendency to the renewal of criminal habits. It is on the assumption that punishment will have the effect of deterring from crime, that its infliction alone can be justified; its proper and legitimate purpose being not to avenge crime but to prevent it" (Report of the Commissioners on Acts relating to Transportation and Penal Servitude 1863: XXI, 85-86).

Further support for this new standpoint was demonstrated by Du Cane who suggested that:

"The system is devised with a view to combine the principles of deterring from the commission of crime and reforming the offender. The latter is an object which for every reason we are bound to follow strenuously, but it must not be effected in such a manner as to interfere with the former, because punishment is primarily to prevent crime by the warning held up to those who might, but for such influences, fall into it" (1872: 12-13).

The Carnarvon Committee's suggestions were embodied in the 1865 Prison Act. In short, they represented a heightening of the "pains of imprisonment" by initiating a regime grounded upon hard fare, hard labour and hard bed (28 and 29 Vict: c. 26). Although separation was to remain the bedrock of all prison discipline, it was not endorsed with the reformation of offenders in mind. On the contrary it was designed to be a repressive and austere experience where all traces of individuality and characteristics were methodically extinguished. In 1877 all local prisons were transferred over to the Home Secretary. Deterrence, the *raison d'être* of punishment following the Carnarvon Report, now operated within "a huge machine working by an automatic regime" (Ellis 1910: 293).

La Science Penitentaire undoubtedly had a profound impact upon penological discourse and the rationalisation of reformatory and deterrent practices. It did not, however, effect universal change and attempts at promoting a greater level of homogeneity with regard to its application proved to be more dilatory in nature than that espoused by academics such as Foucault and Ignatieff. Nonetheless, it is true to say that since Howard's era, penal discourse - although concerned with the efficacy of principles such as deterrence and reformation - was predominantly occupied with the need to promote a greater level of uniformity. This concern manifested itself in a number of ways with regard to prisons and included: the demand for Justices of the Peace to examine the conditions of prisons in their localities; the abolition of gaol fees; the requirement that inspection tours be undertaken; the submission of reports by gaolers, chaplains and surgeons in the county gaols as well as in some town gaols; the provision that rules for the government of prisons be submitted for approval by the

Secretary of State; the establishment of a prison inspectorate; the establishment of codes of rules binding on all prison authorities; the threat of withdrawal of the Treasury grant for non-compliance with particular statutory provisions; and, finally, the nationalisation of the entire prison service in 1877. This last *coup d'essai* was entirely successful. Uniformity of practice was no longer a pivotal concern: this, in turn, enabled new perspectives on penal discourse to take centre-stage. One idea to come to the forefront was that punishment should no longer be devised from concepts such as "rational intellect", "moral consciousness" and "self responsibility" as they presupposed a free moral will which was purely metaphysical in nature. In pursuing a homogenised penal system, the authorities had failed to acknowledge fully that offenders often operated in particular social, economic or psychological spheres that did not make them fully accountable for their actions. By the 1870s, then, as has been delineated in the last section, representations of criminality and deviance were, as Wiener suggests, "increasingly associated with weakness and degeneration rather than inadequately controlled energies, and with a relative lack of autonomy rather than wilful rejection of social limitations" (Wiener 1990: 226). Penal treatment, it was argued, should not be undifferentiated and machine-like but should take account of the etiology of an offender's criminal behaviour. In truth, as we have already seen in the last section, what was required was a process which embodied individualisation of treatment.[53]

---

53. For a criticism of Du Cane's mechanical regime, see Davitt (1885: I. 233-234).

But what aroused this radical undermining of strict uniformity of treatment and the moral free will interpretation of justice? By the 1870s, as we have already seen, great advances had been made by the natural sciences such as anthropology, psychiatry, psychology and genetics. These sciences began to illuminate the idiosyncratic nature of each offender and rejected the conjectural speculation associated with the moral free will concept of criminal justice thinking. A science of criminology emerged which attempted to highlight the individuality of each offender by developing "a positive factual knowledge of offenders based upon observation, measurement, and inductive reasoning" (Garland 1994a: 39-40). It was the beginnings of a movement away from *La Science Penitentaire* and its "algebraic formula" perception of the offender (Ellis 1910: 293) (focusing as it did on the most proportionate, rational and uniform means of deterring and reforming offenders) to a scientism of criminology which attacked the repressiveness and machine-like features of the prison (focusing as it did on a personal investigation of offenders to determine the most appropriate means of reforming them or preventing them from committing further offences). Early demonstrations of this new archetype of punishment, which was committed to reform "no longer attended upon the visitation of God's grace" (Garland 1994b: 305), can be discerned, as we have already seen, from, *inter alia*, the Habitual Drunkards Act of 1879, the Criminal Lunatics Act of 1884, and the Probation of Offenders Act of 1887.

Moreover, the late nineteenth century was also a period which witnessed a reduction in thefts and acts of violence as the "agencies of law enforcement and social control gained, in both a technical and psychological sense, the upper hand over a significant section of the crime committing community" (Harding 1988b: 591-608).[54] Gatrell suggests that one of the main reasons for such an occurrence was that the origins and practices of Victorian crime had evolved out of "pre-police conditions". As the police became more organised in the late 1800s, crime committing communities were, to some extent, caught unaware and were unable to adapt their techniques fast enough (Gatrell 1990: 263-264):

"Once the railways and highways were thrust through the rookeries, once the police began to probe down alleys never before investigated, once shopkeepers and artisans and publicans on the fringe of the old communities began to accept the notion that satisfactory recourse might be to the law in the settlement of offences done against them - then the ecology of the eighteenth century city was irrevocably altered, and the defences it offered the old fraternities as well as the casual thief were by so much diminished" (*ibid*).[55]

But the fact that England had become a less violent place by the late nineteenth century was not attributed in any way to the deterrent prison regime orchestrated by Du Cane. Rather, factors which influenced the diminution of crime

---

54. Between the early 1860s and late 1890s, the rate of trials for indictable offences declined by 43 per cent (Gatrell 1990: 240-241).
55. For an analysis of the *terra incognito* that was metropolitan life in the eighteenth century, see Chesney (1970); Stedman Jones (1971); Low (1982).

were accredited, as has already been noted, to the appearance of a central police force, but also to changes in the legal processing of criminals, in the criminal law and in societal attitudes to offending (Harding 1988b: 595).[56] Indeed, by the 1890s, the prison itself was increasingly recognised as a failure from a disciplinary perspective (Garland 1985: 59). Two factors, in particular, helped to substantiate such a claim: first, there was a decline in the length of prison sentences - Harding points out that the average length of an ordinary term of imprisonment fell from 48 days in 1880 to 34 days in 1893, a reduction of 29 per cent over that period (Harding 1988b: 594); and, secondly, there was a belief that recidivism was becoming more common - in 1872, 27.9 per cent of commitments to local prisons in England and Wales were for the second time, in 1883, the figure had risen to 31.5 per cent, by 1893, it had dropped slightly to 29.6 per cent (Gladstone Committee Report 1895: LVI, 10; Harding 1988b: 599).[57] The

---

56. But see also Thompson who notes in respect of the reduction in violence: "Much was the result of the work situation: of the discipline, punctuality, regularity and routine of factory work, and indeed of non-factory work in large organisations such as the railways or the post-office; and of the influence of many employers on their workforces through the services they provided outside the workplace in patronising chapels, schools, reading rooms, clubs, institutes, works' outings, not to mention factory villages. Much resulted from the work of larger, professional police forces, enforcing law which in some respects at least - for example, capital offences - became less of an ass and hence more obviously to be respected by rational men. A great deal followed from economic growth, improvement in living standards, and the increasing availability of goods and services" (1981: 189-208).

57. Increasing recidivism rates were attributed, in part, to the development of police methods of identification.

reduction in the length of prison sentences could perhaps be viewed as "inappropriate use of the prison sanction with no necessary implications for the prison as an institution", but recidivism, on the other hand, "was a failure which went right to the essence of imprisonment itself" (Garland 1985: 61).

Finally, new perspectives on penal discourse (and in particular reformation discourse) were also influenced, in part, by a newly emergent professional ethos in the Home Office - nine of the 12 graduates who entered the Home Office between 1880 and 1890 had degrees from Oxford (Pellew 1982: 33) - which quickly distanced itself "from the older traditions of prison governance, exemplified by Du Cane and his military predecessors" (Harding 1988b: 604). Indeed this more professional element displayed a remarkable willingness to question Du Cane on various prison practices and, in some instances, even to exclude him from matters pertaining to prison administration: in 1891, for example, after a prisoner at Chatham had been given 13 days' punishment and lost 360 remission marks for his failure to apply prescribed ointments to a face rash, the Home Office sent a set of queries to Du Cane asking, *inter alia*, was it proper to put the responsibility on the prisoner himself to seek further treatment, and to punish him when he failed to do so; in 1889, after a member of the prison staff at Strangeways had been acquitted of the manslaughter of an inmate, the Home Office was again quick to ask the Prison Commission for their comments on the view that the prisoner's injuries could not have been self-inflicted; and in 1893, it issued a censure to the governor of Portland for remarks made to an Irish prisoner without consulting Du Cane before doing so (McConville 1995: 526-547). These examples illustrate, in many respects, the heightening tension between Du Cane's military style approach to prison management and the Home Office's new breed of graduates who were more amenable to new ideas in penal thinking.[58]

By the early 1890s, then, moral free will perceptions of offending, the appositeness of deterrence as a primary goal of punishment, the military approach to prison management, and homogenised methods of penal discipline, were all creaking under combined and sustained attack; a more welfarist reformative approach not based on the full systematisation of the disciplinary and deterrent regime which manifested itself in the prison system between 1877 and 1895 was now beginning to shape itself.

In keeping with these developments, the Gladstone Committee of 1895 acknowledged at an official level that there had to be a change in the composition and orientation of penal policy. It believed that the systematic repression of offenders should no longer be viewed as a practicable or general goal. Instead it recommended that the entire regime be made more adaptable and more variable so as to be congruent, where possible, with the special cases of individual offenders. In this regard, the Committee championed the cause of scientific observation - although recognising that it was still at an embryonic stage - as an essential component of criminal justice thinking (Gladstone

---

58. For similar changes in Ireland in respect of prison administration, see Smith (1981: 336-337).

Committee Report 1895: LVI, 8). For the first time since 1863, as Sharpe has noted, reform was espoused as a central ambition of penal practice, concurrent with that of deterrence (1990: 75). But contrary to the view expressed by Sharpe, it is submitted that it was not a return to the pattern of reformatory practices prevalent prior to 1863. On the contrary, reformation was now beginning to be embodied under a new archetype of punishment, albeit in a piecemeal manner, which included among its attributes: an increased willingness to adopt scientific methods; the decline of moral free will perceptions of offending; the decline of the idea of attempting to stimulate a spiritual awakening in the offenders; and the rise of more individualised and measured reformatory techniques.

The adoption of science as a proper means of rescuing and reclaiming individual offenders can be seen from the following comments of Ruggles-Brise:

"The modern school of *L'hygiene preventive* holds the field to-day - ie, prevention which will operate (1) by the elimination of the social causes which create an unhealthy environment; (2) by the encouragement of scientific treatment of the feeble in mind or body *(faibles d'esprit et arriérés)* so that, if possible, before it is too late, the germs of anti-social conduct may be diagnosed and, if possible, destroyed by appropriate handling and treatment" (1924: 16).

This medico-psychological approach together with a growing appreciation of the part played by the social environment dominated criminological discourse in the period after 1895 (Ruggles-Brise 1921: xvi).

The growing scientific awareness of societal disorder manifested itself, as we have already noted, in a more intensive approach to the individualisation of reformatory practices. Examples of legislation which exemplified this heightened appreciation of the complexities of criminal behaviour include the Inebriates Act of 1898, the Reformatory Schools Amendment Act of 1899, the Probation of Offenders Act of 1907, the Prevention of Crime Act of 1908, the Mental Deficiency Act of 1913, and the Criminal Justice Administration Act of 1914. All of these statutes, together with the extended range of sanctions which they authorised and the penal philosophy which underpinned them, denoted for Garland a "move from a *calibrated, hierarchical structure*, into which offenders were inserted according to the severity of their offence, to an *extended grid of non-equivalent and diverse dispositions* into which the offender is inscribed according to the diagnosis of his or her condition and the treatment appropriate to it" (Garland 1985: 28). As such, reformatory practices would now operate under a new mode of normalisation which demanded greater levels of knowledge of the offender before diagnosis and treatment could commence.

Garland's exposition is undoubtedly excellent in detailing the transformations which have occurred between the "modern penal complex" and its "Victorian antecedents" (albeit that he failed to recognise that this transformation was already under way before 1895). Although the last few paragraphs have described this movement from a "calibrated, hierarchical structure" to an extended grid of "diverse dispositions", it is important - at the risk of sounding repetitive - to keep such theoretical hypothesising within the parameters of penal practicality. Policy changes, particularly within the penal domain where routine is so commonplace, require a gestation period, in many instances, before new initiatives can be wholly recognised as being discontinuous with preceding initiatives. And more attention must be focused on these gestation periods because they often reveal as much about the functional and pragmatic nature of penal practices (ie, the economic, political and social constraints within which they must operate) as theoretical anatomisations do about penal policy reorientations. Essentially what I am attempting to propose here is that whilst new movements, techniques and discourses that account for a particular transformation will, for the most part, be exhaustively documented by academics up to and including the transformation itself (ie, the 1895 Gladstone report for individualisation and reformation, or the late eighteenth and early nineteenth centuries for the rationalising process), old justifications, resistances, and the unworkability, in many instances, of policy change at a practical level are often minimised within such investigative processes. In particular, revisionists often fail to direct the same intensity of research to the period directly succeeding a described transformation. It is submitted that it is these succeeding events which will often unmask more about how engraved old initiatives were and how enthusiastic, forthright and predisposed the penal authorities were to implement new initiatives. In truth, whilst not denying that

200

transformations have manifested themselves, historians of such transformations must attempt to ensure that penal rhetoric, policy and pragmatism are maintained on a balanced, proximate and applicative level by accounting for reform and resistance in both an impartial as well as meticulous manner.

For example, although the sanction of borstal is correctly identified by Garland as a component of this new grid of non equivalent and diverse dispositions, no attempt is made to examine its operation in the early years after its formation. And it appears for a good many years that it adopted an approach more in keeping with pre-Gladstone prisons than the described new mode of normalisation.[59] It was only in the 1920s under the guidance of Alexander Patterson that borstal detached itself from a severe discipline-orientated regime and from its prison roots: in these years it adopted a more educative outlook into its attempts at reform by implementing the "house system", by employing staff from universities and public schools, by allowing borstal officers to wear ordinary uniforms so as to promote a better atmosphere, by opening summer camps, and by placing more responsibility on the boys (Hood 1965:

---

59. See also Osborough who noted of Clonmel Borstal in Ireland: "When the Irish authorities decided to copy the English experiments at Bedford and Borstal, premises had to be found and the No. 2 prison at Clonmel was chosen ... The building had been unoccupied for many years and the accommodation ... was far from ideal. The noise of heavy locks being turned, the effect of iron bars on the windows, stone flags in the yards and the total absence of grass in the main square [conditions which persisted until 1947] were all in striking contrast to the charm of the town itself and its attractive setting in the Suir valley" (1975: 10).

xi-32). Moreover, although the introduction of probation in 1907 was a great breakthrough in terms of its potential as a reformatory technique, it was rather inhibited in its formative years. In 1922 the Report of the Departmental Committee on the Training, Appointment and Payment of Probation Officers noted that the use of probation varied considerably from locality to locality. As a consequence, it recommended that every court should have a probation officer at its disposal (1922: Cmd 1601, 4-6). As Rose noted:

"It would be wrong to suggest that anything like a profession of social work had developed by 1921, but there was a growing recognition that it was a job which required training, and to which a professional attitude would be taken. The actual progress of professionalisation was very slow and is now clearly apparent, but the germ was there. What is more, what might be described as the social workers' attitude to the job, a combination of objectivity and sympathy, often insistence upon effecting a close enough contact to diagnose the problem before attempting to deal with it, were beginning to be perceived, as yet dimly (1961: 95)."

A more bureaucratic framework was established with the enactment of the Criminal Justice Act of 1925 which made it mandatory for each petty sessional division to appoint a probation officer (15 and 16 Geo. V: ch 86). It is only in this era, as Newburn notes, that one sees the movement from the "missionary ideal" to a more therapeutic or diagnostic approach with regard to the treatment of offenders under probation (1995: 85-87).

Similarly although the Gladstone Committee stated its concerns about solitary confinement, it was not until 1922 that it was finally abolished. From then on it was only to be employed as a method of maintaining discipline (Elkin 1957: 118). Fenner Brockway served 28 months in prison from December 1916 until April 1919 for resisting conscription. He described his experience of solitary confinement as a "gross instance of the inhumanity of prison". In terms of reform, he suggested:

"The truth is - and every prison officer and doctor knows - that solitary confinement encourages the growth of the vicious side of the prisoners' nature and develops the tendencies in their minds toward crime (1919: 10-11)."

He also criticised the silent system - which was only substantially reduced around the same time as solitary confinement was abolished - on the grounds that it invited prisoners to practise deception and it created a contempt for the laws of the state as "every prisoner with any mentality at all realises the inhumanity and futility of the silence rule" *(ibid)*. It is no surprise, then, to hear the 1932 Departmental Committee on Persistent Offenders calling for the creation of prison conditions in which the prisoner would have some liberty of action and some kind of communal life so as to combat the evils of imprisonment which included, *inter alia*, a deadening of the senses of responsibility and a starving of the social instincts (1932: Cmd 4090, 23). In the appendage to the same report, Dan Griffiths suggested that it was time "we tackled crime scientifically, drastically, at its source as a disease is tackled, as tuberculosis is being tackled with such excellent results, and as cancer has begun to be tackled" (*ibid*: 68). Finally the sluggish and intractable nature of reformatory changes following the Gladstone Report may also be discerned from widespread perceptions of penal labour. As we shall see more clearly in the next chapter, although the Gladstone Committee repudiated the use of unproductive labour in the prison system and called for the wider adoption of associated work practices, it was unable to propose how such changes were to be brought about - a difficult task, given that the prisons were based on a Victorian cellular confinement system that made association of any kind extremely arduous. As such, although labour was not employed as a punitive technique after 1895, prison authorities, on the whole, continued to view work as essentially deterrent in design. It was only after a report by the Departmental Committee on the Employment of Prisoners in the early 1930s that labour came to be regarded as one of the more salient factors in the reformation of offenders. Thus, it must be stressed that whilst reformatory discourse did undergo a profound transformation in the late nineteenth and early twentieth centuries, it was a number of years before reformatory practices found their footing in the modern penal complex. This is succinctly encapsulated by Harding:

"The significance of the Gladstone report for the British penal system, therefore, was not that it signified immediate change, certainly as far as the everyday experience of most prisoners was concerned. But the sudden demise of the Du Cane administration and the blueprint offered by the report meant that the prison system was in a position to be absorbed into a 'penal welfare' structure, which was to become a dominant means of social control exercised by the State for the first three-quarters of the twentieth century" (Harding 1988b: 608).[60]

Nonetheless by the 1930s and 1940s it can be said that penal optimism regarding the rehabilitation of offenders was high. Psychologists, probation officers, social workers and educationalists were all directing their professional skills towards treatment of the individual offender. This commitment to the potential of therapy and training is evident in the Criminal Justice Act of 1948. To begin with, it formally abolished penal servitude, hard labour, prison divisions and whipping (11 and 12 Geo. VI: ch 58). In addition, it provided for the extension of the positive reformatory experience of borstals to more young offenders. Borstal was now available to any young offenders between the ages of 16 and 21 who had satisfied the courts that it was expedient to their reformation and the prevention of crime that they should undergo a period of training in such an institution, regardless of whether or not they had already formed criminal habits (*ibid*). Moreover, corrective training

---

60. For further support, see Sim who noted: "The regime behind the prison walls in the 1920s and 1930s was still hard, uncompromising and underpinned by violence when order was threatened" (Sim 1990: 68).

and preventive detention were established for persistent offenders (*ibid*). Both of these sanctions were aimed at reform. Even the "incorrigible" preventive detainee was expected, as Ryan suggests, to respond to positive and constructive training (Ryan 1983: 9-10). The Act also restricted the use of imprisonment for young offenders by providing that no court should impose imprisonment on any person under the age of 21 years of age unless it was of the opinion that no other method of dealing with the offender was appropriate (11 and 12 Geo VI: ch 58). Finally, the Act also provided for the payment of money by Parliament towards the expenditure of any body or person approved by the Secretary of State conducting research into the causes of delinquency and the treatment of offenders (*ibid*).[61] This spirit of reform can also be discerned from the comments of Sir Lionel Fox, Chairman of the Prison Commissioners, who suggested that:

"Reform is not some specific which can be prescribed either from the prayer-book or the pharmacopoeia. It must come from something inside the man ... The conception of 'training' therefore seeks to provide a background of conditions favourable to reform, and where necessary and possible to foster this delicate and very personal growth by personal influences rather than by specific features of treatment labelled 'reformative'. Then, leaving deterrence

---

61. One should note, however, that detention centres, designed with a more punitive disciplinary intention in mind, were also introduced under section 18 for young offenders who were not regarded as suitable for either borstals or a prison sentence.

to speak for itself, it concentrates on the social rehabilitation of the prisoner, so as to remove as many obstacles as possible to the maintenance, after discharge from prison, of such will to do right as may have become established or incipient therein. Whether a prisoner has been reformed or whether he has been deterred by his experience, or even if the effect has been quite negative, the protection of society is not well served if he comes back to it unfitted rather than fitted to lead a normal life and earn an honest living, or as an embittered man with a score against society that he means to pay off" (1952: 72).

This commitment and confidence in the reformative ideal remained resolute throughout the 1950s despite rising crime rates. In 1959 a White Paper, *Penal Practice in a Changing Society*, noted that methods of training in prisons had expanded, particularly in the application of psychology and psychiatry, in the advancement of skilled industrial training, in engaging prisoners in associated activities, in the creation of evening education classes, and in the preparation for release through pre-release programmes (Home Office 1959: Cmnd 645: 12).[62] In outlining the direction of the criminal justice system for the succeeding decades, the White Paper advocated a quasi-scientific approach which would be founded upon research into the causes of crime and reinforced by careful appraisal of the results already achieved

---

62.   In addition the White Paper pointed out that three psychiatric clinics with qualified medical teams had been established at Wormwood Scrubs, Wakefield and Holloway.

by existing methods (*ibid*: 7). Thus any future alterations in the techniques of punishment should be firmly rooted in careful planning, and a criminological and penological knowledge of the behaviour of the offenders to whom it was hoped that any proposed techniques would apply.

This scientific approach to the treatment of "diseased" individual offenders can also be discerned from the establishment of Grendon prison in 1962 as an experiment in the psychological treatment of offenders. Central to its ethos, as we shall discover in more detail in the next section, was the creation of an artificial therapeutic community in which offenders were encouraged to take an active role in their own treatment, backed up and supported by a team of psychiatrists (Genders and Player 1995: 11-13). In the same year the Morrison Report noted that the duty of probation officers to "advise, assist and befriend" offenders obfuscated many of the major transformations that had occurred in the ways in which probation officers established and employed the personal relationships upon which their success was based. By the 1960s, a probation officer's dichotomy of duties had to be discharged in an era of increased understanding of the complexities of human behaviour. This, in turn, had resulted in a more professionalised approach being employed in the practice of social work. Accordingly, the "probation officer must be seen, essentially, as a professional caseworker employing, in a specialised field, skill which he holds in common with other social workers; skill which, if it opens up to him hopes of constructive work which were not enjoyed by his predecessors of twenty years ago, also makes more complex and subtle demands upon him, reflecting as it does, growing awareness of the difficulty of his task" (Home Office 1962: Cmnd 1650, 23) .

This recognition of science in the treatment and curing of individuals was rather ironically noted in Baroness Wootton's Winchester Address in 1963:

"Today, personal problems, moral problems, marital problems, problems of deviant behaviour, are constantly brought to the doctor's consulting room, while social workers, with their 'case-work' and their 'diagnostic' and 'therapeutic' techniques, adopt medical poses and express themselves in medical language. In every broadcast discussion on moral issues, be it teenage sex, illegitimacy, adoption or anything else, the presence of a psychiatrist now tends to be thought indispensable. Indeed, one has only to look at last year's Reith lectures to see that the practice of psychiatry now confers a title to make authoritative pronouncements on a range of social problems that extends from adolescent unchastity to world government; and for millions of readers throughout the world Dr. Spock continues to resolve, in effortless prose, the fundamental problems of human relationships. Today Freud and Marx might fairly compete for the title to the biggest popular success since Jesus Christ; and Freud, I think, would win" (Seal and Bean 1992: II, 73).

The 1960s was the decade, as Ryan indicates, when all offenders were expected to be cured of their criminality with the professional help of psychiatrists, social workers, psychologists and probation officers (Ryan 1983: 42). Yet Ryan fails to appreciate that the 1960s was also a decade, as shall become more evident in the final chapter, when increased concern evidenced itself with regard to rising crime rates. The total number of indictable offences known to the police increased from 545,562 in 1957 to 1,199,859 in 1966. In the same period the number of offences against the person increased from 10,960 to 26, 716 (Home Office 1968: 4). Moreover, this rise in the total number of offences was accompanied by a spectacular growth in the prison population. Between 1956 and 1966 the average population in prisons rose from just over 15,000 to well over 22,500 and in the same period the total average population of prisons, borstals and detention centres rose from 20,000 to 33,500 (Home Office 1966: Cmnd 3175, 54). Overcrowding and security became serious issues for consideration in penal establishments. They were compounded by a number of highly publicised escapes: between August 1964 and July 1965, Charles Wilson and Ronnie Biggs escaped from Birmingham prison and Wandsworth prison respectively; in 1966, the spy, George Blake escaped from Wormwood Scrubbs (Newburn 1995: 18-19). Not surprisingly, the Home Secretary quickly established a Committee under the chairmanship of Earl Mountbatten of Burma to investigate prevailing security arrangements.

The Committee reported that there was no "real secure" prison in the country for the confinement of a very small number of high risk prisoners. As a result, it recommended that all such offenders should be confined in one top security prison on the Isle of Wight (Home Office 1966:

Cmnd 3175, 4). Two years later, a Report of the Advisory Council on the Penal System rejected the proposal to concentrate the most difficult and dangerous prisoners in one maximum security prison. Instead it argued for a policy of dispersal among a number of training prisons on the grounds that it would be detrimental to the interests of the prisoners themselves and it presupposed a degree of accuracy in the process of selection for this proposed maximum security prison which was unlikely to be achieved (Home Office 1968: 15). The unwanted "side-effects of these directives were to heighten security across the system, prioritise control and surveillance at the expense of other objectives (such as work, training, education, recreation, and better rights and conditions), and, in combination with the impact of adverse research findings, halt the spread of therapeutic regimes while leaving intact the differentiation between local and training prisons based upon that ideology" (Downes and Morgan 1994: 219).

Furthermore, penal policy began to rely more upon non-custodial sanctions to alleviate the sharp rise in imprisonment. But in the context of widespread public anxiety, such sanctions began to embody more punitive characteristics. As McClean and Hood suggested in 1969, a balance had to be maintained between deterrence and reform if factors such as rehabilitation, prison overcrowding, rising crime rates and public angst were all to be catered for within the criminal justice system (1969: 87). By the late 1960s, as crime rates and prison numbers escalated, and as the effectiveness of the rehabilitative ideal was increasingly challenged as a result, the criminal justice system gradually became less ambitious in its expectations. This is not surprising. In an environment such as the late 1960s, rehabilitation was having to cope with other aims such as deterrence and incapacitation. Unable to establish its actual effectiveness as a penal policy initiative, it found itself being pushed to the periphery in the administration of criminal justice. The notion that the system would operate as a scientific treatment milieu for offenders by acting as an antidote for their failings and a restorer of their values and social skills was steadily displaced by more moderate and practical goals of preventing reoffending and easing prison overcrowding (Trasler 1974: 132).

In November, 1966, the then Home Secretary, Mr Roy Jenkins, commissioned the Advisory Council on the Penal System to deliberate over changes which could be made to the range of non-custodial penalties. Implicit in his reasoning was the desire to restrict the use of imprisonment. One of the proposals which the Wootton Committee, a sub committee of the Advisory Council, submitted was the notion of community service. It believed that such a sanction could provide a means of altering the outlook of offenders by affording them the opportunity of engaging in constructive activity in the form of personal service to the community (Home Office 1970: 13). With this in mind, the report went on to suggest that it should be carried out in association with volunteers as the performance of community service by groups consisting entirely of offenders would "be likely to give the whole scheme too strong a punitive flavour, and would cut off offenders both from the more constructive and imaginative activities, and

212

from the wholesome influence of those who choose voluntarily to engage in these tasks" (*ibid*). It can be argued however that reform played a subsidiary role to the task of alleviating prison overcrowding. Moreover, non-custodial sanctions - designed as measures which would palliate this exigency of overcrowding - had to be introduced in a period of widespread concern about crime and the growing scepticism *vis-à-vis* rehabilitative techniques. Essentially what is being suggested is that the aim of replacing custodial with non-custodial penalties in the late 1960s had to ensure that these replacements embodied some element of "bite" in order to maintain a proper balance between deterrence and reform. It is very difficult in an era of widespread public disquiet about growing crime rates to endorse a policy of non-custodial sanctions without moving towards a more punitive standpoint with regard to their implementation. Indeed community service was seen as punitive in that it deprived an offender of his or her leisure time and would be a "welcome alternative in cases where at present a court imposes a fine for want of a better sanction or again in situations where it is desired to stiffen probation by the imposition on the offender of an additional obligation other than a fine" (*ibid*: 14). Given the political climate, the Wootton Committee was extremely keen to point out the flexibility of this new sanction:

"In general the proposition that some offenders should be required to undertake community service should appeal to adherents of different varieties of penal philosophy. To some, it would be simply a more constructive and cheaper alternative to short sentences of imprisonment; by others it would be seen as introducing into the penal system a new dimension with an emphasis on reparation to the community; others again would regard it as giving effect to the old adage that punishment should fit the crime; while still others would stress the value of bringing offenders into close touch with those numbers of the community who are most in need of help and support" (*ibid*: 13).

Barbara Wootton later described this statement, of which she was always slightly ashamed, as "an undisguised attempt to curry favour with everybody" (Wootton 1978: 228). The introduction of the sanction did not, however, achieve this function. First, there was an element of resistance from probation officers:

"For some years the offenders had more often than not been thought of as emotionally or mentally disturbed, even ill and therefore in need of cure. This had led to the professionalisation of the various treatment services; the prison service with psychiatrists and psychologists, the probation officer trained with psychoanalytical bias to be used in one-to-one casework situations, and so on. Obviously, not all probation officers took kindly to the idea that the criminal could now be 'treated' by 'mucking in' under the 'wholesome influence' of other community volunteers" (Ryan 1983: 50).

Moreover academics criticised the Wootton Committee on

the grounds that it failed to justify the introduction of community service in terms of criminological and penological knowledge as recommended by the 1959 White Paper, *Penal Practice in a Changing Society*, preferring instead to rely upon opinion and the ideological appeal of the sanction. As Hood noted:

"[I]t is hard to resist the conclusion that the deliberations of the Wootton Committee, which provided the justification for the introduction of an entirely new penal measure in the Criminal Justice Act, 1972, failed to provide a coherent and convincing criminological argument for its proposals. And this is not simply an indictment of its distinguished chairman and members, among them a number of notable criminologists, but rather of the method of approach and resources traditionally associated with the government advisory bodies which at best can only lead to suggestions for 'unstructured experiments'. Without facilities for research and academic enquiry their conclusions and recommendations will probably remain a 'potpourri of intelligent suggestions': their acceptance or rejection will depend more upon their political appeal than their likelihood of making a major impact upon what is in danger of becoming an intractable problem: the provision of alternatives ... [to imprisonment]" (Hood 1974: 417).

At a theoretical level, then, what we have witnessed is a shift from the rationalisation of reformative techniques to reformation within an extended grid of non-equivalent and diverse dispositions. What has been described is a whole host of transformations that have impinged upon reformative techniques. They include the decline in the role of the prison chaplain and the rise to prominence of psychologists, probation officers, social workers and educationalists, the movement from *encellulement* to association, the displacement of the moral consciousness concept of criminal behaviour with a more individualised approach, the emergence of more positive factual knowledge on the offender and the adoption of science as a proper means of reclaiming offenders. These have been well documented and need no further analysis here. But they illustrate once again the problem of historiographic anachronism and the distortions which viewing the past with the present very much in mind give rise to. The purpose of this book so far has been to develop a more sensitive approach to the past which, whilst recognising that the present is constructed out of the past (and is in some respects continuous), also recognises the need to develop a different historical framework (so as to account, for example, for the processes delineated in respect of reformative techniques and their influences on the construction of the historically specific sanction of community service) to that expounded by academics such as Vass and Pease in their attempt to portray all penal labour as the progression towards an apogee - that apogee being the sanction of community service.

There are, however, a number of other points that can also be made at a general level. First, from our brief perusal of reformative practices, it has been observed that in some instances reformation has been espoused as an actual goal without requiring much effort from the authorities. Transportation, particularly to America, and the hulks both displayed little in the way of a capacity to reform. The former was utilised on the basis of its ability to remove offenders from the shores of Britain and its advantage in providing a labour force for the colonies, the latter on its capacity to contain offenders until transportation could resume or until transportees could be shipped. Yet both were purported to embody reformative aspirations, albeit at a secondary level. It illustrates, in my view, the insouciance with which reformation can be expounded as an objective of criminal justice. Other forms of punishment, it is suggested, such as deterrence or incapacitation require some form of outward endeavour before being justified as objectives. Secondly, it has been observed how quickly reformation can become a peripheral issue once the authorities are faced with a purported increase in crime. Both in the early 1860s and again in the late 1960s (this will become more evident in chapter 6), impressions of widespread disorder prompted the authorities to demote reformative practices to a secondary role. These examples emphasise the chameleonic nature of penal policy and its distrust, to some extent, of the malleability of human nature particularly in times of crisis. Thirdly, the extent to which reformative practices can be applied have often be circumscribed by economic limitations: the process of rationalisation was, among other things, continually unsettled by the local authorities' financial inability to make the necessary changes; restorative work practices after 1895 were impeded by the lack of resources necessary to turn the isolatory work practices of pre-1895 prisons into the associative work practices of post-1895 prisons; and, as we shall see more clearly in the final chapter, the severe overcrowding in prisons, particularly at a local level, and the lack of resources available to alleviate the problem also impinged upon rehabilitative aspirations in the mid to late 1960s.

None of the points highlighted in the last paragraph are to be found within revisionist accounts of the penal complex. If the reader wishes to pick up on such issues within discontinuous penal practices, then he or she must rely on histories at a detailed local level, such as those written by individuals such as Beattie, Ireland and De Lacy, or legal historians at a more general level, such as those written by Harding, Rawlings, Priestley, McConville, McLynn, Wiener and Emsley. What is needed is for these phenomena (ie, penal pragmatism, economic limitations and the dilatory nature of implementing new policy initiatives) to be incorporated into theoretical accounts of transformations because they often say as much about penal practice as the changes themselves - albeit that they are not as exciting.

Conclusion

From what has been delineated it should be apparent that criminal justice policy cannot be viewed as a linear course of progress and rectification but must be construed in the social, economic and political contexts of the period being anatomised. Like the history of criminology, it must be seen as "a story of constant reformulation in response to shifting political pressures, changes in institutional and administrative arrangements, intellectual developments occurring in adjacent disciplines, and the changing ideological commitments of its practitioners" (Garland 1994a: 28). Within this chronicle of reformulation, broad transformations, which gained credence in the late 1800s and first half of the 1900s, are discernible. These transformations act as demarcations between old and new archetypes of punishment and enable us to illuminate, to some degree, different modes of constructing criminal justice policy. It is axiomatic, however, that we do not over-schematise. Undoubtedly these transformations occurred, but they did so in a dilatory manner and often encountered much resistance and antipathy. Revisionist historiographies are laudable in that they highlight the deficiencies in Whiggish interpretations but more must be done to bridge the gap between transitional discourse and practice: the two have often proved more tortuous than that conceded by individuals such as Foucault.

Having taken account of the complexities of historical transformations in punishment, a broad framework has been created within which the introduction of community service orders can be understood. To begin with, as has been observed in chapter 1, it has been subjected to the external cultural determinant of leisure. By the 1960s the phenomenon of leisure formed a separate and distinct segment of people's lives. It is only within this epoch, when leisure was enshrined as a veritable right of society, that the Wootton Committee could begin to contemplate depriving individuals of it as a plausible means of punishing them for wrongdoings. Moreover, from a penological perspective, general characteristics of a new archetype of punishment can also be discerned from the decline of the moral consciousness concept of punishment, presupposing as it did the free moral will of offenders, and the emergence of a more welfarist approach based on individualisation of treatment. Algebraic formula perceptions of the offender and the spiritual awakening techniques which went with them increasingly gave way to more scientific, factual and inductive strategies towards offending. Finally this new general framework of punishment also witnessed the elevation of reformation to one of the foremost objectives of the entire penal apparatus and the extension of the network of penalties as well as the employment of psychologists, probation officers, social workers, doctors and educationalists to facilitate, *inter alia*, the treatment of deviant behaviour. All of these different rules, characteristics, ideologies and discourses - which were destructive of the previously established penal paradigm and which resulted in "significant shifts in the criteria determining the legitimacy both of problems and of proposed solutions" (Kuhn 1970: 109) - must be construed as components of the modern penal complex. It is only within this described loose schema that one can begin to analyse community service orders; to do otherwise is to engage in an anachronistic and unworkable historiography of the genealogy of the sanction. Having examined broad changes in penality and defined the modern archetype of punishment in general terms, it is now necessary to focus on some of the more specific characteristics of community service and how they should be explained in a historical setting.

CHAPTER 3

HISTORICAL SPECIFICITY AND PARTICULAR TRANSFORMATIONS

In keeping with the view that the structure of modern penality is founded upon specific discourses, aspirations, techniques and sensibilities, this chapter will also deliberate over Vass and Pease's claim of historical continuity in their quest for the genealogy of community service orders. Like the previous chapter, their theses will be tested from a historical perspective. Unlike the previous chapter, however, the analysis will focus on more specific aspects of criminal justice thinking which have had a direct bearing on the introduction of the sanction of community service. These include the ratification of the "community" as an admissible means of social control, the employment of labour as a means of deterring and rehabilitating offenders, and the emergence of international rights concerning the use of forced labour. It is hoped that this chapter - in harmony with the previous two - will provide further support for the supposition that sanctions must be construed in a historically specific context: before one penal complex can be collated with another there must be an acknowledgement that the passage of time has significantly transformed the substructure of penality. Again it will be demonstrated that searches for continuities and precedents over a wide past is a fallacy in that it is founded upon the false assumption that history can be viewed as a linearity; the teleological approach to criminal justice history that it inspires enables academics like Vass and Pease to draw support from analogies which are superficial and perfunctory at best, whilst eschewing fundamental dissimilarities which prevent sanctions such as transportation, hulks and houses of correction being duplicated in every detail in the modern penal setting.

Forced Labour and Penal Sanctions

One of the limitations in expounding the argument that community service orders can be understood from the perspective of a linear view of penal work history is that it cannot account for fundamental transformations that have manifested themselves in respect of international rights and their influence on forced labour. Neither Vass nor Pease attempt to incorporate such transformations into their respective theses. Indeed Pease suggests, as we shall see more clearly in the next chapter, that the consensual element embodied in community service and the consensual element of impressment for debtors supports his claim that both sanctions have some intriguing characteristics when considered together (Pease 1980: 1). The purpose of the following section will be to demonstrate that the emphasis of international law has increasingly shifted from a formalised structure between States primarily concerned with the regulation of national sovereignty and the maintenance of public order to the development of substantive rules concerning the rights of individuals and the promotion of higher standards of living, full employment, and cultural, economic and social standards. But not only do Vass and Pease fail to recognise that transformations have occurred in human rights, they also do not comprehend that rights arise in specific historical circumstances. This point has already been highlighted in respect of the cultural right of leisure. As Kamenka has noted:

"[Rights] are claims made, conceded or granted by people who are themselves historically or socially shaped. They are asserted by people on their own behalf or as perceived and endorsed implications of specific historical traditions, institutions and arrangements, or of a historically conditioned theory of human needs and human aspirations, or of a human conception of a Divine plan and purpose. In objective fact as opposed to some (subjective) feeling, they are neither eternal nor inalienable, neither prior to society or societies nor independent of them. Some such rights can be singled out, and they are often singled out, as social ideals, as goals to strive toward. But even as such, they cannot be divorced from social content and context" (1988: 127).

As such, in this section it will be demonstrated not only that transformations have occurred but that these historically specific rights have, to some extent, influenced the nature of community service in that they prohibit forced labour imposed for private individuals, companies or associations and prohibit forced work of a kind not carried out in the ordinary course of detention or during conditional release from such detention.

One of the distinctive features of the sanctions delineated by Vass and Pease as containing the germs of the community service idea is that they involved the forced or compulsory labour of offenders. Often this labour was hired out to private associations or individuals. In the houses of correction, for example, the authorities foresaw the need to develop strong links with the economic life of the surrounding districts in order to exploit the supply of forced labour at their disposal. Masters in a wide variety of trades, especially textiles and rope making, contracted with the houses of correction for the labour of its inmates (Ignatieff 1978: 31). As well as hiring the labour of inmates, contractors could, on occasion, rent the entire institution from the city authorities. In 1602, Bridewell was leased for 10 years to four promoters who promised to set the idle to work. Within months it was rumoured that prostitutes entertained in the rooms of these promoters. It was also suggested that only a small number of inmates were held in the institution and those who were did not have sufficient clothes or food. As a result the authorities had to recall it from the lessees amidst disgrace and accusation (O'Donoghue 1923: 190-192). Thus the hiring out of labour or the institutions themselves formed an integral component of the administration of the houses of correction. Indeed one of the reasons postulated for their decline in the mid- to late-1700s was that contractors became despondent with the lack of effective work carried on there.

Similarly impressment and the hulks were founded upon forced labour. Such action in respect of impressment was justified on the following grounds:

"War itself is a great evil, but it is chosen to avoid a greater. The practice of pressing is one of the mischiefs war bringeth with it. But it is a maxim of law, and good policy too, that all private mischiefs must be borne with patience for preventing a national calamity" (*R. v. Broadfoot* 1743-1753: cols 1326-1330).

The decision to use the hulks was embodied in an Act "to authorise for a limited time, the punishment by hard labour" of offenders who were liable to transportation (1776: 16 Geo. III, c. 43). Until 1802, supervisors or contractors could contract with the authorities to take convicts off their hands at so much per head, appoint their own wardens and organise accommodation for the prisoners. In view of his losses sustained in the unsuccessful transportation contract to America, the government offered the post to Duncan Campbell who anchored two ships, the *Justitia* and *Censor*, near Woolwich in August 1776 and placed prisoners on them (Sharpe 1990: 52).

Transportation, too, involved the employment of what would now be regarded as forced labour. On arrival in America, convicts were put up for auction and sold to the highest bidder. Convicts with specific work skills were in great demand and always sold for the highest prices. In contrast, women, the lame, sick, old, and troublesome offenders were the most difficult to sell and generally fetched poorer prices (*ibid*: 42-43). Once it was decided to establish a penal colony in New South Wales, the practice of forced labour resumed again. Indeed it has been argued that without the use of a convict's forced labour, the colonisation of Australia would have taken a half century longer, as the Government would have found it very troublesome to find enough settlers to carry out the required tasks (Hughes 1987: 1-2). In 1789, Governor Phillip introduced the assignment system which survived until 1840. Assignment, as the name implies, provided that felons upon arrival in Australia were allocated to the Government or to settlers as labourers. The system had a number of advantages for the government: it was cheap since it transferred some of the cost of keeping the convicts to settlers on their farms; it scattered the prisoners throughout the colony thus reducing their chances of rebelling; and, it taught the convicts habits of labour (Shaw 1966: 217). The most striking feature of assignment, however, was the inequality in the treatment of offenders which differed remarkably from master to master and eventually led to its removal. Indeed the Molesworth Committee in 1838 noted the comments of Captain Machonochie who stated:

"[T]he practice of assigning convicts to masters is cruel, uncertain, prodigal, ineffectual either for reform or for example, can only be maintained in some degree of vigour by extreme severity; ... it defeats, in consequence, its own most important objects; instead of reforming it degrades humanity, vitiates all under its influence, multiplies petty business, postpones that, which is of higher interest, retards improvement, and is in many instances, even the direct occasion of vice and crime" (Molesworth Committee Report 1838: XXII, viii).

Interestingly, workhouses may be distinguished from such sanctions in relation to forced labour. It is possible to argue, albeit tentatively, that workhouses did not involve forced labour as there was an element of implied consent. An individual was not confined in a workhouse as a result of a penal sanction. It only imposed work as an obligation on paupers who decided of their own accord to benefit from the relief that such an institution could offer. Paupers realised that upon entering the workhouse they had to work in order to assist in financing their upkeep. Therefore, although work was imposed, it is arguable that it may not be regarded as forced, as inmates chose voluntarily to carry it out in order to exist. Moreover, once they gave proper notice of their intention to quit, they could leave the institution when they desired.[1]

In the late nineteenth and twentieth centuries, however, the coercive practice of utilising and exploiting the labour of offenders became more contentious as humanitarian considerations developed in importance. It was in these years that national States set about cultivating and

---

1. The author does accept that the element of real choice was often negligible. Yet it is possible to make a distinction between the compulsory nature of work and the placement of offenders at the disposal of private individuals in relation to houses of correction, transportation and hulks, and the nature of work embodied in workhouses where an individual could enter or leave of his or her own free will.

promoting such rights through the forum of international law. The predominant view prior to this was that each State had an autarchial right to govern its citizens as it deemed appropriate. At this juncture it would perhaps be appropriate to highlight the transformations that have occurred. In the late nineteenth and twentieth centuries, the growth of welfare philosophy increasingly began to evidence itself in an international setting. Across a broad spectrum - including labour, education, science, refugee assistance, civil aviation, communications, agriculture, banking and ethnic minorities - the substructure of international law began to shift from a formalised, State orientated approach to one which was increasingly willing to acknowledge the rights of citizens. It was only from the 1940s onwards, however, that this transformation began to make real headway. In these years, Josef Stalin's development of full Marxist-Leninist collectivist socialism and Adolf Hitler's development of national socialism perpetrated acts of suppression of the most outrageous kind (Robertson and Merrils 1989: 2; Friedman 1964: 60). What was now clear was that the "international community constituted by all those States could not afford to continue to leave it to each of them to choose alone, in the exercise of its unfettered sovereignty, between the absolutist strand and the strand of constraints: a superior and extended set of constraints had to be imposed on each of them, in the interests of all" (Sieghart 1985: 36-40). Moreover, not only were these constraints to act as a custodian against the reactivation of pre-war dictatorships, they were also now to be imposed as a bulwark against the advancing tide of communism

(Robertson and Merrils 1989: 102; Szabo 1982: 21).

But how did this more welfarist approach impact upon the design of international law? Baron Frederik M. Van Asbeck has proposed that six new characteristics were discernible. These were, the extension of intergovernmental consultation and co-operation, which had previously been restricted to "foreign relations", to incorporate social, economic and technical matters; the emergence of consultation and co-operation in a more general framework, instead of only in bilateral dealings, "thereby creating an opportunity for a generally shared opinion on higher public policy" which would have an influence upon national opinion and policies; the expansion of interest in the non-European world; the emergence of technical experts on the international scene; the development of institutions such as the League of Nations and the United Nations and their embodiment of features such as regular periodical conferences of fixed composition, permanent secretariats and independent officials; and, the emergence of quasi-parliamentary conferences such as the I.L.O. and their representation of social groups, employers and employees (Van Asbeck 1962: 1058-1059). To these must be added fundamental changes in the approach to individuals under international law. Since the commencement of the Laws of Nations, one of its defining characteristics was that of national sovereignty (Sieghart 1983: 13). This form of international law merely regulated the membership of the family of nations, the rules denoting territorial jurisdiction, the diplomatic immunities of foreign sovereigns and the modification of rights in respect of the rules of war and neutrality (Friedman 1964: 60). As Drost has noted:

"Before the international community in modern times received its first constitution under the League of Nations, human rights did not appear as a distinct set of rules within the Laws of Nations. This is not surprising because international law was traditionally considered to deal only with the rights and duties of States. The States were the only subjects of the Laws of Nations; the individual did not derive any rights from international law. In so far as the individual entered as a party to an issue under international law, his status did not amount to a *positio standi in judicio*. It was the national or territorial State which derived rights or obligations under international law when the individual was injured in, or entitled to, rights under municipal law" (Drost 1965: 15).

Gradually, however, the individual began to acquire a stronger position in respect of his or her position to demand international protection for his or her elementary human rights. Accordingly, and as Van Asbeck has suggested:

"[O]ne can observe that there has been a transition from a stage where a multitude of separate States existed side by side, towards the beginnings of permanent association and unity, but it is the first beginnings only. There has been a transition from unstable and temporary forms of organisation towards the establishment of permanent institutions, and from the looseness of mainly unwritten rules towards the beginnings of a definite body of international law. One can observe further the advance from a political system based mainly on power towards the beginnings of a legal system underscored by power. The traditional individualistic law of States is now coupled with the beginnings of a social law of men. In short, one can observe the passage from a world of separate States, weakly linked together and weakly bound by *State Law*, towards a world in which the possibilities are being explored of establishing an order in which public authority is exercised by strong institutions under a *genuine law of nations*, which binds peoples and governments by its own force and authority" (1962: 1055).

The reasons for such a transformation are manifold. Albeit, as we have already noted, that real transformations did not occur until the 1940s, much of the impetus for change had already begun to manifest itself after the First World War. This impetus included the emergence of a belief that domination was no longer to be taken for granted; the notion that the most appropriate means of preventing further outbreaks of war was to restrict the abilities of States to engage in warfare; the gradual opening up of democracies in some Western European countries and the decline of individualistic and utilitarian notions of liberty; the demotion of Europe to the rank of merely one of the areas of power; and, the avocation of principles by the Soviet Union after 1917 such as the right to self-determination, the substantive equality of States and socialist internationalism (Cassese 1986: 55-59; Birch 1993: 103). As Cassese noted:

"In actual fact, after the First World War, a new wind began to blow through the international community, bringing with it a drive towards limiting equalities between States and towards a greater concern for the demands of individuals" (1986: 63).

The rate of transformation accelerated after the Second World War as a result of the creation of the Atom bomb and its potential for widespread destruction, the developing political power of the United States and its espousal of anti-colonialist ideology, the movement towards a Welfare State in many countries, the brutal nature of fascist regimes both before and during the war, and the growing fear of communism (Cassesse 1986: 64-69; Humphrey 1973: 75-105). But, again, in recognising that fundamental changes have occurred, it is necessary to emphasise that the success of a more welfarist approach to human rights encountered - and continues to encounter - resistance, criticisms (including its Eurocentrism, grounded as it is in western legal, cultural, social and political traditions), dramatic interruptions, continued injustice, and inadequate implementation in many instances. But these phenomena do not, as Rorty would maintain, negate the fact that a "human rights culture" has emerged;[2] it undoubtedly remains the case that

---

2.   Recognition of such a culture, in Rorty's view, does not require a belief in human rights *foundationalism* - what Nietzsche would refer to as the "longest lie". Indeed, in this regard, Rorty argues that there is a "growing willingness to neglect the question *What is our Nature?* and to substitute the question *What can we make of ourselves?*" Rather than being grounded in the "existence of morally relevant transcultural facts", this pragmatic culture of

international law has undergone a metamorphosis in respect of individual citizens and the imposition of international standards established by common consent.[3]

After the First World War, the League of Nations considered the establishment of international legislation for the protection of labour and the creation of commensurate measures to secure its *bona fide* enforcement as some of its foremost aims. The International Labour Organisation was launched in 1919 with the expectation that it would not only contribute to the welfare of humanity but that it would also create a charter for the prosperity and contentment of all workers. It may be regarded as the forerunner of organisations created to safeguard economic, social and cultural rights. In so far as its ultimate aim was to strengthen and consolidate world harmony, the work of the organisation was closely linked with that of the League of Nations. Indeed the affirmation of "universal peace" and "social justice" are both evident in the preamble of the

---

human rights - which acknowledges the continuing nature of abuse and limitations in respect of implementation- owes "everything to hearing sad and sentimental stories" (Rorty 1993: 111-134).

3.   See also Dorr who notes: "Since 1945, there have been some appalling abuses of human rights and much unnecessary human suffering. What we can say, however, is that over the same period, despite the limitations imposed by State sovereignty, the promotion of human rights and the ending of abuses have been formally acknowledged by the international society of States for the first time in history as a matter of legitimate, global concern; standards have been set; and structures and mechanisms have been developed which put pressure on individual States to confront them. The pressures and mechanisms are not always effective ... Man's inhumanity to man will no doubt continue. But since 1945, by instituting rules and procedures, the world is beginning to build barriers at international levels against it" (Dorr 1994: 19-20).

International Labour Organisation's constitution. It reads:

"Whereas universal and lasting peace can be established only if it is based upon social justice; and whereas conditions of labour exist involving such injustice, hardship, and privation to such large numbers of people as to produce unrest so great as that the peace and harmony of the world are imperilled ... [and] whereas also the failure of any nation to adopt humane conditions of labour is an obstacle in the way of other nations which desire to improve the conditions in their own countries; the High Contracting Parties, moved by sentiments of justice and humanity as well as the desire to secure the permanent peace of the world ... agree to the following Constitution of the International Labour Organisation" (Constitution of the International Labour Organisation 1919; Perigord 1926: 72-111; International Labour Office 1931: 22-35).

The foundation of this organisation together with increasing humanitarian awareness in the international environment acted as stimuli for increased condemnation of slavery and forced labour as methods of exploiting the labour market. Slavery was finally prohibited on a world-wide basis by the International Slavery Convention which opened for signature during the Assembly of the League of Nations on September 25, 1926 (Art. 2). Moreover, and more pertinent from our viewpoint, the signatories also agreed that recourse to compulsory or forced labour had grave consequences and contracted to take all the necessary measures to prevent such labour from developing into conditions analogous to slavery (Art 5).

Following the adoption of the Slavery Convention, the International Labour Organisation, at the request of the Assembly of the League of Nations, investigated the issue of forced labour. Its work led to the adoption in 1930 of the Forced Labour Convention. The term "forced or compulsory labour" is defined as "all work or service which is exacted from any person under the menace of any penalty and for which the said person has not offered himself voluntarily" (Art. 2(1)).[4] The Convention undertook to suppress the use of forced or compulsory labour in all its forms within the shortest possible period (Art. 1(1)), but authorised recourse to such labour during a transitional period for public purposes only and as an exceptional measure (Art. 1(2)). In relation to forced or compulsory labour for private purposes, the terms of the Convention are indubitable. Forced labour shall not be imposed for the benefit of private individuals, companies or associations; where such forced labour exists at the date on which a Member's ratification is registered, the Member shall completely abolish such forced labour from the date on which the Convention would come into force for that Member (Art. 4). In addition, work or service exacted from any person as a consequence of a conviction in a court of law is exempted from the Convention provided that the said work is carried out under the supervision and control of a *public authority and that the*

---

4.   It was ratified by the United Kingdom on June 3, 1931. See Bowman and Harris (1984: 88).

said person is not hired or placed at the disposal of private individuals, companies or associations (Art. 2(2)(c)).[5]

Human rights took on a new significance at the end of the Second World War. Many statesmen of the post-war epoch were extremely cognisant of the need to thwart any resumption of war or atrocities in Western Europe. They realised that so long as human rights were recognised and complied with, democracy and peace were assured. It was essential, therefore, to formulate and stipulate the rights and freedoms that would be respected in Western Society and to establish organisations to ensure their enforcement. On 4 November, 1950, the Foreign Ministers of the Member States of the Council of Europe met to sign the European Convention on Human Rights.

Article 4 prohibits forced or compulsory labour and demonstrates the Convention's desire to prohibit the evil of concentration camps from reoccurring. It also reaffirms the International Labour Organisation's condemnation of such labour. The article provides that:

1. No one shall be held in slavery or servitude.
2. No one shall be required to perform forced or compulsory labour.
3. For the purpose of this Article the term "forced or compulsory labour" shall not include:

---

5. Other exemptions include: (a) work exacted in virtue of military service; (b) work which forms part of normal civic obligations of the citizens; (d) any work or service exacted in cases of emergency and (e) minor communal services of a kind performed by the members of the community in the direct interest of the said community.

(a) any work required to be done in the ordinary course of detention imposed according to the provisions of Article 5 of this Convention or during conditional release from such detention;

(b) any service of military character or, in case of conscientious objectors in countries where they are recognised, service exacted instead of compulsory military service;

(c) any service exacted in case of an emergency or calamity threatening the life or well-being of the community;

(d) any work or service which forms part of normal civic obligations (Art 4).[6]

The exception formulated under Article 4(3)(a) for the work of detainees and conditionally released persons is phrased in quite general terms. It does not, unlike Article 2(2)(c) of the International Convention of 1930, exclude work on behalf of private individuals, companies or associations. In 1968, in the case of *Twenty-One Detained Persons v. The Federal Republic of Germany*, the applicants complained that part of the work required of them during their detention was performed on behalf of private firms under contracts concluded with the prison administration and alleged that such a labour contract system amounted to a state of slavery. The Commission observed, in this respect, that Article 4, paragraph (3)(a), contained nothing to prevent the State from entering such contracts. Indeed such forms of prison

---

6. It was ratified by the U. K. on 8 March, 1951.

work were widely prevailing in many Member States of the Council of Europe. Thus the Commission found that the form of prison labour of which the applicants complained, whatever its merits or demerits from a penological point of view, clearly fell within the framework of work normally required from prisoners under the Convention (1968: Application Nos. 3134/67 and 3188 to 3206/67 joined). In some contracting States such as Britain, however, the courts will have to apply the restriction concerning work on behalf of private individuals, companies or associations on the ground of the direct applicability of the International Convention of 1930 ratified by them.

The exception under (a) applies only to work "in the ordinary course of detention ... or during conditional release from such detention". These words were interpreted by the European Court of Human Rights in the *Vagrancy* cases in 1971 to mean that it must be work directed at the rehabilitation of the detainee. It also incorporates a European standard by which a particular State's practice can be compared with that of several other Council of Europe Member States (De Wilde, Ooms and Versyp 1971: XII, 44-45). Thus if a State went beyond what was normal in Europe, it appears that an attempt to rely on Article 4(3)(a) as a justification for requiring prisoners to work might be unsuccessful. Moreover, the Commission had previously found that the detention for vagrancy did not take place under the conditions laid down in Article 5, and in particular under paragraph (4) of Article 5, and thus concluded that their detention could not be justified under the above-cited provision, and that consequently this was a violation of Article 4 (De Wilde, Ooms and Versyp 1969: X, 96-97).[7] The European Court of Human Rights, on the other hand, although similarly finding a violation of the rights guaranteed by Article 5(4), did not deem that it should deduce therefrom a violation of Article 4. It in fact considered that paragraph 3(a) of Article 4 authorises work ordinarily required of individuals deprived of their liberty under Article 5(1)(e) and it found, on the basis of the information before the Court, that no violation of Article 5(1)(e) had been established in respect of De Wilde, Ooms and Versyp (1971: XII, 44-45). As such, according to the Court ruling, the fact that a person whose detention is permitted by Article 5(1) is, in breach of Article 5(4), not

---

7. Article 5(1) states: "everyone has a right to liberty and security of person. No one shall be deprived of his liberty save in the following cases and in accordance with a procedure prescribed by law: (a) the lawful detention of a person after conviction by a competent court; (b) the lawful arrest or detention of a person for non-compliance with the lawful order of a court or in order to secure the fulfilment of any obligation prescribed by law; (c) the lawful arrest or detention of a person effected for the purpose of bringing him before the competent legal authority on reasonable suspicion of having committed an offence or when it is reasonably considered necessary to prevent his committing an offence or fleeing after having done so; (d) the detention of a minor by a lawful order for the purpose of educational supervision or his lawful detention for the purpose of bringing him before the competent legal authority; (e) the lawful detention of persons for the prevention of the spreading of infectious diseases, of persons of unsound mind, alcoholics, or drug addicts or vagrants; (f) the lawful arrest or detention of a person to prevent his effecting an unauthorised entry into the country or of a person against whom action is being taken with a view to deportation or extradition." Article 5(4) states that: "everyone who is deprived of his liberty by arrest or detention shall be entitled to take proceedings by which the lawfulness of his detention shall be decided speedily by a court and his release ordered if the detention is not lawful."

provided with a remedy to challenge the legality of his or her detention, does not render any work required of him or her in detention forced labour. Finally, the work carried out by offenders under Article 4(3)(c) of the European Convention must not be disproportionate or oppressive.[8]

The Abolition of Forced Labour Convention, 1957, further reiterated the call for the abolition of forced labour. The pre-amble defined the purpose of the 1957 Convention as being to secure the abolition of certain forms of forced or com-pulsory labour constituting a violation of the rights of an individual referred to in the Charter of the United Nations and enunciated by the Universal Declaration of Human Rights.[9] It was concerned especially with forced labour as a means of political coercion. Each member of the Inter-national Labour Organisation which ratified the Convention undertook to suppress labour employed: (a) as a means of political coercion or education or as a punishment for holding or expressing political views or views ideologically opposed to the established political, social or economic system; (b) as a method of mobilising or using labour for the purposes of economic development; (c) as a means of labour discipline; (d) as a punishment for having participated in strikes or (e) as a means of racial, social, national or religious discrimination (Art 1). Each ratifying member further promised to secure the immediate and complete abolition of such forced or compulsory labour (Art.2).

The International Covenant on Civil and Political Rights

---

8.   See *X v. Switzerland* (1980: Application 8500/79).
9.   Britain ratified it on 30 December, 1957.

also refers to forced labour in great detail.[10] Its provisions follow closely the wording of the European Convention on Human Rights. It should be noted, however, that Article 8 of the International Covenant on Civil and Political Rights also gives a wider latitude than the International Labour Organisation's standards in that it does not (similar to Article 4 of the European Convention on Human Rights) outlaw work on behalf of private individuals, companies or associations. In contrast, the American Convention on Human Rights, signed in November, 1969, follows more closely that of the International Labour Organisation's Forced Labour Convention (no. 29.), to the effect that any work or service exacted from a person imprisoned in execution of a sentence or formal decision passed by the competent judicial authority must be carried out under the supervision and control of public authorities, and any person performing such work or service shall not be placed

---

10. Britain signed on the 20 May, 1976. Article 8 states: "1. No one shall be held in slavery; slavery and the slave trade in all their forms shall be prohibited; 2. No one shall be held in servitude; 3. (a) No one shall be required to perform forced or compulsory labour; (b) Paragraph 3(a) shall not be held to preclude, in countries where imprisonment with hard labour may be imposed as a punishment for a crime, the performance of hard labour in pursuance of a sentence to such punishment by a competent court; (c) For the purpose of this paragraph the term 'forced or compulsory' labour shall not include: (i) Any work or service, not referred to in sub paragraph (b), normally required of a person who is under detention in consequence of a lawful order of a court, or of a person during conditional release from such detention; (ii) Any service of a military character and, in countries where conscientious objection is recognised, any natural service required by law of conscientious objectors; (iii) any service exacted in cases of emergency or calamity threatening the life or well-being of the community; (iv) any work or service which forms part of normal civil obligations."

at the disposal of any private party, company, or juridical person.[11]

When introducing community service orders in England and Wales, it was necessary to establish whether the work which was required to be performed by an offender could be deemed to be forced labour within the meaning of various international agreements decided upon from the start of the twentieth century. To begin with, the participation of voluntary organisations would have been prohibited by the I.L.O.'s 1930 Convention, as the offender would have been placed at the disposal of a private association. The creation of such a sanction may also have been contrary to the European Convention for the Protection of Human Rights and Fundamental Freedoms in that it was

---

11. Article 6 of the American Convention states that: "(1) No one shall be subject to slavery or to involuntary servitude, which are prohibited in all their forms, as are the slave trade and traffic in women; (2) No one shall be required to perform forced or compulsory labour: this provision shall not be interpreted to mean that, in those countries in which the penalty established for certain crimes is deprivation of liberty at forced labour, the carrying out of such a sentence imposed by a competent court is prohibited. Forced labour shall not adversely affect the dignity or the physical or intellectual capacity of the prisoner; (3) For the purpose of this article the following do not constitute forced or compulsory labour: (a) work or service normally required of a person imprisoned in execution of a sentence or formal decision passed by the competent judicial authority. Such work or service shall be carried out under the supervision and control of public authorities, and any persons performing such work or service shall not be placed at the disposal of any private party, company, or juridical person; (b) military service and, in countries in which conscientious objectors are recognised, national service that the law may provide for in lieu of military service; (c) service exacted in time of danger or calamity that threatens the existence or well-being of the community; or, (d) work or service that forms part of normal civic obligations."

possible to construe the work as of a type which was not carried out in the ordinary course of detention or during conditional release from such detention. It was felt that the concept of "conditional release" from detention, whilst including such situations as release on licence, would probably not extend to sentences of community service. It may now also violate Article 8 of the International Covenant on Civil and Political Rights for the same reason. Breach of Article 8 was not, however, a relevant consideration at the time of introducing community service, as the Covenant was not ratified by Britain until the 20 May, 1976. It was partly to avoid the issue of forced labour that the British legislation provided that an offender shall not be required by a court, to carry out an order without his or her consent.[12] By consenting to the orders, offenders offered themselves voluntarily, thus allowing the criminal justice system to neatly circumvent the difficulty of forced labour.

Criminal Justice and the Community Ideology

The concept of "community" has gained in momentum and dominated to some extent British social and penal policy over the last 50 years. Involving communities in the pursuit of antidotes to contemporary difficulties has become compelling in our time. A wide variety of communal units including hospitals, schools, prisons, and churches, have all

---

12.   See section 15(2) of the Criminal Justice Act, 1972. See also section 14(2) of the Powers of the Criminal Courts Act, 1973 which largely consolidated and superseded the 1972 Act.

experienced the ideology of community in some form or other.[13] The belief in such an open course of treatment is evidenced by the proliferation of panaceas which have manifested themselves since the Second World War to cater for the myriad of societal dilemmas confronting policy makers. Community care, community correction, community work, community policing, community development, community education, community politics and community architecture may all be cited as examples of this increased appeal to the ideology of community. It alludes - the word "community" itself is not only rich in "symbolic power" but also lacks any "negative connotations" (Cohen 1983: 110) - to the existence of an interfusion of analogous social relationships which authorise and encourage the endorsement of mutual aid, co-operation and interaction, the reduction of stigma, and the furtherance of integration. The purpose of the following section is to describe the emergence of this ideology of community and its impact on social control discourse.

Before describing its emergence, it would perhaps be pertinent briefly to ask why the ideology of community had become such an important facet of both social and correctional processes by the 1960s? One may begin by alluding to the dramatic broadening in community organisation practices in America in the late 1950s and 1960s as a result of the growing disillusionment with the New Deal's failure to implement a proper welfare programme in

---

13. For a general examination of the positive features of the "community", see Peck (1987: 59-76).

respect of issues such as poverty, dependency, inner city decay, ghettos, discrimination and unemployment (Kramer and Specht 1969: 16-17); the belief that the Welfare State had also fallen short of its expectations also evidenced itself in Britain as calls were increasingly made for the community to fill in the gap left by the inflexible statutory welfare apparatus (Brenton 1985: 36). Outside of the welfare realm, growing fears about "environmental nuisances" (Baudrillard 1998: 37-47) and "eco-catastrophes"; concerns about the bureaucratic and inaccessible nature of the democratic structure and the desire for more popular participation (Richardson 1983: 54-57); the diffusion of counter-cultural values[14] - for example, the *turn on, tune in* and *drop out* nature of the Hippie way of life (Hall 1972: 595-602); the advance of urbanisation and the alienatory features inherent therein[15]; the conformism and repetitive nature of suburbia and its "commoditization of everyday life" (Medhurst 1997: 240-268),[16] and; the espousal by many

---

14. Indeed Cohen notes that the 1960s, to some extent, was characterised by all sorts of radical populist ideas: "[S]mall is beautiful, people are not machines, experts don't know everything, bureaucracies are anti-human, institutions are unnatural and bad, the community is natural and good. Radicals no longer had to shout about the evils of the standardised, synchronised, centralised nightmare of the 'system'. Everyone appeared to be listening. Society could be redeemed by what Illich nicely called 'organisational disestablishment'" (Cohen 1994: 35).
15. For modernity's "lifting out of social relations from local contexts of interaction and their restructuring across indefinite spans of time-space", see Giddens (1996: 109; 1991: 18-20).
16. As Baudrillard noted in 1970 in examining the process of consumption and the meaning of anomie: "We may, therefore, suggest that the age of consumption, being the historical culmination of the whole process of accelerated productivity under the sign of capital, is also the age of radical

social commentators, often ahistorically, of *Gemeinschaft* over *Gesellschaft* and *organic* over *mechanical* ways of life, all, *inter alia*, increased the appeal and potential of the ideology of community (Milson 1974: 69-113; Ross and Leppin 1955). In the domain of criminal justice, the appeal to the ideology of community was heightened by pragmatic concerns about the ineffectual nature of closed institutions, by humanitarian and civil liberty critiques, by labelling and stigma theory which demonstrated the futile and damaging effects of isolating inmates, and by economic considerations given the high cost of such institutions (Cohen 1994: 117). With this in mind, then, the remainder of this section will examine the emergence of specific practices which harnessed the potential of the community ideology as a remedy for all forms of deviancy.

Pioneering work in the advancement of group psychotherapy commenced in 1940 under the guidance of Dr. Maxwell Jones at Mill Hill near London. He was given responsibility for a hospital unit studying effort syndrome in cases of war neurosis. All patients were diagnosed as having congruous symptoms, including pain over the region of the heart, breathlessness, palpitations and postural giddiness. These features were essentially psychological

---

alienation. Commodity logic has become generalised and today governs not only labour processes and material products, but the whole of culture, sexuality, and human relations, including even fantasies and individual drives. Everything is taken over by that logic, not only in the sense that all functions and needs are objectivised and manipulated in terms of profit, but in the deeper sense in which everything is *spectacularised* or, in other words, evoked, provoked and orchestrated into images, signs, consumable models" (1998: 191).

rather than corporal in cause. As such it was psychosomatic as opposed to physical treatment that was necessitated. Jones soon discovered that positive progress could be made with therapy by altering the social configuration of the hospital to enable more two-way interaction between the staff and inmates (Rapoport 1960: 2). At the termination of hostilities, he was requested to lead a unit staffed from the Maudsley hospital to rehabilitate the most disturbed of the British prisoners of war returning from the prison camps of Europe and the Far East. In order to reintegrate such men back into society, Jones, emboldened by his previous success with army personnel, developed a "transitional community". The institutionalised and disciplined nature of hospitals was relaxed and the patients were encouraged to partake in the active running of the venture. Thus it acted as a conventual stepping stone which aided their adaptation back into a world which had to some extent passed them by (Jones 1968: 16-17; Jones and Tanner 1948: 53; Jones 1982: 3-5). At the same time, sociologists, particularly in America, were beginning to delineate and portray the existence of inmates within institutions of various kinds and their polarisation from society. Patients were regarded as institutionalised as a consequence of the restricted, detached, dispassionate and bureaucratic nature of the administrative networks which governed them.[17] The mid

---

17. For the impact of the total institution on its inmates including the breakdown of the barriers ordinarily separating three social arrangements (work, sleep and play), the "mortification of the self" (ie, forced deference patterns), regimentation, the loss of self-determination, and the underlife of such institutions, see Goffman (1974).

to late-1940s marked the beginnings of a series of attempts to actively associate custodial staff with inmates in the belief that it would dismantle such polarity.

In Britain, as a result of his success at Maudsley hospital and the heightened appreciation of the ineptness of prevailing institutional regimes for the physically and mentally ill, Dr. Jones was commissioned by the Ministries of Labour, Health and Pensions to establish a treatment unit for society's nonconformists. The unit was to incorporate and be accountable for an extensive assortment of individuals and practically covered the entire gamut of belligerent and anarchic behaviour ranging from the indolent jobless to the drug and alcohol dependent. Accordingly the Industrial Neurosis Unit was created at Belmont in 1947 as an experiment in community group therapy (European Committee on Crime Problems 1974: 14-15).[18]

The social milieu of a therapeutic community was inherently different from the traditional hierarchical social structure of the hospital. It was designed both to cultivate an atmosphere which would be more conducive to the mutual resolution of differences and to react against the authoritarian and custodial organisation of the traditional configuration of mental hospitals. Therefore a strong emphasis was placed on communication *per se* and groups of doctors, social workers, attendants and patients were encouraged to give voice to their opinions and difficulties.

---

18. For the development of a therapeutic community led by W.R. Bion at Northfield Military Hospital in 1943, see Kennard and Roberts (1983: 40-49).

Moreover, there was a movement towards a more democratic and homologous formation, which would provide the patients with the scope to participate more actively in the operation of the institution thus enabling the maximisation of therapeutic and diagnostic effect. In order "to collapse the authority pyramid" and create this egalitarian environment, it was considered essential that the *pro forma* doctor-patient role had to be abandoned. In this way, once each individual gave a commitment and became included in treatment and administration, it resulted in a process of socialisation. The social phenomena of involvement, coaction, symbiotic learning and reciprocal support ensured that all participants experienced a sense of belonging. It diverged from antecedent forms of treatment in that its emphasis was on "active rehabilitation, as against custodialism and segregation; democratisation, in contrast to the old hierarchies and formalities of status differentiation; permissiveness, in contrast to the stereotyped patterns of communication and behaviour; and communalism, as opposed to highly specialised therapeutic roles often limited to the doctor" (Jones 1976: 88; Zeitlyn 1967: 1083-1086; Miles 1969: 22-38).

The formulation of the internal operation of hospitals along self-responsible, self-governing community lines brought about great changes in the organisation of mental health. The theoretical impetus, upon which the ideology was based, was derived in the main from social psychology and the works of Bion, Foulkes and Anthony. By fostering a policy centred on therapeutic community groups, it was hoped that the patients could establish co-operative and communicative relationships so as to broadcast their grievances, lose their inhibitions and confront their specific problems. Group therapy, involving the entire hospital community in some form or other, provided, according to Foulkes, a number of important benefits:

(a) It stimulated social integration and relieved isolation.

(b) It acted as a "mirror image" - participants would realise that other individuals had similar anxieties and impulses and suffered in the same way, if not more, than themselves. Recognitions of this nature relieved feelings of guilt and sorrow and made for a resolution to improve.

(c) Because themes were discussed again and again, it enabled individuals to feel comfortable about their problems. Even deep unconscious material could be expressed more readily and more fully - this process was referred to in psychologists' terminology as the "condenser phenomena".

(d) Finally it promoted an element of exchange between the participants facilitating fuller discussion (Foulkes 1964: 33-34).[19] In short, it brought neurosis out into the open where it could be considered and confronted.

---

19. Bion advocated that good group techniques which invoke a community spirit should incorporate the following characteristics: a common purpose; common recognition by members of the group of the boundaries; the capacity to absorb new members and to lose members without the trepidation of displacing group individuality; freedom from internal sub-groups; an important emphasis placed on each individual member and the capacity of the group to confront discontent (1961: 25-26; Jones 1993: 152).

Community treatment was now given the status of a radical and modernistic therapeutic panacea in the domain of mental health. In 1957 the Royal Commission on the law relating to Mental Illness and Mental Deficiency explicitly advocated the employment of the community technique. There should, they suggested, be a general reorientation away from institutional care towards community care. It was expected that this would result in a considerable expansion of the local authority services, which would include, *inter alia*, the provision of residential accommodation for a number of patients who although still requiring residential care no longer needed residential in-patient care and the provision of training facilities in centres or at home for severely subnormal children who were unable to benefit from education at school (1957: Cmnd. 1969, 245).[20] Could this "therapeutic community" ideology which existed as an ersatz milieu within a hospital setting now be transferred to other relevant social units which also treated anti-social behaviour?

Community care was quickly seen as a flexible, adaptive and convincing means of treating social dilemmas and a variety of groups including the mentally ill, retarded and delinquent began to be accepted into the heart of society. Observation over a number of years had shown that incarceration within institutions resulted in the polarisation and alienation of individuals or groups of individuals and was not a functional or pragmatic solution. A stratagem of

20. The Mental Health Act of 1959 gave effect to many of the Commission's recommendations.

a directed progression, where possible, away from restrictive institutionalism towards diversion led to what many anticipated would be the advent of an analeptic millennium in the community. Benedict Alper, for example, suggested that:

"Nothing succeeds like an idea whose time has come. The institution as a means of coping with the problem of specific sectors of our population seems at this point to have run its course. Whether one is aged, below par intellectually or emotionally delinquent, alcoholic, or drug-addicted, the source - and the remedy - of the problem lie in the communities where such people come from. By bringing them back into the community, by enlisting the goodwill and the desire to serve, the ability to understand which is to be found. in every neighbourhood, we shall meet the challenge which such groups of persons present, and at the same time ease the financial burden of their confinement in fixed institutions" (Alper 1973: vii-viii).

In particular, the community-based approach began to take root in western crime control discourse. Confidence was gradually undermined in what could be achieved by regimented cellular confinement. Incarceration in a prison involved, among other things, a severe loss of liberty, existence in a Spartan environment, involuntary celibacy, stigmatisation, exposure to various other forms of deviancy and a loss of autonomy. In addition these hardships would further raise the barriers against reconstructing a normal life upon release. It is not surprising then that the community domain was increasingly viewed as a more practical and humanitarian mode of treating offenders and that the criminal justice system began a progressive movement in that direction.

In penal institutions, the emphasis took the form of the activities known collectively as "correctional community". It derived its assumptions from the "therapeutic community" initiated by Jones at Belmont hospital. In California, the Department of Correction under the guidance of Norman Fenton began some of the first experiments with this method of social therapy in the 1950s (Conrad 1967: 107). It attempted to utilise all the experiences of inmates and staff in a therapeutic manner with the expectation that it would better instruct and prepare inmates for their re-establishment in society. Regular communal meetings became the forum through which all prisoners could communicate their encounters and ordeals. It was anticipated that by confronting the implications and repercussions of their own conduct and by discussing their findings with fellow community members that progress would be possible in curtailing misanthropic inclinations.

Attempts were also made in England and Wales to emulate the therapeutic groupwork conducted in Californian prisons. The psychiatric treatment units established at Wormwood Scrubs and Wakefield for men and Holloway for women experimented with the idea of group therapy and it was recognised as having a significant impact on work with offenders. In 1956 the Report of the Commissioners on Prisons warned, however, that the type of offence and the expressed desire for treatment of this nature - especially before sentence - should not *ipso facto* be symptomatic of the individual's appropriateness for participation in the group. More detailed information on the offender's personality and his or her probability of succeeding on the scheme were required before any decision could be taken (Home Office 1957: Cmnd. 322, 122-123; Morrison 1961: 279-297; Whitley 1970: 60-64). In 1956, in Norwich prison, attempts were made to construct a more wholesome and positive environment within the institution. This was achieved by allocating more personal freedom to the prisoners, by restricting the locking and unlocking of doors, by reducing prison counts and by assigning prison officers to groups of offenders whom they were expected to befriend (Hall-Williams 1970: 155-156). In December, 1957, Pollington borstal introduced the use of group discussion into its training programme. Ninety-minute discussions were organised three times a fortnight for 12 groups of boys, each group consisting of seven to 10 members. Issues covered included family and social relationships, rejection experiences, appraisal of other group members, and practical problems such as finding employment on release (Bishop 1960: 185-193; Jones 1962: 58-63). As Jones noted:

"What is happening here is that group members are gaining real social experience through the group from which they may learn, just as we all learn from our social experience in the community. But the experience they are now gaining, differs from the experience they have had previously, and from which, as they are delinquent, it appears they have not learned very much. Their experience in the group is, first of all, a specially designed, and therefore highly concentrated taste of real life. It is also experience which occurs in a small group and in a highly simplified setting, so that the lessons to be learned from it are more obvious and less easily evaded. Finally there is a group leader present, whose aim it is to point out the lesson, skilfully and carefully: who mobilises experiences for the group, so that its learning can be maximised" (1962: 61).

More permanently, a therapeutic community was actually established at Grendon psychiatric prison in the early 1960s. The participants were predominantly recidivist offenders and were regarded as being more clinically disturbed than inmates from other prisons. Considerable demands were placed on the staff in making receptive the therapeutic venture to the detainees. Many of the cases displayed an aggressive hostility towards the organisers and authority, precipitated in the main by various previous terms of confinement (Home Office 1964: Cmnd. 2381: 58). Nonetheless they achieved their aim of creating a suitable artificial milieu in which to further treatment. Within this environment, the staff could strive to diminish offenders anti-social tendencies and thus better enable the likelihood of their effective reintegration on termination of sentence.

But it was felt that genuine community life could not exist, no matter how much formal roles were abandoned, within the sealed environment of a prison or mental hospital. One of the first penal projects to occur outside the confines of such institutions took place with the introduction of a Community Treatment Project in California in 1961. It contrasted the effectiveness of a period of intensive treatment in the community with a period of detention for similar groups of seriously delinquent male and female offenders who had been committed from the juvenile courts to the State correctional system. As opposed to being incarcerated for a fixed interval, the former group was accommodated on a demanding community based parole scheme where they were subject to individualised as well as extended treatment. An "interpersonal maturity level" classification system was employed to establish treatment aims and objectives (Palmer 1971: 74; Haxby 1978: 154-155). It formulated seven levels on a scale of increasing maturity in order to determine their suitability for the project. Each "I - level" alluded to the different ways in which delinquents conducted their relationships with others and how they construed their environment (Home Office 1974: 249-250).[21] The results for the most part tended to favour the group in the community. Among those on parole for at least 15 months it was found that there was a failure rate of 31 per cent for the experiment group and 50 per cent for those undergoing ordinary treatment. Similar differences were discovered in comparing the experiment and control groups who had been on parole for at least 24 months (39 per cent

---

21. The I-level classification system has been criticised on the grounds that it provided no adequate definition of "potential for change" during an individual's normal psychological development. Moreover, the methods of assigning delinquents to the various I-level types were subjective in nature and as such could not be used as a routine method for classifying offenders.

and 61 per cent respectively) and those who had been on parole for 36 months (46 per cent and 63 per cent respectively) (*ibid*: 254). Accordingly, for many supporters of the corrective community ideology, these figures provided a justification for their conviction that offenders could be treated not only more cost effectively but also more beneficially in a community as opposed to a custodial environment.

In England and Wales it was increasingly recognised that there were great difficulties associated with the reintegration of offenders back into society after a period of incarceration. Many required special attention in the form of support as well as economic assistance such as accommodation, employment, clothing and financial help. The likelihood of after-care being called upon was extended by the 1948 Criminal Justice Act which made provisions for release on licence of prisoners under twenty-one on conviction, men and women sentenced to preventive detention and corrective training, and persons serving life imprisonment. But the most meaningful advance in the development of after-care occurred with the publication of a report by the Advisory Council on the Treatment of Offenders in 1963. Voluntary after-care for offenders discharged from prison had for a number of years been co-ordinated by branches of the Discharged Prisoners Aid Society which supported prisoners in their locality by providing financial assistance. Following the 1948 Criminal Justice Act, increased emphasis and consideration was given to the employment of after-care in facilitating discharged offenders make the transformation from a custodial to a community-based environment. Because of the profound effect which institutionalism had on the lives of prisoners and their ability to readjust, it was deemed axiomatic that after-care be given greater priority within the criminal justice domain. The 1963 report proposed that it should be administered by an expanded, reorganised and more professionalised probation service. In addition, in order for such like schemes to be effectual, they had to be amalgamated with the penal system where the offender carried out his or her sentence and had to be devised as a process which commenced upon sentence and ripened upon release (Home Office 1963: 10-31).[22] Treatment and after-care were now components of the same process aimed at shaping each individual prisoner to conform and adapt to societal norms after completion of his or her sentence.

Moreover, the 1960s marked the beginning of a period which saw the Home Office more prepared to experiment with penal alternatives and in particular to adopt a community oriented approach. As early as 1962 the Morrison Committee suggested that there was a moral case:

---

22. See also the statement of the Home Office in 1959: "It has been said with truth that it is easy to imprison a man; the difficult thing is to release him. Special attention must therefore be devoted first to preparing prisoners for release, and then ensuring that the difficult transition from closed institutional life to free life in society is eased and guided. For many men and women the effort will be wasted unless they receive this help (Home Office 1959: Cmnd 645, 19)." See also the 1961 Criminal Justice Act which made provision for the introduction of compulsory after-care under section 20; it was never implemented owing to the lack of resources available to the probation service at that time.

"in a society founded upon respect for human rights, for a system which allows an offender to continue to live and work in the community. Such a system is also desirable on social and economic grounds. *A priori*, the system will be better if as does the probation system, it brings helpful influences to bear upon the offender while at liberty" (1962: Cmnd. 1650, 9).

As such, a new impetus emerged endorsing the community as a social control apparatus which functioned without having to remove the miscreant from society. It was, in part, assumed that the aim of counselling the offender to refrain from criminal deviancy would best be achieved in a non-custodial setting. This was supported by research and investigation in California which, as has already been delineated, implied that offenders might well be controlled in the community without any upsurge in crime rates or recidivism. There was no reason for presupposing that the same rationale would not work in Great Britain.

The introduction of the 1967 Criminal Justice Act witnessed salient developments in the history of non-institutional responses to crime. Parole, for example, although not a revolutionary departure from established tradition, was an important and innovative penal measure as it permitted the early release from custody of suitable offenders into the community under specified conditions contained in the parole licence (Secs. 59-64). It was intended that the release of offenders under parole supervision would facilitate a diminution in the prison population together with a reduction in the incidence of crime. This trend was further reiterated in 1968 by the Seebohm Committee which stated:

"The feeling of identity which membership of a community bestows derives from the common values, attitudes and ways of behaving which the members share and which form the rules which guide social behaviour within it. Such rules are the basis of the strong social control over behaviour which is characteristic of highly-integrated and long-established communities" (1968: Cmnd. 3703, 147).

In 1969 the Children and Young Persons Act also established new methods of treatment in the community. It enabled civil care as opposed to criminal proceedings to be taken where a delinquent child was suspected of having committed an offence. If the child was found guilty, the juvenile court could make a care order making the young wrongdoer the responsibility of the local authority to be supervised and cared for in the community.[23] Similarly probation was fitted out with additional conditions with the specific intention that it would act as a medium for the management of offenders in the community. Under section 20 of the Criminal Justice Act of 1972, for example, the court could include in a probation order a requirement that an offender attend a day training centre provided consent was given

---

23. The policy was controversial and was never fully implemented due to political hostility from a Conservative government (Bainham and Cretney 1993: 29).

and it was for a period not exceeding 60 days. In addition, section 53(1) of the said Act made provision for probation and after-care committees, with the approval of the Secretary of State, to "provide and carry on day training centres, bail hostels, probation homes and other establishments" for use in connection with the rehabilitation of offenders.[24] As a consequence, the probation service, in order to contend with the increased responsibility placed on it in ensuring the protection of society and the offenders, began to assume a more active and accountable role than in former times.

The belief in the employment of community as a panacea for criminal deviancy was firmly entrenched by the early 1970s. Its furtherance was greatly succoured by penologists on both sides of the Atlantic who demonstrated a volition to experiment with it in order to harness and maximise its potential. By 1972 it was accepted, to some extent, that miscreants could be rehabilitated in association with their communities, thus enabling them to be reconciled with society. Community was commendable and beneficial and promoted a sense of social responsibility and self-reliance by demarcating what was and was not tolerable. Indeed, through, in part, the iconography of Tonnies' *Gemeinschaft* which consisted of all kinds of association in which natural

---

24. The widening scope of probation had been recommended by the Wootton Report in 1970. This is a development, they suggested, "that we heartily welcome; and we believe that it accords with our specific proposals some of which will, we hope, enable the probation and after-care service to take within its scope a wider range of offenders who would otherwise be given custodial sentences" (1970: 64).

as opposed to rational will predominated, "benevolent rhetoric" began, to some extent, to portray the correctional process in Manichean terms with the forces of light of the community (open, inclusive, natural, cultivating a sense of belonging and fraternity) ranged against the forces of darkness of the prison (stigmatising, closed, cultivating a sense of alienation and estrangement). This rhetoric is succinctly and correctly encapsulated by Vass who stated:

"Prisons punish, but *alienate*. Community punishes, but *reintegrates*: it helps to create a moral conscience and assists offenders in rebuilding their social networks; boosting their morale; engaging in good deeds for others; and treating themselves and others with the respect they deserve" (1992: 41).[25]

Community participation was regarded as an integral component of community service at its inception in 1972. This was recognised by Winifield who postulated that the sanction embodied "the maxim of work with the community as opposed to work for the community" (1977: 128). Broadly speaking it was hoped that by associating with members of the public, it would prove to be a salutary experience for offenders sentenced to perform community service orders and would encourage them to foster a sense of social responsibility and alter their perspectives on society as a

---

25. See also Cohen who noted: "In the hagiology and demonology of 'progressive' crime control talk, the contrast is between the good community - open, benevolent, accepting - and the bad institution - damaging, rejecting, stigmatising" (Cohen 1994: 116).

whole. If they could be persuaded to comprehend the consequences of their criminal exploits and develop respect for other people, then they may begin to realise the error of their ways and become less likely to reoffend. Work relationships with volunteers, supervisors and those in need of assistance could be cultivated in an *esprit de corps* as opposed to the negative experience undertaken in the aberrant and artificial confines of a prison environment. The tasks themselves, which were to include gardening and decorating old peoples' homes, helping disabled people to go shopping, hospital visits and clearance work, would enable the offender to make reparation to the community and enhance his or her own sense of self-esteem. The benefits to be derived from being sentenced to serve a community service order were highlighted in a speech given by Mr John Fraser in the House of Commons in June 1972:

"I think that the attractions of community service orders are that community service should enable the offender to win approval for his service. The problem with offenders often is that they have been unable to win approval from the community around them. The new concept will be useful because it will enable them to make reparation in an atmosphere of co-operation with the community and not in confrontation with authority. The problem with many offenders once again, is that they are alienated from authority; and if an attempt is made to bring about a reconciliation, this means an attempt being made by the offender as well as by authority" (House of Commons

Parliamentary Debates 1972: 838, 1964-1965).[26]

Thus community service attempted, by restoring the self worth of offenders in a co-operative, approving and interactive environment, to reintegrate them into society from which they were estranged or alienated.

Before concluding this section of the chapter, it is worth noting that there has been much polemical debate among academics about the locus of community corrections within the penal domain. The ideological appeal of community corrections has been considered by some as an assault on the hegemony of the crime control apparatus itself. Scull, for example, in his book titled *Decarceration. Community Treatment and the Deviant: a radical view*, has suggested:

"Viewed in historical perspective, the shift away from a social control apparatus placing heaviest emphasis on segregating deviants at institutions like prisons, asylums, and reformatories is clearly a development of potentially far reaching significance ... [and is] dependent upon and a reflection of more extensive and deep-seated changes in the social organisation of advanced capitalist societies" (1977: 151-152).

He subsequently revised this conclusion in a later edition of the said book by admitting that it failed to incorporate the

26. See also the Wootton Report which stated: "[w]hat attracts us however, is the opportunity which it could give for constructive activity in the form of personal service to the community, and the possibility of a changed outlook on the part of the offender" (Home Office 1970: 13).

complexities which the introduction of the new community programmes had entailed:

"With hindsight, one could argue that I fell victim to exactly the danger I warned of - that of taking reformative rhetoric at face value and as a result, assuming that the language of radical non-intervention closely coincided with everyday practice" (1984: 176).

On the other hand, Cohen, for example, adopting a Foucauldian perspective, suggests that community treatment only resulted in a "gradual expansion and intensification of the system; a dispersal of its mechanisms from more closed to more open sites and a consequent increase in the invisibility of social control and the degree of its penetration into the social body"(1994: 87):

"But every one of the major patterns ... - expansion, dispersal, invisibility, penetration - is indeed continuous with those original transformations. The prison remains - *a stubborn, continuous presence seemingly impervious to all attacks* (my italics) - and in its shadow lies 'community control'. Together they make up what appears in Foucault as the 'cercarial archipelago', 'net', 'continuum', 'city', 'circle', and 'pyramid'. The creation of all these new agencies and services surrounding the court and the prison, the generation of new systems of knowledge, classification and professional interests, is little more than a widening and diversification of the last century's archipelago, made possible by resources, investment, ingenuity, technology and vested interest on a scale that befits 'post-industrial society'" (*ibid*: 85).

Such a standpoint is also supported by Mathiesen:

"The change of thinking, from the great reform during the first part of the nineteenth century to the principles of reform towards the end of the present century ... mirrors a change from *open to hidden discipline*. It was one of the marks of individual liberalism that its disciplining not only was individualistic, but at the same time still relatively *open*. The disciplining was focused, as a direct measure, on the individual, and could thereby be clearly recognised by him or her, and by others in the environment. It was one of the marks of social democracy that its disciplining not only is societal, but - precisely on the basis of the specific type of societal understanding which underlies it - that it is also *hidden*. The new control out there in society is either completely outside the individual's range of vision, or at least quite a bit less visible than the control forms of pure individual liberalism" (1983: 139).

This approach does have its advantages. It can be argued, with some merit, that community service orders may constitute a heightening of intervention and an increase in the "total criminal justice system" (*ibid*: 134) in that they can be imposed in place of other non-custodial sanctions. Moreover, it can also be argued that community service does penetrate more deeply into the informal networks of society in that many of the organised work projects are carried out in the community and involve association with volunteers and ordinary citizens.

But are these phenomena, as Bottoms inquires, consistent with and an extension of Foucault's disciplinary ideology (1983: 179)? Consider the following. Prior to the emergence of the disciplinary nature of total institutions, Foucault suggested, in relation to penal labour, that classical reformers had "always proposed public work as one of the best possible penalties" (1991b: 109; Bottoms 1983: 179-180):

"Public works meant two things: the collective interest in the punishment of the condemned man and the visible, verifiable character of the punishment. Thus the convict pays twice; by the labour he provides and by the signs he produces. At the heart of society, on the public squares or highways, the convict is a focus of profit and signification. Visibly, he is serving everyone; but, at the same time, he lets slip into the minds of all the crime-punishment sign: a secondary, purely moral, but much more real utility" (Foucault 1991b: 109).

But, according to Foucault, under the carceral project:

"Work is neither an addition nor a correction to the regime of detention: whether it is a question of forced labour, seclusion or imprisonment, it is conceived, by the legislator himself, as necessarily accompanying it. But the necessity involved is precisely not the necessity of which the eighteenth-century reformers spoke, when they wished to make imprisonment either an example for the public or a useful reparation for society. In the carcarial regime, the link between work and punishment is of another type" (*ibid*: 240).

So what purpose does work serve under the carceral regime?

"It is intrinsically useful, not as an activity of production but by virtue of the effect it has on the human mechanism. It is a principle of order and regularity; through the demands it imposes, it conveys, imperceptibly, the forms of a rigorous power; it bends bodies to regular movements, it excludes agitation and distraction, it imposes a hierarchy and a surveillance that are all the more accepted, and which will be inscribed all the more deeply in the behaviour of the convicts, in that they form part of its logic ... Penal labour must be seen as the very machinery that transforms the violent, agitated, unreflective convict into a part that plays its role with perfect regularity. The prison is not a workshop; it is, it must be of itself, a machine whose convict-workers are both the cogs and the products. ... If, in the final analysis, the work of the prison has an economic effect, it is by producing individuals mechanised according to the general norms of an industrial society ... For a machine-society, purely mechanical means of reform are required ... (in England the treadmill and the pump provided a disciplinary mechanisation of the inmates, with no end product)" (*ibid*: 242; Bottoms 1983: 179).

With this in mind, then, is it logical to assume that the nature of work under community service is simply an extension of the carceral project in that it too acts as a "machine" and a "disciplinary mechanisation" without any corrective aspirations? In my view, and as we shall see more clearly in the next section, the nature of work on a community service order is of a constructive non-punitive type designed to instil in offenders a sense of social responsibility and the possibility of a changed outlook on their part. The sanction, from this perspective, cannot simply be viewed as disciplinary in the Foucauldian sense.

Furthermore, critical criminologists adopt a very negative logic in respect of the ideology of community and its net-widening implications. Of course, very often they are correct in identifying that the rhetoric of benevolence and humanitarianism minimises the correlation that exists, in many instances, between community corrections and penal expansion. Nonetheless, there has been a tendency in such literature to over-indulge in nihilism and impossibilism. Critical criminologists deny, for the most part, the importance of "human agency", "progressive accomplishments" and ideological values (such as the ideology of community which was deeply influential even if it smacked of benevolent sounding rhetoric and was ahistorical in representation) (McMahon 1992: 45).[27] For

---

27. As McMahon noted: "Sophisticated conceptual means have been developed for identifying resilient, changing and expanding mechanisms of penal power: the themes of wider, stronger, and different nets, as well as that of the dispersal of discipline, are important examples of this. But the conceptual ability to recognise resistance to such trends and movements

example, and as shall become more evident in chapter 6, a study concluded in 1975 on community service orders which noted that it was utilised by sentencers in about half of the cases as an alternative to other non-custodial dispositions is often seized upon by critical criminologists to support the "dispersal of discipline" thesis. Yet such an argument minimises the apparent success of the sanction in the other 50 per cent of cases. In other words, critical criminologists seek to deny *all kinds* of progress rather than simply *teleologically oriented* progress; as I have stated previously, progress of one kind or another is always possible provided that it does not manifest itself in some form of foundationalism. As such, whilst the supporters of the "dispersal of discipline" thesis can recognise the *mote* in the progressivist's eye, they have become blind to the *beam* of nihilism and pessimism in their own.

Finally, and perhaps most importantly, both Scull and Cohen's arguments fail to appreciate the new hegemonic penal project that manifested itself in the late 1800s and early 1900s and resulted, as discussed in chapter two, in the movement from a "calibrated, hierarchical structure" to an "extended grid of non-equivalent and diverse dispositions" founded upon more scientific, factual, observative and inductive strategies towards offending. For example, by highlighting the imperviousness of the prison to all assaults as support for his belief that the "dispersal of discipline"

---

towards the realisation of progressive values has been sorely lacking. A more open perspective on power, and one that acknowledges the potential for it to be exercised in admirable, as well as in ominous ways, might help to transcend this partial perspective" (1992: 225).

thesis is an extension of original Foucauldian transformations, Cohen disregards the argument that both the nature of these assaults and the authorities' response to them changed dramatically in the late 1800s. In this period, when the prison system was distributed in homogenous circuits, a new assault emerged which no longer demanded a rationalisation of disciplinary techniques, but rather called into doubt the very use of homogenous disciplinary techniques themselves. The result was not simply a continuum of the disciplinary prison apparatus that emerged according to Foucault in the early 1800s. Rather the focus came to bear more on the need for new, extended and more specified measures capable of operating within a more welfarist mode of penalty.

Of course throughout the twentieth century new technologies of surveillance and new custodial and non-custodial sanctions have emerged. But they do not, in my view, constitute a major realignment. Rather they are, by and large, consistent with the transformations of the late nineteenth and early twentieth centuries, and it is, accordingly, within the contours of this penal complex that the operation of community service can be understood. This is not to deny the existence of disciplinary mechanisms within this modern penal complex. One can refer, for example, to Richard Ireland's article, titled *The Felon and the Angel Copier: Criminal Identity and the Promise of Photography in Victorian England*, for perhaps one of the best examples of the extension of disciplinary mechanisms into the modern penal system. He describes how photography emerged in the mid to late 1800s as a response to the difficulties that the identity of criminals posed to the authorities. In these years - and as a result of the demise of transportation, the challenge presented by "urban anonymity" and "geographical migration", the utilitarian drive towards uniformity and proportionality of punishment, and the expansion of opportunities for mobility through improvements both in roads and railways (Ireland 1999: 7-12) - the photographic art found favour as an aid to the maintenance of criminal justice order: it was cheaper and more humane than branding and could be utilised to "remind the offender of a difference in power - the cultural sophistication of those who had technology over those, increasingly regarded as the century wore on as for the most part degenerate rather than frightening, who did not" *(ibid:* 26). The disciplining potential of photographic art in defining criminals has now expanded into more sophisticated techniques that have "gradually become closer, more physically invasive" (ie, fingerprinting and DNA testing) *(ibid:* 32); it has also expanded to include surveillance mechanisms (ie, video cameras, tracking and bugging devices, satellite monitoring and computer techniques in intelligence) which provide a disciplinary potential not only in identifying criminals but also in identifying *potential criminality and criminality itself.* In this sense, modern penalty undoubtedly embodies disciplinary characteristics.

Yet it is my contention that a Foucauldian analysis of disciplinary society as it emerged in the late eighteenth and early nineteenth centuries provides only a limited basis upon which to analyse the introduction of community service orders. For example, such an analysis fails to account for cultural (the emergence of leisure as a right), social (notions of participation that emerged in the late 1950s and 1960s) and legal (the emergence of human rights, particularly in respect of forced labour) phenomena which place limitations on the extension of, and full exposure to, disciplinary practices. This viewpoint is better encapsulated, and expanded upon, by Garland:

"Foucault's reluctance to acknowledge the role of any values other than power and control in the development of punishment leads him to neglect the political and ideological forces which put up a principled opposition to the introduction and extension of disciplinary practices. Disciplinary strategies have only ever been partly implemented in most modern penal systems and, in practice, they exist within what is still a predominantly legalistic, judicial framework. These limits of implementation - which make disciplinary practice far less extensive than Foucault implies - are largely the result of a sustained opposition on the part of the liberal political establishment, and particularly by the legal profession and the judiciary. And this resistance stems, at least in part, from a refusal to accept the violations of legal and liberal principles which a full-scale disciplinary program would entail. These principles - of due process, the rule of law, the rights of the individual, equality of treatment, and so on - have formed a historical counterpoint to the demands of power, and have been used to oppose 'discipline' not just by its working-class targets, but also by important sections of the dominant class" (Garland

1990: 167).

To conclude, then, the ideology of community has become increasingly apparent since the Second World War. Academics such as Scull (who believed that the emergence of community programmes represented a complete apostatise with past penalty) and Cohen and Mathiesen (adopting the extension of Foucauldian discipline hypothesis) all attempt to identify the locus of "community corrections" in the penal domain. From my own perspective, whilst recognising, in some instances, the extension of discipline hypothesis, I believe that such disciplining mechanisms must be incorporated into a broader framework of penalty. It is, in my view, within the extended grid of "non-equivalent and diverse dispositions" that first manifested themselves in the late 1800s, as described in chapter two, that the ideology of community, in general, and community service, in particular, can be understood. Thus, rather than being considered as a major realignment, or simply an extension of discipline, the ideology of community should be understood as occurring within the contours of the modern penal complex, originating as it did at the end of the last century. In saying this, I do not mean to imply that penalty is not subject to new techniques (ie, surveillance), new ideologies (ie, community), new policies (ie, the heightening of security, control and surveillance in the 1960s following the Mountbatten Report) and shifting penal aspirations (ie, the decline of rehabilitation in the late 1960s and early 1970s); rather what is being suggested is that these changing techniques, ideologies, policies and aspirations cannot be understood in terms of the major transformation that occurred in the late 1700s and early 1800s (the Foucauldian shift). Accordingly, they should instead be understood in terms of the last radical transformation, occurring as it did in the late 1800s and early 1900s (this may be referred to as the Garlandian shift, albeit that the transformation manifested itself before 1895 and was not complete by 1914).

Yet polemical debate of this nature is anathema to academics such as Vass and Pease given that they view the entire penal process as a linearity. Even if they attempt to enter such discourse - Vass, in particular, does attempt to furnish us with his grasp of penal complexities by citing Foucault in his historical analysis of community service (Vass 1992: 13; Vass 1984: 21) - by adopting a Foucauldian or Garlandian perspective, they are plainly acting in a discordant manner with regard to their assumptions and beliefs concerning community service and its genealogy: both Foucault and Garland reacted against progressivist, presentist views of history and attempted to construct the modern penal complex (albeit that both approaches differ as to the time and nature of the shift between "old" and "new" penalty) within which modern sanctions could and indeed should be understood. In essence, what I am suggesting is that Whiggish and revisionist interpretations of penal history are mutually exclusive in terms of approach; if one adopts the former interpretation, then it would be chimerical to argue, at the same time, that the emergence of community as a panacea for crime control represents a complete apostatise with the past (Scull), an extension of the

Foucault's disciplining mechanism (Cohen and Mathiesen), or a component of modern penalty as constructed in the late 1800s and early 1900s (Garland), given that the Whiggish interpretation does not account for radical transformations in its progressivist, presentist historiography. As such, Vass cannot have his cake and eat it; if he wishes to portray the introduction of community service as only in detail a novel disposal, given its affinity with penal work sanctions throughout history, then, in the interests of consistency and intelligibility, he should stay clear of revisionist discourse and its attempts to locate phenomena within the penal complex.

Transformations in the Use of Penal Labour

A variety of justifications for the role of penal labour have been expounded throughout the ages. To some, it was primarily based on the premise that economic benefit could be derived from its utilisation. To others, it was perceived as edifying in as much as it could be used to inculcate a work ethic. To yet others, it was exclusively a deterrent to be made as deliberately irksome as was humanely possible. Alternative explanations included that it was merely a means of ensuring that offenders were kept "hard at it" so as to prevent boredom and mischief; that it could be employed to extract uniform and proportionate amounts of punishment; that it provided a contribution to the community; or, that it was reformative in that offenders gained from the social value inherent in useful work.

Finally, in some instances, labour has been regarded as valuable in that it enabled offenders to gain vocational training in skilled trades which would equip them with the wherewithal to earn a livelihood on release. These aforementioned justifications for penal labour did not, however, exist in isolation. Criminal justice practice, as we shall see, often embodied an amalgam of labour objectives with different degrees of emphasis placed on each one at different transitional points in time. The purpose of the ensuing passage is to describe the transformations that have materialised in respect of penal labour with a view to enabling a greater appreciation of the framework within which community service manifested itself.

In determining these transformations, attention will be given to the revisionist historiographies which have attempted to support their respective claims by reference to the changing nature of penal labour. Foucault, for example, in describing the emergence of the "carceral archipelago" in the late 1700s and 1800s, suggests that in this period penal labour began to be utilised as "a power relation, an empty economic form, a schema of individual submission and of adjustment to a production apparatus" (1991b: 243). Marxist interpretations - such as those espoused by Rusche and Kirchheimer, and Melossi and Pavarini - simply view penal labour as being dictated by the mode of production: "every system of production tends to discover punishments which corresponds to its productive relationships" (Rusche and Kirchheimer 1968: 5). Garland proposes, in keeping with his views on the modern penal complex, that in the period between 1895 and 1914 prison labour "changed its effect from that of a punitive imposition to that of a basic element of an educational and training regime" (1985: 30).

With these revisionist historiographies in mind, then, this section will provide a brief description of various penal work practices that existed in the sixteenth, seventeenth and eighteenth centuries in order to highlight the deficiencies in Vass and Pease's approach to criminal justice history, particularly their inability to account for radical transformations that have manifested themselves in respect of penal work practices. However, it will also be demonstrated that revisionist accounts of transformations in penal labour, particularly Foucauldian and Marxist accounts, are also too reductionist and linear in approach. It will be suggested that the utilisation of any form of penal labour by the authorities at any given moment in penal history is dictated by a variety of determinants. These can include: what is possible from a legal perspective (we have already seen how treaties on forced labour to some extent impacted upon the shaping of community service); what is possible from technological and architectural perspectives (associative work practices in the early twentieth century, for example, were difficult to organise given that many of the prisons had been built in the nineteenth century with isolation very much in mind); the ideological commitments of the penal authorities (compare, for example, the militaristic Du Cane era with the professionalised Home Office era that emerged in the late nineteenth century); the enthusiasm and ability of penal staff to implement policy change (although penal labour was no longer to be purely punitive in design after 1895, it was still carried out for the next 30 years with deterrence very much in mind), and; what society is amenable to accepting in respect of penal labour at any point in time. All of these factors, it will be argued, must be incorporated into any discursive analysis of transformations in penal labour. This section, then, will commence with a brief description of various penal work practices in houses of correction, workhouses, transportation and the hulks.

The principal aim of the house of correction was to habituate the idle to a less dissipated way of living by subjecting them to compulsory labour. In this way, they could be infused with the rudimentary habits of work - habits which were perceived by the authorities as being paramount for the preservation of social order.[28] To provide sufficient labour, the creators of Bridewell foresaw the necessity to develop strong links with the economic life of the surrounding districts. Indeed the petition to Edward VI requesting the use of Bridewell Palace promised that caps would be made ("at as low a price or lower than French caps are") especially by the maimed who still had use of their hands. It would also engage in the manufacture of ticking for featherbeds, wool carding, wire drawing, silk winding, and other "profitable devices". Rougher tasks such as the making of nails and other iron work were to be

---

28. As Foucault noted: "For the first time, purely negative measures of exclusion were replaced by a measure of confinement; the unemployed person was no longer driven away or punished; he was taken in charge, at the expense of the nation but at the cost of his individual liberty. Between him and society, an implicit system of obligation was established: he had the right to be fed, but he must accept the physical and moral constraint of confinement" (1991b: 130).

undertaken by "the stubborn and fouler sort" of inmate (Tawney and Power 1924: 307). Marxist accounts of the emergence of the houses of correction have portrayed them "as part of the development of capitalism" and a "valuable part of the economy as a whole" (Rusche and Kirchheimer 1968: 50; Melossi and Pavarini 1980: 29). For them, the fundamental premise upon which the entire enterprise was based was capitalism and commercial exploitation. Yet such accounts fail to appreciate that in addition to simply having commercial motivations, the houses of correction also emerged to provide for the disadvantaged in seeking employment by *creating* work opportunities as opposed to simply *supplying* the existing demand for labour, and to provide educative work experience so as to accustom the idle poor to habits of work (Innes 1987: 52). Moreover, Marxist interpretations fail to appreciate that in terms of capitalistic aspirations, houses of correction proved to be dismal failures. The labour of inmates subscribed only partially to the upkeep of the first bridewell, the bulk of the income being drawn from endowments, regular levies imposed by the city and gifts of money and stock (McConville 1981: 37; Leonard 1900: 65-66).[29] Yet even such assistance never proved sufficient. Furthermore, the government was tentative and unwilling to donate the necessary funds required to put the unemployed population to work. Howard noted:

---

29.   See also Cornish who suggests that the remunerative aspect of productive work was of particular interest to the Justices whose "concern was less for the souls of the prisoners than for the state of rateable pockets" (Cornish 1978: 28).

"[that] there are few bridewells in which any work is done, or can be done. The prisoners have neither tools, nor materials of any kind, but spend their time in sloth, profaneness and debauchery to a degree which in some of the Houses that I have seen is extremely shocking" (1977: 8).

This is also supported by Innes:

"It is unlikely that most bridewells were hives of industry. Certainly, nothing very adventurous and impressive could be expected in a manufacturing way when small numbers of prisoners of very different ages and conditions, past experience, and states of health were committed for brief periods under the not very zealous care of a bridewell master, who must often have had other things on his mind. ... There may well have been bridewells in which no work was carried on. But it seems realistic to assume that in many there was *some* work performed, if perhaps irregularly, with uneven skill, and yielding little profits" (1987: 76).

The same criticism was directed at workhouses in the 1700s:

"As economical cures for poverty, workhouses proved duds. One problem was that the inmates were - by definition - the nation's most unpromising work-force: a rubbish tip including the very young and aged, the chronic sick and infirm, rogues, vagrants, and village simpletons. Many were unemployed and on the parish because of trade slumps: the hope that self-financing workhouses could somehow buck the economic trend was moonshine. In any case workhouses readily became nests of jobbery, run by contractors who pocketed allowances and provisioned them in their private capacity as tradesmen" (Porter 1982: 147-148; Rule 1992: 128; Poynter 1969: 15).

Marxist interpretations also view transportation "as a method of punishment made necessary by ... colonial expansion" (Rusche and Kirchheimer 1968: 58). Undoubtedly they had a point. Convicts could be employed in a vast array of salient and indispensable undertakings which were deemed ineluctable with regard to the development of the colonies and which would have proved very expensive on the mother country in the absence of a labour force of this kind. The economic interest in transportation was further borne out by selection procedures which governed the type of offenders regarded as appropriate for embarkation to Australia. It was mostly the healthy who were singled out and this is evidenced by the low mortality rates (far lower than emigrant voyages) on board the convict ships. In fact the surgeon inspectors who examined offenders on the hulks were pertinacious in their assignment of espousing only the able-bodied since part of their commission was paid on the basis of the number of live convicts who reached the colonies. Nicholas and Shergold allude to the unique age distribution of the convicts: over 80 per cent were aged 16 to 35 years, with 56 per cent aged 16 to 25 years. What was circumvented by the authorities, according to their findings, was the influx of ineffective labourers; less than 9 per cent were under 15 or over 39 years of age (Nicholas and Shergold 1988: 47-51).[30] In addition to being selected on the basis of their age, many convicts were also transported because of their specific work skills. Mechanics, the term given to skilled labourers, were composed of workers with all forms of diverse skills and specialisations and were well suited to the development of a new colony. The building skills, in particular, which convicts brought with them were regarded as most valuable. This separated them from other felons as they were able to bargain with employers and exercise job authority. So great was the divide in the 1830s that a Select Committee saw fit to state:

"As a mechanic can scarcely be compelled by punishment to exert his skill, it is in the interest of the master to conciliate his convict mechanic in order to induce him to work well; in too many cases this is effected by granting to the skilled convict various indulgences; by paying his wages; by allotting to him task work; and by permitting him, after the performance of the task, to work on his own account; and, lastly, by conniving at, or overlooking disorderly conduct; for the most skilled mechanics are

---

30. One should note, however, that most nineteenth century crime was committed by young adults and that this will be reflected in the percentages referred to. Yet even with this in mind, the figures do tend to illustrate the bias for selecting offenders within the 16 to 35 years category. With regard to the mortality rates on board ships, see Robson who points out that between 1782 and 1852 only 1.8 per cent of convicts were lost on the voyage (1965: 5).

generally the worst behaved and most drunken" (Molesworth Committee Report 1838: XXII, vi).[31]

Besides skilled labour, there was a commensurate demand for labourers who could engage in menial and burdensome toil. Because the colonies were still at an embryonic stage, many tasks, including digging, sawing, clearing and carrying were all performed by the offenders. Yet transportation cannot simply be understood in terms of work and the economic advantage to be derived therefrom. Marxists fail to appreciate that it was also devised, in part, as a response to the perceived need of the authorities to rid Britain of its dangerous classes: as we have already noted this can be understood in terms of the unsystematical and ineffectual nature of methods of identification, detection and policing employed in the seventeenth and eighteenth centuries in England and Wales. As Hughes has noted:

"The authorities hoped that it would swallow a whole class - the 'criminal class', whose existence was one of the prime sociological beliefs of late Georgian and Victorian England. Australia was settled to defend English property, not from the frog-eating invader across the Channel but from the marauder within. English lawmakers wished not only to get rid of the 'criminal class', but if possible to forget about it" (1987: 1).

---

31. For an account of the extent of skilled workers in Australia, see Mudie who suggests that: "There is no species, either of labour or enterprise, which there are not to be found persons in the colony capable of undertaking" (1965: 187).

The hulks were recognised as propitious, partly because they relieved the pressure on the gaols, but also because of the perceived value of the labour of their convicts. This latter reason was even more evident as regards the hulk establishments in Bermuda and Gibraltar. In both places an adequate supply of local labour was unavailable, whilst the ventures undertaken were regarded as being of high military, naval and political concern. Such was the significance placed on these considerations that the overseas hulks outlasted the home establishments by several years (McConville 1981: 201-202).[32] The 1847 Report on the General Treatment of Convicts in the hulks at Woolwich conceded that the value of convict labour was extremely beneficial and generally underrated. It suggested that:

"the utility of having a body of men who may be ready upon any sudden public emergency to supply steamers with coal, or to assist in extinguishing fires, has been fully shown in the evidence - the convicts have been called upon and employed for many hours in assisting to extinguish a fire in a large quantity of coal, which had ignited from spontaneous combustion; and also in coaling one of Her Majesty's war steamers, loading with provisions for Ireland" (1847: XVIII, xix).

---

32. Furthermore, the economic expense of preparing an old ship so as to enable it to perform the functions of a prison bore no relationship to the high cost of erecting a penitentiary or house of correction. In addition, the fact that the hulks were removable, allowed the authorities to transfer them to wherever they may have been of benefit to the public with regard to the employment of convicts (Third Report from the Committee on the Laws relating to Penitentiary Houses 1812: II, 145).

Similarly, Sir Herbert Mackworth, having personally visited the hulks, observed many men employed using carts and wheelbarrows to move soil, some working on the bank of a river to make a wharf, and that "upon the whole he thought their work of great use to the warren, and of real public service" (Journals of the House of Commons 1778-1780: 37, 309). But it is important to note that the nature of the work was often arduous, that is to say, it was of an onerous and oppressive kind demanding endurance and stamina, rather than the application of any self-gratifying skills (Mayhew and Binny 1862: 202).[33] Thus whilst the work was not of a wholly futile variety, it afforded scant opportunities for offenders to develop or hone their skills. In this way, it displayed an affinity with the work of unskilled manual labourers in the penal colonies. Similarly convicts completed tasks in the knowledge that failure to do so would result in a whipping or some other equivalent form of punishment (1776: 19 Geo. III, c. 43). But one of the central deficiencies of the hulks pertaining to the utility of labour did not emanate from the ineptness of the convicts but rather from the difficulty in employing all the offenders at the same time. Those who were called upon to toil were selected arbitrarily while the remainder waited on board. Although they were meant to be kept busy by scrubbing the decks and gangways, they were frequently left to their own devices (Branch-Johnson 1957: 13).

---

33. See also Bentham who suggested that the hulks were designed for the worst type of offenders and that the labour was regarded of being of a kind which was more irksome than the labour in the houses of correction (1962: IV, 15).

What then can be said about penal labour from this brief review up to the early nineteenth century? Undoubtedly, one can propose that the economic benefit to be derived from its utilisation was always viewed as advantageous and punitive, non-productive labour does not appear to have been a serious component of the criminal justice system. Labour was also employed as a means of acclimatising paupers and convicts to less dissolute ways of living. Specific policies, however, such as the training of offenders in particular work skills and the utilisation of labour from which social value (rather than habits of labour) could be obtained were not as of yet primary concerns of the system. Finally, labour was, for the most part, public and associative in nature. Yet criminal justice in the sixteenth, seventeenth and eighteenth centuries was also characterised, as we have already seen, by a lack of homogeneity of practice. Such a phenomenon also evidenced itself in respect of penal labour and it is not surprising given the unpromising nature of the workforce, the practice of hiring out offenders to private settlers or entrepreneurs, the lack of financial resources, and the lack of government interest. All of this, however, was about to change. By the late 1700s a reformulation and reorganisation of punishment techniques began to manifest itself. As we have already seen, a more rationalised, uniform and proportionate system of punishment was beginning to be advocated in these years. This new mode of punishment - *La Science Penitentiare* - was to be directed at the prison (this focus on prisons grew ever greater in intensity after the decline of transportation), at the offender's mind and soul, and at enclosure, classification, regulation, surveillance and separation. To accommodate such a transformation, a new accentuation was placed on architecture, on uniformity, on spiritual vivification, and on labour. It is to the attempts to reduce the act of labour to a rationalised process of movements - which may be termed, in Foucauldian terms, the "function of *dressage*" (Foucault 1980: 161) - and to equalise its distribution throughout the penal system that must now become the focus of our attention.

To begin with, we can allude to individuals such as Howard, Blackstone and Eden who did much in the late eighteenth century to champion the right of imprisonment to be considered as an appropriate alternative to execution or penal transportation. Their doctrine gained legislative approbation in the 1779 Penitentiary Act which provided for the construction of two penitentiaries where prisoners could be confined in solitary cells. The Act required the governors of both penitentiaries to keep each offender "so far as may be consistent with his or her sex, age, health and ability, to labour of the hardest and most servile kind, in which drudgery is chiefly required, and where the work is little liable to be spoiled by ignorance, neglect or obstinacy, and where the tools are not easily stolen or embezzled, such as treading in a wheel, or drawing in a capstern, for turning a mill or other machine or engine, sawing stone, polishing marble, beating hemp, rasping logwood, chopping rags, making cordage, or any other hard and laborious service; and those of less health and ability, regard being also had to sex and age, in picking oakum, weaving sacks, spinning yarn, knitting nets, or any other less laborious employment" (19 Geo III: c 74). The venture was a failure, however, due mainly to the unwillingness of the government to consign itself to such a massive capital outlay. Nonetheless following the recommendations of the Holford Committee, an Act was introduced which enabled the establishment of Millbank penitentiary in Middlesex in 1816 (56 Geo III: c. 63). This Committee, greatly impressed by the work of Sir George Paul in Gloucester and by Rev. John Becher at Southwell, was satisfied that "many offenders may be reclaimed by a system of penitentiary imprisonment, not confined to the safe custody of the person, but extending to the reformation and improvement of the mind, *and operating by seclusion, employment and religious instruction*" (Holford Committee Report 1810-11: III, 4). Interestingly, one of the grounds upon which it rejected Bentham's plan was that pecuniary gain was made the "most prominent object of attention" under his regime, and, accordingly, "the experiment of reformation could not fairly be tried" (*ibid*: 14). It recommended, instead, both the Gloucester method of labour - "where it was considered an occupation of the mind, without which, solitude, even in the limited degree imposed by the arrangements of that prison, could be injurious, and in which an individual separated from others will gladly seek relief from the pressure of reflection" - and the Southwell method - where prisoners were offered a share of the profits from their work and thereby the opportunity to learn habits of industry and self-restraint which they would be likely to practice on their return to society - could both be advantageously applied at successive stages in the course of the same imprisonment (*ibid*: 14). In a Report from the Select Committee on the State of the

Penitentiary at Millbank in 1823, it was stressed that the "system of labour should be as productive and useful as possible" in order to combat the possibility of discharging convicts from the institution "without any means of gaining their subsistence"(1823: V, 5).

Further evidence of this movement towards rationalisation in respect of prison labour is provided by the 1823 Gaols Act. In order to promote uniformity, and carry into effect a proper system of discipline so as to secure the reformation of offenders in such institutions, section 10 outlined a series of rules and regulations, the fifth of which provided for the provision of hard labour (4 Geo. IV: c. 64). In addition, section 16 enabled the appointment of Justices to visit and inspect each prison at least three times a year and to examine, *inter alia*, the proper organisation of labour. This was further supported by the 1835 Prison Act - following the recommendations of a Select Committee of the House of Lords on the State of the Prisons (1835: XI, iv) - which appointed a prison inspectorate to ensure, *inter alia*, a more homogenised system of penal labour in the prisons throughout England and Wales (5 and 6 Gul IV: c. 38). Similarly workhouses began to be subjected to a greater degree of rationalisation. In respect of workhouse labour, the 1834 Poor Law Report noted:

"[I]n by far the greatest number of cases, it is a large almshouse, in which the young are trained in idleness, ignorance and vice; the able-bodied maintained in sluggish indolence; the aged and more respectable exposed to all the misery that is incident to dwelling in such a society, without government or classification" (1905: 53-54; Bruce 1972: 54).

In respect of parish employment (outdoor relief), the report suggested that superintendence was rarely given, little or no work was carried out and that the associative nature of work practices were more likely to "degrade the good, not elevate the bad" (*ibid*: 36). Not surprisingly, it called for the termination of all outdoor relief. As regards workhouse institutions, the report recommended the appointment of a central board to control the administration of the poor laws, to regulate, *inter alia*, the labour to be exacted from inmates, and to ensure that regulations governing the management of such institutions were, as far as practicable, uniform throughout the country (*ibid*: 297). The Commission went on to suggest:

"[E]mployment of some kind can, indeed, be always provided, but it appears to us it ought to be useful employment ... The association of the utility of labour to both parties, the employer as well as the employed, is one which we consider it most important to preserve and strengthen; and we deem everything mischievous which gives it a repulsive aspect" (*ibid*: 450-451; Crowther 1981: 198).

Finally, the rationalisation of acts of penal labour can also be discerned from the marks system advocated by Maconchie (and adopted, in part, by Sir Walter Crofton in the Irish convict system)[34] which replaced a time sentence with a labour sentence and embodied a disciplinary stage, a social stage, and an individual stage; the progressive stage system introduced in Australia in 1842 involving two years public work gang service, and three stages in private paid service through which a convict had to pass before obtaining a ticket-of-leave; and, penal servitude, introduced in 1853, and involving, first, hard labour and separate confinement, followed by associated but silent labour composed of four stages at a public works prison.

Care should be taken, however, in discussing this movement towards a more rationalised criminal justice system. As we have already witnessed in the last chapter, rationalisation was difficult to attain given the heavy financial burden placed on local authorities and the dominant political philosophy of the period in question. Impediments to the realisation of a more homogenous system of punishment also manifested themselves in respect of penal labour. The Select Committee on Prison Discipline in 1850 noted, for example, in a reply to comments by the Duke of Richmond regarding the "approximation towards a uniform system":

"Are you aware that in the county of Middlesex, at the house of correction, the sentence of hard labour is carried out by the prisoners stepping upon the treadmill 7,680 feet of ascent per day? ... Is your Grace aware that in Berkshire, the county immediately adjoining Middlesex,

---

34. See Hinde (1977a: 115-147; 1977b: 295-337).

the only way approximating to hard labour is, that, each alternate day, 10 prisoners work at a pump, which is stated by the magistrate and the chaplain to require the power of only two. Did your Grace ever hear of any two systems more diverse than these two?" (1850: XVII, 607).

And this leads us on to our next obstruction to the rationalisation of penal labour techniques - the debate concerning productive or punitive labour. Consider the following in respect of crank labour. The Director of Government Prisons, Dan O'Brien, suggested, before the 1850 Select Committee on Prison Discipline, that crank labour "was applicable to every description of prisoner, provided it was judiciously applied" (*ibid:* 114). He was supported in this contention by Rev. William Fox at Leicester gaol who argued that "it is manifested to me that the prisoners feel it a very heavy punishment, and the immense reduction that has taken place in the number of committals to prison also proves that it has a deterring effect" (*ibid:* 282). On the other hand, J. G. Perry, an Inspector of Prisons, suggested:

"I think there is a very great difference between employing the cranks merely for the purpose of inflicting painful labour, and employing them for producing some useful result ... I think that the prisoner feels himself more degraded by being put to labour that is totally unproductive, and that it is more irritating to the mind, and more calculated to arm all the bad passions of the prisoner against the authorities, than if he felt he was doing some good by his labour" (*ibid*: 73).

He was supported by William Merry, Chairman of the Visiting Justices of Berkshire, who suggested that he would be very sorry to see the use of cranks in prisons:

"I think you are sure to be defeated in your object of reformation of the prisoner if you produce nothing but irritation in his mind. I have seen the machine, and my principal objection to it is, that the man knows at the time he is turning it that it is simply for punishment" (*ibid*: 222).

Such disparity was also noted by the Carnarvon Committee who pointed out that in some prisons such as those at Warwick, Rutland, Spilsbury and Canterbury, the treadwheel was the predominant and, on occasion, only provision for labour; in other prisons, the cellular crank formed the principal implement of punishment, and finally, in some cases, industrial occupation prevailed (1863: IX, iii-iv).

Given this dissociation at a local level, the general cynicism that was emerging regarding reformative practices, the London garrotting panic, and the two articles that appeared in *The Times* on the 16 and 26 December, 1862, which condemned the inefficient and disparate nature of hard labour in prisons (McConville 1995: 48-49), it is not surprising that the Carnarvon Committee favoured a heightening of the pains of imprisonment and the imposition of a more uniform and austere regime across the penal domain. The first requirement, it believed, in moving towards such a system would be to bestow upon the term "hard labour" an authoritative definition which could be embodied in an Act of Parliament. This was duly achieved. The 1865 Prison Act differentiated first-class hard labour, defined in terms of "work at the treadwheel, shot drill, crank, capstan, stone-breaking or such other like description of hard labour as may be appointed by the Justices in Sessions assembled, with the approval of the Secretary of State", and second-class hard labour which was defined "as such other descriptions of bodily labour as may be approved by the justices and was regarded as less punitive, fatiguing and irksome (28 and 29 Vict: c. 26). An example of this distinction may be seen from the use of prison labour in Carmarthen prison after 1865. First-class hard labour consisted of treadwheel labour and stone-breaking, and second-class hard labour was made up of mat and brush making, tailoring, sewing, clog making, painting and washing (Thirty-Eighth Report of the Inspectors of Prisons 1874: XXIX, 50-51). This commendation of first-class hard labour as an instrument of discipline and deterrence is evidenced in the following statement by the Carnarvon Committee:

"Productive labour, indeed, holds out to the local authorities the hope of some profit, and is somewhat less irksome to the prisoner: it is therefore frequently urged, that the crank and wheel, if used at all, should be confined to the pumping of water, or the grinding of corn, or some other remunerative work. The Committee cannot subscribe to this view. If the local authorities can make use of the crank or treadwheel for productive work, the Committee sees no objection to such an arrangement, but they think it essential that every prisoner sentenced to hard labour should be employed upon the crank or treadwheel for a minimum period, and that in no case should the regular enforcement of this system be relinquished or impaired for the sake of making the labour remunerative" (1863: IX, 134).

In rejecting evidence that the punitive use of labour both degraded and demoralised offenders, the Committee had, for the most part, endorsed the reduction of the act of penal labour to a serious of futile body movements which was, on the whole, to be employed within a calculated and systematic regime of austerity - I say, *on the whole*, because even after 1865 complete homogeneity had not, as we have already seen, been achieved.

But how have revisionists described this transformation? Foucault, as we have already witnessed, argued that penal labour's usefulness under such a regime was derived not from its use as an activity of production, but from its use as a means of order and regularity. Penal labour was now, in effect, a power relation that bended bodies to regular movements and made them submit to a production apparatus. Marxists, such as Melossi and Pavarini, argue that as a result of an extraordinary increase in the supply of labour, penal labour was rendered obsolete. Given the demise of its economic role, penal labour inherited punitive and disciplinary characteristics:

"[T]he movement in favour of reform was bound to clash increasingly with a reaction in favour of repression which arose out of the socio-economic situation created by the industrial revolution. The fear of Jacobinism, the extreme growth of pauperism and criminality accompanying an immense industrial reserve army and an extremely low standard of living for the proletariat, the appearance of forms of crime which had an unmistakable class content even if they were not yet *political*, made the demands for a return to the good old days of terror and harsh methods grow ever more numerous ... Work in the system of isolation in cells retains only the repetitive, fatiguing, monotonous aspects of work outside. In brief it is still punitive but completely useless. The treadwheel or crank were simple structures which could be installed in a cell and whose real purpose, despite the appearance of being instruments of labour, was torment and torture. In the period 1840-1865 the principle of terror and with it those of cellular isolation and useless work triumphed in England" (Melossi and Pavarini 1980: 29; Rusche and Kirchheimer 1968: 112).

Yet in respect of penal labour transformations, revisionists, such as Foucault, Melossi and Pavarini, again appear to have over-idealised what is a complex and tortuous history. No attempt is made, for example, to highlight resistance to the imposition of a more homogenised, deterrent regime. And there is ample evidence to suggest resistance at a number of different levels. To begin with, one may allude to the prisoners themselves who counteracted the system on many occasions through working as slowly as possible, through stealing others' work and through breaking the strict rules of silence whilst labouring (Priestley 1985: 139-140). Secondly, one may refer to the lack of requisite funds to implement the necessary changes, and the number of prison statutes, such as in 1815, 1823, 1835 and indeed 1865, which all engaged, to some extent, in a balancing act between the desire, on the one hand, to rationalise, and the need, on the other hand, to refrain from completely usurping the power of the local authorities. It resulted, as we have already noted elsewhere, in a great want of uniformity within the criminal justice system. This fact is further borne out by Lord Carnarvon who in October, 1868, in *The Times*, was still calling for a uniform and effective system of criminal justice:

"Henceforth we must provide for our criminal population within the geographical limits of the United Kingdom, by greater certainty of punishment, by a scale of sentences better proportioned to the nature of the offence, by a more effective police supervision than that already in force, by uniformity and completeness of penal discipline, by greater sternness in repressing habitual crime ..." (McConville 1995: 52).

Nor did attempts at the imposition of such a regime encounter widespread approval. Indeed Bentham had criticised the employment of punitive labour 84 years prior to the publication of the Carnarvon report, arguing instead that it should reform offenders and accustom them to habits of industry by teaching them that work was a pleasure (1962: IV, 12-13). Similarly Mayhew and Binney suggested:

"It needs no one to tell him (an offender) that the treadwheel work, and crank work, and shot-drill have nothing at all to do with the procuring of his food, and that really none of them are sufficiently valuable even to furnish the salt he consumes. If the Almighty ordered that labour should be a curse, at least he attached the eating of our bread to it. But in prison the sweat of our brow brings no food as its rewards; and, therefore, the labour naturally becomes intolerably irksome to the prisoner, so that his whole nature rebels at it; and when the period arrives for his liberation, he has not only learnt to expect his food to be supplied to him without labouring for it, but he has also learnt to look upon industry that he is bound to avoid as much as possible, so that he may taste the sweets of liberty" (1862: 302).

J. G. Perry, an Inspector of the Prisons, who gave evidence before the Carnarvon Committee, also suggested that unproductive hard labour was most undesirable and of a kind to awaken all the detrimental susceptibilities of offenders against the authorities, and therefore produced a deterioration of their moral characters (1863: IX, 61).[35] Nor

---

35. This is not to argue that such criticism amounted to any turn about in penal policy. As McConville noted, Carnarvon "treated his inquiry like a theatrical production: he wrote the script, designed the sets, chose the players and directed their delivery, and to carry the metaphor further, his was the only show in town" (McConville 1995: 104).

did such criticism cease after 1865. In 1874, for example, Henry Briscoe, an Inspector of Prisons for the Southern District, contended that as a result of the 1865 Prison Act with regard to punitive labour, the hands of the gaol authorities were tied to such an extent that they were precluded daily from employing the services of various tradesmen, tailors, shoemakers, and carpenters, who were required for the completion of tasks in prisons (Thirty Eight Report of the Inspectors of Prisons 1874: XXIX, vii). Even Du Cane, who imposed the Committee's recommendations with unflinching rigidity, noted that there was a limit to the time for which a prisoner could be subjected to strictly penal labour:

"If it is desirable to resort to it for its penal effect, it must not be continued for too long a period. To men of any intelligence, it is irritating, depressing, and debasing to the mental faculties; to those already of a low type of intelligence, it is too conformable to their state of mind, out of which it is most desirable that they should be raised" (Du Cane 1872: 33).

In this sense, both Marxist and Foucauldian accounts of historical transformations in penal labour are unbalanced and overschematic in their respective approaches. This is not to deny that their hypotheses are persuasive and contain many important elements of truth. Rather my argument merely attempts to demonstrate that they need to be qualified and refined so as to take proper account of historical actuality.

Moreover, it is possible to highlight further limitations in respect of Marxist arguments. It is my contention that such an approach is too exclusive in that its focus and appraisal is purely confined to an economic anatomisation, with little or no analysis from a political or ideological standpoint. It leads, in my view, to a mischievous interpretation of history in that it gathers material (often dramatic) which supports its cause, but overlooks that which creates tension or incongruity. Consider, for example, the following statement from the Carnarvon Committee:

"The Committee are of the opinion that it is desirable to establish without delay *a system approaching as nearly as may be practicable to an uniformity of labour, diet and treatment*; and, that whilst *industrial occupation* should in certain stages form part of prison discipline, the more *strictly penal element* of that discipline is the chief means of exercising a deterrent influence, and therefore ought not to be heightened, as it has been in some gaols, still less to be entirely withdrawn" (1863: IX, iv) (my italics).

This statement is composed of three central components: (a) rationalisation; (b) the productive use of penal labour which would embody, in many instances, reformative connotations (an issue completely disregarded by academics such as Melossi and Pavarini) and; (c) the unproductive use of penal labour embodying purely deterrent connotations. Of these, the essential key (although not the only key), in my view, to not only the period of the 1860s but the greater part of the nineteenth century is (a), rationalisation. What had changed, as is obvious from the above statement, was the movement from the rationalisation of *reformative practices* as the primary goal to the rationalisation of *deterrent practices*. In this sense, the adoption of deterrent penal apparatuses, such as the treadwheel and the crank, cannot simply be comprehended from the perspective of economic considerations and the belief that penal philosophy in respect of work is only determined by the supply and demand of the labour market. It is my contention that the choice of punitive instruments was governed, not in relation to their non-productivity, as Marxists would have us believe, but in relation to their forte in exacting an equalised quantum of toil from each individual offender: as the Carnarvon Committee suggested, and as has already been alluded to, *"if the local authorities can make use of the crank or treadwheel for productive work, the Committee sees no objection to such an arrangement"*. It is here that Marxists' so-called interrelation between deterrence, non-productivity and the labour market is inconsistent, because labour could be *productive* and yet a deterrent (regardless of the labour market), provided that it was inescapable, measured, uniform and designed to heighten the pains of imprisonment. In short, academics such as Melossi and Pavarini, have underestimated the desire for rationalisation and overestimated the potential of the labour market to affect change in the penal domain.

To return, then, to the main body of the text. By 1877 rationalisation was, for the most part, complete in respect of penal labour. An austere and uniform regime was now in place, embodying as it did deterrence as its primary objective. But almost as soon as uniformity had been achieved, it began to operate against its own universalist principles. In the late 1800s, as we have already seen, there was a growing belief that prison was a failure from a disciplinary perspective. There was also a growing belief that England and Wales were becoming less violent places. These beliefs, of course, were also aided by the newly emergent professional ethos in the Home Office. They were also augmented by the growing awareness of monopoly groups and cartels, the social problems created by industrialists, the advance of the professional ideal, the decline of England's hegemony in world trade, advances made in the natural sciences, the desire to protect the individual from the full effects of a *laissez faire* political philosophy, and the movement from moralism to causilism.

Not surprisingly, penal labour policy went under review again in 1895. Having taken on board the pronouncements of individuals such as Michael Davitt, a former political prisoner, who suggested that he was totally opposed to the "abominable and inhuman punishment of treadmills and cranks" (Gladstone Committee Report 1895: LVI, 18-19) and Colonel Garsia, an Inspector of Prisons, who proposed that the 1865 Act should be altered so as to facilitate the industrial employment of prisoners (*ibid*: 412), the Gladstone Committee set about change:

"[W]e start from the principle that prison treatment should have as its primary and concurrent objects, deterrence and reformation. It follows, therefore, that it is desirable to provide labour which in conjunction with general prison discipline does not impair the one, and which does include the other" (*ibid*: 16-19).

Accordingly, it recommended that all purely mechanical labour, such as treadwheels, should be abolished entirely as it kept the prisoners in a state of "mental vacuity" (*ibid*: 19). In addition, it recommended the use of industrial labour - it was morally and physically beneficial and ought to be found - and the wider adoption of associative labour which could act, *inter alia*, as a welcome relief from constant isolation and as a privilege, liable to suspension (*ibid*: 21).

Penal labour, for Garland, was one of the elements that combined in the period between the Gladstone Committee Report of 1895 and the start of the First World War to form the "basic structure of modern penality in a distinct pattern which is discontinuous with the Victorian system, while being continuous with that of the present day" (1985: 5). There is a certain element of truth in this as the periodisation did witness the elevation of reformation to a level equal with deterrence, the abolition of unproductive toil, and the espousal of associative and industrial work practices. But again, in my view, he has minimised the nature of resistance both during and after the period of his described transformation. It is my contention that penal labour following the Gladstone Committee Report of 1895 provides us with another example of the gestation period required before new initiatives take root and become discontinuous with past penal practices. Consider, for instance, the 1895 report itself. Although it renounced the use of unproductive toil and commended the wider adoption of associated work together with approving the use of industrial training,[36] the Committee was "compelled to admit that no satisfactory alternative has yet been suggested", nor could they forecast how industrial labour might be developed (1895: LVI, 19). Hence by procrastinating over the pivotal concern, no concrete proposals were expounded as to how governors could best utilise labour within their prison regimes - toil of an irksome and vexatious nature was to be ousted but subrogated with what and how? What was called for was an audacious proclamation delineating the reformative influence which had to be brought to bear on the offenders through the medium of constructive labour, thus aiding their reintegration back into society. Unfortunately no such policy was, at that time, forthcoming. This is supported by McConville. He stated:

"[T]he [Gladstone] report evaded central issues, either by calling for further inquiries; or by ignoring them; or by a fudge; or by indecisively elaborating obvious pros and cons. This evasiveness probably came from some

---

36. Borstals can be differentiated from prisons of that era in that they were organised exclusively to reform and train and, as such, were more akin to schools governed by strict discipline with industrial instruction as their primary goal. The underpinning ideology behind their inception was that the sentence itself was not perceived as a punishment but as a means through which the offender could derive a positive and constructive experience. For judicial approval of the reformative rationale of work in borstals, see Darling J. in *R v. Watkins, Smallwood and Jones* (1910. 5 Cr. App. 93: 95) and the dicta of Lord Chief Justice Avory and Justice Sankey in *Observations on detention in Borstal Institutions and the terms of sentences* ((1919) 14 Cr. App. R. 84: 84). But for elements of resistance, see the succeeding pages of this chapter.

realisation of the inadequacy of their work. A strong committee does not hesitate to take up a clear, even if controversial position; a weak one, like a weak child in the playground, tries to be inconspicuous and certainly picks no fights" (McConville 1995: 648).

Yet Garland fails to appreciate this point. He simply states in respect of penal labour following the Gladstone Committee:

"Unproductive labour was officially abandoned, to be replaced by work which was both useful and educative; labour and education in local prisons were put on an associative basis, in line with the traditional practice of convict prisons" (1985: 23).

But this weakness of the Gladstone Committee is fundamental to our understanding of penal labour in prisons during the period. As a consequence, the early years of the twentieth century were symptomised by a dearth of any committed direction or orientation as to the status of labour within prisons. The recognition of its restorative value was counterpoised and indeed suppressed by the presumption that deterrence formed the nucleus of the regime. This is supported by the first systematic enquiry of the prison system after the Gladstone Committee report, undertaken by Hobhouse and Brockway between 1919 and 1922:

"The Commissioners are supposed to have thrown over

the penal view of labour ..., as long ago as 1896, but the punitive element still characterises practically all prison work. There are many monotonous processes performed by hard labour which would be performed by machinery in an up-to-date factory. This is partly due, no doubt, to the difficulty of providing sufficient work for rapid manufacture, and of running well-equipped workshops by the low conditioned and constantly changing prison population; but it is certainly due also (despite all theoretical repudiations) to the punitive conception of the work, and to the system of silence and separation which could not possibly be fitted in with any remunerative form of co-operative production" (1922: 113; Rose 1961: 104-117).

This is not to deny that penal thinking was, for example, increasingly directed towards work in association. But it must be remembered that most of the prisons built in the nineteenth century focused upon the cellular confinement of inmates. As a result, although workshop employment emerged in the early twentieth century, it remained incapable of providing for all incarcerated prisoners.[37]

---

37. Similar problems were evident in Ireland. The Thirty Fourth Annual Report of the General Prisons Board (1912-1913: XLIII: 714) noted: "The number of industries that can be carried on in our prisons is limited. The prisons are mostly of old construction and were designed for purposes of safe custody at a time when useful employment was regarded as a matter of minor importance. They are generally situated in cities or towns with little or no land available for tillage, which is all the more to be regretted in a country like Ireland where a practical knowledge of agriculture is so necessary for the greater number of its inhabitants" (as quoted in Smith 1981: XVI, 340).

Furthermore, the nature of work undertaken in these workshops was often of an effectless and banal kind, more capable of being construed as prison concocted tasks than *bona fide* work tasks.[38] Yet the authorities seemed content to comply with the proposal that work should not be solely of a brutal or irksome nature. Thus whilst they organised work outside the ambit of unproductive punitive labour, little was undertaken which was composed of restorative or positive attributes. They certainly made no claim to the teaching of trades that could be followed up on release or to the employment of work which would aid in rehabilitating offenders. In 1932, the Report of the Departmental Committee on Persistent Offenders remarked that if a labouring man was employed for a lengthy duration in work such as sewing mailbags, he would become "soft" and incapable of doing any work on discharge. To alleviate this, the report stressed the importance of fitting each offender for work on the outside and recommended that the employment of prisoners should not be contemplated in isolation as an internal prison administrative dilemma without considering the prisoner's subsequent career as a free individual (1932: Cmd 4090, 34-37). The creation of a special inquiry to review the system of prison industries and the employment of prisoners was the follow up response by

---

Moreover, it was also noted that prisoners' sentences were as a "rule so short that [they] are incapable of undertaking anything but the simplest kind of work" (Thirty-Third Annual Report of the Prisons' Board 1911: XXXIX, 787, as quoted in Smith 1981: XVI, 340).

38.   For similar criticisms in respect of the early development of the borstal system, see Hood (1965: 103); in Ireland, see Osborough (1975: 14-16).

the Home Secretary to this report on persistent offenders.

In 1933, the Departmental Committee on the Employment of Prisoners reported. Its fundamental argument was that continuous and useful employment must be regarded not as a punishment but as an instrument of discipline and reformation:

"We cannot stress too strongly the consideration which has constantly been placed before us that suitable employment is the most important factor in the physical and moral regeneration of the prisoner" (1933: Cmnd 4462, 64).[39]

In addition, the Committee recommended that training in industry as opposed to production on an economic scale should be the dominant concern of employment in the case of borstal inmates and prisoners under the age of 30 with comparatively long sentences (ibid: 87).

As such, what should now be apparent is that though the use of entirely punitive labour was rendered obsolete within a short time after the publication of the Gladstone Committee's Report, and the reform of prisoners elevated to the position as primary and concurrent objective (along with

---

39. This was concurrent with the view expressed by Mr Maxwell, late Chairman of the Prison Commission: "if work is treated as a form of punishment, the inevitable consequence is that as little as possible will be done and interest and effort will be discouraged, ... if the prisoner feels that the task is of an artificial character invested by the prison authorities either for the purpose of punishing him or merely for the purpose of keeping him occupied, he will perform it in a restless and listless spirit, and the effect both on his character and on his usefulness as an industrial character will be bad" (ibid: 55).

deterrence) of the penal system, prison authorities remained reluctant to view work otherwise than as containing essentially deterrent features. The organisation of work, notwithstanding that it was not irksome to the same degree that treadwheels and cranks were, was still of an unimaginative and ineffectual kind, designed merely to occupy the prisoners without consideration for its significance on their future assimilation back into society. In this way, it illustrates, once again, the need to refrain from over-idealising the nature and speed of transformations. As Kuhn noted in examining paradigm change in science, "novelty emerges only with difficulty, manifested by resistance" (Kuhn 1970: 64); in other words, transformations do not result in new paradigms *ex nihilo*. From our own perspective, rather than viewing any penal paradigm change in terms of monolithic conversion, it is perhaps more apposite to view it from a variety of different foci - thus revealing more about the dialectal nature of change in the penal process - including organisational structure, professional allegiance, political will, economic feasibility, cultural context, intellectual arguments and counter arguments, staff and offender dispositions, and the persuasiveness and inscribed nature of the previous penal paradigm. In this way, we can highlight discontinuities within the penal process whilst also positing the contradictions, dialogues and reciprocal interactions which are inherent therein.

In the years after 1933, however, penal labour policy began to focus more directly on the possibility of regarding it as an instrument of reform and restoration which would facilitate prisoners in securing employment on discharge. In this sense, the most positive and constructive prison work which could be arranged was that which corresponded with and was modelled upon labour undertaken in the free market. Noteworthy improvements followed the Departmental Committee Report on the Employment of Prisoners in 1933. A Director of Industries was appointed with a staff of supervisors and managers to promote the introduction of a wider variety of trades. Workshops were augmented and refurbished to bring them up-to-date with the contemporary labour market (Home Office 1945: 14). It marked, as Grunhut suggests, the beginnings of a twofold objective: "training for work and training by work" (Grunhut 1948: 219). Greater attempts were also made in borstals to train and instruct young offenders in a trade and experiments in vocational guidance were initiated so that inmates could be directed towards the form of employment for which they displayed most aptitude (Hood 1965: 126). The commencement of the Second World War and the heightened demand for labour which it effectuated provided an excellent opportunity for prisoners to engage in useful and constructive toil. They were employed in direct munitions work for government contractors in the assembly of radio equipment, electrical equipment for tanks and fire fighting equipment. Six month courses were established for selected offenders in engineering fitting at three prisons. With the assistance of the Ministry of Labour and National Service these prisoners were placed on skilled engineering work on release. Indeed it was expected that the possibilities for providing each offender with a genuine vocational training in a skilled trade would prove even more plentiful after the war (Home Office 1945: 16). A further development created out of the war effort's necessity for labour was the release of offenders from a large number of prisons into the countryside where they engaged in agricultural work under the auspices of the War Agricultural Executive Committee or on timber reclamation for the Timber Control. Again it was hoped that post-war circumstances would warrant the furtherance of penal labour expansion along these lines (*ibid*).

Yet prison labour was encumbered by many restraints and it would be a fallacy to overstate its progress within the system. To begin with, prisons were not factories and they could not regulate the influx of their labour force. They were required to admit whatever quantities were sentenced by the courts. They also frequently had to contend with the difficulties caused by overcrowding, shortage of workshop space and the unsuitable layout of nineteenth century buildings. Moreover, those received were often composed of individuals with an assortment of work skills and abilities - ranging from the professional to the utterly inadequate - all of which had to be catered for within the confines of one institution. Besides this, many also displayed little or no willingness to actively commit themselves to work programmes provided and for those who received short sentences, the scope for instruction in trade was limited. Finally the system also had to contend with the polemical and formidable assignment of implementing training courses which would be of assistance to offenders on completion of their sentences in an environment where such courses were not always available to law-abiding citizens. The authorities were often confronted with the "less eligibility" argument - prisoners should not be placed in a more advantageous position as a result of their misdemeanours than ordinary citizens who had done no wrong (Report of the Departmental Committee on the Employment of Prisoners 1933: Cmnd 4462, 82-84). It was difficult to justify and advance prison labour policy initiatives in such circumstances. Consequently, although clear policy issues had been formulated as to the function of labour within the penal system, the pursuit of such principles were hindered by a number of obstacles which made their implementation much more difficult.

The period after the Second World War commenced with the enactment of the 1948 Criminal Justice Act. For many years no applicative distinction could be discerned between the conditions under which a sentence with and without hard labour was served as the use of treadwheels and cranks were long repudiated adjuncts of the system. It was reckoned, therefore, that the time had approached when statutory law should be brought into line with practice as it existed in the late 1940s. Section 1(2) of the Act duly abolished the sentence of imprisonment with hard labour and any legislation which required or permitted prisoners to be kept to hard labour ceased to have effect. The Act however contained no compendious statement of the purpose of labour within the prison system. The 1949 Prison Rules were much more detailed and specified the nature and duration of work. Rule 56 declared that every prisoner was required to engage in useful work for not more than 10 hours a day, of which, so far as practicable, at least eight hours were to be spent in associated or other work outside the cells. Yet the practice of employing prisoners according to such regulations raised many complex and intractable difficulties. With the exception of training prisons, workshop hours did not normally exceed 28 per week and as prison numbers continued to escalate above and beyond prison building programmes, the prospect of finding sufficient work for each individual offender which would comply with recommended standards appeared daunting. Moreover, whilst all prisoners were employed with useful employment, it could not be alleged, particularly in local prisons, that it was edifying in the wider sense of securing the inmates' interest or providing them with a vocational predilection (Home Office 1950: 25).

In the 1950s a general impression emerged that the potential of prison labour was not being comprehensively utilised. Too many inmates were engaged in tasks of a repetitive and demoralising nature such as the sewing of mailbags whilst sewing machines remained inoperative within the same workshops. In 1951-52 the Select Committee on Estimates proposed that closer liaison and consultation should be arranged between the prison authorities and government purchasing departments with the intention of determining what regular orders were required. This would facilitate a process of forward planning with regard to prison industry (1951-52: VI, xx). Following this report, the Government Contracts Co-ordinating Committee, with the assistance of the Treasury, attempted to secure as far as possible all work from government departments (Home

Office 1956: Cmnd 10, 20). While the upshot of these adjustments was a decided betterment in prison industries, it was left exposed to some degree by the demand created by the departments concerned. Any slackening of demand from this sector would be evidenced by an analogous reduction in prison productivity. It was necessary therefore to pursue contracts with outside firms. Mr. A. Healey, a former director of Dunlop's, was appointed to the position of prison industrial advisor in November 1957 in the hope that his diffuse experience of the general industrial field would prove fruitful in attracting industrialists (Home Office 1958: Cmnd 496, 24-25). This campaign to expand the use of prison labour on contracts from outside industries had resulted in work for 1,300 men by 1959 on various useful projects which included land drainage, highway works, agriculture and forestry (Home Office 1959: Cmnd 645, 16).[40] Prisons also continued to extend the development of vocational training courses in skilled trades which were designed to enable trainees to take the examinations of the City and Guilds of London and other recognised examining bodies. By 1959 the training was such that over 350 prisoners entered external examinations, with over 70 per cent passing and 30 receiving distinctions or credits (*ibid*).[41] After the war vocational training in borstals, which included brickwork, carpentry, farming, motor mechanics work,

40. Yet it was still beseeched by problems. Much of the work of this nature was diminishing on account of difficulties felt by some of the Trade Unions concerned, and owing to growing unemployment in some areas.
41. Note, though, that the prison population stood at 25,453 in 1959 (Home Office 1960: Cmnd. 1117, 9).

painting and plumbing, also expanded considerably. It was regarded as providing:

a) a good preparation for a boy's getting a worthwhile job on release;
b) a good general training in the use of tools and in the application of techniques which would serve a boy well in most industrial jobs;
c) a helpful method of getting boys interested and used to work, and;
d) a good general character training (Home Office 1962).[42]

Indeed Wolff maintained that the most striking dissimilarity between borstals and prisons was the provision made and consideration allocated to work. Rarely, he suggested, was a borstal unable to occupy its inmates in a full and effective working week and the tasks undertaken were consistently of a more skilled variety than those of their counterparts in prisons (1967: 79).

The 1960s opened with a Report by the Advisory Council on the Employment of Prisoners. This report deemed it necessary, before any positive recommendations could be

---

42. See also the Report of the Work of the Prison Department in 1966 which suggested: "In the earlier years of this century when the routine for establishments for young offenders was being worked out, the view was taken that hard work on the land or long hours scrubbing floors was a cure for most evils. If this was true then it is certainly not true today. The present generation of young men are very critical when their work is not fully productive or modern methods are not employed. They see the work training they are given in borstal in relation to the work they hope to obtain on release" (Home Office 1967: Cmnd. 3408, 18).

proposed, to reiterate the problems with which prison labour was beset:

"The general local prisons are grossly overcrowded; they are old buildings never intended for modern penal methods (including the provision of work in conditions comparable to those of modern industry); and there is a shortage of prison officers...there is little space for new workshops; that movement about the prisons under secure conditions is a very slow process; and that frequent transfers of prisoners from one prison to another are necessary in order to equalise the burden of overcrowding. The old buildings were intended primarily for cellular confinement and not for the freer movement and association of prisoners which is a feature of the modern penal system and is essential to worthwhile employment" (Home Office and Scottish Home Department 1961: 5-6; Morris and Morris 1963: 28).

Despite such difficulties, the Advisory Council continued to hold the view that policy should be directed towards competing on the outside market. Prison industries were not to be considered in isolation. Although separated by necessity from factories employing a free labour force, they should nonetheless be construed as part of the industries of the country and, accordingly, should be managed on similar lines (*ibid*).[43] Some encouraging developments did indeed take place over the subsequent years. Staff numbers were strengthened and new modern industrial techniques, such as line production, costing and work measurement, were introduced. At Manchester, for example, the provision of modern workshops and advancements in organisation made it possible to dispense with unsuitable work and employ more prisoners on industrial production. At Liverpool, a large metal reclamation industry was established which employed 300 men and restricted the hand sewing of mailbags to small numbers of prisoners (Home Office 1964: Cmnd 2381, 49; Home Office 1965: Cmnd 2708, 44). The gravitas which surrounded the whole issue of industrial labour was accentuated by the publication of a second Advisory Council Report on the Employment of Prisoners in 1964. It was contended that Swedish experiments had confirmed the belief that prison industries could favourably compete on the open market given certain conditions. To attain the requisite standard, it was first of all essential to acknowledge that it was proper for prisoners to engage in useful and productive work and assurances needed to be given that prison industries would prove to have an adjuvant and not disruptive influence on the national economy. Secondly, the adoption of modern market techniques were called for in order to ascertain where demand for prison labour lay and, finally, it was necessary

---

43. See also the views of a number of ex-prisoners who similarly stressed the need to bring prison industries into line with modern industries (Prison Reform Council 1962: 18).

to secure the continuation of that demand, once identified, by the satisfactory execution of all orders received (Home Office and Scottish Home and Health Departments 1964: 4-5). Some of these recommendations were incorporated into the creation of Coldingley Prison in 1969 (the first prison of its kind in England or Wales to have a predominantly industrial regime). Light engineering workshops were designed to produce articles for the prison service, government departments, local authorities and for private industry. It also employed the use of work-study incentive pay schemes and improved training arrangements for operatives, as well as a modernised management structure which was compatible in many respects to that displayed by sizeable commercial concerns of the period (Home Office 1970: Cmnd 4486, 23).

Moreover, the scope for employing prisoners on work of social value outside the institutions appeared to increase. Work of this nature was thought to be beneficial in that it enabled offenders to develop a sense of social responsibility in a relatively unrestrained environment and it also profited the general community in as much as it was frequently work of a kind which would not otherwise be completed. The restoration work on the Stratford-on-Avon canal was successfully completed with the assistance of a party of prisoners from Birmingham. Other parties were also engaged in archaeological digs carried out under the direction of the Ministry of Public Building and Works, and on maintaining the grounds of places in the care of the Ministry (Home Office 1968: Cmnd 3774, 46-47). During 1967, prisoners and borstal inmates were employed in archaeological digs, the donation of blood, the maintenance of churchyards, assisting local organisations, the maintenance of hostels, the making of toys for handicapped children and helping the elderly (*ibid*: 8).[44]

Similarly a pre-release scheme was initiated which enabled prisoners to take outside employment for the last six months of their sentence, in some instances from a hostel attached to the prison, in others from normal accommodation within the prison itself. It was devised to neutralise, where possible, the feeling of institutionalisation which offenders suffered from by enabling them to resume such common commitments as the support of their families, tax, insurance and travel to and from work. In 1971, approximately 61 per cent of prisoners who were eligible and had not been considered suitable for release on parole were accepted on to the scheme. However, as a result of the perpetration of serious offences by some offenders on such a pre-release scheme in 1971, the criteria for selection were made more demanding (Home Office 1972: Cmnd 5037, 24-25).

Great changes have occurred in the sphere of work in the penal system. Prior to the nineteenth century it was predominantly focused on the desire to habituate the dissolute to more industrious ways of living and on the remunerative benefit to be derived by the authorities from

---

44. Yet it was also suggested that whilst the government favoured work of a social value outside prison establishments, the progress which could be made in this area was restrained by security considerations, shortages of supervisory staff and the need to devote resources to improving work within the institutions (Home Office 1969: Cmnd 4214, 31).

utilising the large body of labour at their disposal. It was also anticipated that the arduous nature of the work would deter others from either committing crimes or seeking poor relief. The punitive and deterrent attributes of labour became even more conspicuous as the prison emerged as a proper punishment for the confinement of all types of transgressors. The entire regime by 1877 was founded upon a system of uniform rigidity which advocated the practice of separate confinement and punitive hard labour: the first required the complete segregation of each individual offender; the second encouraged work which could be administered in the most precisely measured fashion and designed thereby to be both fatiguing and burdensome. Albeit that segregated unproductive work of this nature was discouraged by 1895, it was replaced with labour which was contrived simply to occupy the prisoners and was still, for the most part, understood as an essential part of the punishment. Hence it was useful in that it did not employ the determinedly useless characteristics of entirely punitive labour but it did little in the way of rehabilitating offenders or preparing them for life after release. By 1933 however, it was urged that work practices should be both constructive and positive as it formed the basis of an offender's training. Accordingly, the invention of tasks for the purpose of occupying prisoners and thereby punishing them was repudiated. Moreover, training in industry, which aided the reintegration of offenders into the community, was now considered the primary principle of employment policy. In this sense, the most advantageous form of work was that which equated with free labour on the outside. The commencement of the Second World War greatly assisted this ideology by enabling offenders to engage in purposeful toil both inside and outside the confines of prisons and borstals. The aims of penal labour between 1945 and 1972 can be summarised as the provision of useful and efficiently organised work which would contribute to the training and treatment needs of offenders whilst at the same time making the greatest possible use of labour, thereby subscribing to the financial costs involved in supporting the penal system. These aims, it was hoped, could be attained by extending the development of vocational training courses, by competing as far as possible on the open market and by employing prisoners on work of social value in the community. Yet it would be a falsehood to allege, even by 1972, that the principles and practice of penal labour had converged. Indeed in many instances they appeared as polarised as ever. Problems still included the prison population which continued to rise at a level which outstripped the rate at which workshop spaces could be provided, the shortage of prison staff, the lack of up-to-date equipment, the controversial role of penal labour in the economic market and the number of monotonous tasks still undertaken.

Post-1945 attitudes to penal labour are very evident in the perceived use of work under a community service order. In general, the work, which displayed striking similarities with that undertaken by prisoners in the community, was of a kind that if it were not done by unpaid labour it would not be carried out at all. The Wootton Committee suggested that a community service order was appealing in that it offered offenders the opportunity to engage in constructive activity in the form of personal service to the community (Home Office 1970: 13). It was anticipated that such activities would instil in the offenders a sense of social responsibility and the possibility of a changed outlook on their part (*ibid*). Moreover, their association with non-offender volunteers would, the Sub-Committee felt, facilitate the reformative value of the sanction and whilst they did not reject the performance of community service by groups consisting entirely of offenders, they were of the opinion that it would be likely "to give the whole scheme too strong a punitive flavour, and would cut off offenders, both from the more constructive and imaginative activities, and from the wholesome influence of those who chose voluntarily to engage in these tasks" (*ibid*). The tasks from which social value was to be derived were to be of a kind which would range from "constructional enterprises for the benefit of the community as a whole to acts of personal service to individuals", and included: constructing adventure playgrounds; clearing beaches and country paths; helping with reclamation projects and restoring canals; cleaning up churchyards; redecorating and restoring churches and church halls; landscaping hospital grounds; clearing bomb-sites; planting trees; repairing railings; making and repairing children's toys in hospitals and children's homes; helping in hospital wards and kitchens, and in clubs for the physically handicapped; maintaining the meals on wheels service at week-ends; and helping the elderly or needy in various ways, eg, visiting, decorating their homes, gardening and distributing clothing (*ibid*: 12). Finally, as the concept of community service was being put forward, its designers were assiduous in their efforts to demonstrate that the work itself was not to be understood as a punishment. The deterrent elements were to be provided from depriving an offender of his or her leisure time. Indeed Baroness Wootton illustrated the possibility of misunderstanding the use to be derived from the work by describing an interview between herself and the B.B.C:

"The interviewer, unfortunately, was not very happy at home in this kind of topic, and the opening question was: 'You are not proposing are you, to put convicts to work on the roads?' This immediately called upon an image of men with broad arrows on their clothing working in chain gangs on the highways. The interview, which was very short, was a disaster because I had to spend the whole time explaining that this was not what we were proposing, but that we were hoping that the work provided would not be punitive or humiliating in its own nature. The penalty involved is the deprivation of leisure, and nothing else ... it is proposed that people who are subject to these orders should work, side by side with volunteers. I think it is possibly one of the most important aspects of the whole proposal that people are doing it because they think it worthwhile. They may make friendships with other people, and they may possibly in consequence - this is our most optimistic hope - get a rather different outlook on their role in society (House of

Lords Parliamentary Debates 1972: 322, 610).[45]

In concluding this section, it seems fair to suggest, in my view, that the history of penal labour is a history which demonstrates the complex and tortuous terrain that is criminal justice's past. It does not lend itself quite so easily to clean discontinuities with older practices, or over-deterministic or one-dimensional accounts of transformations. Instead penal labour history must be read at a much lower level of theoretical abstraction so as to account for issues such as resistance (financial, individual and political), disparities in practice, internal debate, and the dilatory nature of criminal justice reformulations. And although these issues are far less dramatic and intoxicating than accounting for the transformations themselves, they are just as crucial, if not more, to our understanding of any period in penal labour history. Accordingly, any historical investigation of penal labour phenomena which attempts to depict change must not confine such issues to the periphery of its analysis. If it to be wholly accepted as a plausible argumentative thesis, then the author must be prepared to get his or her "hands dirty" in order to account for the

---

45. See also the comments of Mr John Fraser who suggested: "There is a danger that if this form of treatment is regarded as a punishment it will have a kind of chain gang image which will stigmatise not only the offender but also community work and then volunteer workers who would otherwise co-operate in this kind of venture. It is something to be seen as a method of co-operation ... One wants to avoid the idea that it will stigmatise the work itself or the persons participating, whether they be former offenders or volunteers from the community" (House of Commons Parliamentary Debates 1972: Vol 838, col. 1966).

complex processes inherent in penal labour practice. In this way, it can extend our vista of understanding by identifying broad structural changes, whilst simultaneously accounting for specific labour practices and particular institutional and non-institutional labour features which do not, in every instance, sit comfortably with deterministic theory.

This leads me on to my second point. By employing specific historical penal labour illustrations to highlight deficiencies in revisionist texts, I am not implying that these anatomisations, particularly Garlandian, can never be substantiated in respect of penal labour. Rather substantiations are indeed possible, but they necessitate a more diacritical emphasis, so as to incorporate tensions and inconsistencies in to their respective hypotheses. Finally, it is possible, in my view, under this revised revisionist schema of interpretation to highlight broad structural transformations - transformations which cannot be accounted for under a progressivist interpretation - in penal labour history. At a general level, and bearing in mind the qualifications already made, these include the movement towards a rationalisation of reformative labour techniques; followed by the movement towards a rationalisation of deterrent labour techniques; followed by the employment of constructive and positive labour practices in a greatly diversified penal domain which was more capable of accounting for the peculiarities of each specific offender. It is in the last of these movements that labour under a community service order can be understood.

Conclusion

It should be apparent by now that any perception of a march of progress with regard to the genealogy of community service is a misconception. The types of punishment utilised by society at any period in history are determined by a pot-pourri of objectives and activities. They emerge in conjunction with what is technologically, scientifically, geographically, economically and culturally feasible in any given time perspective. In addition, they are moulded by society's sensitivity to crime and its perceived tolerance or intolerance of different modes of punishing deviancy. Within this complexity of interests and intentions, wide-ranging transformations are discernible which enable us to determine the contours of modern penality. This, in turn, facilitates an appreciation of the introduction of community service within a broad framework of understanding. It has already been demonstrated in chapter 2 that modern penality is no longer premised on the moral consciousness and contractual right views of punishment. Instead the substructure is founded upon the following characteristics: a more welfarist approach aimed at producing normalisation through individualisation of treatment with the aid of a wide variety of professional help and greater levels of knowledge concerning the background and personality type of each individual offender; the establishment of reformation as one of the primary aspirations of penological discourse and practice; the systematical operation of sanctions throughout the courts with professional guidance and standard setting emanating

from the centre - the Home Office; and, the extension of penal sanctions to promote and authenticate the aim of individualisation.

The present chapter, adopting a more specific approach by examining particular aspects of the community service order, provides further countenance for the notion that the sanction must be understood in a particular time perspective. To begin with, we have seen that the emergence of an ideological movement for human rights law - thought to be antithetical prior to the early twentieth century - and in particular rights governing forced labour, backed up by proper enforcement mechanisms, had a direct impact on the introduction of community service in that the various treaties and agreements had to be complied with by the authorities. Moreover, the post-1945 appeal to the ideology of the "therapeutic community" as a social control technique, with its emphasis on co-operation, interaction and mutual aid to counteract what was seen as the polarisation of offenders in institutions from society at large, can also be viewed as a phenomenon of the modern penal complex. Finally one may allude to the recognition by the penal authorities of the restorative value of work. Penal labour was, by the mid-twentieth century, no longer viewed as a punishment but as a positive and constructive experiment which would aid offenders' reintegration back into society. All of these beliefs and ideologies, which are incommensurate with views and beliefs of former epochs, have had a profound effect on the shaping and substance of the community service idea in the late 1960s and early 1970s. They illustrate, once again, that the history of penality must not be construed in a linear, abstract and doctrinaire way. With this in mind, the practical implications of what has been delineated in the last three chapters will now be applied to the specific sanction of impressment.

CHAPTER 4

THE PRACTICE OF IMPRESSMENT

Ken Pease has proposed that community service order's forebears include slavery, transportation, penal servitude, and houses of correction. But rather than discussing their persuasiveness as legitimate germs, he chose instead to focus on impressment which he believed had some "intriguing characteristics" when considered in relation to community service (Pease 1981:1). His hypothesis, which attempted to highlight the analogies that could be drawn between both sanctions, was founded primarily upon Radzinowicz's treatise on impressment (Radzinowicz 1968: IV, 79-104; Radzinowicz 1968b: 287-313). At the outset, he alluded to a Commission, which was appointed by Queen Elizabeth in 1602 to arrange that "except when convicted of wilful murder, rape and burglary" an offender might be reprieved from execution and impressed to the navy:

"wherein, as in all things, our desire is that justice may be tempered with clemency and mercy ... our good and quiet subjects protected and preserved, the wicked and evil disposed, restrained and terrified and the offenders to be in such sort corrected and punished and even in their punishment they may yield some profitable service to the Commonwealth" (Pease 1981: 1; Ives 1914: 9).

This quotation was proof for Pease that impressment was an "intriguing precursor" of community service. He regarded the strands of thought in the quoted passage as "eerily similar" to those of the Wootton Report where it was argued that community service:

"should appeal to adherents of different varieties of penal philosophy. To some, it would simply be a more constructive and cheaper alternative to short sentences of imprisonment; by others it would be seen as introducing into the penal system a new dimension with an emphasis on reparation to the community; others again would regard it as a means of giving effect to the old adage that the punishment should fit the crime" *(ibid)*.

Moreover, Pease also argued that, like community service, impressment embodied a consensual element. The Insolvent Debtors Relief Acts of 1670 and 1696 made impressment voluntary for certain categories of debtors. Indeed he proposes that for these prisoners at least, impressment was "more humane than the present scheme, in that prisoners were more aware of the alternative to impressment in 1700 than they are aware of the alternative to community service in 1978" *(ibid: 2)*. In addition, he also had an answer for readers who argued that impressment was an indeterminate sentence whereas community service is limited at 240 hours. He suggested that the degree of indeterminacy was reduced by a statute of 1703 (Insolvent Debtors Relief Act) "in which enlistment of debtors was for the duration of the war rather than for an indefinite period" *(ibid)*. Pease also believed that besides having similar "rehabilitative overtones", references to the quality of the work of those impressed and the desire not to mix offenders with the "older corps" had a "remarkably modern ring" and "the parallels with community service here are fairly remarkable" *(ibid:* 7). Finally, he again quotes Radzinowicz who suggested that long after impressment had fallen into desuetude there remained a "nostalgic regret for so convenient and economical a method of eliminating those considered a social danger, combined with a genuine belief in its reformative value" *(ibid).*[1] These analogies, in particular, led him to the conviction that community service was not inimitable but rather had a lineage dating back some 400 years. His views were endorsed by Van Kalmthout and Tak who also accepted that community service and impressment showed a "remarkable similarity of purpose" (Van Kalmthout and Tak 1988: 12). Hoggarth, similarly, has argued that community service orders' "antecedents go back a long way in penal history" - in a chapter dedicated to such antecedents, she alludes to the parallels which can be drawn between impressment and community service (1991: 41). Finally, in Ireland, Professor Max Taylor has noted that impressment may be seen as a "military community service" (1999: 16). Before commencing with a scrutiny of such a claim, it is necessary to provide a contextual, albeit brief, synopsis of the practice of impressment in the navy.

---

1. This quote is taken from Radzinowicz (1968: 6 103).

Context, Contingency and the Specific Practice of Impressment in the Navy

By the seventeenth century trading by sea had become so prevalent that its advancement and preservation were acknowledged as being of fundamental national significance. Britain, because of its insular geographical position, did not, unlike France or Holland, have to preserve a large army to protect itself from invasion by land. It was free to concentrate its resources on maintaining the "great highway" between itself and trading posts in America, Asia and Africa; these resources would be employed to establish and maintain a strong naval fleet to protect trade routes and prevent the threat of invasion by sea (Mahan 1890: 25; Kennedy 1983: 3). Significantly, however, Britain had nothing approaching a full-time naval crew. In times of international harmony, its warships remained docked in naval ports and were operated by skeleton crews. The outbreak or threat of hostilities was always a crucial affair because the search for a sufficient number of sailors proved to be a continual shortcoming of naval administration. The lack of any cogent structure regarding the recruitment of sailors was as a result of government anathema to the huge financial costs involved as well as the absence of any central machinery to ensure proper recruitment and retainment procedures. While the government would accede to expenditure on all other forms of naval outlay, it would not endorse the use of a naval reserve or register. The navy, as a consequence, found itself having to turn to the skills of maritime sailors in the form of merchant seamen, fishermen, boatmen and lightermen. Indeed a number of resourceful techniques were employed to ensure that the wartime fleet was adroitly prepared for conflict (Baugh 1977: 90; Marcus 1975: 99).

In 1694 Greenwich hospital was founded. It was an endeavour to encourage seamen to enter the Royal Navy by providing medical care for them when they were wounded or crippled whilst serving their country (Lewis: 1960: 117). In 1696 an unsuccessful attempt was made by the Admiralty to create a registry scheme for seamen in which each individual who voluntarily registered was given two pounds. Twenty-four years later a bill was introduced in Parliament for the compulsory register of seamen but it was rejected; the same fate befell another bill aimed at initiating a mandatory register in 1740 (Baugh 1995: 134). In 1758, a statute for the recruitment of seamen was enacted. It may be viewed as a further calculated attempt at enticing professional seamen to volunteer for the Royal Navy by authorising a proper method of wage payment and establishing facilities which enabled seamen to remit their salaries back to their wives and children (31 Geo. II: c. 10). Larger bounties were also provided as a carrot to encourage volunteers with seafaring skills to enlist and greater attempts were made at conserving manpower by increased attempts at enforcing higher standards of hygiene and diet (Gradish 1980: 1-2).

Press gangs were also employed to secure an adequate supply of seamen for the Royal Navy. The pressing of seamen was accomplished in a number of ways: homeward-bound sailors employed by trading companies were the prey of warships or specially hired tenders operating in the Medway, the Downs, or Spithead; villages and towns along the coast were foraged for experienced deck-hands; and, fishermen and watermen operating anywhere in the country or along its coasts were often abducted to support the war effort (Ehrman 1953: 112-117; Davies 1991: 71-72). In certain instances, the Navy felt compelled to invoke the démarche of embargo. This measure, known as compounding, forced ship owners to relinquish a percentage of their crews in return for the protection the Royal Navy afforded to merchant shipping. This technique of manning could not, as Baugh noted, be employed for a long duration as it had a detrimental effect on commercial trade (Baugh 1995: 137). Moreover, the Royal Navy would, on occasion, impress foreign seamen in the South China Seas or in ports such as Lisbon and Madeira (Steel 1957: XXXVII, 47). Most of the foreigners, however, who served on British naval ships were drawn from among the non-French seamen on board French captured warships (Gradish 1980: 80). Finally, the Quota Acts of 1795 and 1796, enacted when the manning crisis was at its nadir, compelled the authorities in various counties in England to provide additional quotas for the fleet from their own districts (1795: 35 Geo. III, c. 5; 1796: 36 Geo. III, c. 115).

There were many protests at the practice of abducting men for service at sea. Obviously those impressed objected and viewed it as a restraint upon their natural rights. Ship owners and merchants also resented it in that it greatly weakened their sailing crews. But on the whole it was seen as a public good in that it preserved the safety of the entire nation. This perception is evidenced in Mr Justice Foster's judgment in *R. v. Broadfoot* in 1743:

"The question touching the legality of pressing marines for the public service is a point of very great national importance. On the one hand, a very useful body of men seem to be put under hardships inconsistent with the temper and genius of a free government. On the other, the necessity of the case seemeth to entitle the public to the service of this body of men, wherever the safety of the whole calleth for it ... [T]he only question at present is, whether marines, persons who have freely chosen a seafaring life, persons whose education and employment have fitted them for the service, and inured them to it - whether such persons may not be legally pressed into the service of the crown, whenever the public safety requireth it. For my part, I think they may. ... War itself is a great evil, but it is chosen to avoid a greater. The practice of pressing is one of the mischiefs war bringeth with it. But it is a maxim in law, and good policy too, that all private mischiefs must be borne with patience for preventing a national calamity. And no greater calamity can befall us to be weak and defenceless at sea in a time of war, so I do not know that the wisdom of the nation hath hitherto found any method of manning our navy, less inconvenient than pressing; and at the same time, equally sure and effectual" (1743-1753: 1326-1330; Anonymous 1814: 3).

The important point to bear in mind is that impressment

was founded, for the most part, on the Navy's proficiency in singling out accomplished seafarers. Shipboard life and shipboard duty necessitated such an arrangement. Captain Matthew Connolly, referring to the employment of landsmen on board warships in 1858, stated:

"Now to suppose that such men as these will ever make sailors is a mere delusion - they will never do so - a sailor must be bred to it from a child, as all our officers and smart men-of-war are; but to take a man from the ploughtail and think, by the mere fact of sending him on board ship, to make a sailor of him, is, as I said before, a mere delusion" (1974: 247; Rodger 1986: 150).

Similarly, Rodger, albeit perhaps overstating the case, noted in respect of criminals:

"In no part of the Sea Service were criminals ever accepted, and an attempt by London magistrates in 1759 to dispose of a notorious gang of pick-pockets, the Black Boy Alley Gang, was firmly countered. Nothing more quickly destroyed the mutual trust of a happy ship's company than the presence of a thief among them, and it was the one crime for which a prime seaman might be discharged without hesitation" (1986: 50).[2]

---

2. In respect of the Army, it was noted: "Most of those obtained by duress were not criminals but rather came from the next category in the current state of values - that is, all such able-bodied, idle and disorderly persons who cannot upon examination prove themselves to exercise and industriously follow some lawful trade or employment; and these the JPs and the

Thus, for the purposes of morale and efficiency, the Navy, where possible, only wanted seafarers on board their ships. This is not difficult to understand. Seafaring men required no elaborate training or instruction when they were transferred from a merchant ship to a man-of-war. A landsman, on the other hand, had no seafaring experience whatsoever. Maritime skills could only be acquired after years of sailing, something which the Royal Navy could not afford those it impressed during a mobilisation.[3]

It is no surprise, then, to learn that impressment was directed first and foremost towards those who had specific seafaring skills. The principle, however, of only recruiting men with nautical experience was not always feasible during wartime and the authorities were sometimes

Constables took up and pressed into service (Houlding 1981: 18)." It does appear, however, that the Army was more susceptible to accepting criminals than the Navy (Gradish 1980: 83).

3.   These skills included: "A vocabulary of several hundred words unrecognisable to the landsman. A sailing ship ... had many miles of rope rigging, and a good seaman was expected to know it intimately, to find the right line in the dark, in a storm, or in the rain. He could tie twenty or thirty different knots without hesitation, and perform various kinds of splices. He could prepare ropes by worming, parcelling, and serving. He could grapple with a wind-filled sail, helping to furl it or reef it as a storm threatened. On coming down from the rigging, he could swab decks, push at the capstan bars, row the ship's boats, rig all kinds of tackle for hoisting weights or for raising or lowering the anchor. That was enough to make an ordinary seaman, but an able seaman needed more. He had to be able to take over as main helmsman and keep the ship on course with her sails filled; to stand in the main chains and heave the lead so that the navigator could know the depth of the water; and to carry out these tasks with the utmost reliability, for the safety of the ship could depend on him alone" (Lavery 1989: 133-134).

pressurised into exercising more drastic techniques of manning. In some instances, they had to recruit landsmen and criminals in order to meet the numbers demanded of each ship's company. With regard to offenders, the Admiralty was always very interested in procuring the release of seamen from gaols and it was even disposed to settling their fees and debts so as to gain their discharge (Gradish 1980: 61). Apart from actual seamen it was also willing to take the smuggling fraternity on board because of their undoubted seamanship skills and because their transgressions were not perceived as belligerent in the way that crimes such as theft and murder were (Lavery 1989: 124). Debtors, too, were admitted and could gain their release from prison by using their bounty to pay off creditors (*ibid*). But aside from these, the Navy was always careful to restrict the reception of offenders. It is necessary to highlight this detail, as Rodger suggests, "to counter the hyperbole which has sometimes passed for fact" (1986: 171). During the French Revolutionary Wars, however, the manning of the Royal Navy proved to be an intractable dilemma. In 1793 Britain found itself in a war with the French which lasted for 23 years and which required all of its efforts. Numbers of seamen rose from the peacetime 16,000 to a peak of 145,000 in 1810-12. Financial funding for the Navy was even more graphic and rose from £1,943,882 in 1792 to a height of £20,096,709 in 1813 (Webb 1988: 207). Faced in the early years of the war with the crisis of having ships tied up without sufficient resources to man them, the authorities sanctioned an Act which required several counties to raise and levy able-bodied and idle persons to serve in His Majesty's Navy (1795: 356 Geo III, c. 34). This, together with the Quota Acts, provided a nonpareil opportunity for the magistrates to dispose of undesirables, such as vagabonds, paupers and criminals, from their parishes. In this way 42 men were sent from Dublin in November 1795 and 30 were impressed from Newgate in April of the same year (Lavery 1989: 124).

The principal stumbling block for the magistrates was convincing the Royal Navy to take their disreputable characters. By all accounts it was averse to employing such individuals - during the French Wars, it was reported that only a "trickle of men" were taken from the gaols and courts (Emsley 1980: 200-205). The Admiralty believed that such persons not only brought "distempers and immoralities among their companies", but also discouraged "men of irreproachable characters from entering Her Majesty's service", seeing that they were "to be ranked with common malefactors" (Roberts 1881: III, 228; Lloyd 1968: 136). The Army felt somewhat similar. Viscount Barrington suggested that "the commanding officers of the several corps abroad are very much averse to accept men under such circumstances". He went further and stated that it would introduce "great uneasiness and confusion into the service if these convicts should be put into His Majesty's regiments for a limited period of time, when the honest volunteer engages to serve for life" (Roberts 1879: II, 469). Indeed, it was disreputables like these who were held accountable for the mutinies of 1797, and in subsequent years the Royal Navy became even more attentive and particular about who it recruited from prisons and those it accepted from magistrates (Lavery 1989: 124; Gill: 1913). In particular, it appears that the Admiralty were not susceptible to accepting criminals accused of Jacobinical offences, seditious behaviour, homosexual offences or theft (Emsley 1980: 205). But even if the Royal Navy was recalcitrant about accepting them, there is also evidence to suggest that during the French Wars, magistrates, in some counties at least, would not give its more ignominious parishioners the opportunity to enlist (*ibid*: 200-205). Emsley, for example, noted during a detailed study of the records of eight borough and 36 county sessions during the wars between 1793 and 1815 that seven of the sessions - Bedford, Bedfordshire, Cambridge, Cumberland, Herefordshire, Norwich and York - had no record of any men being enlisted from the courtroom:

"There appear to have been considerable differences in policy between different county benches. In the populous, and often turbulent, county of Lancashire, magistrates appear to have given very few offenders the opportunity to enlist. In the neighbouring West Riding, however, whose populous, industrialised villages were also contributing enormously to the burgeoning industrial revolution, magistrates gave the opportunity to many more. Within the county of Lincolnshire, the Parts of Holland and Kesteven sent only one man, while Linsey sent 25" (1980: 201-202).

Thus, the practice appears, to some extent, to have been an anomalous and discrepant means of disposing of offenders. What can be elicited from this discussion on the use of impressment? To begin with, it should be apparent that it was simply a stratagem used to enable the Royal Navy to maintain control over the High Seas. Secondly, it should be evident, given the skilled nature of the work involved, that the Admiralty, where possible, was only amenable to admitting seafarers: the wholesale ransacking of crews from the merchant navy by the press service both on inward and sometimes outward journeys bear testimony to this historical reality. Seafarers could also be procured by searching the prisons for mariners and smugglers and the Admiralty would, on occasion, tolerate debtors who were regarded, to some extent, in the same light as landsmen. In times of a severe manning crisis, such as the commencement of the French Revolutionary Wars in 1793, the authorities were given licence to draw upon all types of idlers, paupers and offenders from local parishes and prisons. However, they were often staunchly opposed by the Navy itself who believed such offenders merely offered the menace of mutiny, lowered the morale on board ships, and lacked the requisite nautical skills necessary to serve on board. As such, impressment was strictly exploitative in motive and rather arbitrary and unsystematic in character. It did not have objectives which were explicable or indeed tolerable in terms of modern day punishment. But one must not seek to understand it in terms of modern day penal phenomena. Instead impressment must be construed in its historical context, free from the fabrications and falsehoods of a presentist historian who endeavours to understand it from the perspective of community service. With this in mind, this chapter will conclude with an analysis of Pease's assertions *vis-à-vis* the use of impressment and its genealogical claims in relation to community service. In doing so, I intend to prove that Pease's *soi-disant* similarities are in fact dissimilarities. I am mindful that such an approach is also ahistorical in that it too disregards historical specificity. But since impressment has already been placed in a context, and in order to avoid a "greater evil" - to parrot Mr Justice Foster in *R. v. Broadfoot* - it is felt that by highlighting these dissimilarities, it will, in keeping with the leitmotiv of the argument, facilitate the shattering of myths concerning the lineage of community service.

Anachronism, Ahistoricism and Impressment's Genealogical Claims *vis-à-vis* Community Service

What is particularly striking about Pease's historical approach is the complete lack of reference to historical works on the subject of impressment. He unashamedly professes to rely almost solely on the work of Leon Radzinowicz as countenance for his suppositions. Leaning entirely upon one individual's views to buttress his arguments is surprising in itself. It is particularly so when it is considered that the individual concerned, Radzinowicz, left himself open to a particular type of criticism - that of Whiggish analysis. His monumental five volumes on the history of criminal law administration was assessed essentially from the standpoint of a modern criminologist anxious to delineate the developments that had occurred throughout the ages. He displayed little or no inclination to elucidate the social, economic and cultural history of the society he was representing, or of correlating such a history with the prevailing perceptions of crime and punishment. His history was "a simple linear view of reform as progress" (Philips 1985: 51-52). Radzinowicz's progressivist, presentist view can be discerned from his belief that in England, "as a result of the uninterrupted continuity in its developments, the past, the present, and the future of every important legal institution are intimately interconnected" (Radzinowicz 1944: VIII, 181). It can also be discerned from the opening passage of Volume I of *A History of the English Criminal Law and its Administration from 1750*:

"Lord Macaulay's generalisation that the history of England is the history of progress is as true of the criminal law of this country as of the other social institutions of which it is a part" (Radzinowicz 1948: I, ix).[4]

As Rawlings suggested:

"The chief problem with this perspective is that it looks at history backwards. The historian takes an event ... and sifts through history looking for those things which seem to fit in well with that event. Two piles of information are built up. The first and most important, is of those things which seem - or are made to seem - to predict the event. The second is of those which seem opposed to the event:

---

4. Macaulay's version of Whig history celebrated Britain's progression into modern constitutional reasonableness, economic prosperity and stability after the Glorious Revolution (Macaulay 1858-1862).

those either are discarded or are included so that the path to the selected event can be shown to have been a struggle, even if the end result has an air of inevitability" (Rawlings 1990: 73).

Because Pease is so influenced by Radzinowicz's perception of the development of criminal justice history, he, too, is guilty of operating within a teleological and linear paradigm. As a result, any of the analogies that he has drawn between community service and impressment must be treated with the greatest of scepticism.

Take, to begin with, the notion that both impressment and community service would appeal to adherents of different varieties of penal philosophy. The broadness of community service's objectives, as will be discussed in more detail in chapter 6, must be construed in the context of the social, economic, penal and political milieu of the late 1960s and early 1970s, and, in particular, in the context of historically specific determinants such as increased crime rates, the sensitisation of moral panics, the politicisation of law and order, the crisis of hegemony which manifested itself in the prison system (ie, overcrowding and prison escapes), increased calls, particularly by the New Right, for a return to economic and social *laissez faire*, and the decline in influence of the rehabilitative ethos. Any non-custodial sanction being introduced in 1972 had, from the policymaker's perspective, to combine a number of different philosophies to satisfy the public at large and meet the demands of a pressurised national penal system. This is not to imply that some local parishes did not find themselves impelled to eliminate their criminal classes in the 1600s and 1700s: they undoubtedly were. But impressment was not specifically designed as a measure to palliate these exigencies; rather it provided an opportunity for magistrates, as a result of the pressures of war and the manning crisis that it invariably brought with it, to disgorge its complement of disreputables. The historical reality was that impressment was primarily exploitative in nature - whatever the rhetoric it was dressed up in - in that it provided a ready-made panacea for the manning problems that obtained for a government antipathetic to maintaining a navy during peace time. It was not specifically created as a means of punishing offenders; rather offenders were seen as one further means (albeit a means of last resort) of manning crews in times of emergency. To suggest otherwise, or to propose that it would appeal to a variety of different penal philosophies is to fail to appreciate the true motive of impressment and the true nature of the society in which it endured.

Moreover, Pease also insists that for debtors, at least, impressment is analogous to community service in that they both embody a consensual element. He fails to appreciate, however, that debtors, prior to the mid-nineteenth century, were regarded as a special class of prisoners. Imprisonment of a debtor was primarily regarded as being of a coercive nature, as a means to compel payment rather than as a punishment for the previous failure to discharge a debt. (Harding *et al* 1985: 78; Cohen 1982: 153-171). The position was summed up by Mr Justice Page in his charge to the jury during the trial of John Huggins, Warden of the Fleet, for the murder of Edward Arne in 1729:

"A prisoner for debt is only taken like a distress, and kept there till he or his friends can pay the debt for him. Imprisonment is no punishment, it is not taken as part of the debt... He [the debtor] is kept only in such manner as he may be forthcoming and safe" (Thomas 1972: 149).

One must bear in mind that the economy during this epoch was founded upon a "ramified network of credit and debit" and it was the courts' responsibility to regulate the repayment of outstanding debts (Innes 1980: 251-253). As Levi suggested:

"What could England do without credit? Credit is the life of commerce. In a country where private credit is accessible to all useful enterprises, a person active and intelligent may undertake commercial or industrial operations with comparatively small resources. Where, on the contrary, there is no credit, commerce languishes and becomes the exclusive domain of rich capitalists, the effects of which are a want of competition and comparative dearness of every article of consumption. It is by credit that the whole capital of the country is rendered productive. It is by credit that the great machinery of human transactions is supported and speeded. Although not of itself a productive power, credit is a great purchasing power, which at the command of the merchant creates commodities" (1880: 358-359).

The motives for such a pervasive approach to borrowing and lending included a shortage of specie and a scarcity of financial institutions (Innes 1980: 251-253). This demand for credit is succinctly summed up by Cornish and de. N. Clark:

"In a world where income was often seasonal or spasmodic, where currency could still be hard to find, where sources of borrowing were limited, credit was an inevitable aspect of daily living at every level, as well as of agriculture, industry and commerce" (1989: 226).

Any individual who threatened the debtor/creditor nexus was confined in prison. The courts viewed such an arrangement as necessary to uphold the spirit of commercialism that prevailed. In this way, they provided a cogent redress for creditors and fostered a greater sense of credence in that system of lending. Yet the imprisonment of debtors was not designed as a strict punishment, but rather as a medium through which they could be detained until their debts had been discharged. Indeed certain privileges - not ordinarily given to convicted felons - were afforded to imprisoned debtors. These included extended visiting rights - Lady Hamilton, mistress of Admiral Lord Nelson, who found herself a debtor after the battle of Trafalgar, played hostess to HRH the Duke of Sussex whilst imprisoned (Barty-King 1991: 108) - the opportunity to work at their chosen trades, day trips out of the prisons, and the right, in some instances, to live outside the prison walls (Innes 1980: 251-253; Cohen 1992: III, 153-171; McGowen 1995: 81). The reason why debtors received concessions over and above those awarded to ordinary prisoners was down to the considerable sympathy they invoked in the public at large. Moreover, critics of imprisonment for debt in the late 1600s (the period in which the Insolvent Debtors Acts, that Pease refers to, were enacted) pointed out that it "was paradoxical to confine a debtor who lacked assets for the ostensible purpose of compelling him or her to pay his debts" (Cohen 1992: III, 157). Society recognised that individuals were not always entirely culpable for their insolvency: "some suffered through accidents of fire or theft; trade or health, or even from the vindictive action of an enemy who had chosen to exploit a debt unfairly" (Innes 1980: 251-253). Mishaps of this nature were not surprising:

"Anyone could be disabled and become insolvent by casualties and acts of honest and good intention such as standing surety for a friend, lending money which was not repaid, defending a just suit of law in which delay consumed him, suffering shipwreck or robbery, selling land or merchandise unprofitably, making accounting errors" (Barty-King 1991: 108).

It is within this context that we can begin to understand parliamentary initiatives at discharging debtors from prisons. By enabling them to enlist, it eased public conscience regarding their plight in prisons, removed them from the clutches of their creditors who they were often completely incapable of reimbursing, and provided the navy with a means of manning its crews in times of difficulty.[5]

Now let us focus more ardently upon the consensual element of community service. There are two reasons for this provision:[6]

(i) It was thought that such a sanction would be completely inefficacious in the case of a dissatisfied and uncooperative offender.

(ii) It was also introduced to enable the authorities to circumvent prohibitions on forced labour.

Can it be said, with these reasons in mind, that the voluntary elements of community service and impressment for debtors are "remarkably similar"? The answer must be no. The fact that community service was motivated, in part, by the desire to gain the full co-operation of offenders so as to ensure the satisfactory completion of their sentences cannot ring true for debtors and impressment. It was well known that all impressed men were dispirited with their

---

5. In respect of the impressment of non-debtor offenders, there appears to have been considerable differences in sentencing policy *vis-à-vis* any consensual element. For example, in Gloucestershire (presumably in the 1790s), William Brown was given the choice of six months in gaol or joining a regiment overseas. On the other hand, Joseph Burn, a shoemaker in Northumberland, was found guilty of larceny in 1793 and was *ordered* to be sent on board a warship. Finally, William Maxwell was convicted of misdemeanour at the Devon Assizes in 1794 and his sentence recorded that he was to be imprisoned until such time as he entered His Majesty's Seas Service (Emsley 1980: 201-203).

6. See section 14(2) of the Powers of the Criminal Courts Act 1973, which provides that a court shall not make an order in respect of an offender unless the offender consents.

situation, but they co-operated nonetheless because they realised - or at least most of them did - that dissent or mutiny was futile and would end in death or severe punishment. It would be a deception, then, to propose that the authorities demanded the consent of debtors with the expectation that they would satisfactorily carry out their tasks, when all around them there were men who were deeply dissatisfied with their own predicaments. Secondly, it would be an absolute fallacy - as well as being wholly anachronistic - to propose that impressment was concerned with complying with international conventions concerned with forced labour and offenders. Only in the recent past, as delineated earlier, has Western Society begun to acknowledge and apotheosise human rights, and only recently have these rights come to play a crucial role in criminal justice discourse and criminal justice policy.

Pease also argues that, like community service, impressment was to some extent determinate in that enlistment was for the duration of the war rather than for an indefinite period. There is nothing delimited, however, about the duration of a war. Indeed, one of the reasons cited for the greater number of desertions in the Navy was the lack of a stated period of enlistment. As Usher noted in respect of the period between 1792 and 1814:

"While it is true that all but 20,000 men were discharged after the War [The American Revolutionary War], there was no guarantee to any individual that he would not be held on after the duration. In those days, a seaman had few rights ..." (Usher 1950-51: XXXVII, 686).[7]

The essential point to be cognisant of is that the explicit quantifying of a penal sentence in leisure hours is, as we have already alluded to in chapter 1, very much a feature of contemporary Western societies in which temporal organisation, order, and synchronisation form integral elements. It is only in such a quantified, spatialised setting that the determinacy of community service can be envisaged. As Whitrow suggested:

"Until the rise of modern industrial civilisation people's lives were far less consciously dominated by time than they have been since. The development and continual improvement of the mechanical clock and, more recently, of portable watches has had a profound influence on the way we live. Nowadays we are governed by time-schedules and many of us carry diaries, not to record what we have done but to make sure that we are at the right place at the right time. There is an ever-growing need for us to adhere to given routines, so that the complex operations of our society can function smoothly

---

7.   If Pease was more conversant with the history of impressment, he would have been mindful of a statute in 1835 which provided that no person would be liable to be detained against his consent in the naval service for a period longer than five years (5 and 6 Will IV: c. 34). At least this form of impressment was more determined than that which he proposed. Nonetheless, even this five-year duration was not thoroughly fixed in that the commanding officer was given power in any special emergency to detain an impressed man for a further six months or until such an emergency ceased.

and effectively" (1988: 17-18).

Two further points can be made. First to suggest that "rehabilitative overtones" are present in both community service and impressment is anachronistic and untenable. The modern appearance of the rehabilitative ideal can be differentiated from earlier reformatory appearances in that it emanates from occurrences in other scientific disciplines engrossed in human behaviour and it has been influenced by academic inquiry (Allen 1973: 174).[8] Secondly, the suggestion that the policy of mixing offenders with regular soldiers has a "remarkably modern ring" - and in this regard "parallels with community service are fairly remarkable" - fails to appreciate the motives for mixing or the practices of mixing in both community service orders and impressment. Indeed, with regard to impressment, there is evidence to suggest that certain regiments in the army were entirely composed of convicts. The Secretary of State, Richard Ryder, referred in Parliament in 1812 to three regiments consisting entirely of offenders (Cobbetts Parliamentary Debates: XXI, 1255-1256). Sir Samuel Romilly objected to such a method of recruitment on the grounds that "it would appear more like a certain number of recruits

---

8. The reformative intentions of impressment can be questioned. For example, Thomas Barnes, in 1626, argued for the impressment of vagrants on the ground that it was both pious and prudent "to spend the worst first, and spare the best to the last extremity" (Barnes 1983: 14). A similar view was expressed by a correspondent, "Lenita", in a letter to the *Gentleman's Magazine* in 1762 in which he noted that undesirables should be impressed on the grounds that they "might stop a ball, and prevent the loss of better men" (1762: 53-54).

being wanted for the army, than if it was the good conduct of such a number that had recommended them to a more honourable situation" (*ibid*: 1257-1258). Wilberforce suggested that it would be dangerous to leave these men in regiments of their own and recommended instead that they should be mixed with other corps (and not "older" corps as Radzinowicz and Pease suggested) to form special regiments (*ibid*: 1258). General Tarleton, however, disapproved of mixing those men in the army as they did not want "gaol-birds" to lower the tone of the regular regiments now that their moral prestige "had been much improved" (*ibid*). It is difficult to elicit from these parliamentary debates that mixing was a clear policy with regard to impressment. On the contrary, it appears that offenders, if they were to be taken, were recruited into separate regiments so as to maintain the morale and stature of the regular army.

In respect of community service, the Wootton Committee did not "rule out entirely the performance of community service by groups consisting entirely of offenders". But it regarded it as a "mistake if this became the normal style of the new proposal; for this would, in our view, be likely to give the whole scheme too strong a punitive flavour and would cut off offenders, both from the more constructive and imaginative activities, and from the wholesome influence of those who chose voluntarily to engage in these tasks" (Home Office 1970: 13). The reason for mixing offenders on a community service order with volunteers, then, are as follows: to ensure that the sanction did not embody too many punitive characteristics, to conceal, to some extent, the identity of the offenders and to enable them to be influenced by those who voluntarily gave their free time to perform constructive and imaginative tasks in the community. The motives and practices of mixing under a community service order are, accordingly, incomparable with those under impressment.

Conclusion

Impressment cannot be viewed as forming an integral part of the penal system. It was reserved for offenders as the *ratio ultima* to be utilised on occasions when ships' complements could not be secured with volunteers and impressed seamen alone. As such, its ambitions were strictly exploitative in nature, with occasional lip-service being paid to reformative values. Even when it was practised as the *ratio ultima*, there appears to have been a strong element of rancour from the army and the navy to the employment of the services of offenders in their outfits. Because of its arbitrary character, its exploitative motivations, and its use also of impressed non-offenders, it is a delusion, in my view, to allege that impressment is explicable or rational in terms of modern day punishment. Moreover, as we have already seen in the first three chapters, impressment, at a more general level, is not explicable in terms of community service given that the latter sanction is contained within an archetype of punishment which embodied more factual and inductive strategies towards offending, within a highly rationalised and professionalised penal apparatus which was receptive to historically specific phenomena such as the existence of leisure as a right, the emergence of international rights concerning forced labour, and the emergence of ideologies such as "community participation". And rather than looking back upon impressment with "nostalgic regret", perhaps we should consider it more with the following quotation from J. R. Hutchinson in mind:

"Standing as a bulwark against aggression and conquest, it ground under its heel the very people it protected, and made them slaves in order to keep them free. Masquerading as a protector, it dragged the wage-earner from his home and cast his starving family upon the doubtful mercies of the parish. And as if this were not enough, whilst justifying its existence on the score of public benefit, it played havoc with the fisheries, clipped the wings of the merchant service, and sucked the life-blood out of trade" (1913: 17-18).

It is hoped that this analysis has exposed Pease's hypothesis as an attempt to simplify and distort our understanding of the history of impressment. His truncated, teleological approach to the genealogy of community service orders has failed to account for the complexities - and, in particular, the problems posed by cross-analysis - inherent in historical interpretation. Moreover, and as a consequence of such a linear approach to history, he portrays penal labour dispositions of earlier epochs as being solutions to the same set of "fixed problems" and the same set of "fixed canons" as those concerning community service - of course, as I have already argued, the result is a form of interpretation which is highly selective and deeply distorted.[9] The purpose of this book so far has been to illuminate the ahistorical approach adopted by academics such as Vass and Pease who depredated the past to foster and popularise myths relating to the introduction of community service. Having presented a more historical picture of the past and having outlined the broad penal framework within which community service could operate, the book will now move on to examine more positive and genuine claims of relevance in respect of the germs of the community service order ideal.

---

9. For a similar argument in respect of the history of science, see Kuhn: "The depreciation of historical fact is deeply, and probably functionally ingrained, in the ideology of the scientific profession, the same profession that places the highest of all values upon factual details of sorts ... The result is a persistent tendency to make the history of science look linear or cumulative ... Because they aim to acquaint the student with what the contemporary scientific community thinks it knows, textbooks treat the various experiments, concepts, laws, and theorems of the current normal science as separately and as nearly seriatim as possible. As pedagogy, this technique of presentation is unexceptional. But when combined with the generally unscientific air of science writing and with the occasional systematic misconstructions ... one strong impression is overwhelmingly likely to follow: science has reached its present state by a series of individual discoveries and inventions that, when gathered together, constitute the modern body of technical knowledge. From the beginning of the scientific enterprise, a textbook presentation implies, scientists have striven for the particular objectives that are embodied in today's paradigms. One by one, in a process often compared to the addition of bricks to a building, scientists have added another fact, concept, law or theory to the body of information supplied in the contemporary science text. But that is not the way that science develops. Many of the puzzles of contemporary normal science did not exist until after the most recent scientific revolution. Very few of them can be traced back to the historic beginning of the science within which they now occur. *Earlier generations pursued their own problems with their own instruments and their own canons of solution"* (1970: 138-141) (my italics).

358

PART III

THE MODERN PENAL COMPLEX AND THE INTRODUCTION OF COMMUNITY SERVICE ORDERS

CHAPTER 5

THE SPECIFIC GERMS OF THE COMMUNITY SERVICE ORDER IDEAL

The purpose of the first three chapters was to create a general framework of penal objectives, termed modern penality, within which the practice of community service could be understood. In describing this framework it has been shown that both the "function and constitution" of modern penality are, in many respects, different from penality in earlier times (Garland 1985: 234). The purpose of this chapter is to describe the specific germs of the community service order ideal within the general framework of modern penality. Thus, rather than adopting the anachronistic and unworkable approach of Vass and Pease, which views the germs of the community service as being a history of every work-based sanction which has been established in relation to offenders, this chapter will provide a more historically correct interpretation of the sanction's genealogy by tracing its "conditions of emergence" in terms of a "history of the present" (Garland 1994: 25). As Garland noted:

"This explicit concern to write a history of the present acknowledges that our contemporary problems and practices are quite distinct from those of the past; but equally, it recognises that our present arrangements were constructed out of materials and situations which existed at earlier points in time. The present is continuous with the past in some respects, and discontinuous in others. It is the historian's job to identify the processes of transmutation which characterise change and, in particular, the generation of those differences which constitute our modernity" (*ibid*).

As the general transmutations have already been identified, it is now necessary to focus in on the specific germs of community service. In particular, this chapter will examine enthusiasm for the community service ideal in the 1950s and 1960s in the voluntary sector, in prisons, borstals and detention centres, in the establishment of intermediate treatment programmes, and through international penal experiences. It will be argued that it is to these specific phenomena that the historical conditions of emergence of community service orders can be traced.

The Voluntary Boom

Prior to the late nineteenth century, voluntary work in England and Wales was characterised by the performance of charitable deeds by middle and upper class philanthropists. Voluntary social service - typically manifest in the numerous small charities established by individuals and religious organisations - was, for the most part, the keystone of the administration of welfare, with the State, as "junior partner", filling in the gaps when it was deemed necessary (Brenton 1985: 31; Sheard 1992: 11). But in the late nineteenth and early twentieth centuries, it was apparent that voluntary organisations were ill-equipped to provide the necessary social services. They were essentially "non-systematic, capricious, fragmented, unco-ordinated and competitive, and because most frequently they were aimed at moral reform and social control more than social need, they proved inadequate to the enormous need that existed" (Brenton 1985: 16). As these needs became more palpable and the demand for uniformity of practice more widespread, increased pressure was placed on the State to guarantee minimum levels of social provision. Not surprisingly, then, these years witnessed the growth in State social provision and commercial insurance as a means of support for the destitute, and voluntary organisations increasingly found themselves having to operate in conjunction with statutory authorities (Thane 1982: 290).

This transformation from a principal accentuation on voluntary action to State action was exacerbated in the mid-1940s with the creation of an extensive network of social services by a Labour government (1945-1951) anxious to establish a social nadir below which the conditions of life of any citizen would not be permitted to drop. A series of enactments were passed to ensure that this social nadir was secured and maintained. They included the Education Act of 1944 (7 and 8 Geo. VI: ch. 31),[1] the National Health

---

1. This Act raised the minimum school leaving age to 15 and made State education in secondary schools free.

Service Act of 1946 (9 and 10 Geo. VI. Ch. 81),[2] the National
Insurance Act of 1946 (9 and 10 Geo. VI: ch. 67),[3] the
Children Act of 1948 ((11 and 12 Geo. VI: ch. 43),[4] and the
National Assistance Act of 1948 (11 and 12 Geo VI: ch. 29).[5]
As Owen noted:

"All this meant that Englishmen could now look to the
State for a basic social minimum and it aroused uneasy
suspicions that in at least some sectors private
philanthropy might be on the way to redundancy" (1964:
532).

This is also supported by R.H.S. Crossman, Minister of
Social Services in the Labour Government after the Second
World War, who suggested:

"In the construction of the new social service State we
turned our backs on philanthropy and replaced the
do-gooder by highly professional administrators and
experts. Our principle has been that we would create a
State in which politicians at Westminster, with the help of
elected or nominated amateurs in the regions, would

---

2.   This Act endeavoured to introduce a free and comprehensive health service.
3.   This Act attempted to prevent people dropping below the social nadir
     whenever they were unable to earn; individuals could earn a right to such
     a benefit through their own contributions.
4.   This Act placed central responsibility for children's services with the Home
     Office.
5.   This Act required local authorities to provide residential accommodation for
     the elderly and infirm and to promote the welfare of the blind, the deaf, and
     the general classes of the handicapped.

control services run by paid professionals. In this respect we had considerable success" (1976: 266).[6]

Undoubtedly there remained supporters of voluntarism after the war. Lord Beveridge, for example, stressed the need for the employment of voluntary action to carry out tasks which the State could not be expected to do such as the giving of advice and the organising of leisure (1948: 266-302). Yet voluntarism was, on the whole, treated with cynicism by a Labour administration that viewed it as being too associated with middle and upper class models of philanthropy and benefaction. This antipathy was also identified by Webb who stated:

"A subsidiary but important part of the drive towards statutory social services represented a deliberate move away from voluntary provision not least within the Labour party. Faith was invested in statutory services as a way of guaranteeing provision that was comprehensive and universal, professional and impartial, and subject to democratic control. The immediate post-war implementation of social policies marked an attempt decisively to move away from social policies that were

---

6. See also D. L. Hobman who noted in 1953: "The need for charity is obviously far less today than it was even a quarter of a century ago. *The Times* lately published an account of a hundred cases (histories of persons appealing for funds, which was given in the supplement of the *New York Times*, in December 1952); from an analysis of this list it appeared that in England only 10 per cent of these cases would have required private charity, the remaining 90 per cent could have claimed assistance as their right from the social services" (1953: 104-105).

partial in scope, socially divisive in action, and socially controlling in intent. Voluntary organisations were regarded with not a little suspicion in the process" (1976: 7, as quoted in Brenton 1985: 20).

Accordingly, after 1945 voluntary organisations found themselves faced with uncertainty about their futures as their functions and duties were increasingly usurped by a monopolistic State control apparatus. In order to survive they would have to modify in accordance with the changing nature of governmental control. Thus for the first 10 to 15 years after the Second World War - whilst attempting to adjust to new roles - they appeared, as the Wolfenden Committee pointed out, to be "marking time" (1978: 20).

In the late 1950s and 1960s, however, enthusiasm for the employment of volunteers and community participation prompted revived interest in the nature and role of voluntary service. In this period the range of voluntary organisations expanded and new groups proliferated to provide what were perceived as necessary services to the community. Indeed Stephen Hatch, in a survey of the employment of voluntary organisations in three towns in the late 1970s (the towns were described under the pseudonyms of Anglebridge, Forgeham, and Kirkforth) estimated that although "the history of a few existing voluntary organisations in the three towns goes back to the last century, a majority of them have come into being since 1960" (Hatch 1980: 77). Nationwide, these new or modified groups included the following: (a) the reorientation of some service organisations to differentiate their contribution from that of statutory agencies (ie, the provision of specialist services, not available in the statutory sector, by Barnardo's and the Church of England Children's Society); (b) the growth of pressure group organisations such as Shelter, the National Campaign for the Homeless, Disablement Income Group, Child Poverty Action Group; and, (c) the flowering of mutual self-help groups such as Pre-School Playgroup Association, Gingerbread, Coeliac Society, Spina Bifida Association and Muscular Dystrophy Society (Wolfenden Committee 1978: 20; Younghusband 1978: I, 273).

By alluding to the emergence of a plethora of voluntary organisations in the late 1950s and 1960s, I do not wish to imply that there was a profound reversal of roles for the statutory and voluntary bodies. The State continued to remain the primary administrator of social welfare services. What had changed was the perceived ability and competence of these voluntary organisations - having modified themselves according to the State's activities - to act supplementarily as a partner to the statutory services. But why had this change come about so soon after the creation of a supposedly all encompassing Welfare State?

To begin with, the Welfare State had fallen short of the expectations it had generated. These expectations had been impeded by the economic difficulties that ensued following the Second World War, the effects of the Korean War on public expenditure, the Cold War and inflation (Hadley 1975: 3-4). In addition, the income elasticity of demand dictated that even though there was a growth in prosperity and social and technological improvement, demand would, nonetheless, increase for most social services (*ibid*).

Secondly, the bureaucratic and inaccessible nature of the State system had led to growing frustration and impatience among citizens and politicians alike (Brenton 1985: 36). Thirdly, there was a growing realisation that new social needs - such as the "disintegrating effect of slum clearance policies, rising rates of divorce and growing numbers of single parent families" - could not be tackled comprehensively by an inflexible statutory welfare apparatus (*ibid*). Realisations of this kind were magnified by the knowledge that such "gaps" could not be closed by further expansion of the social services. Need, as Hadley suggests, "is not a static concept; it is redefined as provision improves" (1975: vii). Outside of the realm of welfare provisions, there was also a growing concern about young people and in particular the activities of young people. In the age of consumerism, adult Britain was becoming increasingly alarmed at youth subcultures. It is against this background "that volunteering began to be perceived in a new role: as a safe, constructive outlet for the otherwise unpredictable and destructive energies of a disaffected young people" (Sheard 1992: 12-13). Such a panacea for delinquent youth culture must also be viewed in the light of the development and practice of the idea of "participation". As the Aves Committee noted:

"[T]he process of becoming an advanced industrial society has had effects which contribute to the interest in voluntary work. The degree of control over parts of our lives and the loss of some of the personal element, particularly at work, has produced a desire to counteract these effects by undertaking activities which give scope for spontaneity, initiative and contact with other people" (Aves 1969: 22; Bugler 1965: 18-19; Ministry of Housing and Local Government 1968: Cmnd. 3703, 152).

The need to develop a new social purpose was also highlighted by Richard Hauser:

"Previously there were forces at work in the community which had the effect of often preventing breakdown. These forces moulded personal relationships in families, groups, communities, by producing common objectives. People were united in the fight for better conditions. In wartime they were united by sheer need. The moulding and uniting power of these outside pressures for survival is no longer as acute; the Welfare State, so very necessary from any point of view, has incidentally been instrumental in weakening defensive family and community ties; and the threat of war, while no less real, now seems far removed from the ordinary man's immediate province of action. Thus, the individual comes to have less and less need to defend himself, and less and less need to combine with others for mutual defence. He comes, in fact, to have less purpose to live for. This lack of purpose necessarily causes fragmentation: it hampers the individual in his struggle to live fully, and it makes for a falling apart of the community at the seams. People lack the will for community life; the individual may actually die of boredom. In other words, man needs either to have the incentive of defending himself against hostile forces around him, or to have a new, constructive, social purpose for which to live. We have turned a corner into a new age where - apart from the ever-present, and therefore often half-forgotten need to fight against the threat of war - plain survival is no longer the main purpose of individual life. It may be that it is always the most sensitive people who suffer most from this lack of purpose: the young housewife, for instance, in a new housing estate, living with far greater material comforts than her parents had, may now find that in fact she has less to live for, and that this new existence is thoroughly frustrating; she will not understand the reasons why it is so, and may feel unnecessarily guilty about it. The real disease is *unlived life*" (1963: III, 5).

Not surprisingly, there was an upsurge of interest in "participation" as a political and social issue in the 1960s. Participatory measures were viewed as beneficial in a number of ways. To begin with, they could provide those involved with a sense of dignity and self-respect. Secondly, they could enhance an individual's capacity by helping him or her to "cope intelligently with a new range of issues". Thirdly, they could assist individuals in discovering their own real interests and, fourthly, they provided an expressive function in that they enabled ordinary people to voice their opinions in respect of policy issues (Richardson 1983: 54-57). Finally, all of these factors must be seen in relation to "all kinds of grass roots action" such as anti-poverty and urban renewal strategies in the United States in the 1950s and 1960s. These activities encouraged in part by the civil rights movement and by general social unrest, acted as a stimulus for the expansion of the voluntary sector in Britain (Brenton 1985: 37).

Having briefly described the re-emergence and new role of voluntarism in the late 1950s and 1960s, it is necessary, at this juncture, to become more specific. One aspect already alluded to was the unprecedented interest in the perceived anti-social behaviour of young people during these years. The period had witnessed a widening in the financial and cultural independence of young people as their levels of disposable income increased. The ending of National Service in 1960 - with its aim, *inter alia*, of promoting a sense of social responsibility - accelerated this trend (Roberts 1983: 16-18). This affluence and independence also appeared to create a new consciousness among young people themselves. This was typified by the teddy boys, who responded to affluence and achievement by ascribing importance to the "yob"; the mods in their sharp dressed suits and pointed shoes; the rockers, representing anti-authority and anti-domesticity; and, the bootboys, notorious for their bigotry and celebration of their working class origins (Brake 1980: 72-73; Goldman 1969). All of these groups created panic in the minds of the adult public and were seen as an indicator of the inherent deterioration in the moral fabric of society. Scuffles between mods and rockers, such as those that occurred at East Coast seaside resorts in August of 1964, and their subsequent sensationalised exposure in the press magnified such concerns (Brake 1980: 75). Essentially the problem was seen as one in which young people had begun to earn more money than previous generations and many of them were unable "to find the best means of using this money in a period of ever-increasing leisure" (Hansard, House of Commons Parliamentary Debates 1964: 697, 255). One of the more favoured proposals for the amelioration of this situation can be discerned from the following section of a speech given in the House of Commons in June, 1964:

"What is needed is for a far greater number of good citizens to spend some of their time outside their homes and families in all kinds of voluntary movements. They could engage in such things as helping with youth clubs, helping a local church, or helping the Freedom from Hunger Campaign. One of the failings of our modern society is that there is a lack of people to take part in all kinds of voluntary work. If more were prepared to engage in voluntary work, we would create a new ethic in society which would help to conquer this problem" (*ibid*: 268-269).

By the mid-1960s this "new ethic" was, in part, realised through the concept of community service (non-penal). It was viewed as being valuable in that it would promote a sense of social responsibility in young people by allowing them to participate in the problems of society and it would also act as a useful source of manpower for the giving of vitally needed assistance. Initially, the idea of community service had been directed overseas. The international work-camp ideal, for instance, first became noticeable after the Second World War. It was believed that the collection of groups of young people from various countries in camps where they would work and live together would achieve two goals: first, it would encourage international conciliation by providing the perfect milieu for the cultivation of personal relationships and friendships; secondly, the labour of the volunteers could be utilised to great effect in the crucial task of post-war reconstruction (Thomas 1971: 1). Moreover, Alec Dickson established Voluntary Service Overseas in 1958. At that time many Third World countries were engaged in the transition from colonial to self-rule. It was felt that young people could actively help in this process as well as benefit personally from the period in service (Burley 1980: 13). The nature of the work, however, and the need for selection made it a pursuit for the élite few who could bring particular and badly needed skills with them (*ibid*). Nonetheless the idea of community service was gradually taking hold at home. Even if the jobs young people could be required to do were of a manual nature, such as repairing a youth hostel, gardening for the infirm or decorating a room for a pensioner, it was believed that there still would be personal and educational benefits to be derived therefrom. Community service at home, as Brasnet pointed out, would allow young people to take "their place as a real part of the community" and, in addition, it would revitalise the services "through the special qualities of enthusiastic and sensitive youth" (Brasnet 1969: 250-252). Its growth in the 1960s is evident from the following statement made by Mr Christopher Chataway, the Joint Under-Secretary of State for Education and Science, in 1964:

371

"Young people are taking on a bigger share of responsibility for programmes and there appears to be what I regard as a remarkable growth of interest in schemes whereby young people give assistance to the elderly and others in need in the community" (Hansard. House of Commons Parliamentary Debates: 697, 47).[7]

In 1962 Alec Dickson founded Community Service Volunteers. He endeavoured to alter public perceptions of young people by demonstrating what they could actually achieve in environments such as psychiatric institutions, Cheshire Homes and approved schools. In pursuing this goal he adopted a policy of non-rejection: in his view, to serve overseas, in other people's countries was a privilege, but to serve in your own country was a right (Dickson 1976: 117). He believed that one of the greatest dangers posed by consumerist society was that of isolation and the feeling of not being wanted. As such, it was vital, in his opinion, that young people be enabled to provide service from which they could feel appreciated and of use (*ibid*: 124-125). Accordingly the real difference between C.S.V. and earlier organisations such as V.S.O. was that it was not directed primarily at middle-class, well-educated young people. On the contrary, Dickson was keen to promote

---

7.　See also Thomas who suggested: "[T]he last decade has seen an enormous growth in the numbers of young people involving themselves in community service. Many existing religious, charitable, and voluntary organisations have extended their activities to include community service schemes, and other organisations have been established specifically to encourage and organise community service" (1971: 1).

self-development and responsibility among the less well-off, the less well-educated and the more difficult or anti-social members of society (Sheard 1992: 14).[8] For example, one development in C.S.V. in the mid-1960s was to arrange for boys and girls in approved schools to perform community service themselves (Bugler 1965: 20). Similarly, a place for community service was given a stamp of approval by the D.H.S.S. on intermediate treatment schemes (Burley 1980: 23). In addition to organising work for volunteers in the community, C.S.V. also extended the range of its activities to include an advisory service for schools and youth groups, experimental summer tutoring projects for immigrant children, race relations, work with the police and the production of kits, broadsheets and newsletters which assisted in broadcasting the experience gained in projects to a wider public (Dickson 1976: 137; Bugler 1980: 20).

It would be wrong, however, to hold the view that Dickson had a monopoly on the organisation of the community service ideal. Enthusiasm for community service was also reflected in the publication of a number of education reports in the late 1950s and 1960s. To begin with, the Albemarle Committee, appointed by the Minister of Education in November 1958, recognised - given the changing social and industrial conditions - the valuable and vital need of voluntarism. This need was magnified by the abandonment of National Service in 1960; from then on it was estimated that there would be a further 200,000 young

---

8.   The majority of people, however, who engaged in voluntary activities remained, on the whole, middle class (Gerard 1985: 211).

men annually seeking employment and leisure pursuits in civilian life (Ministry of Education 1963: 68).[9] The Newsom Report, in 1963, suggested that community service in "local hospitals, decorating a community centre, making and repairing toys for nursery and infant schools and individual service in schemes for helping elderly or invalid persons" was of double value to school children, in that they performed useful tasks in the community and derived benefit from the undertaking of more adult responsibilities (*ibid*). On this latter value, one headmistress wrote:

"[T]here have been girls going through a difficult time, and we have found a spell away from school in quite different surroundings has worked wonders. I have a strictly unofficial working arrangement with three infant and nursery schools in the neighbourhood where there are very understanding headmistresses. A troublesome girl can become a most reasonable young lady when helping to tell stories at dinner time to infants, or helping to serve meals, or to dress and undress young children. Most important of all, when she has had the status of a young adult for a few weeks she seems to gain in poise and confidence in herself, which halts the downward trend" (*ibid*).

---

9.   The historical conditions of emergence of community service (non-penal) may, in part, explain the "conceptualisation of community service [penal] as a young man's punishment". For other factors which may have an impact on the under-representation of women on community service orders, including their "domestic responsibilities" and "limited choices regarding placement allocation", see McIvor (1988: XXXVII, 280-290), McIvor (1992: 35), Hine (1993), and Worrall (1995).

From 1963 onwards, increasing numbers of secondary schools began to incorporate community service into the timetables of their curricula (Ball and Ball 1973: 23). Belief and support for the idea of community service in education is also evident in the 1968 Schools' Council Report, titled *Community Service and the Curriculum*, and by the proposals of the Youth Service Development Council in 1969 (Dept of Education and science 1969: 14). Similarly, in 1964, Anthony Steen established Task Force: its aim was to mobilise the work of young volunteers in the service of the old and was founded upon Steen's experience of recruiting working-class teenagers to visit housebound pensioners in the East End of London in the previous three years (Hadley 1975: 15). In this way, it was hoped that the spirit and enthusiasm of young volunteers could be harnessed to tackle pressing social problems - particularly problems concerning services to the old - and both the volunteers and society could benefit accordingly. In the first year of its operation, there were two small teams of full-time staff, one functioning north of the Thames, and the other on the south of the river. In the following three years, seven more centres were opened (*ibid*). By June of 1969, 3,500 old people were receiving assistance from Task Force. Work was carried out by circa 8000 volunteers, involving 164 schools (Dartington 1971: 9). Indeed as a result of the enthusiasm for Task Force in the city of London, Steen decided, in 1968, to establish the Young Volunteer Force Foundation as a national extension of the Task Force ideal (Ball and Ball 1973: 26). Within months Y.V.F.F. centres had sprung up in locations such as Cwmbran, Stoke and Newcastle (*ibid*).

The decline and re-emergence of voluntary bodies in the social welfare system was also parallelled in the criminal justice system. By the 1940s, the penal system had witnessed a striking decline in the recruitment of volunteers. It was thought that with the professionalisation of the probation service their services would no longer be required (Gill and Mawby 1990: 30-31). It was only in the 1960s that active recruitment began again when it was recognised that volunteers could be employed to extend the service offered by the probation service, "enabling it to reach new clients and to offer help additional to what was already available and of a different kind" (Haxby 1978: 73). But unlike earlier generations of volunteers, this new generation embodied larger numbers of young people. Moreover, although most of them were middle class, they were less exclusively so than in the past and were not "a particular breed, but part of the growing army of volunteers working throughout the health and social services" (Barr 1972: 1).

By the mid-1960s, it was clear that there were many practical tasks which could be carried out by volunteers. The Report on the Work of the Probation and After-Care Department, 1962 to 1965, reiterating the views of the Advisory Council on the Treatment of Offenders in 1963, recommended that the number of volunteers acting as auxiliaries to the probation service should be increased. There were, it suggested, a variety of worthwhile tasks that they could engage in and included befriending prisoners' families, providing club-rooms for lonely ex-prisoners, finding ex-prisoners work or lodgings, and providing hostels (1966: Cmnd. 3107, 41).[10] Similarly, in November 1965, the Home Secretary stated in a letter to all the probation committees that he wished to see the inception in each probation area of an experimental scheme in which voluntary workers would complement and reinforce the professional guidance and support offered by probation officers to discharged offenders (Home Office 1966: Cmnd. 3107, 43). In 1966, Teamwork Associates was established in order to recruit, select and train voluntary workers for the Inner London Probation and After-Care Service (Younghusband 1978: I, 113). In the same year, the National Association for the Care and Resettlement of Offenders was established with grant aid from the Home Office. Its aim was to strengthen voluntary effort in the field of delinquency and to encourage greater partnership between the statutory and voluntary services (Home Office 1969: Cmnd. 4223, 51).[11] As such the 1960s witnessed the gradual increase in the employment of voluntary workers. In 1966 there were only 794 volunteers known to be working with the probation service and less than half the probation committees for England and Wales claimed to be using

---

10. The 1965 White Paper, *The Adult Offender*, also stated: "There are many voluntary activities which range from the befriending of individuals and providing material help - including notably help for the wives and families of those still in prison - to the running of clubs where ex-prisoners were welcome, and a housing scheme to help them find a home... Some offenders were so handicapped, mentally or physically, that the chances of their successful establishment in society are necessarily small. They will need continuous and intensive support for a very long time, and there is room for further voluntary effort here" (1965: Cmnd. 2852: 10).
11. It replaced the National Discharged Prisoners Aid Society.

volunteers (Barr 1972: 41). By 1970 the number of volunteers had risen to 2,176 (Home Office 1974: 134), and only four out of 68 probation committees stated that they did not employ volunteers (Barr 1972: 41). As we shall see in the next section, alongside increases in the employment of volunteers, the period in question also witnessed an upsurge in the use of offenders as community service volunteers. It was believed that as a result of working face to face with the old, the sick and the disabled and performing tasks for their benefit, offenders would develop a sense of social responsibility.

Thus, rather than accepting the view, as Vass has done, that the community service principle was a "continuation of a *long standing* (my italics) tradition of self-help and voluntary service" (Vass 1984: 26), I would propose that it was very much a part of the remarkable growth in voluntarism in the late 1950s and 1960s. This voluntary boom was brought about as a result of deficiencies in the State system of social welfare, the emergence of new social needs, mounting disquiet about the habits and activities of young people, the development of community participation projects in the United States and the genuine desire of people to combat the increasingly detached and faceless features associated with advanced industrial society. What is particularly interesting from our viewpoint is the attempt to include young people in this emerging voluntary movement. The ending of National Service and the increasingly independent characteristics of youth culture had created unease in adult Britain: voluntarism was viewed as one possible means of maintaining order and encouraging responsibility. It is within this context that we can appreciate the emergence of the community service ideal. Permitting young people to participate in the social problems of the community was viewed as advantageous in that it would encourage them to acquire and develop social responsibility skills and it would be beneficial in that the tasks undertaken would be of direct value to the community. A whole host of community service schemes were organised by groups such as Task Force, C.S.V. and Y.V.F.F. so as to enable enthusiastic young people to give assistance. Moreover, the spirit of community participation also gained credence in the criminal justice system when it became obvious that a highly professionalised and bureaucratised probation service could not comprehensively provide for all the needs of offenders, ex-offenders, and their families; as a consequence, the mid- to late-1960s witnessed a substantial escalation in voluntary activities in the penal system.

Because this notion of voluntary community service was so much in vogue both inside and outside the criminal justice system, it is not surprising that it had a profound effect on the thinking of the Wootton Committee. Lady Wootton and her colleagues recognised that the idea of voluntary service had come into "fresh prominence" with the emergence of organisations such as C.S.V. and Task Force, and with the involvement of young volunteers still at school (Home Office 1970: 12).[12] The Wootton Committee

---

12. Indeed the founder of C.S.V., Alec Dickson, gave evidence before the Committee (Rutherford 1993: 150).

went on to state:

"For illustrations of the wide variety of projects included in such voluntary community service, ranging from constructional enterprises for the benefit of the community as a whole to acts of personal service to individuals, we are greatly indebted to representatives of a number of the organisations concerned whom we have consulted. The examples quoted included: constructing adventure playgrounds; clearing beaches and community paths; helping with reclamation projects and restoring canals; cleaning up churchyards; redecorating and restoring churches and church halls; landscaping hospital grounds; clearing bomb sites; planting trees; repairing railways; making and repairing children's toys in hospitals and children's homes; helping in hospital wards and kitchens, and in clubs for the physically handicapped; maintaining the meals on wheels service at week-ends; and helping the elderly or needy in various ways, eg, visiting, decorating their homes, gardening and distributing clothing" (*ibid*).

Indeed the Committee was assured by the voluntary organisations concerned that there was an "abundance of opportunity" for community service, both in work with or for individuals and in construction projects (*ibid*: 15).

Moreover, the idealism underpinning the introduction of community service orders is in many respects similar to the idealism which governed the establishment of organisations such as Task Force and C.S.V. What was appealing about a community service order was that it would provide offenders with the opportunity to participate in society by the performance of constructive tasks in the community. It would also enable them, through close personal contact with volunteers and with members of society most in need of help and support, to alter their outlooks and develop a sense of social responsibility. In respect of offenders associating with volunteers, Lord Donaldson stated:

"These volunteers inevitably have a social conscience and a sense of duty which the offender is unlikely ever to have encountered in his home environment, and the close contact and comradeship of working side by side can have a profound effect on many to whom a sense of duty is not only alien but completely unknown" (Hansard. House of Lords Parliamentary Debates 1971: 332, 640).

In the same way it was felt in the 1960s that consumerist society impeded participation and promoted a feeling of isolation. Many believed that alienation and disaffection of this nature could be counteracted through the outlet of voluntary community service. By participating, and by associating with those who of their own volition attempted to improve the lives of those around them, it was hoped that young people, in particular, would develop a greater sense of social responsibility which would enable them to become committed and active members of the community in which they lived. Such a viewpoint is compatible with that expressed by Hood:

"[T]he concept of voluntary community *service*, rather than compulsory community *work*, was a response to the idealistic spirit of the Community Service Volunteers movement: a movement of mainly middle-class educated youth for alleviation of hardship among the old and under-privileged. Attachment to the work of these young volunteers was presumed not only to be of help to the community but mainly to introduce offenders to constructive rather than destructive attitudes towards others in the community" (Hood 1974: 409).[13]

Yet Smith contends that any substantive links or correlations between volunteering and community service orders are tenuous:

"[T]he parallels are arguable. Organised voluntary service is a largely middle-class concept in our society. It depends on a surplus of leisure, a normative framework which rewards service with heightened prestige or respect, and generally at least a small capacity to bear some incidental, if minor expenses. It is not too cynical to suggest that no one gives anything for nothing; volunteers need rewards as much as paid workers, though these may well not be expressed in monetary terms. Traditionally volunteers have been middle-aged, the women attracted by the opportunity to use otherwise excessive free time, the men

---

13. What Hood fails to appreciate, however, is that compulsory community work for offenders would be deemed to be forced labour within the meaning of various international agreements as delineated in chapter 3.

perceiving the benefits to be obtained from a reputation for involvement in activities not directly remunerative. The rapid expansion of further and higher education has added an army of school children and students to the ranks of volunteers, and a whole new range of organisations, specially equipped to cater for the particular contribution of the young. Again it has proved important to recognise the need for projects to offer young people more than merely the satisfaction of doing useful work. Significantly the best-publicised of schemes over the past twenty-five years have provided participants with the chance to travel abroad, with, of course, the very proper additional objective of spreading international understanding or aiding developing countries. Organisations with programmes limited to this country invariably find it easier to recruit for projects offering strong human contact and high immediate job satisfaction" (Smith 1974: 248).

In relation to community service orders, he states:

"In practice, it has to be admitted, the offender placed on a community service order is unlikely to see his service quite as positively as would a volunteer. His participation will be voluntary only in the sense that, as with a probation order, his consent in court will be required (and usually given for fear of a less attractive sentence). Manual work is unlikely to be a refreshing break from a weekday sedentary job, from too much leisure, or from relaxed study; projects will rarely offer offenders the opportunity of travel, and service will hardly bring social prestige, honours, or business advantage. Indeed, it would be easy to see the work demanded under a community service order as little more than forced labour, and it is wise to remember that it may well be so perceived by many of those sentenced" *(ibid)*.

Undoubtedly Smith is correct in suggesting that most offenders are unlikely to see their service in the same light as volunteers. He is also correct in proposing that community service is unlikely to bring offenders social prestige, honours or business advantage. Yet he appears to be making the mistake of looking for unequivocal parallels or absolute imitations between volunteering and community service orders. This, of course, is not feasible. The former must be construed as a body or group of bodies working in conjunction with the statutory services which seek to improve the conditions of life for the community in which we live, whilst the latter must be viewed as a penal sanction which seeks to deprive offenders of their leisure by getting them to perform constructive tasks in their localities. But once this is recognised it is possible to begin identifying a similarity in idealism.

Smith, however, is incapable of recognising such an affinity as he fails to appreciate the specific nature of volunteering in the 1960s. It was not solely concerned with service overseas, with prestige or honour, or with acting as a hiatus from sedentary work routines. Rather the focus also came to bear, to some extent, on employing volunteering as a constructive outlet for disaffected youth, as a medium through which the feelings of isolation associated with advanced industrial society could be counteracted, as a means of promoting social responsibility and integration into the social life of the community, and as a means of providing for social needs not covered by the statutory services. The community service ideal, in particular, was seen as beneficial in that it would facilitate young people by enabling them to undertake more adult responsibilities and it would also result in the performance of constructive tasks in the community. Enthusiasm for this ideal can be discerned from the establishment of C.S.V. and Task Force, and the views of the Newsom Report, the Schools' Council Working Paper on Community Service in the Curriculum, the Aves Committee and the Youth Service Development Council. If Smith could have appreciated that this notion of community service was prevalent around the time the Wootton Committee was established, then he may have been more susceptible to the belief that the idealism behind volunteering and community service orders was, in many instances, similar, albeit that the practices of both were undertaken under very differing circumstances.

Community Service and Offenders

Having outlined the emergence of the community service ideal in broad terms, the purpose of this section is to focus more specifically on the influence of the ideal on penal thinking. In particular, it will focus on the emergence of the ideal as a policy initiative in prisons, borstals and detention centres. Social training projects in such institutions, particularly by the 1960s, offered inmates the possibility of performing constructive work in the community in conjunction with the voluntary services. By performing tasks side by side with volunteers and face to face with the sick, disabled and aged, it was hoped that it would impress upon each offender that there were needs in society, other than those centred upon his or her own personal advantage. Thus, through their participation and contact with others outside the penal system, offenders would be encouraged to develop a sense of social responsibility and feel more a part of the community.

In the 1940s and 1950s prisoners were able to perform constructive tasks in the community as a result of the war effort and as a result of natural disasters such as severe snow storms and flooding. In 1942, for example, the Report of the Commissioners of Prisons and Directors of Convict Prisons reported that 40 convicts from Dartmoor undertook road-making on a War Department gun practice site and received commendation from the military command for the quality of their work (Home Office 1946: Cmnd. 7010, 41). Similarly the harsh winter of 1946 provided an example of the possibility of utilising prison labour in the community in the public interest: in this instance, many miles of snow-bound roads were opened up by parties of prisoners (Home Office 1947: Cmnd. 7271, 41). In 1953, parts of the East Coast of England were badly hit by flooding. Prisoners helped by performing community service in a variety of ways: in Chelmsford they filled sand-bags to stop gaps in the sea wall and also loaded them onto lorries for transport to the flooded areas; other prisoners from Brixton and Wormwood Scrubs helped for several months with the sorting and packaging of parcels of clothing in the W.V.S. depots in London; and, at Eastchurch, where the sea walls had been breached, prisoners worked zealously for long hours in the cold and darkness to repair them and to rescue cattle and sheep that were stranded (Home Office 1961: Cmnd. 1467, 19).[14] By the late 1950s and early 1960s, however, community service, as shall become more apparent, began to take on a more ambitious and policy-orientated role in penal institutions as it came to be viewed as an essential element in the employment and social training of inmates. Prisons, notably Pentonville and Shrewsbury, began to co-ordinate and plan schemes of voluntary social service (Home Office 1965: Cmnd. 2708, 15). In 1963, the deputy governor of a regional prison wrote:

"In late September a group of volunteer staff and prisoners visited the Cheshire Homes with the deputy governor for a meeting with the management committee of the home. The meeting was to co-ordinate and plan the

---

14. In 1962, a group of ex-prisoners made a similar recommendation to the Prison Commission: "Work must be useful and constructive and if possible keep the prisoner in touch with life outside. There are jobs in the community that could be done by prisoners (by all except the dangerous and violent) such as clearing bomb sites, building playgrounds, decorating old people's homes, farming, allotments, etc. The more work done outside the walls of the prison the better, since the prisoner can then feel he is able to play a part in the life of the community and the ordinary citizen outside can realise that the prisoner is not a different animal to be feared and isolated, but a human being who needs help" (Prison Reform Council 1962: 18).

work of groups of volunteers from the staff and prisoners who, since early August, had been giving up their Saturday afternoons to work in the home and grounds. As a result of that meeting, work to an agreed plan has been carried out topping trees, tidying and clearing the grounds, painting and decorating rooms, walls, doors, corridors, removing and making good the wall of an old fireplace, floor laying etc. Tiles bought as a result of the efforts of the drama group have been provided and laid in the kitchen and curtains have been made, together with their pelmets for the nurses' rest room" (Home Office 1964: Cmnd. 2381, 17).

By 1967, the leisure time of prisoners in many institutions throughout the country was taken up with archaeological digs, donating blood, maintaining churchyards, helping local organisations, working in hostels, making toys for handicapped children and helping the elderly (Home Office 1968: Cmnd. 3774, 8).

Nor was this notion of voluntary community service strictly confined to offenders in prisons. Between 1939 and 1940, for example, up to 250 boys in borstals were employed daily digging trenches, erecting anti-tank defences, and making a rifle-range and an anti-magnetic mine for the Admiralty. Much work was also carried out, frequently on bomb or machine-gun sites, making camp roads and drill grounds, salvaging sunken ships, and erecting and camouflaging spirit-tanks (Home Office 1946: Cmnd. 6820, 53). In 1947 the Report of the Commissioners of Prisons and Directors of Convict Prisons noted:

"[T]he corporate spirit of Borstal can have a very different effect. During the floods of 1947, the agricultural land worked for the Ministry of Agriculture by the borstal camp at Gringley Carr, Notts., with much of the adjoining country, suffered disastrously. The borstal came into action at once and the whole of their effort was placed ... at the service of the neighbourhood. Without thought of hours, comfort, or safety, borstal officers and boys worked side by side with the local people for days and nights on end, often in blizzards and waist deep in water, rescuing people and stock, salvaging food and crops, and waging ceaseless battle with crumbling banks" (Home Office 1948: Cmd 7475: 57).[15]

Roger Hood, in describing the idealism underpinning the introduction of community service orders, suggested that the involvement of offenders in voluntary community service had been a "particularly long standing element" of borstals since the 1930s (Hood 1974: 410). He fails to appreciate, however, that community service in these institutions underwent a change of direction, akin to that described in prisons, in the late 1950s and early 1960s: the authorities, rather than relying upon acts of God or sporadic

---

15. Similarly the governor of Hollesley Bay Borstal Camp noted in 1953: "The flooding of some 500 acres of the estate during the great storm of the 31st January/ 1st February put us all very much on our mettle and although no real danger to life was involved it must be placed on record how magnificently all concerned, staff and inmates, rose to the occasion and worked so hard on the estate and in the neighbourhood in an effort to repair the damage to the sea and river walls. Only when there is such a test can one fully judge stability and loyalty" (Home Office 1954: Cmd 9259, 75).

requests for help, began actively to embrace the ideology of community service and view it as an essential element in the employment and social training of borstal inmates.

There are three main reasons which may be cited for the change in direction in prisons and borstals. To begin with, it was motivated by the emergence of the corrective community ideology as a panacea for miscreant behaviour and as an alternative to the isolatory nature of institutional incarceration as outlined in chapter 3. Secondly, and more importantly from the perspective of this chapter, it was influenced by the remarkable growth in voluntarism and, in particular, by the growth of voluntarism concerned with the performance of community service tasks. If enabling ordinary citizens to participate in the social problems of the community could prove beneficial by encouraging their social responsibility skills and by counteracting feelings of isolation and disaffection, there was no reason to suppose that the same process could not prove just as edifying in respect of offenders provided proper safeguards were set in place. As early as 1958, Dr Kurt Hahn spoke to borstal authorities at their conference and encouraged them to promote the use of acts of social service. He believed that if compassion could gain power in the inner lives of inmates, it would weaken all passions which prompted them to acts of inhumanity (Home Office 1961: Cmnd. 1467, 38). The Report of the Advisory Council on the Employment of Prisoners in 1962 provided further support for this reasoning by suggesting that borstal inmates had a substantial contribution to make in the community (Home Office 1962: 7). Every effort was therefore to be made to demonstrate the use to which the product of their labour is put. It could be demonstrated most forcefully, in the Advisory Council's view, by enabling them to produce goods for organisations, such as hospitals, which they would appreciate as being of benefit to the community (*ibid*).

Thirdly, reparation, as an ideology, gained increasing support in a variety of different spheres from the late 1950s onwards. This support can be examined both from the perspective of victimology and penology. In the former case, Margaret Fry had proposed a scheme of State compensation for the victims of crimes of violence as early as 1957 (Rock 1990: 46-90; Newburn 1995: 147; Shapland *et al* 1988: 1-2). It was not, however, until 1964 that a Criminal Injuries Compensation Scheme came into operation following the publication of a White Paper, *Compensation for Victims of Crimes of Violence* (1964: Cmnd. 2323). In 1968, section 28 of the Theft Act, as amended by section 6 of the Criminal Justice Act, 1972, made provision for restitution orders in respect of stolen property. Moreover, following a request by the then Home Secretary, Mr Roy Jenkins, in November 1966, the Widgery Committee examined how the "principle of personal reparation might be given a more prominent role in the penal system" (Home Office 1970b: v). Indeed, and as a result of the Widgery Committee's recommendations, section 1 of the 1972 Criminal Justice Act provided that a court could, in addition to dealing with an offender in any other way, require him or her to pay compensation for personal injury, loss or damage resulting from the offences; section 7 of the said Act also embodied a reparative element, again recommended by the Widgery Committee, in that it provided that criminal bankruptcy orders could be made against convicted persons - this sanction attempted to prevent criminals from benefiting from their ill-gotten gains and to ensure that compensation was paid to the victims of crime named in the orders. In alluding to these orders, I do not wish to posit a belief that the victim's movement enjoyed unfettered success in the 1960s and early 1970s.[16] It was still, in these years, confined to the periphery of criminal justice discourse. Moreover, although reparation did manifest itself in respect of initiatives concerning victims in the period in question, such initiatives were primarily motivated by penological rather than victimological concerns; in other words, altering the penal system for the benefit of victims played an ancillary role to the perception that criminals - particularly criminals such as the "undisciplined hooligan" - *paid back* society for their wrongdoings and recognised their obligations in an affluent society where it was believed that they "never had it so good". Nevertheless, and despite this secondary role, it is still possible to argue that the outlined developments represented the nascent emergence of a backlash[17] - a

---

16. For the problems which still confronted victims in the era, see Prime (1971: XXXXVIII, 880-882).
17. See, for example, Schafer, who noted in 1960: "The State enforces criminal justice in order to maintain law and order, in the collective interests of its citizens. The individual victim is a part of the community, and for that reason criminal proceedings are, in the last analysis, applied in the interests of this individual victim as well as in the interests of the community as a whole. It therefore seems senseless to exclude the victim from the settlement of a criminal case, and to regard him merely as the cause of, or reason for,

backlash which required a further 20 years and an array of other impetuses to come to the fore before the victim began to play a more prominent role in criminal justice discourse - against what Christie would term the "reduction of the victim to a nonentity" (Christie 1977: XVII, 1-15).

More importantly, and without doubt more emphatically, reparation as a concept attracted many supporters in the penological realm. In 1957, the Advisory Council on the Treatment of Offenders questioned whether or not it would be feasible and practicable to provide greater scope in the penal system for offenders to pay compensation or make restitution for the damage they had done (Home Office 1957). In 1959, the White Paper, *Penal Practice in a Changing Society*, noted the redemptive merits of reparation, particularly in an era of increased concern about the fragmentation of the social fabric (Home Office 1959: Cmnd. 645: 7). Such fragmentation was thought to be the result of the breakdown of family discipline, the decline of religion, the "get-rich" quick ethos of "acquisitive society", "growing impersonality", the opportunities for impulsive and organised crime that industrialised nations provide, and the lack of international wars which "meant that the aggressive instinct of our young people breaks out in other forms" (Hansard. House of Commons Parliamentary Debates 1971: 826, 967; Labour Party 1964: 56; Conservative Party 1966: 9-15). Reparation, as an ideology, was to some extent posited as a panacea for such breakdown. For example, in

the criminal case" (1960: 122).

an opinion sample in Northview in the mid-1960s, reparation was the dominant response of those questioned on how best to punish the criminal activities of Mods and Rockers. This would involve "visible restitution (repairing broken windows or sweeping the streets) organised along para-military lines" (Cohen 1973: 90); other work that was suggested "included cleaning hospitals, observing in casualty wards and taking spastic children on holidays" (*ibid*: 91).[18] In 1970, the Widgery Committee noted, in general, that reparation was an "essential element in the punishment of crime",[19] whilst the Wootton Committee,

18. Reparation was also gaining a hold in academic circles. For example, in 1963, Hauser noted: "Training should aim at making a prison into a community service where prisoners can 'pay back' to society by doing work of social value (1963: 13). See also Del Vecchio who argued in 1969: "It is a fundamental maxim of justice that everyone should bear the consequences of his acts; hence comes the duty to repair the harm which one has caused to another and the correlative right to claim such reparation in the most adequate form. In some cases the harm done and consequently the duty of reparation affect only the individuals concerned, as in the non-payment of money due under a contract; in these cases there is obviously sufficient reparation in a civil judgment for ... compensation. But if the wrongful act is done with criminal intent or with such a degree of fault as is equivalent to criminal intent, the resultant harm commonly is the concern not only of the individual who has suffered it but also of all fellow-members of the society, whence comes a need for reparation of a public nature, going beyond private compensation" (1969: 201).
19. It noted: "The feeling that more should be done to require offenders to make reparation reflects a number of different approaches as to the purposes which reparation is intended to serve ... One view is that the primary purpose of reparation has an intrinsic moral value of its own ... On another view, reparation finds its greatest justification in ensuring that the offender does not enjoy the fruits of crime. This is one of the considerations which have led the superior courts to pass exceptionally long custodial sentences in some very serious cases ... Others again would emphasise the reformative

more particularly, justified, in part, the introduction of community service orders on the grounds of its emphasis on reparation - in the form of personal service - in the community (Home Office 1970: 13). As Windelsham noted:

"To the politicians of the 1970s, the notion of community service by offenders was an attractive one. Combining relative novelty with practicality, it seemed evidently constructive as a way of repaying society for a wrong done, while at the same time bringing the offender within reach of the voluntary organisations which are a peculiarly English way of providing services of value to a wider community" (1993: III, 122-123).[20]

Thus, in the late 1950s and 1960s, support for reparative and

value to be attributed to reparation" (Home Office 1970b: 3).

20. Further support for the concept of reparation, as employed in community service, was evidenced in the comments of Mr James Callaghan in the House of Commons in November 1971: "It is a very ambitious and worthy idea that those who have done damage to the community should expiate their offence by giving some part-time service to the community. Such service can ... take the form of constructional enterprises for the benefit of the community as a whole without regard to individual liberty - such as cleaning beaches, restoring canals and helping in hospital kitchens - or in the acts of personal service to individuals - for example, decorating the homes of elderly people. I agree that there is a very strong case for this sort of provision and I hope that it will be implemented" (Hansard. House of Commons Parliamentary Debates 1971: 826, 983). Political support for reparation, however, was not just confined to community service orders. See, for example, Quintin Hogg who argued, in 1967 in the House of Commons, that reparation should be "viewed as one of the principal motives underlying our treatment of serious offences" (Hansard. House of Commons Parliamentary Debates 1967: 745, 1686-1687).

community ideologies, together with a new-found confidence in volunteering as a panacea for many of the alleged "destructive energies" at play in advanced industrial society, all contributed to the active embracement of community service in penal institutions.

As such, within a relatively brief period, most borstals had developed schemes whereby inmates could carry out community work in their spare time. As one borstal governor noted in 1965:

"Service to the community has been the *exciting development of the year* (my italics) and one in which in many ways the lads more than the staff have forced the pace. The role of the staff has been to give freely of their time and energy to support the lads in what they have jumped into on the slightest encouragement. It is voluntary every step of the way, and to the best of my knowledge no lad has ever been asked to participate before he has expressed willingness to do so. Their reliability (with few exceptions), and their sensitivity with the old and with the disabled has been a humbling experience to us. They provide a real ministry to the old people of the district digging their gardens and helping them with their heavy chores; but more than this, in giving them company and friendship. The link with two hospitals having severely disabled men in their care, culminated in two weeks in Chiswick, where 15 to 20 lads were paired in camp by similar numbers of gravely disabled men, which gave them the first holiday they had for years. The immense good and happiness it brought to these men and the real outgoing and persistent friendship that the lads extended towards the patients, many of whom were far more attractive as people, was a remarkable achievement" (Home Office 1966: Cmnd. 3088, 22).

By 1967 the notion of community service had become widespread in borstals. The Governor of one such institution described how up to one-third of the inmate population was annually involved in some form of social service in their free time. Tasks included work at a Polio Training Club on Sunday mornings, at an Old Folks' Home at weekends, at a Darby and Joan Club on Saturday afternoons, and at spastic swimming lessons on Friday nights (Home Office 1967: Cmnd. 3408, 17). Indeed the materialisation of this community service ideal in borstals in the 1960s has been chronicled by the Prison Department in 1969:

"[T]he most encouraging developments have been in *social welfare work and community projects*. These range from gardening and decorating work for the elderly and needy to helping run holidays for paraplegic patients and they can be of great value in helping trainees to develop insights into the needs of the physically and mentally handicapped. Such activities can also provide trainees with an opportunity to mix with young people of their own age, coming in many cases from a very different background and range of experience, and these contacts often prove to be of considerable benefit to both sides" (Home Office 1970: Cmnd. 4486) (my italics).

By the late 1960s the ideal had also found its way into the training projects of some detention centres. In 1968, for example, one such institution reported that some of its youths had engaged in tasks which included cleaning up cemeteries and churchyards, assisting at church bazaars and helping old people with their gardens (Home Office 1970: Cmnd. 4724, 22).[21] In 1970 the Report of the Advisory Council on Detention Centres stated:

"We consider it very important that every centre should make provision for work outside the centre, and that wherever possible it should be work that can be seen to be of service to the community. We recognise that this will not always be easy to achieve, but we are convinced of the value of a gradual transition to liberty, even in a short sentence, and of inspiring in the detainee the sense that he has done something constructive and of value to others. We have been glad to note that a start has been made towards this, and we hope that it will be possible to extend these activities" (Home Office 1970c: 22).

Finally, it also appears that local arrangements were sometimes made under which probation officers arranged placements for clients to participate in voluntary community service schemes.

The descriptive nature of this section was necessary, it

---

21. The Report also listed the creation of a bowling green for local senior citizens among the community tasks performed by trainees in one detention centre.

was felt, to demonstrate how pervasive the community service ideal was in penal thinking in the 1960s. We have observed how this ideal emerged, in part, from an *ad hoc* practice concerned with providing service in times of specific need, such as during a war or severe snow storms or flooding, to an active policy of many penal institutions and treatment programmes by the mid-1960s. Whilst not grounded in any criminological or penological analysis, community service for offenders was viewed expediently for a variety of reasons: it would heighten their awareness of the plight of people less fortunate than themselves; it would enable them to "pay back" society for their wrongdoings; it would help them to appreciate their own potentialities; it would enable them to jettison the belief that they were a source of contumely to all by providing them with the opportunity to engage in constructive projects for the benefit of others, and; it would permit them to benefit from their association with non-offender volunteers and those they were helping by promoting social integration. In many respects, therefore, the blossoming of the community service ideal for offenders in the 1960s directly parallels similar developments in the non-penal sphere where voluntary community service was so much in vogue. It is not difficult to envisage, then, given society's willingness to embrace non-penal voluntary community service, and given the overall trend towards correctional community projects for treating deviant behaviour, how the phenomenon of community service should become such a popular ideology in penal thinking.

Yet both Pease - who was so concerned "with the context

within which community service should be considered" (1980: 5) - and Vass - who was also concerned with highlighting that community service was not a piece of penal policy "which surfaced in the early 1970s as if by chance" (1984: 6) - made no mention of the penal practice of community service prior to the introduction of the actual sanction in 1972. This illustrates, in many respects, the flaws in their belief that the history of community service is the amorphous history of every past penal labour practice. Engaging in anachronistic analysis of this nature of course conceals much more than it reveals in that it fails to appreciate that a sanction such as community service is grounded upon historically specific penal and social practices. By only paying limited attention to the context in which community service should be considered (through the adoption of a broad and sophistically argued position in respect of community service's history), Vass and Pease, not surprisingly, are incapable of exposing more specific and veritable claims of relevance in respect of the sanction's genealogy.

But perhaps they are not entirely culpable for this failure to identify community service practices prior to 1972. It may be argued that the Wootton Committee, in proposing the sanction, overstated the value of its own originality. Its keenness to publicise its own ingenuity of design can be discerned from its tendency to minimise the role of community service for offenders prior to its inquiry. It stated that far from being a "meagre achievement" the introduction of community service represented "a new and radical development" which "broke new ground in this country" (Home Office 1970: 12). Although recognising that the experience of extra-mural work in prisons and borstals was of "some relevance", it believed that the value of this experience was limited, "inasmuch as volunteering affords offenders in custody a welcome opportunity of getting outside the institution for a time, and does not raise the administrative problems inherent in a non-custodial scheme" (*ibid*: 15). Undoubtedly the introduction of a non-custodial sanction demanded forward planning in relation to issues such as the organisation of a sufficient range of tasks, proper supervision and a proper enforcement mechanism. Naturally, too, one must concede that a custodial setting is very different from a non-custodial setting and this did have an effect on the operation of the community service ideal. The crucial point for our purposes, however, is that the central idealism of community service remained unviolated: in both instances, community service was unaltered in respect of its practice (the performance by offenders of useful tasks in the community) and its intention (to change the outlook of offenders by enabling them to participate in the community and make reparation for their wrongdoings). Thus, the Wootton Committee's claim that its proposals in respect of community service were radical is correct; it did, however, over-exaggerate its own ingenuity in that it degraded the significance of the role of the community service ideal in the penal system prior to its proposals.

Similarities in this idealism can be discerned by taking a close look at the Wootton Committee's Report and by examining statements made in the parliamentary debates around the time of the introduction of community service. For example, Lady Wootton, in mentioning the use of borstals, stated in 1972:

"It is found that the sight of persons far more disadvantaged than they are themselves, and the opportunity of helping such people, has a very beneficial effect on their attitudes. It is that kind of thing we are thinking of in making these proposals" (Hansard. House of Lords Parliamentary Debates 1971: 332, 611).

Furthermore, the Wootton Committee itself recognised the "wholesome influence" that volunteers could have on offenders (Home Office 1970: 13). It also saw community service as advantageous in that it would bring offenders into "close touch with those members of the community who are most in need of help and support" (*ibid:* 13) and would provide the opportunity for "introducing into the penal system a new dimension with an emphasis on reparation to the community" (*ibid*). In particular, the Committee stated:

"What attracts us, however, is the opportunity which it would give for constructive activity in the form of personal service to the community, and the possibility of a changed outlook on the part of the offender. We hope that offenders required to perform community service would come to see it in this light, and not as wholly negative and punitive" (*ibid*).

This is precisely the same ideology propounded by the

governors of prisons and borstals in relation to their community service order schemes. As we have already noted, it was seen as giving prison and borstal inmates an opportunity of doing socially constructive work and so of contributing to society instead of taking away from it. It was also seen as enabling them to change their outlooks by participating in the community itself and by associating with volunteers and with people less fortunate than themselves.

Finally, one also may allude to the statement of Roger Hood as support for the belief that the community service ideal was not radical. In relation to the Wootton Report, he suggested:

"The proposition that such service would be effective must, of course, have been based upon some assumptions about why crimes are committed or, indeed, why they are not committed. But none of them are made explicit. One can only guess that the Committee believed, either that offenders failed to realise the personal or social consequences of their actions or that their offences derived from a general lack of consideration for others - rather than from a set of circumstances more specific to the offence, and/or that offenders were not well integrated into the social life of the community within which they lived and that joining with volunteers might effectively change the pattern of their previous associations and leisure activity" (1974: 409).[22]

Hood is, of course, correct. The question it begs, however, is why the Wootton Committee - which was so intent on formulating a radical new sanction - did not provide any analysis for its proposals in terms of criminological and penological knowledge?[23] The most obvious answer must be that because the ideological appeal of community service was so popular, there was no need to justify it in scientific terms. It had already gained authenticity, albeit on non-scientific grounds[24], from the Albemarle and Aves Committees, from organisations such as C.S.V. and Task Force, and from the Report of the Advisory Council on the Employment of Prisoners in 1962, and from the Home Office. If, however, the idea of community service had been

---

22. He also stated, referring to the Wootton Committee: "Did they believe, for example, that such offenders are any different from the majority of the population in the value they place upon mutual support and in the sympathy they feel for the sick, disabled and incapacitated aged? ... Was the offender viewed as basically lacking empathy, and that this could be remedied by revealing the true state of the sick? Or was he seen as labouring under a feeling of inferiority, with a 'chip on his shoulder' which would be dispelled by revelation of the truly underprivileged? Or was he simply hedonistic and selfish; a fact to be brought home to him by the selflessness of volunteers? Where was the considerations of the problem in the light of criminological and penological knowledge?" (*ibid*: 410-411).

23. The 1959 White Paper, *Penal Practice in a Changing Society*, demanded that any substantial changes being considered in the penal system should be founded upon criminological and penological knowledge and should provide an analysis of why existing methods needed changing (Home Office 1959: Cmnd. 645, 7).

24. On the "sentimentality" of the support for the community ideology, see Beck (1979, I, 1-14).

wholly original, then, in my view, the Committee would have been under much more pressure to justify its assumptions in an analytical manner. It was the fact that the Committee could rely upon the approved, somewhat "sentimental", idealism of community service which enabled the community service order sanction to be so readily acceptable, albeit as "a mass of unexplained and unfounded assumptions" (Hood 1974: 412). As such, in addition to being closely associated with the emergence of voluntarism in the 1950s and 1960s, the community service order sanction was also derived from the practices of borstals and prisons where it was viewed favourably by many governors. Indeed so popular was the idealism of community service, that it led the Wootton Committee, without proper analysis, *inter alia*, of its effects on reconviction rates or the type of offender it most suited, to formulate and shape a non-custodial sanction around it.

Intermediate Treatment

In the run up to the 1969 Children and Young Persons Act, there was a growing belief - particularly in the Labour Party, the Child Care Service, and among social scientists - that formal court prosecutions and sentences were undesirable in respect of juveniles. In its place, a less interventionist technique was called for which would be founded more upon a "welfare oriented jurisdiction" (Bottoms 1974: 118). Such a movement, as Pitts points out, was motivated by the following factors: the belief that social inequality and social deprivation were instrumental in encouraging delinquency among young people and children; the fear that the stigma associated with the court system merely aggravated such inequality by highlighting and confirming the delinquent's identity; and, the view that the State had an obligation to counteract the causes and consequences of social inequality (1996: 255). One mode of treatment to emanate from such a movement was that of "intermediate treatment". The purpose of the following section is to describe its operation and highlight, if possible, how it provided support for and to some extent resembled the Wootton Committee's idea of community service. Again it must be noted that little attention has been devoted among academics to the notion of intermediate treatment and its affinities with community service. Pease, for example, having delineated the context in which community service could be considered, attempted to describe the reasons why the sanction emerged as an attractive penal option (1980: 5). Yet no attempt was made to view it in the light of intermediate treatment or, more generally, in the light of the 1969 Children and Young Persons Act. Vass's effort to describe the specific context of community service was an improvement on this. He noted in *Sentenced to Labour* that the Children and Young Persons Act introduced new methods of treatment in the community (1984: 23). He did not, however, actually mention intermediate treatment. Similarly neither Young in *Community Service Orders* nor McIvor in *Sentenced to Serve* made a note of intermediate treatment.[25] Lawrence Frayne, in *Paying Back: twenty years of community service,* does appreciate that since 1969 "there had been semi-formal provision for community service by juveniles in schemes of intermediate treatment" (1993: 27). Nevertheless he does not endeavour to discuss it in terms of its impact on the Wootton Committee. In this section, it will be argued that this inattention or laxity in respect of intermediate treatment was a fundamental oversight which should not have been omitted from any contextual analysis of the introduction of community service.

In 1965, the White Paper, *The Child, the Family and the Young Offender,* was published. It suggested that the previous 10 years had seen greater calls for changes in methods of dealing with children and young persons who came before the juvenile courts. Children should, where possible, be spared the stigma of criminality. As such the White Paper proposed, *inter alia,* to remove young people from the jurisdiction of juvenile courts. In *lieu* thereof, it suggested that each local authority, through its Children's Committees, should be empowered to appoint local family councils to consider each case (Home Office 1965: Cmnd. 2742, 5). This and several other radical proposals met with a furore of disapproval, particularly by magistrates. The White Paper's ability to succeed was further hampered by the general lack of enthusiasm for its proposals among Home Office civil servants, by the appointment of a new

---

25. McIvor, however, was not primarily concerned with the introduction of community service in England and Wales, but rather with the operation and practice of the sanction in Scotland.

Home Secretary in 1965 (Mr Roy Jenkins), and by the fact that the Labour government, at the time, had a very slender majority in Parliament (Thorpe 1980: 6). Not surprisingly, it was abandoned. Three years later, however, another White Paper, *Children in Trouble*, was published. It discarded the polemical family council notion and retained the juvenile courts. It also, for the first time, officially mentioned the concept of intermediate treatment. Prevailing forms of treatment, it suggested, distinguished sharply between those which involved complete removal from the home and family and those which did not. It recommended that a middle ground be found for those at risk of becoming, or those who had already become, "delinquent" (Home Office 1968: Cmnd. 3601, 9-10). Intermediate treatment was, it conjectured, that middle ground in that it could act as a supplement to normal supervision and as an alternative to committal to care (*ibid*). One year later, the intermediate treatment ideal found legislative support in the Children and Young Persons Act. It enabled juvenile courts to include in a supervision order that a child or young person up to the age of 17 live in a single specified place for not more than 90 days in a year, or live, present himself or herself to a person specified, or participate in activities specified for not more than 30 days in a year. In general terms, intermediate treatment was directed towards those who required a more group-orientated or practical activity approach to their difficulties and who were considered likely to respond to "short term placement or regular brief contact with a different environment" (Dept of Health and Social Security 1973: 15). It was not likely to be acceptable for a child or young person whose personality problems were deeply ingrained or whose home and family problems were considered intractable *(ibid)*.

The objective of intermediate treatment was to bring young persons into contact with a different environment by participating in a wide variety of constructive activities of a social, educational or therapeutic nature. It was hoped that such an environment would provide delinquent youths with "the opportunity of forming new personal relationships and developing new interests" (Dept of Health and Social Security 1972: 14). It was vital, therefore, that intermediate treatment should be directed at all children and young persons, and not just children and young persons subject to a court order. This would also enable the latter category to participate in activities which bestirred their interest beyond the time when they were formally instructed to do so *(ibid)*. Moreover, it was considered important to secure the children and young persons' acceptance of their treatment. Otherwise they would regard it as something they had to do because of a court order. As such, it was essential that the activities be of social value and should not in themselves be perceived as punitive (Mays 1975: 136). Part of the philosophy underlying this form of treatment can be discerned from the following statement by Dan Jones, a youth worker appointed by the Tower Hamlets Children's Department to develop an intermediate treatment project:

"I believe groups of irresponsible young people can only learn responsibility through being given the opportunity to shoulder it. If they are to have confidence in themselves to develop any control over their own social situation, the worker has to build on positive links that powerfully bind them together, links which despite their delinquent label show the youngster to have loyalty, courage, dignity and enormous potential" (Dept of Health and Social Security 1976: 14).

The opportunity to shoulder responsibility would be given to young people by providing them with a means of broadening their experiences in human relationships and beneficial activities in their own community. But what were these activities to consist of and how were these relationships to be formed? To begin with the range of activities could include special interest groups, adventure activities, remedial teaching, community service and group counselling (Younghusband 1978: I, 61). Dan Jones wished to pursue the following at Tower Hamlets:

(a) Playgrounds and pre-school activities for young children.
(b) Adventure playgrounds and outdoor programmes to attract and help aggressive or withdrawn youngsters.
(c) Unconventional youth clubs used to reach "unclubbable" youngsters.
(d) Detached work with groups of difficult young people in their own environment and on their own terms.
(e) A wide range of recreational programmes including sport and the arts to attract and stimulate the participation of difficult youngsters and also ordinary children.

(f) Activities involving youth in service to the community.
(g) Informal educational programmes for youngsters having difficulty in coping with school or work.
(h) Involvement of parents and members of the local community as volunteers or paid workers in controlling projects, fund raising etc.
(i) The co-operation of the wide range of existing statutory and voluntary services with the aim of co-ordination and innovation (Dept of Health and Social Security 1976: 13).

All of these activities would require children in trouble to interact and participate with others. In this way, it would facilitate the cultivation of personal relationships based on trust, loyalty and responsibility.

Yet intermediate treatment, in spite of all its possibilities, had a rather dilatory beginning. In some areas by the mid-1970s, the local authorities had either not organised a scheme, or had done so on traditional forms of youth service not designed to cater for constructive activities (Adams *et al* 1981: 20-21; Morris *et al* 1980: 17; Haxby 1972: 172-186). Part of the reason for such confusion was the return to power of the Conservatives in 1970. They announced that they would not bring into force the decriminalising sections (4 and 5) of the 1969 Children and Young Persons Act (Morris and Giller 1987: 91). These sections had intended to prohibit or restrict criminal proceedings for offences committed by children and young persons by the provision of diversionary services through local authority social work intervention. As a result of the change of government, criminal proceedings were not prohibited for offenders under 14 or restricted for offenders between 14 and 17. Similarly, the minimum age qualification for a borstal sentence was not increased from 15 to 17, and detention centres and attendance centres were not phased out. In practice, as Morris and Giller point out, the social welfare philosophy inherent in the Act never materialised (1987: 91). Other sections, such as intermediate treatment, were given the go ahead, but it was left to the discretion of the "police, magistrates, probation and social services departments to find means of altering the patterns of sentencing as well as of liaising to develop a process for deciding whether or not to prosecute" (Thorpe 1980: 8). Obviously these aspirations could not be achieved instantaneously. Furthermore, local government reorganisation in 1972 meant that the social services itself was too unfocused and inexperienced to "grasp the opportunities inherent in intermediate treatment" (Adams *et al* 1981: 20-21). Accordingly it was not until the mid- to late-1970s that any real headway was made with the idea of intermediate treatment.

Nevertheless, despite its difficult beginnings, it is possible to argue that the intermediate treatment movement provided some impetus for the introduction of community service orders. This is not to imply that both sanctions were irrevocably linked or completely homologous in design. Undoubtedly they were different sanctions both in shape and in the types of offenders for whom they were intended. But it is still possible to recognise similarities; one such similarity was the belief inherent in both sanctions that offenders stood a better chance of being integrated back into the community after completion of their sentences if their actual sentences offered them the opportunity of engaging in constructive activities in the community while still living at home among their families and friends. With this in mind, let us look more closely at what intermediate treatment was attempting to achieve. To begin with, it endeavoured to act as a middle ground between normal supervision and committal to custodial care for children and young persons. It also desired to offer such individuals contact with a different environment through constructive activities in the community, be they of a social (ie, community service), educational (ie, pre-school activities for young children) or therapeutic nature (sport and the arts). These activities, moreover, provided an opportunity for forming new relationships and new interests. It was considered vital in this regard to ensure that all activities were of a social value and were not simply considered punitive or retributive. Finally, by broadening their experiences in a whole range of constructive activities and by developing personal relationships, it was hoped that children and young persons would begin to develop a sense of social responsibility.

In many respects, therefore, it reflects the ideology, albeit on a more general scale, of the community service ideal. This innovation also attempted to encourage a sense of social responsibility and a changed outlook among offenders through the performance of constructive tasks in the community. Again, it was important that the tasks performed were not seen as negative or punitive and were to be performed in association with the wholesome influence of those who voluntarily engaged in such activities. Moreover, the Wootton Committee also sought the middle ground in that its enquiry was essentially a "search for forms of disposal which are alternatives to complete deprivation of liberty with its disruption of family life" (Home Office 1970: 2). To this extent, it noted that its terms of reference had been diminished by the Children and Young Persons Act of 1969:

"The development of the Government's plans for dealing with offenders who are children or young persons, which has culminated in the Children and Young Persons Act 1969, has enabled us to concentrate our attention on methods of treatment of offenders aged 17 and over" (*ibid*).

The Committee was also prepared to highlight more specific similarities with the 1969 Act. The following statement is undoubtedly a reference to intermediate forms of treatment:

"We recognise that community service might be particularly valuable in the treatment of the young offender, especially in view of the association which we envisage with volunteers, many of whom are teenagers: indeed, such service is one of the forms of treatment which are envisaged for offenders under 17 by the Children and Young Persons Act, 1969. But we do not think that it should be confined to any particular age group" (*ibid*: 14).

Further support for the view that similarities exist can be discerned from Lady Wootton's comments on the White Paper, *Children in Trouble,* in the *Criminal Law Review* in 1968:

"Perhaps the most original section of the Paper is that which deals with 'intermediate forms of treatment', ie, something between supervision and long-term removal from home ... These provisions open the door for a variety of experiments and their flexibility is much to be commended. Experience of their possibilities may even prove helpful in the desperate search for new and constructive forms of treatment of offenders in higher age groups. Today it is generally conceded that offenders are constantly sent to prison, not because this will do them any good, but for want of any more hopeful alternative; but as the relevant Sub-Committee of the Advisory Council on the Penal System is only too well aware, few and far between are any original and promising suggestions for non-custodial and semi-custodial treatment. *Is it too much to hope that, if local authorities or social service organisations get accustomed to employing 16-year-olds under court orders, they might in time extend this to include young men of slightly more advanced years? It would not be the first time that innovations in the treatment of young offenders have been copied by adult courts and penal institutions*" (1968: 471) (my italics).

Its extension to higher age group offenders was indeed not too much to ask for. Lady Wootton, herself, provided confirmation of this fact in the *Criminal Law Review* in 1973:

"[Community Service] also has affinities with what has come to be known as 'intermediate treatment' proposed under section 12 of the Children and Young Persons Act 1969; and it looks as if, not for the first time - nor maybe for the last either - treatments designed originally for dealings with the erring young may be creeping their way up into the adult ranges of the age-scale" (1973: 18).

In the last section it was argued that the Wootton Committee's idea of community service was only wholly original in the sense that it transplanted the ideal from a custodial to a non-custodial setting. Yet this section demonstrates that even that process was not *entirely* original given that intermediate forms of treatment already existed in England and Wales. And although intermediate treatment was not simply based on community service, involving as it did other activities besides, it did embody many of the same ideas and aims. As such, it acted as a source of support and encouragement for the Wootton Committee in introducing community service. The only transition that now had to be made, apart from administrative changes, was to transplant the idea of constructive tasks in the community during an individual's free time from a children and young persons' age scale into the adult ranges of the age scale. But even the originality of this transition can be questioned. As we shall see in the next section, the Committee was also able to rely on international experiences in New Zealand and America which employed adult offenders in constructive tasks in the community.

International Experiences

To date, we have observed that the Wootton Committee, in putting forward its proposals for community service orders, could draw encouragement from the emergence of practices of voluntary community service in the 1960s and from the emergence of practices of community service as a policy initiative in prisons, borstals, and detention centres. It was also established that the community service order ideal had affinities with the practice of intermediate treatment, albeit that intermediate treatment incorporated a broader range of activities and was designed for children and young people. As shall be evident in this section, the idea of community service was also not without parallels abroad - parallels which the Wootton Committee could draw upon as a means of support and encouragement for its own "radical" innovation. Indeed Baroness Wootton openly admitted knowledge of such experiences:

"The sentence is frankly experimental. But there are parallels in the European, the American and the Australian continents, though in some cases they only involve juveniles" (*ibid*: 18).

A review of international encounters of community service type schemes is intriguing in that it highlights a debate as to the origins of the community service order. For instance, Hans Jorg-Albrecht and Wolfram Schadler believe it to be a British innovation (1986: vii). Similarly American academics such as Carter, Cocks and Glaser believe that the specific use

of community service emerged conceptually in England in
the late 1960s and operationally in 1972 (1987: 4; Silberman
1986: XII, 131-132). Such a belief is also supported in
Germany:

"Im Gegensatz zu den Deutschen Experimenten ist das
Englische Community Service Programm einzig und
allein darauf ausgerichtet, die Freiheitsstrafe als
Primarstrafe zurückzudrängen" (Fuchs 1985: 359).[26]

In France it has been suggested:

"Historiquement, le premier programme de travail
d'interêt général a été etabli en 1966 à Alameda en
Californie" (Marc 1985: 109, 113).[27]

In 1983, the then Minister for Justice in the Republic of
Ireland, Mr Michael Noonan, suggested whilst addressing
the Dáil that community service orders originated in New
Zealand (Dáil Debates 1983: 342, 320). Yet the 1985
"Whitaker Report" in the Republic stated that it was an
Australian innovation (1985: 50). Some Dáil deputies,
however, suggested that it was a British idea. Mr J Kelly, for
example, referring to Irish legislation concerning
community service, stated:

---

26. "Contrary to German experiments, the English community service order
was unique in that it was entirely focused on pushing custodial sanctions
into the background."
27. "Historically, the first programme of community service orders was
established in 1966 in Alameda in California."

"[T]his is simply one more example in the ignominious parade of legislation masquerading under an Irish title ... which is a British legislative idea taken over here and given a green outfit with silver buttons to make it look native" (Dáil Debates 1983: 342, 169).

The purpose of this section is to highlight international experiences of community service prior to the Wootton Committee's Report and to determine which, if any, of these experiences can lay claims to be the actual origins of the community service order sanction.

In the 1950s, New Zealand initiated a programme of combining a sentence of probation with a condition which required the completion of a number of hours community work. However, there were, as Armstrong points out, a number of difficulties associated with the employment of such a sanction:

1. It was not actually embodied in the law.
2. That in order to impose the condition relating to community work the court was imposing greater restraints (presumably in relation to paid employment and family life) on the freedom of the offender than was really justified in many cases.
3. The issue of forced labour had to be negotiated, New Zealand being a signatory to the international labour convention (1983: 10).

Nonetheless the need to develop sanctions which embodied the use of constructive activities in the community remained strong. In 1962, as a result of an amendment to the Criminal Justice Act, the sentence of periodic detention was established. Initially it was only deemed suitable for offenders aged between 15 and 20 but an amendment to the Act passed in 1966 made it available for adults also. It was viewed as being suitable for offenders who had been convicted of offences punishable by imprisonment or who had failed to pay a fine (Home Office 1970: 101). The sentence compelled offenders to attend a designated centre during their leisure time in the evenings or at weekends where they engaged in a number of constructive activities. Importantly, from our viewpoint, the activity of work, both inside and outside the institution, was advocated. It was believed that such an activity would give offenders a "sense of social responsibility and respect for persons and property" (*ibid*: 102). A typical work activity included, for example, community service alongside volunteers in projects such as assisting at hospitals, charitable or educational institutions, or helping in the home or garden of an old or handicapped person (*ibid*). By 1970, 10 such centres had been established: five accommodating young offenders; two for those aged 17-25; and three for those aged 21 and over (*ibid*: 101). Lady Wootton referred to the scheme in the House of Lords in 1972:

"But I want to say that we made a few references, in passing, to the New Zealand experiment of weekend residences, where young men engage from these centres in various forms of community service at the same time as having educational discussions, particularly on social topics. Conditions are of course very different from those in this country because of the smaller population and the large rural element in the economy, but we were impressed with what we heard: we did not see it at first hand" (Hansard. House of Lords Parliamentary Debates 1972: 332, 611).[28]

In relation to Australia, Lady Wootton noted:

"[T]his is an original provision in this country but it is not without parallel abroad: I always recall right in the centre of Australia in a juvenile court two young boys who had noticed that the collecting box for the Flying Doctor Service had a rather fragile front - and a glass front so that everybody could see when they were intending to put in a 5s. that everybody else had put in a £1. They noticed this, and took the opportunity, when it offered, to break the glass and steal the contents. The juvenile court at Alice Springs after long deliberation (how greatly I envied this when I thought of our metropolis lists of 40 cases) decided that these boys should pay for what they had done by spending their Saturday afternoons doing chores for the Flying Doctor Service. So there are these parallels abroad" (*ibid*: 612-613).

It appears, however, that such a practice was, similar to

---

28. The Wootton Committee itself thought that "there might be a place for a new form of weekend residential care as a focus for outdoor community service activity on the lines of the New Zealand periodic detention work centre" (Home Office 1970: 21).

community work practices as a condition of probation in New Zealand, rather *ad hoc* in nature and not a feature of statute law.

In the early 1950s in Germany (Federal Republic), Judge Karl Holzschuh began the practice of sentencing young offenders to perform constructive tasks in the community. For example, he sentenced a 16-year-old caught breaking street lamps in Darmstadt to work for three months cleaning street lamps with city maintenance employees. Similarly, "Lena", a 16-year-old housemaid found guilty of stealing money from her employees to purchase sweets, was ordered to buy chocolate and take it every Sunday to a local orphanage (Little 1957: 29). Holzschuh's belief in positive activities for offenders can be discerned from the following statement:

"Die Tiefenpsychologie lehrt uns, dass unser Tun und Lassen weitgehend vom Unterbewusstsein bestimmt wird. Bei Anwendung der Hypnose hat man die Beobachtung gemacht, dass es nicht möglich ist, den Unterbewusstsein eines Menschen einzuflüstern: du willst nicht rauchen - du willst nicht trinken - du willst nicht Motorrad fahren. Dieses nimmt keine negativen Suggestionen und Befehle an. Es hört nur die Wörter, die sich auf ein Handeln beziehen: rauche, trinke, fahre Motorrad. Eine Positive Suggestion ist deshalb weit und wirksamer. ... Hier liegt die einmalige und einzigartige Bedeutung der Weisungen: Statt der negativen Repressivmassnahmen mehr und mehr die gesunden Kräfte, die positive Leistung, die gute Tat zum Einsatz zu bringen" (Holzschuh 1960: 295-296).[29]

Holzschuh was greatly aided in 1953 by the passing of legislation which enabled German judges to apply a form of community service to juvenile delinquents (Rentzmann and Robert 1986: 12).[30] It also, importantly, made the Government's Youth Authority and certain welfare societies responsible for ensuring that the court orders were implemented (Little 1957: 29; Dunkel 1985: I, 45-256). It was not long before the employment of such practices began to be called for in England and Wales. Indeed an anonymous article written in the *Journal of Criminal Law* in 1958 stated:

"Whether the English courts should enliven their comparatively humdrum methods by the introduction of Judge Holzschuh's intriguing practices is a matter perhaps

29. "Psychology teaches us that our doings are determined, in part, by the subconscious. It has been observed through the use of hypnosis that it is not possible to influence the subconscious of a human: you do not want to smoke - you do not want to drink - you do not want to ride a motorbike. The subconscious does not accept negative suggestions or commands. It hears only the words that relate to an action: smoke, drink, ride a motorbike. A positive suggestion is therefore more effective. ... Here lies the unique meaning of Weisungen [forms of community service]: instead of more and more negative repressive measures, it seeks to bring healthy forces, positive benefits and good deeds to the forefront."

30. Section 12(2) of the German Constitution prohibits forced labour except for general military service. It appears, however, that community service imposed as an educational measure by a juvenile court was not unconstitutional in itself provided that it was not discriminatory, overtaxing or degrading (Van Kalmthout and Tak 1992: II, 499). For a closer examination of section 12(2), see Youngs (1994: 165).

worth considering by those interested in the problems of juvenile crime" (Anonymous 1958: XXII, 170).

Moreover, the first study to put forward definite proposals for the creation of a community work sanction for adult offenders was in Germany. In 1966, Jurgen Baumann *et al* published a report titled Alternative Draft of the Penal Code. Section 52 provided:

"(1) Auf Antrag des Verurteilten ordnet das Gericht an, dass gemeinnützige Arbeit, insbesondere in Krankenhausern, Erziehunganhalten, Alterheimen oder ähnlichen Einrichtungen ganz oder zeitweise an die Stelle der Geldstrafe tritt, wenn dadurch der Strafzweck erreicht werden kann. Der Antrag kann auch während der Laufzeit der Geldstrafe in der Regel jedoch nur einmal, gestellt werden.
(2) An die Stelle eines Tagessatzes tritt ein Tag freiwilliger gemeinnutziger Arbeit. Von der Entlohnung ist der Mindestsatz nach S.49 Abs. 2 einzubehalten.
(3) Das Vollstreckungsgericht kann die Art der Arbeit nachträglich durch Beschuss ändern. In Hartefällen kann es die Arbeit erlassen" (Baumann 1966: 17).[31]

---

31. "(1) On application by the offender the court shall, if the purposes of corrections can thereby be achieved, order community service in hospitals, educational institutions, old-age homes or similar organisations, as partial or complete satisfaction of a fine. Application may also be made during the term of payment of a fine, as a rule only once. (2) One day of voluntary work shall be the equivalent of each unit of a daily rated fine. Payment shall at least conform with the minimum provided for under Section 49(2). (3) The court charged with supervision of the execution of the sentence may

Hamburg adopted such a scheme in 1968. It allowed offenders who were unable to pay fines to carry out a form of community service provided they consented. Much of the reasoning behind the creation of such a sanction was to enable fine defaulters to avoid "ansteckenden Gefängniskontakt mit Schwerkriminellen" (Fuchs 1985: 324). To begin with, 150 offenders were selected to work in parks, cemeteries, hospitals and public soup kitchens (*ibid*; Pfohl 1983: 36-38).

In October, 1966, a Court Referral Programme was established in Alameda County in the United States through the combined efforts of the Volunteer Bureau and the Municipal Judge, Jacqueline Taber. This programme, although not a part of the criminal justice system, was created so as to enable selected offenders to perform unpaid labour in the community (Beha 1977: 6-7; Corry McDonald 1986; Maher and Dufour 1987: 23). It primarily served female offenders convicted of traffic and parking offences. Later on, those convicted of misdemeanours, such as petty theft, and disorderly conduct, also became eligible (Harris 1979: 12). Participation was voluntary and offenders could opt, if they so desired, for a traditional form of sentencing (Beha 1977: 6-7). The idea quickly took hold and judges

---

subsequently modify its order concerning the type of work. In cases of hardship the court may revoke the work." This alternative draft proposed that a fine could only be imposed in daily, weekly or monthly sentences. Section 49(2) provided that a judge, in imposing such a fine, should take account of the means of an offender at the time of pronouncing the sentence. The minimum amount of a day sentence was to be fixed at 5 deutschmarks, a weekly sentence at 35 deutschmarks and a monthly sentence at 150 marks (*ibid*: 16). See also, for a translation of section 52, Mueller (1977: 41).

began to impose forms of community service for a variety of offences. For instance, six Nebraska contractors convicted of rigging their bids for highway construction jobs, were each given tasks such as the creation of jobs for released prisoners and road improvements on a local Indian reservation (Corry McDonald 1986: 7). Similarly, executives of a firm who were convicted of criminal violations were ordered to donate 200 hours to a youth training project and to hire a number of paroled felons in their firm (*ibid*).

The Wootton Committee itself recognised that such practices were in operation:

"In some State and Municipal Courts in the U.S.A., for example, it is a common practice to require offenders to carry out work in hospitals; and in West German juvenile courts the power to issue directives to young offenders has been used for similar purposes in an imaginative and sometimes striking fashion eg, by sending youth drunks to help in homes for inebriates in order to bring home to them the consequences of alcoholism, or by sending those who rob old people to help at weekends in old people's homes. We are alive to the attractions of such proposals but it is not our primary intention to make the punishment fit the crime; should this occur we would expect it to be as much a matter of accident as of design. We are particularly anxious to avoid decisions which smack of gimmickry and so undermine public confidence. The scheme that we have in mind, therefore, is intended, not to compel the offender to undergo some form of penance directly related to his offence, which would only have limited application, but to require him to perform service of value to the community or to those in need" (Home Office 1970: 14-15).

Although the Wootton Committee drew support and encouragement from international experiences, credit for the introduction of a specific sanction of community service orders must go, in my opinion, to England and Wales. Despite the fact that the jurisdictions referred to all had adopted community service practices in one form or other by the late 1960s, it was only after the Wootton Committee's Report that they specifically established (with one exception, Germany) specific community service order sanctions, and these sanctions were, by and large, modelled on the English and Welsh design. For instance, as a result of the Criminal Justice Amendment Act of 1980, community service orders were introduced in New Zealand. The model which they adopted was an English and Welsh one, a good deal of attention being devoted to Barbara Wootton's "widely publicised" report. It could be imposed for offenders convicted of an offence punishable by imprisonment and the sentence was administered by the probation division of the Department of Justice (Armstrong 1983: 11-12; Leibrich 1985: XVIII, 85-94; Leibrich *et al* 1984: 4). The community service sanction could be distinguished from periodic detention centres on the grounds that it was more accessible and flexible, and it did not involve an element of compulsion (Leibrich *et al* 1984: 61). Similarly, much of the legislation for community service orders in Australia was founded on the English and Welsh model. Community service was provided for in Western Australia in 1977 (as a result of the Offenders Probation and Parole Act, 1963-1977) "where it was closely modelled on the British law" (Jones 1983: 71); in Queensland (The Offenders Probation and Parole Act of 1980) and New South Wales in 1980 (as a result of the Community Service Order Act of 1979), and in Victoria (on a pilot basis) and South Australia (in two metropolitan districts) in 1982 (Bevan 1983: 2).

By the late 1970s in Germany "haben sich immer mehr Bundesländer an eine Initiative des Staadtstaates Hamburg von 1969 errinert" (Fuchs 1985: 357). Such a scheme was introduced in Berlin in April 1978, in Hessen in August 1981, and in Bremen in August 1982 (Pfohl 1983: 36-45). These initiatives enabled persons on whom fines had been imposed and who were unable to pay them as a result of financial difficulties, unemployment or maintenance obligations to perform community service instead (Jorg-Albrecht and Schadler 1986: 174-175). Yet there was a reluctance to introduce community service as a principal sentence similar to that established in England and Wales. Bishop explains this by suggesting that fines in Germany filled the role played by community service in other countries. Thus the possibility of using community service as an alternative to imprisonment was greatly restricted (Bishop 1988: 207). Moreover, doubts still existed about whether or not an independent sanction of community service would be prohibited by the constitutional ban on forced labour and there was also the belief that the introduction of such a sanction was inappropriate given the poor situation of the job market (Van Kalmthout and Tak

1994: II, 471).[32]

By the mid-1980s in America, it was believed that community service was on the verge of becoming a "permanent institution", largely as a result of reports of the English and Welsh experience (Corry McDonald 1986: 9). As Silberman noted in 1986:

"Community Service, as it exists in the United States, is based on a British programme" (1986: XII, 132).

It had been recommended by organisations such as the American Bar Association (it also recognised that the specific sanction of community service was an English and Welsh innovation) and it received widespread acclaim in popular and academic literature (Harland 1980: XXIX, 426). In 1976 the Law Enforcement Assistance Administration made funding available for the establishment of community service programmes for adult offenders. In 1978 the Office of Juvenile Justice and Delinquency Prevention provided resources to enable the development of community service programmes for juveniles in 85 counties and states. By the 1990s, "community service orders were statutorily authorised options, in many, if not most, American jurisdictions" (Feeley *et al* 1992: 155-207).

Thus the process in respect of New Zealand, Australia and America had come full circle: England and Wales, initially

---

32. Although not imposed as a principal sanction, community service could, in addition to being imposed for fine default, also be imposed as a special condition of a suspended sentence, parole, a caution with conditional deferral of sentencing, a conditional waiver and a conditional pardon.

having been inspired, in part, by the international experiences delineated, exported community service in its new form back into these countries. Germany, however, has proved to be a more reluctant importer. This is not surprising given its preference for fines as an alternative to imprisonment and its constitutional doubts regarding forced labour. As such, it was in England and Wales that community service order sanctions first began to be statutorily institutionalised as an alternative sentencing option to imprisonment. Further support for this belief can be discerned from the whole host of jurisdictions which have drawn encouragement from, and for the most part imitated, English and Welsh practices concerning community service.

For example, in the mid-1970s in Canada some individual judges began to use community service as a condition of probation. It was sporadic though, many judges being sceptical about the legality of such a practice. By 1977, however, their suspicions had been allayed when the Court of Appeal upheld the legality of community service as a condition of probation (*R. v. Shaw* (1977) 26 C.R.N.S. 358). In June 1977, the Minister of Correctional Services and the Attorney General "set out to initiate the *English experience* (my italics) by introducing pilot projects in six areas and petitioning the Federal government (of Ontario) to create community service as a sanction independent of a probation order" (Menzies and Vass 1989: 28, 207).[33] To date community service remains a part of a probation order for adult offenders but it has been established both as an independent sanction and as a condition of probation for young offenders (*ibid*). Similarly, in Scotland, the Community Service by Offenders (Scotland) Act of 1978 was "comparable to the earlier legislation that had been introduced in England and Wales" (McIvor 1992: 8). Section 1(1) provided that a court could make an order for any person, of 16 or older convicted of an offence punishable by imprisonment, requiring him or her to perform unpaid community work for such number of hours (being in total not less than 40 or more than 240) as may be specified in the order."[34] In Scotland, however, in addition to being imposed as an independent sanction, community service could also be imposed as a condition of probation (section 7).

Community service orders in the Republic of Ireland were also based on the English and Welsh model. The Criminal Justice (Community Service) Act of 1983 provides that community service must be unpaid work and the number of hours to be completed should not be less than 40 hours or more than 240 (section 3(2)). The legislation further declares that the work should be completed within a period of one

---

33. See also Marc who suggested: "L'example anglais a traversé l'Océan et incité le service de Probation du Quebec a conduire en 1977-78" (the English example crossed the ocean and acted as an impetus for the probation service of Quebec to take the lead in 1977-78) (Marc 1985: Vol. 109, 113).
34. Section 1(2) provides, *inter alia*, that a court cannot make an order unless the offender consents.

year (section 7(2)).[35] Moreover, Rule 4 of the District Court (Criminal Justice (Community Service) Act 1983) Rules of 1984 requires a District Court judge to specify in an order the particular sentence of imprisonment for which community service is being substituted. The following types of offences are excluded:

(i) An offence where a fine may be imposed. In these cases the penalty imposed by the court is not a custodial sentence but a monetary fine. Committal only ensues when the offender fails to pay the fine within the time allowed. Since the penalty imposed was not a custodial sentence, a community service order cannot be made.

(ii) Offences for which there is a mandatory sentence, for instance a life sentence imposed following a conviction for murder.

(iii) Sentences imposed on offenders under 16 years of age at the time of sentencing.

(iv) Sentences imposed by the Special Criminal Court (O'Donovan 1990: 42-43).[36]

---

35. However, on application by the offender or relevant officer, and if it is in the interests of justice having regard to the circumstances to do so, the one year period may be extended.

36. In relation to sentences imposed in the Special Criminal Court, Mr Michael Noonan stated that he would be "reluctant to involve a civilian type service like the Probation and Welfare Service in the supervision, and possibly in the prosecution before the courts of breach of orders, of offenders who have associated with illegal organisations or other organised groups engaged in serious crime" (Dáil Debates 1983: 342, 324).

In the introduction to this section it was noted that Mr Kelly had suggested that the Act introducing Irish community service orders was simply taken out of the statute books in England and Wales and given an Irish title. Undoubtedly the introduction of community service orders in the Republic of Ireland was based on the English and Welsh model. But Mr Kelly's statement is not entirely true for two reasons: first, from the outset in Ireland a 16-year-old offender could receive a sentence of 240 hours;[37] secondly, in Ireland community service is employed as a direct alternative to imprisonment and the court must state the prison sentence it would have prescribed (had it not felt community service to be suitable) when imposing the order. This contrasts with England and Wales where community service is viewed as an alternative to offences "punishable with imprisonment" (Section 14(1) Powers of the Criminal Courts Act, 1973).

As a result of the Community Service Act of 1989, community service orders can now also be imposed in the Netherlands in two forms: as a principal sentence imposed by a judge, and as a special condition imposed under a conditional pardon. The maximum number of hours that can be imposed for a criminal case is 240 but no minimum has been set. Before imposing a sentence of community service the judge must state the prison sentence that he or she considered imposing prior to deciding upon community

---

37.   Section 10(2) of the Criminal Justice Act of 1991 similarly raised the number of hours for 16-year-olds in England and Wales to 240. Prior to this the number had been fixed at 120.

service (Van Kalmthout and Tak 1992: II, 743-746; Kelk 1995: 15-16). Other jurisdictions that have introduced community service order sanctions since 1972 include France, Denmark, Belgium, Norway, Portugal and Luxembourg. Although Sweden introduced community service orders in 1992 (Whitfield 1993: 92), prior to this it had shown a marked reluctance to develop such a sanction. Yet even its reservations, as we shall see, were reservations about the English and Welsh model. The B.R.A., a working party of the Swedish National Council for Crime Prevention, highlighted these reservations in 1977:

"[T]he system of community service is not entirely without objections so far as Sweden is concerned. The report pays particular attention to the practical problems entailed by this form of punishment. The system presupposes that there exist suitable and meaningful tasks, that a control system exists, that supervisory staff are available and not least that we can count on voluntary effort prepared to be involved in this kind of activity. Sweden is a pretty professionalised society where most work is performed by trained workers. Offenders often lack necessary qualifications and find it difficult to obtain suitable employment. The system presupposes that the person sentenced to community service has the other necessary qualifications to fulfil the tasks. The groups in Sweden that one wishes to transfer from imprisonment to other forms of sanctions often lack the social preconditions for community service. The risks thereby become great for a socially unjust application of the sanction system. Sweden also lacks the structure of strong and vigorous voluntary organisations that are one of the basic conditions for *Community Service in England*. It is also clear that a number of objections from the standpoint of the criminal law principles can be made to community service. It is hard to reconcile it with the demands for legal security, justice and equality since its contents varies from case to case and it is hard to assess it from the standpoint of punishment value"(Council's Working Group for Criminal Policy 1978: 63) (my italics).

By the late 1960s, then, the Wootton Committee was in a position to draw encouragement from community work practices in periodic detention centres and as a condition of probation in New Zealand; from *ad hoc* arrangements in Australian courts; from the experiences of Judge Holzschuh and other judges (from 1953 onwards) in Germany; and from the Court Referral Programme initiated in Alameda County in the United States in 1966. In this sense, as we have already seen in previous sections, *the community service ideal* was not radical. Yet the specific sanction of *community service orders*, as embodied in England and Wales, was novel in that it combined all of the following:

(i)   it was a statutorily institutionalised non-custodial sanction;
(ii) it formed an integral part of the criminal justice system;
(iii) it was made available to the courts for sentencing offenders of 16 and older;

435

(iv) it made use of voluntary organisations;

(v) it took account of the issue of forced labour;

(vi) it set out the hours and procedure for non-compliance;

(vii) it provided that the sanction should be administered by the probation service;

(viii) it was not aimed at making the punishment fit the crime.

Albeit that most jurisdictions made some alterations, it was this general model, or the impetus that this general model had created, that was one of the key factors in the introduction of the specific sanction of community service orders in: (a) countries with an experience of community service practices such as New Zealand, Australia and the United States, and (b) countries with little or no such experience including Canada, Ireland, France, Denmark and Belgium.

Conclusion

It has already been demonstrated in the first four chapters that the prefatory history approach to community service orders, as adopted by Vass and Pease, is, in the words of Garland - he was actually referring to prefatory histories in relation to the development of criminology - "a kind of foundational myth, developed for heuristic rather than historical purposes" (Garland 1994: 22). Not only does such an approach distort the intentions and aims of earlier penal institutions that adopted labour and hide the fact that their practices were founded upon specific beliefs and ambitions as well as an adherence to specific cultural determinants, it also fails to identify the fact that the introduction of community service orders was structured upon or around specific penal practices (both domestic and international), movements (the community ideal as discussed in chapter 3 and voluntarism in this chapter), as well as a specific cultural backdrop (the punishment of offenders by depriving them of their leisure time). This chapter has attempted to ground the historical conditions of emergence of community service in such terms, albeit recognising that such conditions, even when combined with a whole conjunction of forces (ie, social, cultural, penal, fiscal and political) which will be described in chapter 6, meant only that there was a good, as opposed to inevitable, chance that the sanction would be introduced.

The Wootton Committee, in introducing the sanction of community service, could look, to begin with, to the idea of voluntary community service which was so much in vogue in the 1950s and 1960s. The idealism underpinning such a practice was, in many respects, similar to the sanction proposed by the Committee. It was felt that the alienation and disaffection associated with consumerist society, particularly among young people, could be negated through the outlet of voluntary community service. Secondly, such a development was also reflected in the penal sphere. Many prisons, borstals and detention centres established schemes as a policy initiative whereby inmates could carry out community service tasks in their spare time. The performance of such constructive tasks would help offenders by enabling them to appreciate their own potential, by promoting social integration, and by encouraging in them a sense of social responsibility by making them aware of the existence of people less fortunate than themselves. It is not difficult to appreciate, then, that the notion of community service was well established by the 1960s, given its popularity in penal and non-penal spheres. The ideology of community service was also apparent, albeit on a more general scale, in the initiation of intermediate treatment schemes. In addition to acting as a middle ground between normal supervision and committal to care, this form of treatment also endeavoured to provide children and young persons with a different environment through the employment of social, educational or therapeutic activities in the community. In this way, it was hoped that they would form new interests and relationships, and develop a sense of social responsibility.

All of these described movements and schemes acted as stimuli for the introduction of community service orders in England and Wales. Further impetus, if it was needed, could be drawn from international penal experiments with community work in Australia, America, New Zealand and Germany. But whilst international experiments could act as a source of inspiration for the Wootton Committee, it is suggested that the specific sanction of community service was an English and Welsh innovation. There are three reasons for making such a claim. First, the jurisdiction of England and Wales was ripe for the introduction of such a sanction given that the community service ideal was already so prevalent both in a penal and non-penal sphere. (This is not difficult to understand when contrasted with Sweden which refused to introduce a specific sanction of community service until 1992 on the grounds that (a) sufficient meaningful tasks for offenders did not exist (b) it could not count on the necessary voluntary effort, and (c) many of its prison inmates were not suitable for the type of work involved.) Secondly, the specific sanction of community service, as introduced in England and Wales, was actually exported back to Australia, New Zealand and America. In the case of Germany, there was a reluctance to import community service along English lines because of the country's specific constitutional ban on forced labour and its preference for a system of fines as a principal alternative to imprisonment. Thirdly, the community service order idea, as enunciated in England and Wales, was also transplanted, with some alterations, into a number of other countries such as Canada, Ireland, Scotland, France and Denmark. Thus, whilst the idea was not radical by 1970, given its popularity in non-penal as well as penal thinking, the specific statutorily authorised sanction of community service for offenders 16 and over was an English and Welsh innovation.

CHAPTER 6

THE PENAL, SOCIAL, POLITICAL AND ECONOMIC CLIMATE OF THE LATE 1960s AND EARLY 1970s

The purpose of this chapter is to determine the reasons why the decision to draw upon the germs delineated in the last chapter was taken. Simply because those germs manifested themselves in either the described domestic or international penal and social domains does not explain the motivations and rationale for drawing upon them. More importantly, perhaps, it does not explain the manner in which those germs were fashioned to produce the sanction of community service. We have already witnessed in the first chapter how the cultural determinant of leisure shaped, to some extent, community service orders. We also noted that this cultural determinant has not remained constant and continuous over time. Indeed it has been submitted that it was only with the creation of a particular leisure environment, as existed after 1945 when leisure was established as an actual right of each individual, that the authorities could begin to deprive offenders of it, and justify it as an acceptable means of punishing offenders. In this chapter, penality in the late 1960s and early 1970s will be scrutinised from a variety of different perspectives in an effort to construct a more composite picture of the specific sanction of community service and how it was moulded in the period concerned.

However, rather than adopting a Rankean narrative of the historical process - *wie es eigentlich gewesesen ist* - I am conscious in examining the contours of the specific period in which community service orders were introduced that its "inimitable essence" can never be captured. Moreover, in addition to recognising our inability to extirpate the "whole experience" from the past being described, it is also important to bear in mind that there is, as Garland suggests, "no settled hierarchy of purposes or causal priorities which prevails at every point allowing us to describe, once and for all, the sequence of forces and considerations which determine the specific forms which penality displays (1990: 285).[1] Instead the penal period in question must be construed as a highly differentiated process, composed of a whole purview of referents which were all at work - in varying degrees of "effect", "amplitude" and "breadth" - in shaping the penological climate. For our purposes, these referents include rising crime rates, the sensitisation of moral panics, the politicisation of law and order, the crisis of hegemony which manifested itself in the criminal justice system, growing calls for the need to return to economic and social *laissez faire*, the declining influence of the rehabilitation ethos, and the priority and policy choices adopted by policy makers. Of course, some of these referents, such as the crisis in hegemony and moral panics, have manifested themselves at earlier points in time. Yet it

---

1. On the differentiation and prioritisation of events, see Foucault (1980: 114). For the dilemma in historical interpretation of irrational happenings, casual causes and the "famous crux of Cleopatra's nose", see Carr (1986: 90).

will be argued that it is the combined effect, as well as the specific nature of individual effect, of all of these referents which gave punishment in the late 1960s and early 1970s certain idiosyncratic and specific characteristics not evident in punishment set against earlier penal backdrops (albeit that it can still loosely be understood in terms of the modern penal complex set out in chapters 2 and 3). In this regard, the reader will have to bear with the fractured nature of the text, mindful, it is hoped, of the attempt being made at constructing a composite, albeit incomplete, picture of the penal, social, economic and political forces at work. As such, I make my apologies now for the lack of sequential analysis in this chapter. Any defects in this regard are sacrificed, it is hoped, in the interests of pursuing the various referents under separate headings.[2] Albeit that some element of lucid chronological analysis is lost in the process, the aim of this chapter, then, is to highlight the different starting and transitional points of the referents alluded to. Such an approach will, it is hoped, enable a better appreciation of the penological climate in question and its impact on the shaping of community service orders. Our approach in the first three chapters was diachronic in that it broadly mapped the relevant penal and cultural contours within which community service orders were introduced. The last chapter and the present one are more synchronic in design in that they focus on the specific features of the penal complex in

---

2. As Braudel noted: "Each 'current event' brings together movements of different origins, of a different rhythm: today's time dates from yesterday, the day before yesterday, and all former times" (1980: 34).

the late 1960s and early 1970s which impacted upon the introduction of community service orders. The discursive framework that follows, it is hoped, will enable us to develop a broad understanding of the different forces acting upon the penal domain in the period in question; it will not, however, be possible within the ambit of a single chapter to do much more than highlight the various referents and emphasise their impact upon the sanction.[3] These provisos aside, however, it is hoped that such an approach will provide a proper basis upon which to understand the decision to draw upon the germs of community service. It is also hoped that such an analysis will provide a more pluralistic framework in which to understand the manner in which those germs were moulded together.

Law and Disorder

By the late 1960s, as we shall see, the public had become extremely concerned about the rising incidence of crime (McClintock and Avison 1968: 272; Morris 1989: 97-98). In 1949 the number of recorded indictable offences stood at 114,294 (Central Statistical Office 1951: 58). This figure had increased to 130,920 in 1957 (Central Statistical Office 1958: 69); to 182,217 in 1961 (Central Statistical Office 1962: 65); to

---

3.   In saying this, I do not wish to imply that that these referents, or indeed the germs discussed in chapter 5, made the introduction of community service a *fait accompli*; rather what I wish to argue is that these referents and germs made a *strong case* for the introduction of such a sanction.

218,435 in 1965 (Central Statistical Office 1967: 67); and to 242,208 in 1967 (Central Statistical Office 1968: 67). In 1969 the figure stood at 283,825.[4] The Labour party viewed this escalation in the number of indictable offences as a result of the "get rich quick ethos of the affluent society" (Labour Party 1964: 5-6). Such an outlook was compatible with R. H. Tawney's 1966 monograph on "acquisitive society":

"The will to economic power, if it is sufficiently single-minded, brings riches. But if it is single-minded it destroys the moral restraints which ought to condition the pursuit of riches, and therefore also makes the pursuit of riches meaningless" (1966: 35).

The Conservative Party, on the other hand, put it down to a wide variety of factors. These included the growing impersonality of society and the anonymity of the individual within it, the decline in the agencies of direct social control and moral instruction, the growing emphasis on success, the decline of family influence, the values of youth culture, and the opportunities provided for crime in industrial and prosperous societies (Conservative Party 1966: 11-15). Undoubtedly increasing crime rates had an effect on societal anxieties. Criminal statistics, however,

---

4. This is an adjusted figure: direct comparisons between 1969 and those of earlier periods are not possible given that the 1968 Theft Act redefined theft and incorporated virtually all offences of larceny, breaking and entering, robbery, embezzlement, and fraudulent conversion. The real figure for 1969, then, was 304,070 (Central Statistical Office 1973: 82). Recorded non-indictable offences also showed a remarkable rate of growth. The figure increased from 523,563 in 1949 to 1,337,445 in 1967.

were insufficient in themselves to cause the anxieties that prevailed in the late 1960s and early 1970s. The purpose of the following section, then, is to demonstrate how a fear of disorder was engendered in the masses through a variety of different phenomena. In doing so, it is necessary to refrain from drawing an amnesiac and ahistorical picture of order, civility and respect for authority prior to the period in question. Of course there never has been a "Golden Age" of compliance and security: Jack the Ripper, the garrotting panic, escaping convicts from the hulks, Fenian upsurges of violence on the mainland, the number of ticket-of-leave men roaming the streets, the number of criminals using aliases, to name but a few, all bear testimony to such a reality. What is striking about the 1960s and early 1970s from our perspective, however, is the number of events which came together to give the "20 years ago" brigade so much ammunition with which to invoke indignation and anxiety (Pearson 1983: 4-11).

One may begin by alluding to the perceived disorder that manifested itself in relation to the youth of Britain. In the early 1950s it was the "Teddy Boy" and the perceived images of mindless violence that he personified. In fact, as Chibnall noted, the "moral panic surrounding the Teddy Boy carried such momentum that it continued long after the style began to decline in 1957" (1977: 62). In the 1960s, notions of disaffected youth were associated with the Mods and Rockers. As Cohen has suggested:

"The Mods and Rockers symbolised something far more important than what they actually did. They touched the delicate ... nerves through which post-war social change in Britain was experienced. No one wanted depressions or austerity, but messages about 'never having it so good' were ambivalent in that some people were having it too good and too quickly" (1973: 192).

Generalised beliefs about youthful violence and the deterioration in the moral fabric gained widespread coverage in the press. This coverage often amounted to misconception. For example, with regard to the Mods and Rockers and their clashes in Margate in 1964, Cohen argues that a whole series of fallacies were portrayed in the press; although it was believed that the Mods and Rockers caused widespread damage at Margate and that the resort suffered a loss of trade, it appears, in truth, that only £100 of damage was caused and more visitors turned up at the resort than ever before (Cohen 1971: 229-230). In this sense, press sensitisation fuelled the hysteria generated.

Albeit that it was not a new phenomenon, the theme of violence was also perpetuated through the intensity of football hooliganism in the 1960s (Chibnall 1977: 33).[5] It was, no doubt, sustained and to some extent amplified by the press through their techniques of portraying the phenomenon to the public - these included amassing

---

5.   In 1969, the Minister of Sport, Mr Howell, who viewed a football supporter who wore "hobnailed boots or ... [sung] obscene songs as anti-social as the driver drunk in charge of a car", called for magistrates to show "a bit more" imagination when dealing with hooligans: by imagination he meant custodial sentences as opposed to fines which were, in his view, "often quite ridiculous and inappropriate" (*The Daily Telegraph* 1969: Oct 6, 13).

separate offences in a wide variety of locations into one report under a joint heading such as "40 arrested in football riots", and also by publishing the views of magistrates, politicians and football managers (Roshier 1973: 35-36). Racial consciousness, such as the Rhodesian House demonstrations and anti-police harassment demonstrations, together with the emergence of a more black militant consciousness with the establishment of the British Black Panther Party and the Black People's Alliance, and Enoch Powell's "rivers of blood" speech in Birmingham in 1968, also contributed to the unsettled atmosphere being created in Britain (Hall *et al* 1981: 248-252; Marwick 1998: 231-238). Further concerns were raised by the number of political demonstrations that evidenced themselves. These included the anti-Vietnam demonstrations in 1968, the "Stop the Seventies" tour (Springboks rugby tour) in 1969, and the break up, by Cambridge students, of a dinner promoted by the Greek government in 1970 (Chibnall 1977: 94; Halloran 1970; Downes and Morgan 1994: 203). The anti-Vietnam demonstrations in Grosvenor Square in October, 1968, in particular, highlighted the increased anxiety being felt about the breakdown of law and order. Although there were not many violent encounters, the media, expecting agitation from the outset, directed their attention to what violence there was, neglecting almost entirely any issues raised by the demonstration itself (Murdock 1973: 162). Moreover, urban guerrilla warfare began to raise its ugly head in the period concerned. In August, 1971, four revolutionaries were convicted of conspiring to cause explosions at the home of Robert Carr, architect of the Industrial Relations

Bill. Five further bomb attacks occurred between the explosion of two bombs at Carr's house in January, 1971, and the arrest of the revolutionaries in August of the same year. Such acts were carried out in response to the belief that the ruling classes continued to exploit and oppress the interests of the masses (Chibnall 1977: 96-103). In reporting the planting of bombs at Carr's house, the press was, as Chibnall noted, "unanimous in identifying the attack as something alien to the British way of life, a threat to the freedom we all enjoy under the rule of law" (*ibid*: 98). Finally, the shooting of three policemen in Shepherds Bush in August, 1966, the bestial accounts of child murder in the Brady and Hindley trial, and the sensational and violent lives of the Krays and Richardsons, all helped to compound the feeling that British society was increasingly witnessing a period of subversion and moral degeneracy.

Two further themes in law and order also began to find resonance in the late 1960s. First, the growing phenomenon of drug abuse began to be perceived as a social problem. In the 1930s and 1940s there were only about 350 known addicts, but by the 1960s this had increased to 3,000 (Bean 1974: 1). Moreover, much of the anxiety was perpetuated by the drug culture inherent, *inter alia*, in much of the popular music of the period - it could be seen, for example, in such song titles as *Lucy in the Sky with Diamonds* (the initials spelling LSD) and Procul Harum's *A Whiter Shade of Pale* (Marwick 1990: 143-144). Indeed 1967 is generally regarded as the year when panic about drugs reached new heights.[6] It was the year, for example, that Mick Jagger was tried on drugs charges - no figure, as Hall points out, "was more designed to fit the stereotype and trigger moral alarm: overtly if androgynously sexual, flamboyant, hedonistic" (Hall *et al* 1981: 240).[7] It was also the year that the Regional Drugs Squad was formed; that section 2(5) of the Criminal Law Act, 1967, was introduced to enable a police constable to arrest anyone believed with reasonable cause to be about to commit an offence of possessing cannabis; and, that section 6(1) of the Dangerous Drugs Act, 1967, was introduced to enable the police to search persons without a warrant on reasonable suspicion of possessing any of the controlled drugs.[8] Awareness of a growing drug culture was also aided by the media which, as Auld noted, succeeded in "creating a situation where almost any form of behaviour, provided it ...[was] sufficiently abnormal, unexpected or bizarre, ... [was] a candidate for explanation in terms of the effects of drug intoxication" (Auld 1973: 157; Young 1973: 314-323). Secondly, images of anarchy and violence began to manifest themselves in relation to Northern Ireland. These images included: the participation of 4000 people on a civil

6. See also Marwick who noted: "The late sixties was the first era in which almost everyone in certain age groups, and in certain professions (mainly to do with the arts, entertainment and education) had at least some contact with drugs, even if it amounted to no more than the offer, and refusal, of a joint or a few amphetamines" (1998: 496).
7. In the same period, Marianne Faithful was apprehended after an overdose, and Keith Richards, also of the Rolling Stones, was found guilty of drug offences (*ibid*).
8. For judicial views on drugs in the period concerned, see Teff (1975: 24-26).

rights march protesting about housing discrimination, local government appointments, the absence of one man-one vote, and gerrymandering on August 24, 1968; fierce rioting by Republicans in the Bogside, Coalisland, Armagh, Dungannon, and Belfast on the 14-15 of August, 1969; the use of CS gas on the citizens of the Bogside during those riots - this was the first time that CS gas was officially used on British soil; the emergence of the Provisional I.R.A., anxious to remove itself from the less active Official I.R.A. (thought, in jest, to stand for the *Irish ran away*); the death of Ensign Robert Curtis on February 4, 1971, the first British soldier to be killed in Ireland since the 1920s, quickly followed by the gruesome killing of two R.U.C. officers in Belfast and three off-duty soldiers, two of them teenagers and brothers, in Ligoniel; the rising death count - by 1970, 25 deaths were directly attributable to the "troubles", by the end of 1971, there were 174; and the killing of 14 people on an internment protest march by British paratroopers in Derry on 30 January, 1972 (Coogan 1995: 26-161).[9] All of these incidents in Northern Ireland undoubtedly heightened the sense of crisis being felt in Britain as a whole. They helped considerably, as Hall *et al* noted, "to sharpen the tenterhooks on which the British public, by now, had become thoroughly impaled" (*ibid*: 297).

In questioning the way people think about the decline of law and order in England and Wales, Pearson's cogently

---

9.   Anne Edwards, a Sunday Express columnist coldly wrote about the event in the following terms: "this sort of loudmouthed, lunatic hooliganism is festering all over the country", under a headline, "When thugs hide behind a cause" (Hall 1981: 300).

argued thesis is correct in proposing that there never has been a "Golden Age". By alluding to a plethora of concerns in the 1920s and 1930s, such as riots at football matches, dismay about crime, gambling, dog tracks, amusement arcades, and the "Americanisation of English morality" through cinema, he concluded that contemporary problems are not a break with the past in respect of issues of law and order (1983: 25-48). There is much to commend in what he proposes, particularly in relation to the ahistorical approach adopted by the "20 years ago" brigade. Yet it is my contention that the intensity of the violence, crime and unrest that I have described in the 1960s and early 1970s, together with the close proximity of events in temporal terms, their cumulative impact, and the effectiveness of the "20 years ago" brigade in transmitting messages of disorder, all had very real consequences in respect of the criminal justice system. Furthermore, these phenomena in the late 1960s and early 1970s were covered by a newspaper system more adept at covering a wider range of law and order issues, more specialised in nature, more capable of identifying collective values, more visible with large pictures and more prominence given to the issues focused upon, and more personal in nature with the decline of anonymity outside the leader columns (Chibnall 1977: 46-74; Mathiesen 1995: 339; Curran 1978: 74). In addition, these law and order phenomena had become more visible through the arrival of television into the homes of most British citizens in the 1960s. As Alderson noted:

"Being both audio and visual, television leaves less to the

effort of the person receiving the message than do radio or newspaper, which require more action on the part of the listener or the reader. Since television is delivering its message to the eye and the ear, it has a special impact" (1982: 8).

Finally, I.T.N. introduced *News at Ten* on 3 July, 1967. It was the first half-hour news bulletin and was quickly followed by the B.B.C.'s decision to extend its own 9.00 p.m. news bulletin. Such developments had important consequences for the dissemination of news via television. As Seymour-Ure noted:

"News was no longer an illustrated supplement to radio and newspapers. Newscasters worked as journalists and interviewers, not just announcers. Satellite transmission even added immediacy and a much extended range of sources and material. 'The news' became less of a bulletin and more an integrated programme of 'reporter packages', capable of delivering large audiences in peacetime" (1996: 10).

Thus whilst Pearson was correct in noting the amnesiac manner in which anxiety was often generated by the "20 years ago" brigade, the fact remains that it was generated and there was a cornucopia of ammunition which they could draw upon, and more importantly, which the masses could relate to given the nature of the press and television.

Moreover, it is submitted that there are two fundamental flaws in Pearson's approach. First, many of the moral panics indexed by him in the early part of the 1900s did not manifest themselves in a crisis of hegemony in the penal domain. In this sense, such panics cannot simply be viewed as continuous with the panics that evidenced themselves in the late 1960s which did, in part, result, as will be argued, in a crisis of hegemony. Secondly, even if one attempts to categorise panics that have effectuated penal change (and Pearson makes no attempt), one will be faced with a number of discontinuities which prevent simple linear comparisons. Contrast, for example, the garrotting panic of the early 1860s with the panics of the late 1960s and early 1970s. Albeit that we can make superficial correlations in that both sets of panics were promoted by the press, judiciary, police and public, it is submitted that a number of phenomena make schematism impossible at a more purposeful level. These include the intensity and variety of the panics, their occurrences throughout the country as a whole, the methods used to disseminate information about the panics to the public at large, the political climate of the periods concerned, the politicisation of panic, their combination with other dominant penal aspirations (in the early 1860s, it was the desire to rationalise; in the late 1960s and early 1970s it was the more pragmatic consideration of bifurcation) and the manner in which panics magnify penal dilemmas (in the early 1860s, it was the lack of uniformity across the system as a whole; in the late 1960s, the panics were magnified by a crisis of containment, by the demise of rehabilitation as an effective policy goal, by the over-crowded nature of prisons, and by the need to curtail expenditure). Many of these factors will be discussed in more detail as we proceed through this section and indeed the chapter as a whole. Suffice it to say, at this juncture, that Pearson's approach is ahistorical in that he views panics in a simple linear paradigm. No attempt is made: (a) to account for the fact that historical actuality dictates that not all panics instigated, even in part, specific shifts in penal thinking; and (b) to account for the fact that when they did (such as in the early 1860s and late 1960s), the panics were sustained by specific penal, historical, technological and social forces which render comparisons within a narrow teleological framework nugatory. With this in mind, then, it is now necessary to examine the impact of the described phenomena on the criminal justice system. The crisis that manifested itself in the system in the late 1960s and early 1970s will be dealt with at a later point in the chapter.

To begin with, we may allude to post-war general elections in Britain. In the 1945, 1950, 1951 and 1959 elections, little or no attention was devoted to the issue of law and order. In political terms the years in question were characterised by "Butskellism", a form of consensus politics which supported the expansion of the Welfare State, State planning and intervention (Downes and Morgan 1994: 39; Taylor 1981: 39). But by 1966, the Conservative party, albeit that it concentrated its policy on the eve of the election on the topics of economy, Europe, trade union reform, social services and housing, began to assume the mantle as the law and order party: 40 per cent of Conservative candidates broached the issue in their campaign addresses with not one Labour candidate doing likewise (Butler and King 1966: 103). Such an increase in Conservative addresses on the topic of law and order must, for the most part, be attributed to widespread media coverage of crime issues, in particular issues such as disaffected youth, football hooliganism, the Moors murders, the Shepherds Bush police murders, and the exploits of the Krays and Richardsons. It was the 1970 election, however, that set the real agenda for law and order. The Conservatives again placed a strong emphasis on the framework of order, with 60 per cent of its candidates mentioning the issue as opposed to 15 per cent of Labour candidates (Butler and Pinto-Duschinsky 1970: 90). Moreover, law and order was now firmly entrenched as the sixth most important issue in Conservative thinking; it had not, as yet, got into the Labour top ten (*ibid*).[10] In this way, the Conservatives had recognised the electoral rewards to be gained from forceful leadership in the domain of law and order, whilst still advocating the need for individual responsibility. This is illustrated by Quintin Hogg's speech in Trinity College, Dublin, in December, 1966, in which he argued that society was faced with a "slide into anarchy", partly as a result of Labour M.P.s' "deliberate detestation of all forms of authority save their own opinions" (*Sunday Times* 1969: 7 December, 3),[11] and by Enoch Powell's speech on June 13, 1970, in which "he made an onslaught on the

---

10. For a general analysis of the 1970 election, see Conley (1994: 55-64).
11. See also Rhodes Boyson who suggested: "Not only is the present Welfare State inefficient and destructive of personal liberty, individual responsibility and moral growth, but it saps the collective moral fibre of our people as a nation ... The predictable outcome is seen as disorder, crime and lack of civic duty, and in the palsied inefficiency so often visible throughout the public service, nationalised boards and even private industry. We have been heading for economic and moral bankruptcy" (Boyson 1971: 1-8).

enemy within, the small minority who were infiltrating and brainwashing decent people into accepting the collapse of law and order as exemplified in Ulster and in the cancellation of the South African tour" (Butler and Pinto-Duschinsky 1966: 161; Himmelweit 1981: 94-95; Aughey and Norton 1984: 137-148).

Along with the politicised nature of law and order, the period in question was also symptomised by marked changes in police functioning and organisation. In the 1950s, the police, given their consensus style of policing, were generally regarded as "national mascots" and "totems of patriotic pride" (Reiner 1994: 710). However, in response to rising rates of crime, particularly violent and organised crime in the 1960s, the emphasis was turning, albeit slowly, to "technology, specialisation and managerial professionalism as the keys to winning the fight" (Reiner 1992). There was, for example, a series of amalgamations which reduced the number of police forces in England and Wales from 159 in 1945 to 49 in 1970 (Lea and Young 1984: 182). More directly relevant was the increasing specialisation within the force itself: the Regional Crime Squads were created to deal with serious crime in 1964; the élite Special Patrol Group was established by Scotland Yard as a highly mobile unit for hard-line operations such as political or racial disturbances in 1965; the Drugs Squad was formed in 1967; Task Force was established in Bristol in 1967 consisting of an armed police unit of 40; and, the Bomb Squad became a permanent feature of the police forces in the late 1960s (Hall 1981: 46-47; Manwaring-White 1983: 44). In addition, the police became more military minded in their response to crime and disorder. Until the mid-1960s, they held a very limited supply of weapons, but from 1966 onwards they began to acquire surplus army rifles (Uglow 1988: 55). They also began to utilise more advanced types of weaponry. In 1968 36 different police forces held stocks of CS gas, the R.U.C. used a water cannon on the streets of Derry on October 5, 1968, a gas gun was discharged by the police in Willenden, London, in 1971, and rubber bullets which could be discharged from baton guns became a common weapon of the R.U.C. in the late 1960s in Northern Ireland (Manwaring-White 1983: 117-154). Finally, police information collection, surveillance methods and communication systems all underwent a massive overhaul in the 1960s. In 1968, for example, the Greater London Council ratified the installation of a system referred to as CITRAC (Central Integrated Traffic Control Scheme) which it aimed to operate from Scotland Yard's Area Traffic Control room. When it was completed, CITRAC consisted of 145 cameras capable of surveying 200 square miles for 14 hours a day, six days a week. In 1969, the Labour government authorised the construction of a national computer unit to be stationed at Hendon, North London. In 1972, the first police command and control systems were introduced in Birmingham. In the same year the A8 Operations System was established by the police in London. It employed close circuit video cameras at numerous locations throughout London, such as Trafalgar Square, Whitehall, Hyde Park Corner, and Grosvenor Square, so as to monitor any protest marches (*ibid*: 84-115; Emsley 1991: 166). The consequences of these changes culminated, to some extent, in the demise of the "Dixon of Dock Green" perception of policing, focusing as it did on a consensual approach, and the emergence of the specialised "technocop" approach which was more willing to employ modern scientific developments, often at the expense of community relations, in the fight against crime. Albeit knowingly oversimplifying the transition, Hall *et al* noted:

"These changes combined to decrease the traditional independence of the policeman on the beat; to accentuate the move away from 'peace keeper' to 'crime fighter', and to weaken the remaining links between police and community. The 'typical' policeman was no longer the friendly, helpful 'bobby', keeping the peace and thereby preventing crime, knowledgeable about 'his' community and sharing some of its values, with a large degree of 'on the spot' independence from his immediate superiors. Today, ... the 'typical' policeman is a professional 'cop', member of a crime-fighting unit, whose cultural contact with the people he polices is minimal" (1981: 46).

Finally, the crisis was also reflected in widespread anxiety about growing social permissiveness. The 1960s had evidenced a sustained programme of libertarian criminal law reform: the acquittal of Penguin books in 1960 over the decision to republish *Lady Chatterly's Lover* (Robertson 1993: 218); the Abortion Act, 1967, which enabled the medical termination of a pregnancy if two medical practitioners were of the opinion that it would involve risk to the life, physical health, or mental health of the pregnant woman, or if there was a sustained risk that if the child were born it would suffer from such physical or mental abnormalities so as to be seriously handicapped; the Murder (Abolition of Death Penalty) Act, 1965, which suspended the use of the death penalty for five years; the National Health Service (Family Planning) Act, 1967, which enabled the local health authorities of England and Wales to supply contraceptive substances and appliances; the Sexual Offences Act, 1967, which provided that a homosexual act between two consenting adults in private would not be a criminal act; the abolition of censorship of the theatre under the Theatres Act, 1968; and the Divorce Reform Act of 1969, which provided, *inter alia*, that if a married couple had lived apart for a continuous period of two years, they had a legal right to get divorced. In the public domain, the effects of these reforms quickly became discernible. Gays began to 'come out, advertisements began to appear providing information on contraceptives and abortion', explicitness became more palpable in books and in the theatre, and more freedom was afforded to both sexes after divorce reform. In short, "British society seemed to have broken out of the straitjacket of dullness and conformity which had pinioned it since Victorian times" (Marwick 1996: 152; Marwick 1998: 265; Hall 1980: 1).

But from our perspective, these reforms also had another important consequence - the commencement, or "mapping together" as Stuart Hall *et al* would call it (1981: 222), of a moral backlash. It is submitted that seeds of dissensus quickly began to combat the new found belief that permissiveness promised a novel platform for freedom to express itself. We have already seen in the last chapter that the emergence of participation as a social and moral issue in the 1960s was brought about as a result of the belief that the age of consumerism precipitated the loss of some personal element in people's lives. Anxiety and dissensus also evidenced itself in Mary Whitehouse's "Clean Up T.V." campaign which grew into the National Viewers and Listeners Association (Davies 1975: 47), in the growing attack on "pornographic Britain" (Longford Report 1972; Capon 1972: 5-6), in the religious ideologies of the Lord's Day Observation Society, S.P.U.C. and the Festival of Light movement (one march by the Festival of Light movement in 1971 consisted of 10,000 people headed by the Bishop of Blackburn and the Chief Constable of Lancashire), in discontentment with divorce legislation, particularly among the Married Women's Association (which organised a petition of 12,000 names) and the Mothers' Union with its 400,000 members (Pym 1974: 85), in disgruntlement with the abolition of capital punishment (opinion polls suggested that 65 per cent of the people opposed it), and in the convergence of the criminal violence issue in the mid- to late-1960s to create the "Violent Society" theme among anti-permissives (*ibid*: 69; Crick 1974: 27). Such dissensus was encapsulated in Flo Dobbie's, *Land Aflame*, in 1972:

"In our factories, machines are fitted with proper guards to prevent people from injuring themselves. Parliament supports this by law. Yet in the realm of the mind we are told: 'Remove all guards! Let anything happen! This is not liberty but licence, not freedom but slavery. Enough of it.

Let us strive to achieve a land in which our children are free of moral corruption'" (1972: 93).

This backlash, as we shall see later on in this chapter, also helped to shape, *inter alia*, judicial action in England and Wales: as Hall *et al* noted, "they seemed to share public anxiety about permissiveness, they took a stringent line in implementing legislation which they interpreted as too soft; they helped to generate, by some of their statements on violent crime, the initial concern" (Hall 1981: 37; Ryan 1983: 118). Moreover, there was a growing consentience in Conservative circles, as we have already touched upon, that Labour rule was effectuating disunity through the subversion of traditional social authority. The New Right, and in particular individuals such as Law and Boyson, argued that the Conservative party needed to break with the consensus if it ever hoped to attain power. It could do this, *inter alia*, by appealing to the "silent majority", that great mass of ordinary citizens who increasingly felt dissociated from the decision makers and opinion formers of the era (Gamble 1974: 103; Brittain 1973: 356). Such a standpoint was exploited to the full by Enoch Powell. His "rivers of blood" speech in Birmingham in 1968 had a significance, as Gamble noted, far beyond that of immigration (1974: 103). Within days of his speech, Powell had received 105,000 letters of congratulations for his beliefs *(ibid:* 121). In effect, it opened up the permissive society debate, aided the breakdown of consensus politics, and established a new platform for Conservatism and its image as the law and order party *(ibid)*.

For our purposes, it is important to realise that the period of the late 1960s and early 1970s manifested itself in a perceived crisis of control. Such a crisis was brought about, in part, through dramatic increases in crime, notions of disaffected youth, football hooliganism, racial tension, political demonstrations, the developing drug culture, and the upsurge of violence in Northern Ireland. It would also be sustained, as shall become more evident, by the rise to prominence of containment as a policy goal, by the crisis that arose in relation to prison numbers, and by the growing attacks on rehabilitation as a policy goal. All of these phenomena, it will be argued, combined to manifest themselves in a shift towards a more repressive, authoritarian control culture. Such a shift evidenced itself in the movement from a consensual to a professional, somewhat militaristic, approach to policing, in the palpable hardening of the judiciary, in the politicisation of law and order, and, as we shall see, in the drive towards bifurcation. It is now necessary to turn our attention to more specific developments in the criminal justice system itself.

Penal Crisis

The intention of the following section is to illustrate the crisis of hegemony which evinced itself in the criminal justice system in the 1960s and early 1970s. Such a crisis was, as has been described, provoked, in part, by the perceived escalation in disorder in the period concerned. It would be actuated at a more intense level by a number of phenomena located within the penal complex. These include massive increases in the prison population and the number sleeping two or three to a cell, the extreme pressures placed on the provision of services in the prison system, the degrading conditions to be found therein, the increasing number of prison escapes particularly by high profile inmates, the increasing number of disturbances and the general rise of violence of inmates directed at each other and against prison staff, the substantial growth in gross prison expenditure, the mounting evidence that rehabilitative practices were not having the desired effect, the developing sociological awareness of the contaminating effects of prison life, and the pragmatic, reactive nature of penal policy making in the period concerned. By providing a comprehensive narration of such phenomena, it is anticipated that we will begin to appreciate not only why the decision was taken to devise the specific sanction of community service, but also the specific framework within which the sanction would have to be formulated. Let us begin by examining the issue of overcrowding.

(a) Overcrowding
The purpose of this section is to highlight the expansionist nature of prison system growth, particularly in local prisons, since the Second World War. In particular, it will attempt to demonstrate that by the late 1960s the phenomenon of prison overcrowding had, unlike in the 1940s and for the greater part of the 1950s, come to be perceived as an intractable problem which was incapable of receding of its own accord. The growth of prison overcrowding of course

cannot simply be viewed in a linear or continuous pattern as it is a phenomenon very much confined to the latter half of the twentieth century. As Downes suggests, placing more than one prisoner in a cell prior to the Second World War was "virtually unknown" (Downes 1993: 67). In 1908 the daily average prison population stood at 22,029 but had been reduced to 9,196 by 1918. In 1923, it had increased slightly to a figure of 11,148 (Rutherford 1984: 123). Yet such an increase was not a cause for concern among the prison authorities. In fact, they confidently predicted in 1924:

"[P]resent circumstances and the history of the past few years give us reason to hope that the prison population will not increase in the near future; but will show a steady, if slow, decline" (Home Office 1925: Cmnd 2307, 6-7).

There was much to suggest that their prediction would hold true. In 1938, the daily average population stood at 11,086 (Central Statistical Office 1951: 63), but many prisons had been closed, reducing the number of prison cells by about 5,000 (Stern 1993: 24). The 1940s, however, witnessed a sharp increase in the daily average prison population. In 1944 it stood at 12,915, in 1945, it was 14,708 (Home Office 1947: Cmnd 7271, 14), and by 1948 it had risen to 19,765 (Home Office 1949: Cmd 7777, 11). The prison authorities now found themselves having to deal with a prison population higher than had been known since 1913 and expected to have, as a result, 55 prison establishments under their control by the end of 1947, as opposed to 40 in 1938

(Home Office 1947: Cmd 7271, 14). These included the establishment of open and medium-security prisons which began with Leyhill in Gloucestershire in 1946 (Thomas 1972: 81). In addition to the establishment of more prison institutions, the authorities also found themselves, for the first time officially, having to place more than one prisoner in a cell. In 1948, almost 2,000 prisoners slept three to a cell in local prisons (Home Office 1950: Cmd 8088, 28). It appears, however, that it was looked upon as a temporary expedient rather than as a policy change. As the governor of one prison noted in 1948:

"About 300 men still remain three in a cell. I shall be glad when this overcrowding eases. It is unhealthy and disconcerting both for the prisoners and the discipline of the prison" (Home Office 1949: Cmd 7777, 72).

Indeed another governor even saw the positive side of overcrowding:

"The location of three prisoners in one cell has proved far more successful than I had ever anticipated ... It appears to help them over their apparent depression that used to be so noticeable" (*ibid*).

What was not apparent then was that this so-called temporary phenomenon of overcrowding would so dominate penal policy over the next 50 years. It was brought about and maintained by the growth of crime (by the late 1960s, the number of men convicted of indictable offences was averaging an increase of 7 per cent per year) (Home Office 1971: Cmnd 4724, 3); by longer sentences of imprisonment (between 1938 and 1968 the number of sentences between six and 12 months imprisonment increased from 1,881 to 5,958, the number of sentences between 18 months and three years increased from 581 to 4,059 and, the number of sentences between three and five years increased from 158 to 1,086) (House of Commons Parliamentary Debates 1971: 826, 977; Bottoms 1987: XXVI, 181); by the number of short sentences of imprisonment imposed (in 1964, for example, out of 44,000 persons received into prison under sentence, no fewer than 22,500 had been sentenced to six months imprisonment or less) (House of Lords Parliamentary Debates 1967: 283, 644) ; the number of individuals remanded in custody before conviction (35,000 people each year according to Mr Jenkins in 1966, although only half this number received prison sentences on conviction) (House of Commons Parliamentary Debates 1966: 738, 65); by the sentencing policy of the courts (in 1969, for example, 32,169 suspended sentences of imprisonment were imposed and in the same period 8,742 persons were committed to custody on the activation of suspended sentences - many of these might have received a fine or probation, if the suspended sentence had not been in operation) (Home Office 1970: Cmd 4486, 10); and finally, by the increase in the population of England and Wales which also produced a rise in the number of people in custody (the male population at risk, for example, between 1950 and 1970, increased by 9.7 per cent) (Home Office 1971: Cmnd 4724, 3).

In the early 1950s the prison population continued to increase. In 1951, the daily average figure stood at 21,780 and had grown to 23,670 by 1952 (Home Office 1956: Cmnd 10: 31). The prison authorities dealt with this growth by reconditioning some closed and redundant prisons, by employing open prisons and borstals, and by establishing medium-security prisons adapted from camps, country houses and disused forts *(ibid*: 9). As such, overcrowding still appeared to be viewed as a temporary expedient. As one governor noted in 1953:

"We are *still congested* ... I have had isolated cases of men wanting to share a cell but these requests have been confined to illiterate prisoners who seek companionship" (Home Office 1954: Cmnd 9259, 111) (my italics).

Indeed the trend for the daily average population in that year was downwards, standing as it did at 23,567 (Home Office 1956: Cmnd 10, 31). This pattern continued in the following years, dropping to 22,213 in 1954, to 21,010 in 1955 and 20,642 in 1956 (Home Office 1958: Cmnd 496, 9). This enabled the number of prisoners sleeping three in a cell to be reduced from a figure of 5,638 at the end of 1952 (Home Office 1954: Cmnd 496, 1) to a figure of about 3,000 in 1955 (Home Office 1956: Cmnd 10, 9). This steady downward trend was checked by the end of 1956 and was followed by a sharp upward trend: in 1957 the daily average population increased to 22,428, in 1958 to 25,379, and to 27,088 in 1960 (Central Statistical Office 1962: 67). By 1959 the number sleeping three in a cell had increased to 6,000 (Home Office

1960: Cmnd 1117, 24). As a result, from the 1950s onwards, overcrowding was no longer simply looked upon as a temporary expedient. The prison authorities now realised that they were faced with a building programme of "formidable dimensions and great urgency" if they were to make effective classification and treatment possible (Home Office 1959: Cmd 645, 21).

Matters did not, on the whole, improve in the 1960s. By 1962 the average daily prison population stood at 31,063 (Central Statistical Office 1964: 101). Both 1963 and 1964 saw a decrease in numbers, 30,896 and 29,600 respectively (Central Statistical Office 1973: 70). 1965 saw only a gradual increase in numbers to 30,421 but the curve was by now on a steadily upward trend (*ibid*). By 1969 the numbers had grown to 34,067 and escalated to a massive 39,028 in 1970 (*ibid*: 86). Obviously these increases - prison numbers were now four times what they were before the war (House of Commons Parliamentary Debates 1971: 826, 955-956) - had a huge impact upon the internal administration of prisons. In 1966, for example, the number of persons sleeping three to a cell rose from 5,177 in January to 7,026 in December and the number of persons sleeping two to a cell increased from 364 to 1,494 in the same period (Home Office 1967: Cmnd 3408, 1-2). In 1969 the number of people sleeping two or three to a cell was 10,539 rising to 14,174 in 1970 (Home Office 1978: Cmnd 7290, 4).

The outcome was a rapid expansion in prison building programmes. In 1958/59 £822,000 was spent on prison building (Central Statistical Office 1964: 74). It had increased to £4,257,000 in 1961/62 (*ibid*), to £5,250,000 in 1964/65

(Central Statistical Office 1967: 107), to £7,088,000 in 1968/69, and to £8,738,000 in 1969/70 (Central Statistical Office 1973: 86). This represented an increase of 963 per cent over a period of 11 years. Not surprisingly, official reports acknowledged the need to maintain a prison building programme for the foreseeable future. In 1969, for example, it was noted:

"Whatever may be the changes in our penal system in the last third of the twentieth century, there is no immediate prospect of the prison system withering away. Indeed it is likely that there will be more people in prison in the next few years than ever before. These are unpalatable facts, but they will not be altered by our wishing they were otherwise" (Home Office 1969: Cmnd 4214, 106).

In this respect, it is difficult to see the merit in Scull's 1977 hypothesis that it was only in the 1960s that "the momentum of the drive to shut down institutions and minimise incarceration gathered its greatest force" (Scull 1977: 140). We have already seen that the period in question witnessed a rapid expansion in the prison population and in prison building programmes. In 1969, for example, the prison authorities were responsible for 111 institutions as opposed to 57 in 1950 (Home Office 1969: Cmnd 4214, 13). What in fact was happening in the late 1960s was a much more complex movement than that depicted by Scull. This movement - which may loosely be referred to as a policy of bifurcation - embodied characteristics such as: (a) a belief that there should be a widespread reduction in short-term sentences of imprisonment and on the use of remand before sentencing, and; (b) a belief in the development of non-custodial sanctions to reduce some of the burden of the prison system, as discussed in more detail later in this chapter. It is within the parameters of these first two characteristics that Scull's 1977 thesis operates. But the period in question also embodied other characteristics. For example, it included: (c) a belief in the development of a prison construction programme more capable of providing proper accommodation resources in a criminal justice system that increasingly recognised the prison as an institution of last resort. The Criminal Justice Bill of 1972, for example, embodied two main principles, with a clear and rational distinction between them: "the first is that those who commit crimes of violence should be punished severely, and the second is that those whose offences do not include violence should, as far as possible, be punished by means other than imprisonment" (House of Commons Parliamentary Debates: 1971: 826, 976). It also included: (d) a decline in emphasis on rehabilitation as a primary goal of the prison system and the rise to prominence of the "holding function" of imprisonment (Rutherford 1984: 54-55), and; (e) a growing anxiety about disorder.

The first four of these characteristics will be dealt with in detail as we progress through the chapter. But for now it is important to realise that the movement that was derived from these characteristics was brought about by a number of factors. These include: the realisation that the prison population far outstripped the number of prison places that could be provided - as Lord Mountbatten noted in 1966, even the "remarkable achievement of increasing the number of establishments from 39 in 1945 to 106 in 1966 has not kept pace with the enormous growth in prison population" (Home Office 1966: Cmnd 3175, 54-55); a realisation that overcrowding was not a temporary expedient, but a phenomenon that the prison authorities would have to contend with for a number of years; a realisation that imprisonment - far from being attacked by a decarceration movement as Scull suggests - would play a pivotal role, particularly in an era, as already delineated, of widespread escalation in crime; a realisation that a crisis was developing in prisons - both on security and humanitarian grounds - which would only heighten if penal policy remained the same; and finally, a realisation, as we shall see shortly, that the overall economic situation did not favour, in the late 1960s and early 1970s, massive expenditure on criminal justice, particularly treatment programmes.

From the perspective of this section, it is important to realise that the authorities were faced with a policy choice by the late 1960s. They could either let matters remain the same and risk allowing the prison population to get completely out of hand (between 1964 and 1970, for example, the average prison population had increased by 31.8 per cent , and between 1966 and 1970, the number sleeping two or three to a cell had increased by 155.8 per cent), or attempt, as they did, a strategy which would embody the notion of building prisons so as to accommodate only those that needed to be contained within such institutions (this manifested itself in a 66.2 per cent increase in prison building expenditure between 1965 and

1970) and to develop a system of non-custodial sanctions and other measures (the modification of the bail system, for example) which would attempt to curb the dramatic growth in the prison population. At this juncture, it is necessary to examine in more detail the crisis that was brought about in the management of prisons, particularly on humanitarian and security grounds, as a result of this dramatic growth in prison numbers.

(b) Consequences of the increase in the prison population
It was obvious by the late 1960s that the prison authorities were faced with a mounting crisis. The leading article in *The Times* on October 14, 1970, noted, for example:

> "The prison population has been increasing at an extraordinary rate. It was under 32,000 at the end of 1968. Now it is over 40,000 - a rise of more than a quarter in less than two years" (1970: October 14, 11).

Similarly, Mr Fred Castell, General Secretary of the Prison Officers Association, said the following about prison overcrowding in 1970:

> "The situation is critical and frightening. I do not use the words normally and I am not trying to create a panic situation but something will have to be done" (*The Times* 1970: August 5, 2).

Even the Home Office appeared to appreciate the significance of the increase in prison population:

"Overcrowding is the worst feature of our present system, worse even than the old buildings in which it takes place, and its effects are seen throughout the system" (Home Office 1969: Cmnd 4214, 104).

The purpose of this section is to provide a brief overview of how the effects of such an increase in the prison population evidenced itself in the prison system as a whole. One may begin by examining the conditions in prisons during the period in question. The increase in the prison population undoubtedly placed extreme pressures on the provision of services such as the organisation of clothing, feeding, bathing, recreation and exercise, and the demand for sluices and water points (Home Office 1968: Cmnd 3774, 13). It also impacted upon the provision of industrial and educational services - Lord Stonham, for example, noted that in some prisons it was necessary to increase the number of jobs that could be done sitting on a chair "because there are not enough rooms for anything else" (House of Commons Parliamentary Debates 1967: 283, 665). Such an environment also affected the ability of staff to segregate and classify categories of offenders and frustrated their attempts to rehabilitate them (*The Times* 1971: August 3, 12). In such conditions, as the Commissioners of Prisons noted, it was a difficult task to turn prisoners out improved individuals, both morally and physically (Home Office 1962: Cmnd 1798, 13). By the late 1960s, as we shall see later on, the task of rehabilitation was by and large substituted for the task of humane containment.[12] Perhaps more than anything else, though, increases in the prison population affected the prisoners themselves and their need for sufficient living space, privacy, mobility and visits.[13] The problems created by enforced association with others in a cell designed for one in Gloucester prison was described in *The Times* by Mr. Butler:

"I had occasion during an evening patrol to visit an inmate in his cell to administer medical treatment. The inmate was set up in a bed, situated behind the door, reading a book. He was attired in pyjamas; his bedding was clean and tidy and he impressed me as being a clean young man. On the wall above him were a few photographs of his family and it was evident that he had been used to living in decent surroundings. Adjacent to his bunk was a tier bunk, occupied by two elderly men. The inmate occupying the top bunk was in bed, fully dressed, complete with shirt, tie and pullover, and smoking a cigarette. It was obvious that he had not

12. As Victor Yates noted in the House of Commons in 1966: "if we cannot turn out prisoners better than when they went in, at least we have an obligation not to turn them out worse" (House of Commons Parliamentary Debates 1966: 738, 130).

13. Jimmy Boyle, for example, stated about his first experience of Barlinnie prison: "The blankets were filthy with lots of burn holes from guys smoking. The cell was filthy and there was an overwhelming stench of urine that came from the three stained chamber pots in the far corner. There was no escaping from this stench. There was a table that we were to use for eating on but it was covered with dog ends ... The prisoners were locked up 23 hours a day and allowed out for half an hour in the morning and afternoon to walk around the prison yard" (Boyle 1977: 86).

washed. The occupant of the lower bunk was reading and he too was smoking. By the side of his bed there was a chamber pot, full of urine, with match sticks and sputum floating on the surface. This, to him, was a convenient spittoon and ashtray. The cell table was covered in a mixture of salt, sugar, bread crumbs, spilt tea and tobacco butts. The smell in the room was a combination of 'Black Bell' smoke, stale urine and food rot, and, apart from the small corner where the younger man was lying, the cell was in a filthy condition. As I entered the cell I was compelled to step back on the landing because of the stench. On the pretext of looking at the cell board, I was able to inhale some fresh air before venturing into the room again. How that young man must have longed for the privacy of a single cell and what mental suffering he must have endured as he lay in those unhygienic surroundings" (*The Times* 1970: October 14, 11; Morris and Morris 1962: II, 338).

It led *The Times* itself to state:

"The overcrowding in British prisons has become an affront to human dignity and a threat to the efficiency of the penal system ... The degrading conditions in which some prisoners are forced to live, cooped up two or three to a cell in which they may have to spend up to two thirds of their time must be disturbing to any civilised society" (*ibid*).

The conditions themselves also militated against effective

security and the implementation of the proper custodial function of imprisonment. Lord Mountbatten, for example, noted that "overcrowding, apart from being thoroughly undesirable in itself, is a serious risk to security" (Home Office 1966: Cmnd 3175, 54-55). One sign of the strain manifest in the prison system by the 1960s can be discerned from the increasing number of escapes and attempts at escape. In 1946 only 864 such attempts were made but by 1966 this had grown to 1,871, an increase of 116.5 per cent in the space of 20 years (Thomas 1972: 185-187). Such an increase became all the more alarming with the escape of high profile inmates such as Charles Wilson from Birmingham prison in August, 1964, Ronald Biggs from Wandsworth prison in July, 1965, and George Blake from Wormwood Scrubbs in August, 1966. In respect of Charles Wilson's escape, *The Times*, describing it as a "monumental scandal" which must make the prison service a "laughing stock among the criminal classes", stated, in addition:

"It must also reduce the general public, for the time being, to despair about the capacity of the forces arrayed against crime to deal with it effectively" (*The Times* 1964: August 13, 11).

These escapes, together with the disturbances at Brixton, Gartree and Albany in 1972 (Newburn 1995: 23; Fitzgerald and Sim 1979: 7), and the general rise of violence of inmates directed against each other and at staff - violence was particularly prone to occur during the early morning routine of unlocking and slopping out - all illustrated the degree of pressure that the entire prison system was facing and raised doubts about the capability of the system to carry out even the basic task of confinement. It contributed, as we shall see, to the rise to prominence of control and containment as dominant issues in criminal justice thinking.

One final point can also be made. It concerns the decline in morale and growing militancy among prison staff about the conditions in which they had to administer their duties. Increases in escapes, loss of control of inmate affairs, the growth of specialists, the overwhelming belief that more was being done for the inmate than the staff, the threat of assaults - in 1961, for example, there were 228 assaults on prison officers (Thomas 1972: 190), and the increased difficulty of performing tasks such as bathing, feeding, clothing, and containing prisoners, as a result of the phenomenal growth in prison numbers, manifested itself in increased disquiet among prison staff (*ibid:* 190). This soon translated itself into direct action. In 1972, the Prison Officers Association threatened a national strike following an attempt to increase manning levels at Gartree prison. This was followed a few months later by the same association instructing its members not to work any more overtime than they were required to under the terms of a national agreement during the month of September (Evans 1980: 96-97). As such, apart from an increasing prison population being disagreeable in that more prison places would have to be provided, it also had a number of other repercussions which heightened the effects of the crisis being felt by the late 1960s. They included, to begin with, an increased pressure being placed on the provision of feeding, clothing and bathing services, on the provision of classification and segregative duties, and on attempts at rehabilitation. From the prisoners' perspective, these effects manifested themselves in a heightened tension as a result of the decline in living space, in mobility, in recreation, in exercise, and in the general hygienic conditions of their living accommodation. At an official level, the increase in prison population also made the custodial function of imprisonment much more difficult (evident in the growing number of escapes and disturbances), and led, in part, to a growing disquiet among prison staff.

(c) Costs

So far in this chapter we have highlighted a number of dramatic increases. These include increases in crime, in prison numbers, in prison assaults, in the numbers sleeping two or three to a cell and in the number of escapes and attempts at escape. But perhaps the most dramatic of all increases observed in the criminal justice domain since the Second World War has occurred in relation to gross prison expenditure. In 1943/44 the figure stood at £1,949,000 and had grown to £4,481,000 by 1947/48 (Central Statistical Office 1951: 63). The 1950s witnessed a similar pattern, gross expenditure increasing from £7,924,000 in 1951/52 to &16,995,000 by 1959/60 (Central Statistical Office 1954: 69; Central Statistical Office 1962: 68). In 1961/62 the figure stood at £23,068,000 (Central Statistical Office 1964: 74); in 1968/69 at £49,621,000; in 1969/70 at £57,864,000, and; in 1970/71 at £66,880,000 (Central Statistical Office 1968: 107). It represented an increase of 3331.5 per cent over a 27 year period. Such an increase has been commented upon by Keith Hawkins:

"The economics of the penal system are now assuming much greater importance. Traditionally penal measures have been evaluated in terms of their apparent impact, if any on the behaviour of offenders under study; they have not usually been evaluated in cost/benefit terms" (1975: 70).

Of course such a statement displays a complete insensitivity to historical penal sanctions and distorts or conceals many of their aims and functions. Economy and expediency have always played a role in penal policy making and new penal sanctions have never been devised solely on the grounds of apparent impact on the behaviour of offenders. It is respectfully submitted that the point Hawkins should have made was that these criteria, economy and expediency, were accentuated in the 1960s as a result of the exponential growth in gross prison expenditure. Indeed the inelastic nature of government resources and the concern about rising expenditure on prisons can be highlighted through a number of official reports in the late 1960s and early 1970s. For instance, the Government White Paper, *People in Prison*, stated:

"Many people concerned with the prison system have said, or been tempted to say, that the only thing to do with our Victorian inheritance is to pull it down. But even assuming, and it is a very big assumption, that suitable sites could be found for modern buildings to replace them, the provision of 20,000 new places in secure prisons and borstals would cost something over £100 million. The prison service needs new buildings and they are being planned. But we have to face the fact the resources to replace all unsuitable buildings are simply not available, and that the service will enter the last quarter of the twentieth century with buildings designed in the nineteenth" (1969: Cmnd 4214, 73).

Similarly the Wootton Report suggested:

"Imprisonment is not only inappropriate and harmful for many offenders for whom it is used; often it is a wasteful use of limited resources. Cost is not the only factor but it is worth observing that, quite apart from the increased risk that the State would have to support the family of an offender deprived of liberty, the cost of maintaining an inmate in a prison establishment is on average about £22 a week. No official estimate has been made of the average cost of supervising a probationer but we would judge it to be of the order of £1 a week" (1970: 3).

It is also important to bear in mind that the period in question, the late 1960s and early 1970s, saw the emergence of growing discontent with the Welfare State and its combination of "Keynesianism" - embodying as it did a belief in massive state intervention in the economy - and "Beveridgism" - embodying as it did a belief that the government should guarantee social rights and privileges

(Finlayson 1994: 351-353; Pierson 1991: 142). A growing consensus - which may loosely be defined as the New Right - began to argue that the State was no longer capable of meeting the demands that were expected of it. They supported this contention by alluding to the failure of successive governments to achieve a high rate of economic growth, to curb inflation and to address the issue of the balance of payments (King 1975: XXIII, 288). In addition, they argued that the range of activities and range of responsibilities which British governments had undertaken since the Second World War had resulted in overload:

"The fit between what the Labour Party said it would do in 1945 and what the Labour government actually achieved between 1945 and 1951 is astonishingly close ... Since about 1959, however, the fit has become less close. Not only do parties in office increasingly fail to do the things they said they were going to do: they increasingly do things that they pledged themselves specifically not to do" (*ibid*: 285).

To avert a fiscal crisis they argued that governments needed to curtail their overall level of activities and to concentrate on balancing the budget by reducing expenditure to meet generated revenue (Mishra 1989: 42-43). In short, they argued for a return to economic and social *laissez faire*.

Economic expenditure and attempts to restrict public expenditure undoubtedly gave impetus to the search for alternatives to custody (Conservative Party 1971: 6). Indeed Scull, highlighting the problems associated with the conventional Whiggish account of the emergence of decarceration (which he believed was presented "as an essentially beneficent reform having its roots in the progress of social scientific understanding and/or improvements in medical technology"), argued that its drive in the 1950s and 1960s was brought about primarily as a result of the growth of the Welfare State and the fiscal crisis that manifested itself (1977: 152). In these conditions, segregate methods of social control became much more difficult to sustain. But rather than viewing the continued growth of expenditure on welfare services as being inconsistent with the curtailment of expenditure on social control, he believed they supplemented each other:

> "[I]t is precisely the expansion of one which made possible and desirable the contraction in the other" (*ibid*: 135).

Moreover, Scull also suggests that the liberal rhetoric embodied in the decarceration movement was useful as "ideological camouflage, allowing economy to masquerade as benevolence and neglect as tolerance" (*ibid*: 152). This is the only significance which he bestows upon the ideological forces of the era - a window dressing which would make the real job of curtailment of public expenditure on social control (which would consequently facilitate the redirection of resources in to other welfare services) appear more presentable.

Scull's thesis can be commended on the grounds that he does not view the introduction of non-custodial sanctions purely in benevolent terms. There are, however, from an economic perspective, two fundamental flaws inherent in his thesis. To begin with, he fails to substantiate his belief that the State would want to curtail expenditure on social control so as to facilitate the growth of other welfare services. Indeed there is evidence to suggest that the contrary actually occurred. Comparing prison spending on the social services between 1968 and 1979, the May Committee stated:

"[A]t least in England and Wales, prisons' current expenditure has done better as a whole and compares favourably on capital expenditure. Put in another way, current expenditure in England and Wales on the prison service has risen faster than that on selected social services or total expenditure, whilst capital expenditure has fallen less in the prison service than elsewhere" (1979: Cmnd 7673, 148).

This is supported by Ian Gough in an article written in *New Left Review* in 1975. Examining total expenditure as a percentage of gross national product at factor cost, he detected an increase from 42 per cent in 1961 to 50.3 per cent in 1971 to 50.5 per cent in 1973. At the same time, he noted an increase in justice and law (which included police, prisons, law courts and parliament) from 0.8 per cent in 1961 to 1.3 per cent in 1971 to 1.4 per cent in 1973 (1975: 60). In the same period, he noted that provision for social security increased from 6.7 per cent in 1961 to 8.9 per cent in 1971, but decreased to 8.7 per cent in 1973 (*ibid*). Let us examine the figures more closely. Although more provision was made for social security in the period between 1961 and 1971, expenditure in the area only increased by 32.8 per cent. During the same period, expenditure on justice and law increased by 62.5 per cent. In the period between 1971 and 1973, expenditure on social security actually dropped by 2.2 per cent, whilst expenditure on justice and law increased by a further 7.7 per cent. Similarly, provision for health and welfare only increased by 31.8 per cent between 1961 and 1971 (from 4.4 to 5.8 per cent) and only by 1.7 per cent between 1971 and 1973 (from 5.8 to 5.9 per cent) (*ibid*).

Secondly, Scull underestimates the fact, as we have already seen in the first section, that law and order had or was becoming a pressing issue for concern precisely at the time that he suggests a curtailment in expenditure was taking place. And, again, the facts speak for themselves: prison expenditure, for example, increased from £49,621,000 in 1968/69 to £66,880,000 in 1970/71. In this sense, he fails to appreciate that the prison service is *sui generis* in character, even if a determined policy of bifurcation is in place. As such, it is somewhat of a chimera even to attempt, particularly without substantiation, to suggest that the expansion of welfare services was made possible by the curtailment of expenditure on social control, given the protean nature of the latter service. Although not specifically relating to Scull, Stephen Shaw suggested in 1980:

"It is frequently argued that, as presently established, the prison service operates with different objectives, and under different circumstances from any other part of the government with which it might be compared. Unlike the education service, say, it operates intensively around the clock. Unlike, for example, the hospital service it has little direct control over the admission of inmates in regard to either their numbers or to their type. While a hospital may extend its waiting lists and operate a system of priorities, under present procedures prisons have to increase their inmate numbers in direct response to sentences of the courts" (1980: 3).

Finally, apart from according them with the status of "ideological camouflage", Scull has very little to say about what Garland would refer to as "the importance of ideological and political forces and the internal dynamics of penal administration and their role in determining policy" (1990: 108). Yet ideological and humanitarian forces such as the growing recognition of the potent effects of inmate culture and inmate socialisation processes in prisons; the realisation among politicians, penal reformers and criminologists that there was a large number of prison inmates that should not be incarcerated; the rise to prominence of concepts such as reparation and community; the turmoil of the late 1960s and the waning credibility in existing penal practices, all, also, played a part in the movement towards the development of non-custodial sanctions. As Matthews noted:

"Although we might agree that humanitarianism is not the primary force behind changing control practices, it does not follow that the ideology of humanitarianism is not significant in explaining such developments ... Ideologies such as humanitarianism do not descend from heaven - they have a real material basis, and practical consequences" (1979: 110).

Moreover, this movement was also augmented by pragmatic considerations such as the inability, as we shall see, of prisons to prevent recidivism, problems concerning the availability of sites for the construction of new prisons, and the inability of the prison system to cope with overcrowding, staff unrest, disturbances and escapes. Thus, by only focusing on the economic dimensions of decarceration - which he constructed in order to highlight the deficiencies in Whiggish texts - Scull also falls into the trap of providing an ahistorical interpretation, and consequently, further debases the persuasiveness of his overall thesis.

This is not to deny that economic considerations played an important role in the movement towards non-custodial sanctions. They undoubtedly did, particularly in a political environment such as that prevalent in the late 1960s. But economic pressure is only one of the many pressures which influenced penal policymaking. And more account must be given to these other considerations because they affect the very nature of fiscal involvement itself - as we have seen, fiscal involvement was forced to increase to contend with the overall pressures exerted on the system even though since 1967 attempts have been made, *inter alia*, to curb the level of expenditure through the adoption of a more bifurcated system of criminal justice.

(d) The decline of rehabilitation

It is commonly believed that the period between the Second World War and the late 1960s was one in which "rehabilitation received its fullest and widest support" (Young 1983: 98; Newburn 1995: 16). By the mid-1970s, however, the ideology of rehabilitation found itself under increasing attack. Many would argue that Robert Martinson's article, entitled *What Works? Questions and Answers about Prison Reform*, in which he suggested that, with few isolated exceptions, the rehabilitative ideal had no appreciative impact on recidivism (1974: XXXV, 22-54), had a pivotal role to play in the decline of the ideology. From this point onwards, the nihilism of "nothing works" became a catch phrase in social control talk. It is my contention, however, that the merits of the rehabilitative ethos, particularly in prisons, were being attacked by both conscious and unconscious forces before the 1970s, albeit that their effects and impact were not always readily observable or immediately actionable upon. They would, nonetheless, help fuel the expansion of non-custodial sanctions and the movement from a policy of treatment to containment in the prison system.

One may begin by alluding to the Mountbatten Report in 1966 which was established, as we have already seen, as a result of the growing number of escapes, particularly high security escapes, that had occurred since the Second World War. The Inquiry began by noting that there was no really secure prison either in England or Wales (Home Office 1966: Cmnd 3175, 54-55). As a consequence, it recommended a tightening up of security in all prisons and the construction of a top security prison on the Isle of Wight for the confinement of the small number of high risk prisoners (a number, though, which was increasing as a result of the restriction of capital punishment under the Homicide Act of 1957 and the suspension of the death penalty under the Murder (Abolition of Death Penalty) Act of 1965) that the prison system had to deal with *(ibid)*. Two years later, a Report of the Advisory Council on the Penal System (the Radzinowicz Report) rejected the proposal to concentrate the more difficult and dangerous offenders in one maximum security prison on the grounds, *inter alia*, that it would be detrimental to the interests of high risk prisoners and it presupposed a degree of accuracy in the process of selection which was unlikely to be achieved. Instead it successfully argued for a policy of dispersal among a number of training prisons (Home Office 1968: 115). Nonetheless, although the Mountbatten Report was rejected in favour of the 1968 Radzinowicz Report, it still marked the emergence of a new security consciousness in prisons. As Priestley noted:

"Security was a new watchword; vague sentiments of reform were replaced with a tough-sounding managerialism" (1989: 182).

Accordingly, following these reports, the emphasis on control and security intensified: new locks were fitted; walls were mounted with barbed wire; fences were raised in height; checks on perimeters were stepped up; and, dog patrols, searchlights, T.V. monitoring equipment, electronic gates, infra-red cameras, and specialist prison officers were introduced (Hall-Williams 1970: 96-97). In addition, these measures had repercussions in other areas of prison life. These included restrictions on the employment of outside work parties, restrictions on the availability of recreational and educational facilities, and restrictions on freedom of movement within the confines of imprisonment (Fitzgerald and Sim 1979: 22-23). For Fitzgerald:

> "The importance of the Mountbatten Report lies in the halting of what was perceived as the treatment trend in British penal institutions" (1977: 49).

For Thomas and Pooley, the problem was not so much the Mountbatten Report itself. Rather the problem was vested in the decision to reject the Mountbatten Report in favour of the Radzinowicz Report (in other words, the adoption of a policy in favour of dispersal as opposed to concentration):

> "Had Mountbatten's recommendations been accepted, the need for security measures could have been explored and contained. This would have left the rest of the system to continue to try to achieve a reformative, rehabilitative goal" (Thomas and Pooley 1980: 43).

It is submitted, given the 116.5 per cent increase in prison escapes between 1946 and 1966, given in particular the number of high profile escapes and the alarm it engendered among the general public, and given the fact that the "security clamp down" was already taking place before Mountbatten's findings were published (special maximum security wings, for example, were already established in some prisons), that security would have remained a pivotal issue for concern in the administration of prisons, even if Mountbatten's proposal of concentration had been accepted. Nonetheless, both accounts are correct in that they highlight the rise to prominence of containment at the expense of rehabilitation. But they are too one-dimensional in approach in that they view such a movement only from the perspective of security. Undoubtedly security has a major role to play, but so also had issues such as the conditions that pertained in prisons, the potent effects of institutionalisation, concerns about the permissiveness of society and the levels of crime, and concerns about increasing reconviction rates and negative research findings. Any analysis of the decline in support for rehabilitative practices in the 1960s must also embrace these issues.

The escalation in prison numbers, for example, weakened the ability of the prison service to provide proper educational and industrial facilities. The prisoners themselves, of course, were increasingly confined in an environment without proper living space, recreational facilities or privacy. Prison staff, even if they were fully committed to the task of rehabilitating offenders, increasingly found themselves having to maintain order and carry out basic tasks such as clothing, feeding, bathing, and containing, often at the expense of training and treatment programmes. In such conditions, it is more difficult to dissertate about the effectiveness of imprisonment as a means of rehabilitating inmates. Moreover, as sociological knowledge about institutional procedures gained in momentum, social scientists began to focus on the "total institution" and its limitations in terms of rehabilitation.[14] In 1958 Gresham M. Sykes published a book, titled *The Society of Captives*, in which he studied the social system of New Jersey maximum security prison. After examining this system, in part, from the inmate's perspective, he stated:

"Present knowledge of human behaviour is sufficient to let us say that whatever the influence of imprisonment on the man held captive may be, it will be a product of the pattern of social interaction which the prisoner enters into day after day, year after year, and not of the details of prison architecture, brief exhortations to reform, or sporadic public attacks on the 'prison problem'. The particular problem of social interaction into which the inmate enters is, in turn, part of a complex social system with its own norms, values, and methods of control; and any effort to reform the prison - and thus to reform the criminal - which ignores the social system of the prison is as futile as the labours of Sisyphus. The extent to which the existing social system works in the direction of the prisoner's deterioration rather than his rehabilitation; the extent to which the system can be changed; the extent to which we are willing to change it (these are the issues which confront us)" (1958: 134).

Similarly, Terence and Pauline Morris, writing about

---

14. Donald Clemmer's book, *The Prison Community*, published in 1940, may be regarded as a pioneering work on prisoners from a sociological perspective.

Pentonville prison in 1963, suggested:

"It is at the psychological level that imprisonment is a painful, depriving and destructive experience. The important point here is that while some prisoners actually experience a conscious sense of pain and deprivation, there are others, as it were, anaesthetised to the pains of imprisonment by frequent exposure to it resulting in their being in an advanced stage of prisonisation or institutional neurosis. For these men the problems are serious in that, unaware of the way in which imprisonment is progressively reducing their chances of successful rehabilitation outside, they do nothing to mobilise their resistance to it. What is even more serious is that the prison lacks both facilities and staff resources to identify such individuals or to help them" (Morris and Morris 1963: 183).

The cumulative impact of such studies demonstrated a heightened awareness of the contaminating effects of prison life and the futility, to some extent, of prevailing rehabilitative programmes. As the Home Office noted:

"The 1895 Departmental Committee on Prisons envisaged that the task of the Prison Service should be to release offenders 'better men and women, physically and morally, than when they came in'. But experience in recent years has led increasingly to scepticism about the compatibility of rehabilitation in this traditional, paternalistic form with the practicalities of day-to-day life in custody. The coercion which is inherent in a custodial sentence and in the very nature of "total institutions" tends to direct the whole of the inmates' individual and group energies towards adjustment to the austerely unnatural conditions; towards alienation from authority; and thus towards rejection of any rehabilitative goals toward which the staff may be working" (Home Office 1977: 18).

Although it was only in the mid-1970s that the techniques of rehabilitation began to be questioned, it is my contention that a succession of negative research findings had already demonstrated, in respect of particular sanctions, that different types of treatment had little or no impact upon subsequent reconviction rates. The results, in part, contributed, at a pragmatic level, to a weakening in the commitment towards rehabilitation, albeit that the ethos of rehabilitation was not being questioned *per se.* This weakening in commitment towards rehabilitation is most apparent in respect of prisons. In 1959, the Home Office publication, *Penal Practice in a Changing Society*, still cherished the idea of providing effective training programmes for prisoners as its primary goal (Home Office 1959: Cmd 645, 21). By 1965, another Home Office publication, *The Adult Offender*, put forward the view that whilst long periods of imprisonment may punish and deter offenders, it certainly did not fit them "for re-entry into society" and every additional year that they are detained "progressively unfits them" (1965: Cmnd 2852, 3).[15] By 1969, in *People in Prison*, it was accepted that the first task of the prison service was "humane containment" with other tasks, such as rehabilitation, playing a secondary role (1969: Cmnd 4214, 7). Moreover, many commentators in the 1960s and early 1970s confessed to a "profound scepticism" in respect of imprisonment's ability to effectively rehabilitate offenders (Cross 1971: 84-85; Mattick 1967: VII, 452; Jepson 1971: XIII, 234-245). Such views, no doubt, were in part motivated by reconviction rates in imprisonment. The 1969 White Paper, *People in Prison*, noted that "more than half the men who have served sentences of more than 18 months for an indictable offence were reconvicted within two years of release from prison and that about 75 per cent of young men released on licence from prison were reconvicted within three years" (1969: Cmnd 4214, 53). Similarly, it was noted in 1969, in *The Sentence of the Court*, that except for first offenders over the age of 30, the reconviction rates for those sent to prison were worse than was expected (1969: 53).

Uncertainty was also creeping in as a result of negative research findings in respect of other penal sanctions. For example, Little, in an analysis of the receptions into borstals between 1950 and 1956, argued that there had been a deterioration in the quality of inmates received. He went on,

---

15. It also suggested: "You cannot train men for freedom in conditions of captivity. In these words the late Sir Alexander Patterson stated the paradox which presents itself daily to every prison administration. The paradox cannot be evaded; but it is all the more necessary to overcome it by strengthening links between the prisoner and the free community and by developing new ways to ease the transition back to freedom" (*ibid*).

however, to suggest that even if the "training material" had been as good as it was prior to the period in question, the borstal system would still not have been as efficient in preventing recidivism (Little 1961-62: II, 266-272).[16] Sir George Benson revealed in the late 1950s that imprisonment in Lewes gave results identical with borstal training. He remarked about these findings in the House of Commons:

"The Prison Commissioners did not like that; they were horrified and I was surprised. In effect, the Prison Commissioners said, 'This must be wrong. We have concentrated on reform in borstal. Borstal must give better results'. They asked the research unit of the Home Office to do a check on Stafford Prison, which is the other big prison centre for adults. The check confirmed up to the hilt that imprisonment gave identical results with borstal" (House of Commons Parliamentary Debates 1960: 630, 596-600; Bottoms and Stevenson 1992: 22-23).

He went on to suggest:

"Apparently, institutional treatment of various kinds makes little or no difference to the results" (*ibid*).

Indeed, the published national reconviction rates for all

---

16. See also Mannheim and Wilkins who revealed, after studying the previous records and subsequent careers of 700 boys who were sentenced to borstal training between August, 1946, and August, 1947, that "all classes of risk emerged from the open borstal 10 per cent better than the same risk categories emerged from the closed" (Mannheim and Wilkins 1955: 222).

offenders from borstals during the period 1960-1966 indicate that the reconviction rate was rising - from 52.1 per cent in 1960, to 55.9 per cent in 1963, to 58.7 per cent in 1966 (Bottoms and McClintock 1973: 265). Similarly, reconviction rates for boys who committed further offences within three years of their release from approved schools increased from 57 per cent in 1958 (Home Office 1967: 51) to 68 per cent in 1964 (Home Office 1970: 42), and it was noted in 1969 that between 55 per cent and 60 per cent of young offenders released from senior detention centres were reconvicted within three years (Home Office 1969: Cmnd 4214, 53).

But doubts about the effectiveness of rehabilitation were not simply confined to segregative methods of social control. Between 1948 and 1953 the Cambridge Department of Criminal Science carried out a study of probation involving 9,336 cases in London and Middlesex. Their findings revealed that, of those studied, 26.2 per cent of all adults and 37.6 per cent of all juveniles failed their probation (Report of the Cambridge Department of Criminal Science 1958: 3-4). A further study of probation carried out by Barr and O'Leary in 1966 pointed out that the success rate of men given probation orders declined from 80 per cent in 1950 to 68 per cent in 1961, and for women from 86 per cent in 1950 to 79 per cent in 1961 (Barr and O'Leary 1966: 15). Thus, no form of penal treatment appeared to demonstrate a striking success rate in rehabilitative terms. Indeed Radzinowicz remarked in 1961 that the "similarity of success and failure rates, as measured by the after-conduct of offenders, irrespective of whether they are put on probation, fined, sentenced to short-term imprisonment, or to longer corrective detention, is indeed striking" (Radzinowicz 1961: 169). Likewise, Benson suggested that "the uniformity of results from penal treatment ought to have been revealed many years ago" (House of Commons Parliamentary Debates 1960: 630, 596-600), and McClean and Wood argued in 1969 "that most studies reveal considerable similarities between the effectiveness of penal treatments of various types" (1969: 81). Interestingly, McClean and Wood did not use such findings to condemn rehabilitation outright. Instead they placed the blame on the difficulties in finding a single cause of crime which proved as "chimerical as the search for a single form of penal treatment *(ibid)*".[17] Appraisals of this kind were also evident in the United States before the mid-1970s. For example, George Vold, in response to findings of contained recidivism in a variety of penal programmes in 1958, laid the blame on the lack of research into crime causation (1958: 302). As McMahon noted:

"In sum, the recurrently negative findings of crime causation were not initially used in diminishing commitment to rehabilitation but rather served to justify more of the same: the issue was not whether the idea of rehabilitation itself was conceptually flawed, but how the goals could be better accomplished" (1992: 15).

---

17. Other commentators suggested that the pattern of failure was a result of the "number of granite and steel archaic penal stations bestride the road of social progress" (Alper 1968: VIII, 17).

This is true to some extent, but it does not furnish us with the whole story. Although negative research findings did not, in the late 1960s and early 1970s, amount to a complete nihilistic attack on the rehabilitative ideal at a theoretical level (this is hardly surprising given that until the mid-1970s most studies continued to be written in a benevolent vein), they did act as a contributory factor in the demise of the ideal at a practical level. Thus, if viewed in isolation, it is fair to propose that the consequences of negative research findings did not impinge upon the rehabilitative ideal *per se*, given that most of the attention at a theoretical level was focused on the complexities of crime causation. But when viewed with other phenomena - such as increasing crime levels and the prison crisis - it is also fair to propose that at a practical level, rather than being justified, rehabilitation was, in effect, being debased. And negative research findings also had an important role to play in the debasement. As Bottoms and Stevenson suggest:

"The negative research findings concerning penal treatment produced in the 1960s by Benson and others were indeed shattering to many adherents of a liberal progressive approach in penology. They had advocated research, but they had not remotely expected research to emerge with results of this kind" (1992: 23).

But what pragmatic impact did such findings have? It is my contention that the growing documentation of the restricted and inadequate potency of penal sanctions in rehabilitative terms helped, to some extent, to fuel the expansion of non-custodial sanctions because, for offenders of comparable background, time spent in custody could not, *inter alia*, be shown to produce "any better results than supervision in the community" (Home Office 1974: 5). Even the Wootton Committee itself in 1970 acknowledged that its recommendations "could not be definitely known to be more effective than existing measures", but they could be justified, not on the grounds simply of a continued commitment to rehabilitation as McMahon would have us believe, but on the grounds that there was a widely held view that many offenders were sentenced to imprisonment "for lack of any more appropriate alternative" and imprisonment was "often a wasteful use of limited resources" (Home Office 1970: 3).[18]

Of course there was one other vital determinant in the decision to introduce community service orders - a determinant not immediately apparent from any brief perusal of the Wootton Committee's report. We may allude to it by reference to the following statement from Hood:

"Post-war penal policy has been set upon a task of

---

18. The Wootton Committee has been criticised on the grounds that it failed to justify the introduction of community service in terms of criminological and penological knowledge as recommended by the 1959 White Paper, *Penal Practice in a Changing Society*, preferring instead to rely upon opinion and the ideological appeal of the sanction. Hood, for example, suggested "that the committee's conclusions and recommendations were a potpourri of intelligent suggestions: their acceptance or rejection will depend more upon their political appeal than their likelihood of making a major impact upon what is in danger of becoming an intractable problem ... - the provision of alternatives [to imprisonment]" (Hood 1974: 417).

contriving alternatives to custody in a political climate where the *increasing alarm about crime and the growing scepticism of welfare measures to the criminal of the 'affluent society' has dispelled some of the earlier enthusiasms for dealing with the more serious offender within the community as a problem solely for social casework-supervision"* (*ibid*: 377) (my italics).

The perception of widespread disorder in the period concerned undoubtedly had a profound impact on the Wootton Committee when introducing the sanction of community service. Indeed it was very conscious - given the widespread public anxiety that prevailed, given the negative research findings, given the knowledge that the stereotype of the criminal in the early 1970s created an image "to which social casework hardly seemed appropriate", and given the understanding that it would be very burdensome for a government to justify massive expenditure on the "treatment of offenders" (*ibid*: 378-379) - of the need to provide the sanction with sufficient "bite". Community service was advanced as punitive in design in that it deprived an offender of his or her leisure time and was a "welcome alternative in cases where at present a court imposes a fine for want of a better sanction or again in situations where it is desired to stiffen probation by the imposition on the offender of an additional obligation" (Home Office 1970: 14).

Moreover, instead of justifying the sanction in terms of its rehabilitative potential, the Wootton Committee justified it on the grounds of its appeal "to adherents of different varieties of penal philosophy": it would be cheaper than imprisonment; it had an emphasis on reparation; it would give effect to the old adage that punishment should fit the crime; it would act as an effective deterrent when a fine, for example, was in effect no penalty or probation was viewed as too soft; and, it would provide a possibility for a changed outlook on the part of offenders through the work they undertook and through their association with volunteers (Home Office 1970: 13-14). Even this last objective encountered some resistance:

"For some years the offenders had more often than not been thought of as emotionally or mentally disturbed, even ill and therefore in need of cure. This had led to the professionalisation of the various treatment services; the prison service with psychiatrists and psychologists, the probation officer trained with psychoanalytical bias to be used in one-to-one casework situations, and so on. Obviously, not all probation officers took kindly to the idea that the criminal would now be treated by 'mucking in' under the 'wholesome influence' of other community volunteers" (Ryan 1983: 50).

It indicates, perhaps more than anything else, the demise of rehabilitation as a legitimate and rigorously applied goal in penal thinking. Unable to establish its effectiveness, it found itself being pushed off its pedestal as a primary initiative to being one of a pot-pourri of penal objectives operating in the criminal justice system. The notion that this system would operate as a scientific treatment milieu for offenders by acting as an antidote for their failings and a restorer of their values and social skills was displaced, to some extent, by more moderate and practical goals - a desire to reduce prison overcrowding, to reduce expenditure, and to ease public anxiety about escalating crime rates. Thus, rehabilitation had now to accommodate, and in many respects give way to, these aspirations: if it could fit in and prove successful, this would be an added bonus - if not successful, at least it could be justified on the grounds that it was not more *unsuccessful* than imprisonment and this parity was achieved at a much lower level of expenditure and suffering, whilst maintaining a sufficiently punitive element.

There is one final point that can be made in respect of McMahon's claim that rather than witnessing a diminishing commitment to rehabilitation, the late 1960s and early 1970s actually experienced increased attempts to accomplish the goal of rehabilitation. In putting forward her claim, she completely ignores the extreme sensitivity, as delineated earlier, concerning the rise of crime, particularly crimes of violence. I do not wish here to provide a summation of what has already been described in the first section of this chapter. But there is one angle of the issue of rising crime rates that needs to be addressed in respect of its impact upon the rehabilitative ideal - that issue being the shaping of judicial attitudes in a period of widespread anxiety about crime. Anxious to check the "erosion of moral constraints", the rise in crime, and the spread of permissiveness, there was a palpable hardening, from the 1960s onwards, in judicial attitudes to crime (Hall *et al* 1981: 34). There is ample documentation of this hardening in attitude. For example, after hearing how a 21-year-old man had been put on probation and fined by magistrates for offences of violence, Mr Justice Lawton, in 1969, stated:

"With all this violence young people are indulging in today, I am wondering whether leniency with the young is best for the public. In my view, this kind of violence to other people in our streets is not going to be cured by probation, fines or day attendance centres and the like. Word has got to go round that anyone who commits this kind of offence has got to lose his liberty" (*The Guardian* 1969: October 9, 34).

Similarly, Mr Justice Roskill, a leading High Court judge, urged magistrates not to be afraid of imposing stiff sentences:

"Public opinion through the press has been quick to make itself felt about the violence of youthful housebreakers, mobs of football fans or others going about armed with knives and offensive weapons and bicycle chains. If the courts did not reflect that public opinion by the treatment of crimes of this kind in a way which the public will support, the courts will deservedly lose public respect and confidence" (*The Daily Telegraph* 1969: October 10, 19).

Finally, one can allude to the comments of another High Court judge, Sir Raymond Hinchcliffe, who, harping back to the Golden Age when "people used to have qualities of tolerance and kindness", noted that society in the late 1960s and early 1970s was founded upon "unkindness, intolerance, selfishness, greed and no faith in anyone or anything". He warned the courts not to take a soft line against those committing robbery with violence and dangerous weapons, and urged magistrates, in pursuing a stern sentencing approach, not to fear "criticism which is often unfair, ill-informed, and unfounded" (*The Guardian* 1972: May 20, 8). Comments of this nature, of course, illustrate the premium placed on deterrence in the period concerned. Moreover, it highlights the effects which public opinion can have on judicial attitudes and sentencing policy. Given (a) the rise of crime and the insistent calls by the public for harsher sentences, and, (b) the willingness of the judiciary to reflect public opinion in the treatment of crime, it is not surprising that these two phenomena, when taken together, also acted as a significant contributing factor in the demise of rehabilitation at a practical level.

As such, although not denying that rehabilitation continued to exist as a goal of penal policy, it is submitted that it would be wrong to view it as proceeding at pace in the late 1960s and 1970s. Whilst Martinson's "nothing works" hypothesis may have become a catch-phrase in the mid-1970s for the view that rehabilitation could not have an appreciable effect on recidivism levels, it is suggested, at a practical level, that a number of different phenomena had already combined to devalue and impair the operation of the ideal. These include the rise to prominence of containment at the expense of treatment in the prisons in the 1960s; the sheer difficulty of prison numbers which often made rehabilitation impractical; the growing impact of sociological studies on the pains of imprisonment; negative research findings on the success of rehabilitative research programmes; a political climate increasingly alarmed about crime; and a hardening in judicial attitudes with more emphasis placed on deterrence and incapacitation.

These phenomena, in turn, facilitated, in part, the drive towards bifurcation: in order to reassure the public, the "hard end" became harder by greater investment in prisons, security, police, managerialism, control and by altering definitions of dangerousness (section 28(2) of the 1972 Criminal Justice Act, for example, extended the penalty of possession of a firearm with intent to endanger life from 14 years to life imprisonment), whilst the "soft end" expanded to deal with offenders who should not ordinarily be punished at the "hard end" (the 1972 Criminal Justice Bill, for example, was said to embark "on a new range of non-custodial penalties designed to find methods of awarding punishments to criminals which do not involve incarcerating them") (House of Commons Parliamentary Debates 1971: 826, 966). Accordingly, this policy of bifurcation allowed the authorities to alleviate the pressures on prisons and prison expenditure, whilst still enabling them to eat their "law and order" cake (Pitts 1981: 29).

In this way, penal authorities could allude to the prisons and argue that they were getting tough on serious offenders, such as those who commit robbery with violence. But they could also call attention to the problems in prisons - such as overcrowding, inhumane living conditions, the negative sociological impact of confinement, and high recidivism rates - and employ such criteria to justify the introduction of non-custodial sanctions. For example, a sanction such as community service, as we have already seen, could be justified on the grounds that it: was cheaper ("whatever the administrative cost of success, it could not possibly match the expense of keeping an equivalent number of men in prison") (Wootton 1973: 20); was more humane ("the intention of the scheme is not to humiliate ... but to promote a sense of social responsibility") (*ibid:* 18); and contained an element of "bite" (an important issue, particularly in a period when the fine, the probation order and discharge "were no longer thought appropriate for every situation in which a non-custodial option might be contemplated") (Young 1979: 9).

In addition, the authorities could argue that community service contained nothing that suggested it would be less successful in rehabilitative terms than imprisonment (indeed Lady Wootton proposed that "if it ever did turn out that C.S.O. was *at least as successful a treatment as imprisonment,* judged by the rate of subsequent recidivism, ... the scheme would almost certainly outstrip the facilities offered by the voluntary societies", and it would be essential to enlist the co-operation of local authorities) (Wootton 1973: 20) and also held out the possibility of effective reintegration.

But these justifications are in themselves very revealing and are perhaps also indicative of the demise of rehabilitation in practical terms. In my view, *pragmatic concerns* - such as restricting the use of imprisonment, being seen to be addressing the issue of law and order, and curtailing expenditure - overshadow any *optimistic desire or commitment to rehabilitation.* Indeed a brief perusal of the Wootton Committee report will reveal no firm assurances of any kind, no long-term strategy goals, and no priority choices (Hood 1974: 384). In fact, apart from devising alternatives, it does little more than repeat the same truisms and make the same pronouncements as were being voiced in the House of Lords, House of Commons, media and, to some extent, across society as a whole. For example, if the sanction of community service was still committed to the rehabilitative ideal, then, what type of offenders was it for? How was it to be viewed in relation to other non-custodial sanctions? Was the length of a community service order to be determined on the basis of the offence committed or on the basis of the treatment thought necessary? This is what the Wootton Committee had to say on such issues:

"We have not attempted to categorise precisely the type of offender for whom community service might be appropriate, nor do we think it possible to predict what use might be made by the courts of this new form of sentence" (Home Office 1970: 14).

One final indication of the pragmatic approach taken by the Wootton Committee can be discerned from the following statement by Lady Wootton and her hopes for the future of community service:

"If ... recidivism after a C.S.O. turns out to be at least not significantly worse than that following short sentences of imprisonment, it will be justified on economic grounds alone, because, as the Inner London Report puts it, offenders employed on tasks for the benefit of others... could have been sitting in prison cells, benefiting none, but each costing the nation between £30 and £40 a week and, perhaps, as much again to support their families. If, on the other hand, the record of community service proves more hopeful than that of the ex-prisoner, that should firmly establish the new sentence as an alternative to imprisonment" (Wootton 1978: 132).

This astonishing piece of "hedging" worked, of course, against its own ends; community service, as a result, has never become established purely as an alternative to imprisonment, but forms, to some extent, the middle ground between alternatives to imprisonment and alternatives to other non-custodial sanctions. It illustrates, though, the pragmatic, reactive approach of the Wootton Committee's thinking and its preference for immediate non-committal responses to pressing concerns as opposed to the adoption of more proactive responses which would have embodied a greater analysis of the specific types of offenders for whom community service was intended, its positioning in the penal system, the manner in which it was to be applied, and clear statements about policy strategies (as opposed to simply trying, in the words of Lady Wootton, "to curry favour with everybody") and intended effects. When reactive pragmatism of this nature took hold - with little or no emphasis on assurances, priorities, long-term strategy, proper guidelines or comprehensive analysis - rehabilitation suffered a fateful blow, perhaps more fateful even than any of the other blows that it suffered during the period concerned.

At this juncture it may be useful to provide a compendium of the different forces acting within the penal domain in the late 1960s and early 1970s. On the one hand, we have witnessed the emergence of a more authoritarian control culture which evidenced itself in the tightening up of security in all prisons, restrictions on the employment of outside work parties, the availability of recreational and educational facilities, and freedom of movement within the confines of prisons, the politicisation of law and order, and the palpable hardening in judicial attitudes; by anxiety about government expenditure which restricted the development of treatment programmes; by the demise in general of rehabilitation at a practical level; by the acceptance at an official level of humane containment as a primary goal of prison administration; by the realisation that alternatives to imprisonment needed to embody an element of "bite"; by evidence that the hard end of the system was getting harder; and, by the pragmatic approach adopted, in some instances, by policy makers with their refusal to adopt strategy goals or make firm priority choices, all of which, no doubt, aided the development of a more control centred penal environment.

On the other hand, there was a growing realisation that there was a need to develop non-custodial sanctions. It was brought about by the belief that: there were too many offenders in prison for lack of an appropriate alternative; that imprisonment positively unfitted many prisoners for re-entry into society; that imprisonment actually promoted dehabilitating socialisation processes; that there was a need, where possible, to curtail the level of expenditure; that non-custodial sanctions could be justified on the grounds that they would prove at least as successful as prison in terms of recidivism; and that there was a need to alleviate the degrading conditions in which many prisoners had to live. It is necessary, at this point, to examine more closely the development of non-custodial sanctions and the policy of bifurcation in the late 1960s and early 1970s.

Alleviating the Crisis

It was evident by the mid-1960s that the prison system was in the depths of a crisis. Escalating prison numbers, in particular, were beginning to force the hand of policy makers. In this sense, the Criminal Justice Act of 1967 may be regarded as a meaningful occurrence in penal policy terms, albeit that its ideological aspirations were rather simple in design. In fact, the Home Secretary, Roy Jenkins, in negotiating the Bill's safe passage through Parliament, suggested that it had a single leitmotiv, "that of keeping out of prison those that need not be there" (House of Commons Parliamentary Debates 1966: 738, 64). This is appositely demonstrated in respect of the specific sanction of the suspended sentence which found legislative approval in sections 39-42 of the aforementioned Act. Although not entirely embryonic - the suspended sentence had been proffered in the 1950s but was turned down on the basis, *inter alia*, that there were no compelling reasons for suggesting that it would make appreciable improvements to the prevailing collection of penal sanctions (Windelsham 1993: II, 109; Osborough 1969) - it was now substantiated on the grounds that it would act as an effective stratagem for restricting the use of imprisonment whilst still symbolically signalling the severity of the offence committed. Under section 39, a court which passed a prison sentence of not more than two years could make an order suspending that sentence. To highlight more emphatically the need to reduce the prison population, section 39(3) provided that where a prison term of not more than six months was passed on an offender who had no prior experience of imprisonment or borstal, then a court was compelled to suspend any sentence.[19] It appears, however, that the sanction was not a complete success in respect of its policy aspirations. Early research investigation on the use of the suspended sentence indicated that it was being employed not only in *lieu* of imprisonment, but also in place of fines and probation. Sparks, for example, estimated that of the men given suspended sentences in 1968, only about 40 per cent were diverted from prison. If the suspended sentence had not, *ex hypothesi*, been available to the judiciary, a further 40 per cent would have been given fines and about 12 per cent would have been placed on probation (Sparks 1971:

---

19. However, if the act or acts constituting the offence consisted, *inter alia*, of an assault or a threat of violence to another person, or of having or possessing a firearm, an explosive or an offensive weapon, or of indecent conduct with or towards a person under the age of 16, then the court was not compelled to suspend sentence.

384-401).[20] Thus the merits of the suspended sentence were circumscribed to some extent by its employment as an "alternative to alternatives". Moreover, an offender who ordinarily would have received a fine, probation or discharge, saw his or her chances of a prison sentence increase dramatically on subsequent conviction for offences committed whilst under a suspended sentence. This furtive expansion of the social control network under the façade of decarceration would form, as we shall see, an integral element of Cohen's dispersal of discipline thesis.

The other major change brought about by the 1967 Act was parole. Although its introduction has been defended on rehabilitative grounds (Jenkins suggested that by being released early, offenders were afforded an opportunity to lead "good and useful lives") (House of Commons Parliamentary Debates 1966: 738, 66), it may also be cited, as Bottomley suggests, as a good example of "penological pragmatism" reacting to prison overcrowding (Bottomley 1984: XXIII, 24-40). Indeed Jenkins himself argued that once the 1967 Act became effective, 4,500 offenders would be eligible for parole, albeit that he expected no more than

20. In *R. v. O'Keefe*, Lord Parker, in an attempt to provide clearer guidelines to sentencers on the rationale of the sanction, suggested: "A suspended sentence is a sentence of imprisonment ... [W]hether the sentence comes into effect or not, it ranks as a conviction unlike the case where a probation order is made, or a conditional discharge is given. Therefore, it seems to the court that before one gets to a suspended sentence at all, the court must go through the process of eliminating other possible courses such as absolute discharge, conditional discharge, probation orders, fines, and then say to itself: this is a case of imprisonment, and the final question, it being a case of imprisonment, is immediate imprisonment being required or can I give a suspended sentence" ([1969] 1 E.R. 427-428).

about 20 per cent of this number to be released:

> "Altogether, the reduction in the daily average prison population might be about 600" (House of Commons Parliamentary Debates 1966: 738, 70).

Moreover, in an attempt to alleviate the number of remand prisoners committed to prison (35,000 a year, as we previously noted), it was felt that restrictions should be imposed on the power of the courts to refuse bail. The clear intention of such restrictions was "that magistrates should use remands in custody considerably more sparingly, particularly when a prison sentence was not likely to result" (*ibid*: 66). Accordingly, section 18 of the 1967 Criminal Justice Act broadly provided that a magistrates' court, when trying summarily a person who had attained the age of 17 for an offence which was punishable with not more than six months' imprisonment, or when adjourning an inquiry as examining justices in a case where the accused or prosecutor claimed that the trial should be by jury, should remand the person on bail unless one of a number of conditions set out in subsection 5 of the section applied. Where a magistrates' court refused to commit such a person for trial on bail under subsection 5, the court was required, if the offender was not represented or his or her solicitor or counsel requested it, to provide written notice stating the reasons for refusal (Simon and Weatherrit 1974: 1; Home Office 1974: 5-7).

Furthermore, there was a general belief that the basic approach for dealing with those who did not pay their fines too readily accepted "imprisonment as an alternative to payment" (House of Commons Parliamentary Debates 1966: 738, 68). This is not surprising given that about 10,000 fine defaulters were sent to prison each year (*ibid*: 65). Accordingly, by section 44 of the 1967 Criminal Justice Act, magistrates' courts were, with some exceptions, prohibited from issuing a warrant of commitment to imprisonment for default in payment of a fine, and from fixing a term of imprisonment which was to be served by an offender in the event of default in paying a sum adjudged to be paid by a conviction. It was also provided that even after conviction (where the court had not issued a warrant of commitment for default in paying, or fixed a term of imprisonment which was to be served on any such default), the court should not issue a warrant of commitment for default unless, *inter alia*, it inquired into the offender's means on at least one occasion after the offender's conviction, it appeared to the court that the offender had sufficient means to pay, and all other methods of payment appeared to be "inappropriate and unsuccessful". In addition to restricting the use of imprisonment for fine default, the Act also increased the maximum fines which magistrates' courts could impose for a wide range of offences so as to ensure that such courts would not be "hampered by inadequate maxima" (Home Office 1971: 4), and empowered the same courts, in a case where a person defaulted in the payment of a sum of money, to make an attachment of earnings after inquiring into the means of the said person.

The net effect of these developments would, as Jenkins suggested, "make fines bite harder and thus serve as a more useful alternative to prison, while, at the same time, making it more possible to enforce them without resort to imprisonment" (House of Commons Parliamentary Debates 1966: 738, 68).[21] Indeed by 1968 the reception of fine defaulters had dropped by a third when compared with the preceding year, although it is important to note that such a reduction was due, in part, to the decline in offenders fined by the courts and to the "time lag" which manifested itself as a result of the fine enforcement process initiated by the 1967 Act (Sparks 1971: 77). Finally, section 91 of the same Act removed the penalty of imprisonment for the offence of being drunk and disorderly, to be implemented when the Home Secretary was satisfied that sufficient alternatives were available for persons convicted of such an offence.[22]

Thus, developments such as the suspended sentence, the mandatory suspended sentence, parole, restrictions on the power of the courts to refuse bail, restrictions on the use of imprisonment for fine default, increases in the maximum fines which could be imposed, and the removal of the sentence of imprisonment for the offence of being drunk and disorderly, all, to some extent, bear testimony to the intense desire of the authorities to curb, for various reasons, the

---

21. Dame Irene Ward was a little more sceptical in relation to the changes proposed with regard to fines: "The one consideration that the Home Secretary had in mind is to empty the prisons. Nobody disagrees with his objective, but a person should not set this as his one and only priority and cause tremendous hardship to many unfortunate people who have gone before the courts to get their protection and to get the protection of justice" (House of Commons Parliamentary Debates 1967: 745, 1971).
22. The Home Secretary noted during the passage of the bill through parliament that 5,000 drunks went to prison every year (House of Commons Parliamentary debates 1966: 738, 65).

exponential growth in prison numbers. However, it does appear, in keeping with the criticisms already levelled at the Wootton Committee, that these innovations were very much a result of reactive, pragmatic policy making with little or no evidence of any detailed or meticulous analysis of their likely long-term effects. As Quintin Hogg noted during the second reading of the Bill introducing these innovations:

> "It [the bill] is a pot-pourri of more or less intelligent suggestions, few of them new and mostly from identifiable and almost all from responsible sources. ... But the main burden of my song is that what is wanted is not such a mixture, because I believe that a pot-pourri of intelligent suggestions is not what is wanted at present. ... *What I believe is wanted is a new appraisal of the fundamental assumptions of our penal system, a new rational and coherent approach to English criminal law*" (*ibid*: 76-77) (my italics).

What is striking about the 1972 Criminal Justice Act is that whilst it embodied a desire to alleviate the "crisis caused by the astonishing, almost overwhelming growth of the prison population" (Conservative Party 1971: 6), it demonstrated, in addition, a strong commitment to severe punitive responses - the increases in penalties for possession of firearms, provisions with regard to bankruptcy and compensation, and the allocation of powers of forfeiture and disqualification to the judiciary, all corroborate this toughening in attitudes towards law and order. In this way the 1972 Criminal Justice Act would enable the Conservative government to reduce the pressure on the prison population, thus minimising state expenditure and the burdening effects of overcrowding on the physical conditions of prisons, whilst still allowing them to claim to be getting tough on crime through empowering the courts to deal "with offences on a basis which would appeal to modern society" (House of Commons Parliamentary Debates 1971: 826, 972). This process of bifurcation was encapsulated by Maudling, the Home Secretary, whilst outlining the 1972 Criminal Justice Bill in the House of Commons:

"To recapitulate the main proposals in the Bill, the Government believe that there is a real problem, as the country recognises, in the expansion of crime, particularly violent crime. We therefore propose introducing new measures based on two principles. The first is that those who commit crimes of violence should be punished severely, and the second is that those whose offences do not include violence should, so far as possible, be punished by means other than imprisonment. I believe that this is a clear and rational distinction" (*ibid*: 976).

Let us examine more closely this two-pronged approach to law and order. At the "hard end", new measures were introduced concerning the use of firearms: section 28(2) provided that the maximum penalty for the offence of carrying firearms with intent to commit an indictable offence was to be increased from 10 to 14 years of imprisonment; section 28(3) provided that the maximum penalty for the offence of possessing a firearm while committing certain offences (these included, *inter alia*, some offences under the Malicious Damage Act of 1861 and the Offences Against the Person Act of 1861) was to be increased from seven to 14 years of imprisonment, and that the maximum penalty for the offence of carrying firearms and imitation firearms with intent to commit an indictable offence was to be increased from 10 to 14 years of imprisonment. By increasing the maximum penalties for various firearms offences, an area which had shown a worrying upturn according to Maudling, it was hoped that it would demonstrate how seriously Parliament took the matter (House of Commons Parliamentary Debates 1971: 826, 969). Similarly, in response to public anger over cases which enabled offenders to hold on to some of the proceeds of their crimes even if committed to prison, criminal bankruptcy orders - an issue previously taken up by Lord Widgery's Committee on reparation - were introduced under section 7. The orders were intended to be made against offenders who by their offences caused loss or damage (not attributable to personal injury) to one or more identifiable victims in excess of £15,000. After a judge in the Crown Court had made such an order, in addition to dealing with the offender in any other way (provided it did not also make a compensation order against the offender), the Official Petitioner, who in practice was the Director of Public Prosecutions, was then empowered to proceed in the normal way of bankruptcy proceedings and ensure that compensation was paid to the victim.

Moreover, the powers of the courts were increased through section 1 of the 1972 Criminal Justice Act. This enabled courts to make compensation orders, in addition to dealing with offenders in any other way, for any personal injury, loss or damage suffered as a result of their offences. Prior to the enactment of this section, statutory provisions pertaining to compensation appeared unclear and limited in scope, and were accordingly "sparingly and unevenly used" (Home Office 1970b: 55). It was hoped through providing a more "unified code" that the courts would find them easier to use (House of Lords Parliamentary Debates 1972: 332, 578). Provisions were also made in the Act for forfeiture of property and disqualification, in certain circumstances, from driving. Whilst not considered "major matters", they could also, as Maudling suggested, act as useful additions to the powers available to the courts (House of Commons Parliamentary Debates 1971: 826, 971). From this perspective, the Act assisted in the extension of control mechanisms by either increasing the length of sentences for various offences or by providing additional armoury to the judiciary which could be employed as "add ons" to the existing array of penal sanctions.

But there was also another side to the 1972 Act, a side which, informed by political pragmatism, continued to develop non-custodial sanctions. They could be justified on the grounds that those "who need not be sent to prison, those who are not guilty of violent crimes, should be punished in other ways in the interests of relieving the strain on the prison service and in the interests of the community" *(ibid: 972)*. One can allude of course to the introduction of community service orders, deferred sentences,[23] medical treatment centres for alcoholics, and day training centres as part of a probation order for inadequate offenders who could not cope with the complexities of life. One can also allude to the allocation of power to probation and after-care committees to establish probation and bail hostels themselves as opposed to leaving it simply in the hands of voluntary organisations, the provision that no court should pass a sentence of imprisonment on a person under the age of 21 who has not previously been sentenced to imprisonment unless it is of the opinion that no other method of dealing with him or her is appropriate, the provision that a magistrates' court who sends such an offender to prison must state the reason for its opinion that no other method of dealing with the offender is appropriate,[24] the abolition of mandatory suspended sentences on the grounds that it diminished the responsibility of the courts and it appeared that the employment of probation orders and fines had dropped dramatically since its inception, the restatement of the decision in *O'Keefe* that an offender should not be dealt with by means of a suspended sentence unless the case appeared to be one in which a sentence of imprisonment would have been appropriate in the absence of a power to suspend sentence, and the introduction of the suspended sentence supervision orders which enabled an offender to be placed under the supervision of a supervisory officer for a period

---

23. This had the advantage of allowing the court to "stay its hand" in order to see how the offender would behave (Home Office 1970: 75).
24. Section 14(5) abolished the First Offenders Act of 1958.

specified in the order but not exceeding the operational period of the suspended sentence. These then were the changes and additions which were made to the existing range of non-custodial sanctions in 1972.

Unfortunately they were, for the most part, provisions made in hope rather than carefully construed and analysed penal developments. Of course the Wootton Committee (albeit that many of its sanctions did not find legislative credence in the 1972 Criminal Justice Act) could justify such an approach: "the solution is to experiment with such measures and to evaluate them" (Home Office 1970: 3). For example, in respect of deferment of sentence, the Wootton Committee suggested that "courts, by experimentation, would soon learn what types of offences, and which types of offenders, would respond to this form of penal treatment" (*ibid*: 28). Experimenting with innovations in order to ascertain their "hit or miss" credentials after they have found legislative standing is, in my view, another monumental piece of "hedging". The reason for this may be simply stated. In a period of widespread escalation in prison numbers, any provisions enacted to alleviate the crisis will invariably be adopted into the heart of the criminal justice system, provided they demonstrate some semblance of success. In the long term, however, such an approach is problematic in that it is devoid of clear criminological or penological analysis. For example, the 1972 Criminal Justice Act did not comprehensively address the issue of why suspended sentences were being employed as alternatives to fines and probation. No attempt was made to contend with more esoteric issues such as the inability of policy makers to set down clear guidelines on the use of both discretionary and mandatory suspended sentences in 1967, or the prevailing model of sentencing behaviour and the courts' perceptions of their objectives (Sparks 1971: 394-401). Instead, the 1972 Criminal Justice Act simply abolished the mandatory suspended sentence and restated the principle that a suspended sentence should be used as a direct alternative to imprisonment.

Moreover, it is my contention that an approach which recommends evaluative research after proposals have been introduced is an abdication of responsibility on two grounds: first, it is ambiguous in design. Who is to undertake the evaluative research? How successful do sanctions have to be before they are maintained or perhaps, more appropriately, how unsuccessful do they have to be before they are discarded? What criteria are to be used in measuring the success rate?[25] Secondly, if new innovations are unsuccessful, then nobody is entirely to blame because they were only experimental until evaluative research could demonstrate their potential. Such a stance is convenient in that it enables penal innovators to traverse any negative evaluations of their designs whilst the penal complex, as a whole, is left to bear the brunt of such a vacillating *modus operandi*. This is not to suggest that all evaluative research can be undertaken prior to the introduction of a penal

---

25. Consider again, for example, the Wootton Committee's statement in respect of community service: "We have not attempted to categorise precisely the type of offenders for whom community service might be appropriate, nor do we think it possible to predict what use might be made by the courts of this new form of sentence."

sanction. Of course research must continue on a sanction once it is up and running in order to determine its true potential. But it is suggested that much of the work at a criminological and penological level must have already been undertaken on issues such as likely effects, target groups, how it would be perceived by the judiciary and offenders, how it would be perceived by the public, and its position in relation to other sanctions in the penal domain.[26] Unfortunately, such an approach was not forthcoming in the

---

26. See also Magee who, in examining Popperian practical politics, noted that "detecting mistakes and inherent dangers by critical examination and discussion beforehand is an altogether more rational procedure, and one as a rule less wasteful of resources, people and time, than waiting till they 'reveal themselves in practice': 'For, in this connexion, it is essential to face the fact that any action we take is likely to have unintended consequences. This simple point is one whose implications are highly charged for politics, administration and any form of planning. It can be illustrated easily. If I want to buy a house my very appearance in the market as a buyer will tend to raise the price; but although this is a direct consequence of my action no one can possibly maintain that it is an intended one ... Things are all the time happening which nobody planned or wants. And this inescapable fact should be allowed for both in decision-making and in the creation of organisational structures: if it is not it will be a permanent source of distortion. This again reinforces the need for critical vigilance in the administration of policies, and the allowance for their correction by error elimination. So not only do authorities which forbid prior critical examination of their policies condemn themselves to making many of their mistakes in a more expensive form, and discovering them later, than they need; they also ... condemn themselves to pressing on with mistakes for some time after these have begun to produce injurious unintended consequences'" (Magee 1973: 75-76). Such a discourse of "unintended consequences" is grounded in practicalism, focusing as it does on the design and mechanism of implementation of decisions. Of course, and as we shall see, the discourse of "unintended consequences" in the penal complex is much more oriented towards *sinisterism* - as embodied in the "dispersal of discipline thesis" (focusing as it does on the consequences of decisions).

period concerned and the sanctions that were implemented were grounded on nothing more substantial than a "potpourri of intelligent suggestions". It illustrates, once again, the pragmatic, reactive nature of penal policy making in England and Wales in the late 1960s and early 1970s.

We have now examined a series of measures introduced in the late 1960s and early 1970s to alleviate the prison crisis. Some have argued, as we have already seen, that these developments can be viewed as an extension of Foucault's "panoptic society". In a nutshell, the "dispersal of discipline" thesis puts forward the view, as we have already seen, that such measures have simply resulted in a widening and blurring of the boundaries of the network of social control. Implicit in such an argument is the need to refrain from understanding these new measures in terms of a "benevolent sounding destructuring package" (Cohen 1994: 38). Instead of understanding measures such as community service as an apostatise with Foucauldian transformations in the late eighteenth and nineteenth centuries, writers such as Cohen would argue that:

> "[T]he original structures have become stronger; far from any decrease, the reach and intensity of State control have been increased; centralisation and bureaucracy remain; professionals and experts are proliferating dramatically and society is more dependent on them; information has not made the legal system more formal or more just" (*ibid*: 37).

Of course such a hypothesis can be commended on the

grounds that it does not portray the introduction of these measures in purely progressivist, presentist terms. It can also be commended, as we have already seen, on the grounds that a sanction such as community service can constitute a heightening of intervention in that it may be utilised in *lieu* of other non-custodial sanctions, and it often penetrates more deeply into the informal networks of society. But can these measures be seen as a further consolidation of Foucault's carceral continuum or is a wider explanatory framework required? We have already criticised Foucault's "epistemelogico juridical" technique of interpretation, focusing as it does on the period between 1760 and 1840, on the grounds that: the level of capital punishment under old penality was far milder than commonly perceived; the level of physical punishments (punishment of the body) continued well into the nineteenth century; no account is made of the immense resistance that manifested itself in relation to the extension of the State control apparatus; "disciplinary mechanisation" in the Foucauldian sense cannot simply be extended into the modern penal complex (penal labour, for example); no attempt is made to account for cultural, social and legal phenomena, all of which place limitations on any full exposure to disciplinary practices;[27] and, no attempt is made to account for the new hegemonic penal project, as outlined by Garland, in the late 1800s and early 1900s (albeit that the

---

27. See also Garland who notes that the current process of "defining deviance down" - which occurs at the "shallow end" of the system - is in direct opposition to those who argue that the State is forever seeking to extend its "tentacles of control" (Garland 1996: 456-457).

transformation had manifested itself before 1895 and was not completed by 1914).[28] All of these phenomena acted against Foucault's monolithic interpretation of the transformation between old and new penality. Any attempt, therefore, to extend Foucault's hypothesis in order to account for recent penal developments will founder on the same rocks. In this sense, commentators such as Cohen, who are motivated by the desire to highlight the deficiencies in progressivist texts, fall into the same over-schematic trap - the "photographic negative" approach as Wiener would call it - by accepting unequivocally Foucault's hypothesis. Let us take this argument further with regard to the dispersal of discipline thesis.

Consider, for example, Cohen's belief that "community control has supplemented rather than replaced traditional methods" of social control on the grounds that rates of incarceration are not decreasing (1994: 44). Notwithstanding that more people were being sent to prison per annum, Bottoms' critique of the dispersal of discipline thesis alludes to the fact that the *proportionate* use of imprisonment for indictable offences in England and Wales dropped from 33.3 per cent in 1938 to 29.1 per cent in 1959 to 14.8 per cent in 1980 (Bottoms 1983: 167). Of course such a broad analysis fails to reveal the fact that whilst the proportionate use of imprisonment demonstrated a remarkable decrease from 1938 until the mid-1970s, by 1975 the pattern had been reversed: the proportionate use of imprisonment increased

---

28. For the lack of reflectivity in respect of the dispersal of discipline thesis, see McMahon (1992: 36-38).

from 12.9 per cent in 1974 to 13.4 per cent in 1975, to 13.7 per cent in 1976 and 1977, to 14.6 per cent in 1978, and to 14.9 per cent in 1979. It dropped slightly to 14.8 per cent in 1980 (Sabol 1990: I, 30). It cannot be denied that support for the dispersal of discipline thesis is evident from the figures from the mid-1970s onwards. Yet no attempt is made by supporters of the "extension of Foucauldian disciplinary mechanisms" hypothesis to address the issue of the proportionate long-term drop in prison numbers between 1938 and 1980. And it is clear that these long-term statistical trends cannot simply be viewed in terms of original Foucauldian structures becoming stronger and more intensified given that the period between 1938 and 1974 witnessed a substantial decline in the proportionate use of imprisonment. Whichever way you view the reversal of the trend after 1974, it is not open to argue that it is consistent with the pattern that manifested itself in the preceding years. Yet, if you are seeking to extend Foucauldian disciplinary mechanisms, then you must extend them in a uniform and consistent manner; it is not open to employ such a meta-theory simply in respect of post-1974 trends whilst disregarding pre-1974 trends which are not in keeping with the hypothesis being expounded. Consequently, it is fallacious to argue that post-1974 trends and the nature of the power being exercised by the State control apparatus are entirely in keeping with *original* Foucauldian transformations.

Moreover, Bottoms has also alluded to the fact that the use of fines for adult offenders guilty of indictable offences increased from 27.2 per cent in 1938 to 44.8 per cent in 1959, to 52.6 per cent in 1980 (1983: 167). He uses these statistics to demonstrate that the rise of the fine is not "fully consistent with the dispersal of discipline thesis", because the fine is not "primarily disciplinary" (*ibid*: 180). This is not the only time that the totality of Foucauldian analysis has been criticised by alluding to the use of the fine. Regarding nineteenth century penality, Ireland noted:

"Unglamorous as it may sound, it might be suggested, with only a slight element of mischief, that penality within the nineteenth century as a whole and particularly the latter part should be characterised by the imposition of the fine or the withdrawal of a licence rather than by the construction of Pentonville" (forthcoming: 6).

Yet Bottoms' use of statistics is again not entirely revealing. Between 1938 and 1967, the use of the fine did show a remarkable increase from 27.2 per cent to 67.3 per cent. But the figure dropped to 57.1 per cent in 1968 (no doubt partly as a result of the introduction of the suspended sentence) and to 50.3 per cent in 1969. It increased to 51.2 per cent in 1970 and continued to increase in the following years until it stood at 56.0 per cent in 1974. Thereafter the figure decreased (1977 being an exception) and it stood at 52.6 per cent in 1980 (no doubt partly as a result of the introduction of community service orders) (Pease 1975: 68). Whilst the figures for the periods 1968-1969 and 1974-1980 (with the exception of 1977) do support the notion that other alternatives were being used in *lieu* of the fine, no attempt is made by Cohen to incorporate long-term increases in the use of the fine. And these long-term increases are important because, as Bottoms and Ireland suggest, the fine is not a disciplinary penal disposition in the Foucauldian sense.[29] Cohen's failure to deal with such statistical penal trends is very much in keeping with the criticism levelled earlier at revisionists such as Foucault on the need to close the gap between transitional discourse and practice. Such a contention in relation to Cohen is supported by McMahon:

"While reviewing relevant statistical data appears mundane compared to engaging in literary and metaphorical depictions of transformations in penal control, the necessity of undertaking such prosaic tasks must be considered crucial for adequately analysing and understanding penal trends" (1992: 46).

Finally, in criticising the dispersal of discipline thesis, one can also refer to what Garland would term the place of "non-rational phenomena" (1990: 163).[30] The difficulty with Foucault's panoptic society, and consequently with the approach taken by those who seek to extend his hypothesis into the present penal complex, is that it is premised on a synergetic and undeviating course of execution. Yet there are strong grounds for arguing that such an assumption undermines much of the persuasiveness of the overall thesis given the indubitable fact that "non-rational phenomena" -

---

29. The fine, for example, is not for the most part a penalty which involves "continuing supervision by a penal agent" (Bottoms 1983: 169).
30. See also McMahon (1991: XXX, 145).

which operate at a practical level against the uncompromised implementation of Foucauldian disciplinary mechanisms - have always formed an integral component of our penal system. It is my contention that disciplinary mechanisms have always broken down on two levels: at an individual level (ie, individual offenders or penal officials who impede the course of execution); and, at a general level (ie, difficulties with supervision, fiscal constraints, organisational and pragmatic concerns, and technological mishaps which also impede or alter the course of execution). Let us examine both levels together.

In the 1850s and 1860s, for example, after Foucault's original transformation had occurred, Ireland, writing about the dilemma of identifying prisoners and the way in which it jeopardised "the very drive towards consistency, practicability and uniformity of punishment which marks so much of the nineteenth century discourse of penalty" (forthcoming: 9-10), noted:

"[I]f John Phillips could be George Flynn in Carmarthen, John Stanmore in Merioneth and John Hanley in Montgomery, the whole penal enterprise was threatened by a crucial handicap" (*ibid*).[31]

---

31. See also the Carnarvon Committee Report which noted: "[T]he Committee has so frequently during the course of examination been drawn to the great public inconvenience, which is felt from the difficulty in identifying a previously convicted prisoner, that they cannot close their report without indicating both the extent of the evil and the suggestion of a remedy" (1863: IX, 37). The remedy suggested was that of photographing prisoners, a practice which had been employed in Ireland for a number of years.

Even by the 1870s, when photographing offenders was becoming more commonplace, identification was still subject to "non-rational phenomena":

> "Flaws in the system became apparent. One, which in truth had been troubling from an early period, was related to the technological crudity of the early photographic process. *In the case of an unwilling subject the difficulty of securing the necessary stasis for long exposures might be considerable, a mere jerk of the head sufficient to defeat the process, a distortion of the features sufficient to confound it"* (*ibid:* 31) (my italics).

Nor should these phenomena be simply viewed as part of our penal history. Consider, for example, Sykes's analysis of inmate culture in a prison institution in 1958:

> "The lack of a sense of duty among those who are held captive, the obvious fallacies of coercion, the pathetic collection of rewards and punishments to induce compliance, the strong pressures towards the corruption of the guard in the form of friendship, reciprocity, and the transfer of duties into the hands of trusted inmates - all are structured defects in the prison's system of power rather than individual inadequacies" (1958: 61).

Many of these same forces also operate in respect of community service orders. Between March and December, 1979, Anthony Vass conducted a survey as a participant observer on community service order scheme. Participation involved the completion of 220 hours community service, carried out in two sub-areas of Southdown. In his findings, he noted an unwillingness to work among many offenders, a lack of materials and equipment, a flexible interpretation of the rules which enabled all breaks to be credited to offenders, albeit that official policy stated otherwise (Vass 1984: 90-91).[32] In addition, he noted:

> "[T]he social distance between mainstream society and deviants is symbolically and effectively stressed by the recipients by drawing clearly defined territorial boundaries between offenders and themselves ... The phrase 'keep out of sight' is a standard colloquialism in the social world of community service" (*ibid*).

Whilst discussing the offenders on a community service order scheme, Supervisor D in sub-area B noted:

> They'll do a few bits here and there. Then they'll tell you, 'We've had enough of this. We want tea'. Some of them are complete failures. It's like trying to do miracles with them. I avoid getting in situations...which can spoil my day ... I try to avoid aggravations. I pretend I don't see or hear" (*ibid*: 105).

Consider also the following answer by Offender A when asked about how many hours offenders actually put into

---

32. For similar findings in respect of offender laxity in complying with agreed employment arrangements in Ireland, see Walsh and Sexton (forthcoming).

community service:

"From their [officers] point of view or ours? From theirs whether we work an hour, two hours...makes no difference as long as we are present to sign our [attendance] forms ... From our point of view, community service means an effort to get up on Sundays and make it to the office or the ... pick up spot ... We probably work ... an hour on most days with a couple of hours playing around. If we were paid for what we ... do ..., which [takes] weeks, we could finish the job in a day or, who knows, 10 minutes - depends. Community service is like playing a game. There's give and take. It makes life easier for everybody that way. They [officers] want us to finish our hours. They need us as we need them. It's as simple as that" (*ibid*: 106).[33]

Thus non-rational phenomena such as an unwillingness to work among offenders, a lack of materials and equipment, flexible interpretations of hours worked, isolation from mainstream society, and official avoidance of aggravation, all, to some extent, form components of the fabric of community service orders. In this respect, it is over-schematic to simply view such a sanction from the perspective of totalised discipline alone. But the "expansion,

---

33. Further evidence of resistance to disciplinary mechanisms can be discerned from debates on the use of electronic tagging in 1988. It was resisted successfully on the grounds that half the potential offenders who could be tagged did not have a telephone and by the probation service who preferred to be "helpers rather than controllers" (*The Guardian* 23 February 1988: 18).

dispersal, invisibility and penetration" hypothesis in regard to community control programmes is also over-schematic in that it affords - as has already been stated in respect of Scull - little or no status to ideological or political forces. Yet community participation, as previously discussed, cannot simply be understood in terms of disciplinary society and the "logic of the master pattern" (Cohen 1979: III, 359). It must also be understood as being derived, in part, from the lack of success of the Welfare State, new social needs, growing concern about the activities of young people, the perceived loss of control of people over their lives in an industrial society, the need to promote dignity and self-respect, and the need to voice opinions. Moreover, no attempt is made to analyse the specific nature of penal policy making under the dispersal of discipline thesis. We are simply led to believe that the "logic of the master pattern" is responsible for the extension of Foucauldian disciplinary mechanisms. Yet as we have seen, particularly in relation to the Wootton Committee, pragmatic considerations - such as the desire to reduce prison overcrowding, prison expenditure, and the need to ease public anxiety - sometimes took precedence over strategy goals and priority choices. Pragmatism of this nature, of course, militated against a sanction such as community service ever developing as a true alternative to imprisonment, yet it does not fit neatly into the dispersal of discipline perspective of community control programmes. The outcomes may have been the same - community service being employed as an alternative to alternatives in many instances - but their respective approaches - particularly in respect of the *sinisterism* that the dispersal of discipline thesis embodies[34] - certainly are not.[35]

To conclude, then, the dispersal of discipline thesis is insightful in that it highlights deficiencies in the progressivist, presentist analysis of community control programmes and offers us a more radical interpretation and explanation. A broader framework of analysis is, however, required when explaining community control programmes so as to account for statistical trends, cultural, social and legal phenomena, ideological developments, pragmatic developments, and non-rational phenomena, all of which are inconsistent with the totalised discipline perspective.

Conclusion

In the late 1960s and early 1970s sanctions such as the suspended sentence, the mandatory suspended sentence, parole, restrictions on the power of the police to refuse bail,

---

34. See, for example, Scull (1987: 331) who suggests: "[W]e must look to the ways in which the organisational interests of the professions running the criminal justice system have ensured the transmogrification of yet another generation of 'reforms' in the directions dictated by administrative convenience and bureaucratic aggrandisement."

35. See also Blomberg (1995: 45-46) who notes: "[W]hile these metaphorical characterisations [including those related to the dispersal of discipline thesis] and broader interpretations have been useful, they are often partial and overgeneralised. Specifically, the metaphors and associated theoretical interpretations do not convey the nuances of the penal reforms, their specific origins, their differences in implementation, their distinctive operational features, their potentially mixed outcomes, or the combined effects of broader influences in shaping penal reform processes."

restrictions on the issue of a warrant for imprisonment for fine default, the increase in maximum fines which courts could impose so as to encourage their use, removal of the penalty of imprisonment for being drunk and disorderly, deferred sentences, medical treatment centres, the allocation of power to establish probation and bail hostels, the provision that no court should pass a sentence of imprisonment on a person under the age of 21 who had not previously been sentenced to imprisonment unless it was of the opinion that no other method of dealing with him or her was appropriate (a magistrates' court had to state the reason for its opinion that no other method of dealing with the said offender was appropriate), the abolition of the mandatory suspended sentence, and the introduction of suspended sentence supervision orders, all formed part of a stratagem for restricting the exponential growth in prison numbers and the number sleeping two or three to a cell. Such a process was heightened by the extreme pressures placed on the provision of services in the prison system, the degrading conditions to be found therein, the increasing number of disturbances and escapes, the growing discontentment with the Welfare State and its combination of Keynesianism and Beveridgism, the developing sociological awareness of the contaminating effects of imprisonment, and the growing awareness of the advantages of community participation programmes. Moreover, many of these sanctions, particularly in the early 1970s, had to operate in a climate which was witnessing a shift towards a more authoritarian control culture. Such a shift is palpable, in the period concerned, in policing, judicial, political and penal circles (ie, the movement towards containment in prisons and the declining influence of rehabilitation as a policy goal).

It has been argued that many of these sanctions resulted in an expansion and intensification of the social control network, an increase in its invisibility and its deeper penetration into the social body. Such an approach as we have seen is laudable in that: (a) it highlights the deficiencies in progressivist, presentist analysis; (b) brings our attention to the fact that a heightening of intervention, in many instances, has occurred, and; (c) brings our attention to the fact that they do penetrate deeper into the social body. Yet revisionist perspectives provide only a limited basis within which these sanctions can be understood in that they focus, almost entirely, on economic (Scull) or disciplinary (Cohen) dimensions. In this sense, they are too compartmentalised in approach in that they fail to contend with many phenomena which circumscribe and are inconsistent with either totalised discipline or purely economic perspectives. For example, a sanction such as community service can result in "blurring" in that tasks are carried out by offenders in the community in association with volunteers and the public. It may sometimes be difficult for an outsider to discern who exactly is caught up in the social control net. Yet Vass's empirical research has demonstrated, at least for sub-area A and sub-area B of Southdown, that "clearly defined territorial boundaries" can also be drawn between offenders and the public. As such, it is over-schematic to propose that blurring occurs as an unopposed and undeviating penal process. There is need, as has already been suggested, to incorporate concepts such as blurring within a wider and more representational framework of analysis.

Let us conclude, then, by focusing on the specific sanction of community service. We have already seen in the last chapter that the introduction of community service orders was structured around historically specific penal practices (both domestic and international) and historically specific movements (voluntarism and community participation). As we have seen in this chapter, the actual moulding of the sanction was also determined against a specific backdrop. For example, it was motivated by the desire to curtail prison numbers and to reduce gross prison expenditure in the criminal justice system. It was also motivated by the possibilities which concepts such as community participation and reparation (greatly espoused in the Widgery Committee report) afforded policy makers, offenders and the public. Moreover, the element of "bite" which the sanction embodied, as previously discussed, must also be seen against the backdrop of the politicisation of law and order and rising fears about the level of crime. Indeed the Government itself made changes to the Wootton Committee's proposals on community service in order to demonstrate to the public that their stance was not a soft one. These included, *inter alia*: (a) the restriction of community service to imprisonable offences; and (b) the removal of no minimum period of service (replaced with 40 hours) and the extension of the maximum period from 120 to 240 hours (Menzies and Vass 1981: XXVIII, 205).

It is also worth noting that the sanction itself did result in an expansion of the social control network in that it was employed not only in *lieu* of imprisonment but also in *lieu* of other alternatives to imprisonment. Pease *et al* noted, after conducting empirical research on the six community service order pilot schemes, that "sentencers in many cases seem to regard community service as an alternative to non-custodial sentences at least as much, and possibly more than, alternatives to custodial sentences" (1975: 68). The dangers of such an occurrence had already been seen by Lord Donaldson in 1972:

"[T]he danger of her [Lady Wootton] recommendations is that if they are applied wrongly, or applied without the greatest of care, they are going to be alternative to probation and not alternative to prisons. As the noble Earl, Lord Mansfield, said in his excellent, informed and stimulating maiden speech, it is a very good thing for magistrates to have a number of alternatives in front of them; but variations on the probation theme, though useful, are not fundamental. What is fundamental is to give the wretched magistrates something to do with the man rather than send him to prison ...What we want to do is to give the magistrates an alternative which will enable them to keep a man out of prison. The danger in the whole of the legislation, including the last Government's suspended sentence plan (which has gone rather wrong), is that this will not have that effect" (House of Lords Parliamentary Debates 1972: 332, 635).

Yet rather than viewing such a phenomena from the perspective of the "cunning state", more attention must be given to other causal factors. After all, the Wootton

Committee did express the desire that "non-custodial penalties should be truly non-custodial" (Home Office 1970: 9). Much of the problem in respect of community service orders is, as previously discussed, attributable to the reactive, non-committal approach adopted by the Wootton Committee - a factor conspicuous by its absence in the dispersal of discipline thesis. Such an approach undoubtedly facilitated the expansion of the social control network and must be incorporated into any theoretical anatomisation concerning the issue. One final point can be made. We have just noted that Pease *et al* were of the opinion that community service was employed as an alternative to non-custodial sentences in about half the cases they studied. But what of the other half? Does it not indicate that community service orders were, in part, successful at removing offenders from imprisonment? The problem with the dispersal of discipline thesis is that it is entirely nihilistic in outlook and it eschews all "indicators of reductionist effect" (McMahon 1992: 74). As McMahon noted:

"[L]ittle attention has been paid by critical analysts to the apparent removal of some offenders from imprisonment by virtue of their subjection to other penal measures. Thus, for example, where a program such as community service orders is discussed in any detail, the tendency is to emphasise that, in about half of those cases in which they are used, the offender would probably not have been imprisoned anyway ... This approach ... detracts attention from the point that, in the other half of cases, community service orders have apparently been used in *lieu* of imprisonment. In seeking to criticise such programs, attention to their accomplishments has been minimal" (*ibid: 73*).[36]

Again, evidence of success in regard to community control programmes must find expression in any related analysis - be it empirical, theoretical, or both.

Having already outlined more positive and genuine claims of relevance in respect of the germs of community service, as opposed to those expounded by academics such as Vass and Pease, the purpose of this chapter was to provide a snapshot of the climate within which those germs had to be moulded together. And, again, the constitution of this climate is, in many respects, discontinuous with earlier times. As such, this chapter has attempted to define penal phenomena in their specificity in order to better appreciate the introduction and shaping of the sanction. It should by

---

36. See also Matthews who noted: "The danger of the impossibilist ethos ... is not only that it provides a disincentive to the formulation of realistic and progressive policies, but also that it can similarly lead to the premature abandonment of a search for alternatives to incarceration. It is arguably the persistent pessimism which surrounds deinstitutionalisation and diversion strategies in Britain and North America that has inadvertently lent support to the movement toward a re-expansion of the prison system. By reducing the decarceration process to an epiphenomenon, or by condemning it to a premature burial despite continued and widespread evidence of 'success', many theorists have discouraged debate and ignored the gains which have been made during the 'decarceration era'. Dismissing the potential of these movements, encouraging a belief that everything is getting worse, that 1984 is just around the corner - even if a little late - and suggesting that the only thing which might be worse than living with prisons is living without them, is to exchange the possibility of realistic and progressive interventions for dystopian fantasies" (1987: 357).

now be apparent that many of the described phenomena, such as the cumulative impact and representation of a succession of moral panics (which were sustained by specific penal, technological and social forces), the politicisation of law and order, acute prison overcrowding from the 1950s onwards, the increasing number of escapes and attempts at escape, the rise to prominence of containment as a primary policy issue, growing discontentment with the Welfare State and the emergence of the New Right (intent as it was on curtailing expenditure), the emergence of ideologies such as community participation and reparation, the declining credibility in the rehabilitative ethos, and the lack of long-term strategy goals or priority choices among the innovators of penal sanctions, are incapable of being viewed in a narrow, teleological framework. They must instead be construed in the political, social, economic, technological and penological climate of the period being examined.

CONCLUSION

At a general level, this book has attempted to move away from the irredeemable preoccupation of writing prefatory histories of contemporary criminal justice and criminological phenomena. At a more particular level, an attempt has been made to move away from the notion that the history of work-based penal dispositions is, to some extent, the *causa fiendi* of community service orders. Such a Whiggish methodology, in my view, is fallacious in that it abstains from proper diachronic analysis by utilising the "principle of exclusion" to jettison all that which is not commensurate with its linear schema of interpretation; depicts community service as an "unfolding logic" which was always scheduled to appear as a sanction; and, proceeds with a method of analysis which views all penal labour sanctions as being governed by the same principles and assumptions - albeit that penal authorities in earlier times had a much lesser degree of success in forming penal labour sanctions given that these sanctions must be viewed as the *less reputable forebears* of community service. Again, I would reiterate the belief that community service may have a *long past* but a *short history* in that it was driven by a particular and specific complex of penal strategies, agencies, representations and techniques which render anachronistic any unqualified analogies between it and past penal work practices. As such, I have sought to write a more historical and conceptual account of the introduction of community service orders. Such an approach was attempted by being responsive to context and by utilising discontinuity as a tool of analysis. In this sense, I have alluded to a wealth of revisionist literature, all of which focused on the incidence of interruptions in the criminal justice history process in order to illuminate their respective hypotheses on modalities of punishment.

This book began by examining how societal attitudes and sensibilities have an impact upon penal policy initiatives. This was explicitly demonstrated in respect of the cultural phenomenon of leisure. It was argued that leisure was not a demarcated and separate segment of an individual's daily routine prior to the industrial revolution. Rather it was available in the interstices of the workday which was more often than not determined by agrarian and seasonal rhythms. Between the eighteenth and nineteenth centuries, however, and as a result of the concentration of labour in specialised institutions and the increased emphasis on temporal precision, on time related as opposed to task related toil, on the cash nexus relationship between employers and employees, and on individual and collective work discipline, a marked disjunction manifested itself, in broad terms, between leisure and work. But leisure was still, for the most part, viewed as a threat to the work ethic in the period concerned. It was only in the twentieth century that demarcations between work time and free time became more palpable. Leisure, in its modern sense, was brought about as a result of the substantial reduction in the hours of work, the growing belief that leisure was a suitable non-monetary compensation for work and should, where possible, be a matter of personal choice, the introduction of holidays with pay, increases in the holidays taken, the emergence of a leisure industry, the enshrinement of leisure as a right, increases in discretionary income, and the declining role of the Church. Moreover, and more importantly from our perspective, it has been argued that it was only in leisure's modern sense when it was viewed as a right of the people and was a separate and distinct component of daily routine that an offender could be deprived of it as a suitable means of punishment. Thus, it was only in the modern sense that we can begin to appreciate how this cultural phenomenon of leisure could play such a pivotal role in the operation of community service orders.

Continuing to use discontinuity as a tool of analysis, I then proceeded to demonstrate that the criminal justice system itself has not remained constant and continuous over time. For example, it was shown that the concept of a centralised State was anathema to reasoning prior to the late 1800s given that the State was viewed, for the most part, as simply having safeguarding duties and was weak in its functioning. Gradually, however, the State began to assume a more functionary, proficient and active design as a result, *inter alia*, of the development of monopoly groups, the centralisation of finance, the intensity of the problems created by urbanisation and industrialisation, the professional ideal, the growth of New Unionism, and a growing awareness of the need to protect the vulnerable and defenceless from the increasingly unjust system of individualism, embodying as it did concepts such as self-help and self-reliance. The extension of the power of the State to intervene manifested itself ultimately in a more homogenised system of State control and can be starkly juxtaposed with the local and disparate arrangements that so characterised eighteenth century punishment. Moreover, in addition to examining the intricacies and complexities of human intervention from the perspective of State control and social thinking, this book also viewed it from the perspective of scientific reasoning. It was noted that as a result of the advances made in science in the mid- to late-1800s a more developed awareness of diacritical etiology manifested itself and resulted in the rejection of spiritual and conjectural reasoning on the characters of offenders. Under such conditions, it was not surprising that the criminal justice system moved towards a more inductive and individualistic approach in respect of the treatment of criminal behaviour and consequenced itself, in part, in the emergence of a new archetype of punishment which attempted to punish offenders in a manner more receptive to the intricacies of human nature and human fallibility. Finally, in chapter two, the object of reformation was traced from a modality of punishment which functioned in the absence of homogeneity; to a system (*La Science Penitentaire*) more capable of adopting algebraic formula perceptions of offending in respect of reformative practices by utilising techniques such as *encellulement,* continuous inspection, inscribed architecture, and staged systems; to a more welfarist, individualistic reformative approach which was not based on the full systematisation of disciplinary and deterrent penal practices.

At this juncture, it should be obvious that a Whiggish interpretation of the history of community service orders, and the "principle of exclusion" which it embodies, cannot account for issues such as homogeneity of penal practices, the whole process of individualisation of treatment (and the more "knowledgeable form of regulation" which it led to), and the movement from *encellulement* to association and the adoption of science as a proper means of reforming individuals. Having examined broad structural changes in penality and defined the modern archetype of punishment in general terms, the book proceeded to focus on more specific aspects of criminal justice thinking which have had a direct bearing on the introduction and operation of community service.

It was proposed, to begin with, that the emphasis of international law has increasingly shifted from a formalised structure between States primarily concerned with the regulation of national sovereignty to the development of substantive rules concerning the rights of individuals and the promotion of higher standards of living, full employment, and cultural, economic, and social enhancement. Again it was argued that these historically specific rights influenced the nature of community service in that they prohibit forced labour imposed for private individuals, companies or associations and prohibit forced work of a kind not carried out in the ordinary course of detention or during conditional release from detention. Furthermore, this book alluded to the advancement of the community ideology in the 1950s and 1960s which was brought about as a result of the belief that the Welfare State had failed to meet all expectations, the notion that advanced industrial society was gradually usurping part of the role of individuals living in it, attempts to stimulate social integration in the domain of mental health, and by increased fears about the ineffectual and expensive nature of closed prison institutions. In such an environment, it was argued that a new impetus emerged which endorsed and authenticated the community as a proper social control mechanism. Finally, chapter 3 concluded by tracing the campaign to reduce the act of penal labour to a rationalised process of movements and to equalise its distribution throughout the penal system, followed by its utilisation in the twentieth century as a constructive and positive practice in a greatly diversified penal complex. All of these beliefs, ideologies and phenomena, which can broadly be described as having manifested themselves in the modern penal complex, are incapable of being justified or conceived in terms of principles or sentiments from former modalities of punishment. The practical implications of the arguments expounded in the first three chapters was illustrated, perhaps most dramatically, in respect of the specific sanction of impressment.

Fortified with the components of the present day sanction of community service, Ken Pease believed he found similar constituents in the sanction of impressment without realising that they were not formulated in the same periodisation framework as the present, and had not, therefore, been created with the same objectives or motives in mind. As such, his methodology, in my view, led ineluctably to a distortion of the analogies that were drawn. It was noted, for example, that impressment was simply another stratagem devised by the Royal Navy to maintain control over the high seas, and even then, the Admiralty was only amenable, where possible, to admitting seafarers. Thus, impressment as a penal sanction must be viewed as being exploitative in nature and rather unsystematic in operation. Pease was also criticised, *inter alia*, on the grounds of his failure to allude to historical works on the sanction of impressment; on his failure to recognise that impressment was not specifically created as a means of punishing offenders; on his failure to see that debtors were regarded as a special class of prisoners and that the consensual element for them was brought about as a means to ease public conscience regarding their containment in prisons, to remove them from the restrictive embrace of their creditors, and to assist the navy in manning ships in times of war; and on his failure to realise that impressment was not determinate in the sense that quantifying a penal sanction in leisure hours is. Moreover, it was also argued that it is a fallacy to propose that the sanction of impressment was "remarkably similar" to the sanction of community service given that the latter is embodied in a modality of punishment which contains many features not inherent in earlier modalities of punishment. Having performed this historical catharsis in the first four chapters, and having outlined the modern penal complex within which community service operates, I then attempted to locate the conditions of emergence of the community service order ideal itself.

It was noted, for example, that a remarkable growth occurred in the 1950s and 1960s in voluntarism as a result of the deficiencies in the State system of social welfare, the emergence of new social needs, mounting disquiet about the habits and activities of young people, and a genuine desire of people to combat the increasingly isolated features associated with advanced industrialist society. Secondly, community service in penal institutions began to take on a more policy oriented outlook - as opposed to being founded upon acts of God or infrequent calls for help - as it came to be regarded as an essential element in the employment and social training of inmates. It was motivated by the growth of voluntarism, and in particular voluntarism concerned with community service tasks, and by the emergence of the corrective community ideology as a panacea for deviant behaviour. Finally, chapter 5 also examined developments in respect of intermediate treatment in domestic law and international experiments with community work in Australia, America, New Zealand and Germany, both of which provided further impetus for the introduction of community service orders.

The final chapter attempted to provide a composite picture of how those germs were moulded together to form the specific sanction of community service. The penological period in question, the late 1960s and early 1970s, was portrayed as highly differentiated in character and comprised of a wide array of penal referents which all aided in the specific form that community service displayed. The chapter began by highlighting the fact that the late 1960s and early 1970s manifested itself in a crisis of control which was brought about, in part, by dramatic increases in crime, notions of disaffected youth, football hooliganism, racial tension, political demonstrations, the developing drug culture and the upsurge of violence in Northern Ireland. Turning to more specific developments in the criminal justice system, it was argued that there was a growing realisation that the prison population far outstripped the number of places that could be provided; that overcrowding was not a temporary expedient, but a phenomenon that the prison authorities would have to contend with for a number of years; that extreme pressures were placed on the provision of services and conditions in the prison system; that the Welfare State and its combination of Bevredgism and Keynesianism was not working; and that there was a demise, in practical terms, in the rehabilitative ethos. These developments consequenced themselves in the politicisation of law and order, the shift towards a more authoritarian control culture in penal, political, judicial and policing circles, and in the reactive and pragmatic nature of government responses (mainly by means of expanding the number of dispositions available to the courts). Many of these issues were realised in the shaping or operating of community service. For example, the sanction could be justified on the grounds that it was highly likely that it would not prove more *unsuccessful* than imprisonment in rehabilitative terms; it would be cheaper than a term of imprisonment; it contained a sufficient element of bite; and was more humane than subjecting a non-serious offender to a term of imprisonment. Furthermore, it has been suggested that the introduction of community service was governed by short-term, non-committal concerns which resulted, in part, in the sanction never being established purely as an alternative to imprisonment.

A series of issues have been contended with in this book. These include an attempt to define the parameters of the modern penal and cultural complex in respect of community service; an attempt to highlight the ahistorical approach adopted by Pease and his cohorts; an attempt to formulate more positive and genuine claims of relevance in respect of the germs of the community service order ideal; and an attempt to provide a discursive framework of the plethora of forces which acted upon the penal, social, economic, ideological and political domains in the late 1960s and early 1970s, all of which helped to shape the sanction. All of these issues were grappled with in the hope of writing a history of the present in respect of community service orders. It is hoped that this history has aided our understanding of the key issues and concepts inherent in community service and its relationship with other concerns and practices in the period in question. Moreover, it is hoped that this history will be viewed as being more sensitive to context and written in a manner which does not present the sanction as an "unfolding logic" which was always destined to appear.

Much of my effort to write a history of the present in respect of community service was aided by examining the attempts of revisionists to construct master strategies of social control through highlighting the *incidence of interruptions* in the criminal justice history process. Revisionist analysis is excellent in that it emphasises the need to associate penal developments with prevailing conditions in the broader social structure, provides a more coherent and historical understanding of penality, illuminates the deficiencies in progressivist, presentist history, and provides us with a better analysis of power relations, real intentions and actual consequences in the penal complex. But again it must be stressed that revisionist analysis only provides a partial basis upon which to understand penality. First, revisionist analysis, as we have seen, is too schematic in methodology and fails to account for a series of forces, such as those which are diametrically opposed to change, which require explanation outside that proffered in their respective hypotheses. Although such forces are, in many instances, far less exhilarating than elucidating transitional interruptions in the penal process, they are just as pivotal to our understanding of the penal complex because they enable us to close the gap between transitional penal discourse and actual penal practice. In this sense, revisionist analysis needs to take on a more diacritical emphasis in respect of the criminal justice history process. Secondly, revisionist analysis needs to take on a more reflective attitude in respect of its own internal genre of discourse. For example, Cohen, through metaphorical categorisations, attempts to extend Foucauldian disciplinary mechanisms into the penal domain of the late twentieth century (and suggests that developments in this domain are consistent with *original* Foucauldian transformations) without ever considering Garland's hypothesis which argues that a new hegemonic penal project manifested itself in the late 1800s and early 1900s and resulted in the movement from a "calibrated hierarchical structure" to an "extended grid of non-equivalent and diverse dispositions" founded upon more scientific, factual and inductive strategies towards offending. Albeit that both Foucault and Garland attempt to construct a modern modality of punishment by highlighting the *incidence of interruptions*, it cannot be denied that the respective interruptions which they delineate, the key forces which they believed acted as the impetus for transition, the juxtapositions that they made, and the constituents of the modern that they portray, are highly contrasting in outlook. Yet Cohen is more than happy to engage in discourse about the extension of Foucault's discipline thesis without attempting to substantiate such a claim in respect of the Garlandian modality of punishment. This is not to deny that theoretical perceptions of penality are important. As Harding and Ireland note, we do require a conceptual framework "to provide an overall sense of order and direction", and to "avoid description and quantification for its own sake" (Harding and Ireland 1989: 68). Rather what is being suggested is that there is a need for a more eclectic and self-critical methodology in our investigations into transitions in the penal process which, whilst providing a conceptual framework, also highlight the various components acting upon the penal complex including cultural, political, religious, economic, pragmatic, social and non-rational forces.

But let us not be distracted from the main argument of this book. It has sought to demonstrate the anachronistic historiography deployed by academics such as Vass and Pease in their quest to understand the introduction of community service orders. Instead, and using discontinuity as a tool of historical analysis, an attempt has been made to define loosely the locus of the emergence of the modern modality of punishment in order to demonstrate that the history of community service is not a history of progressive refinement. Once this modality of punishment was in place, it was then possible to trace the historical conditions of emergence of the community service order ideal. It is hoped that a general framework has now been created which will assist in constructing parameters for future study in respect of the sanction. This framework is necessary, in my view, in order to highlight the complex and interrelated nature of community service and to enable it to become a more coherent object of analysis. New avenues of enquiry for future study - not touched upon in earlier monographs on the sanction - have now been opened up in respect of community service and include issues such as the cultural determinant of leisure and its impact, notions concerning community participation, the policy of penal pragmatism, perceptions of human rights in respect of forced labour, the ideology of community as a social control technique, the politicisation of law and order, the growth of voluntarism in the 1960s, and the decline of rehabilitation in practical terms. All of these phenomena need to be incorporated, both at a contextual and empirical level, into any future analysis of the operation of community service in order to appreciate fully both the meaning and prospects of the sanction.

BIBLIOGRAPHY

ABELL, F. (1914) Prisoners of War in Britain, 1756 to 1815: a record of their lives, their romance and their sufferings. Oxford: University Press.

ABRAMS, M. *et al* eds. (1985) Values and Social Change in Britain. London: Macmillan.

ACTON, H.B. (1969) The Philosophy of Punishment: a collection of papers. London: Macmillan.

ADAMS, Robert *et al* (1980) A Measure of Diversion: case studies in intermediate treatment. National Youth Bureau: Leicester.

ALDERSON, J. (1982) The Mass Media and the Police. IN: SUMNER, C. ed. Crime, Justice and the Mass Media. Cambridge: Cropwood Conference Series. No. 14.

ALLEN, Francis A. (1973) Criminal Justice, Legal Values, and the Rehabilitative Ideal. IN: MURPHY, J.G. ed. Punishment and Rehabilitation. California: Wadsworth Publishing.

ALPER, B.M. (1968) Borstal briefly revisited. British Journal of Criminology VIII: 6-19;
(1973) Foreword. IN: BAKAL, Y. ed. Closing Correctional Institutions: new strategies for youth services. Lexington: Lexington Books.

ANONYMOUS (1814) The Right and Practice of Impressment, as concerning Great Britain and America, considered. London: J. Murray.

ANONYMOUS (1958) Let reparation fit the crime. Journal of Criminal Law Vol. 22, pp. 167-170.

ANTHONY, P.D. (1977) The Ideology of Work. London: Tavistock.

ARGYLE, M. (1996) The Social Psychology of Leisure. London: Penguin.

ARIES, P. (1962) L'Enfant et la Familiale sous L'Ancien Régime. New York: Vintage Books.

ARMSTRONG, G. (1983) Community Service Orders in New Zealand. IN: BEVAN, C. ed. Community Service Orders in Australia and New Zealand. Canberra: Australian Institute of Criminology.

ASHCRAFT, R. (1994) Locke's Political Philosophy. IN: CHAPPEL, V. ed. The Cambridge Companion to Locke. Cambridge: Cambridge University Press.

ASHPLANT, T.G. and WILSON, A. (1988) Present-Centred History and the Problem of Historical Knowledge. The Historical Journal Vol. 31. No. 2, pp. 253-274.

ASHTON, T.S. (1948) The Industrial Revolution, 1760-1830. London: Oxford University Press.

ATIYAH, P.S. (1979) The Rise and Fall of Freedom of Contract. Oxford: Clarendon Press;
(1989) An Introduction to the Law of Contract. (4th edn.) Oxford: Clarendon Press.

AUGHEY, A and NORTON, P. (1984) A Settled Polity: the Conservative view on law and order. IN: NORTON, Philip. ed. Law and Order in British Politics. Gower: Aldershot.

AULD, J. (1973) Drug Use: the mystification of accounts. IN: BAILEY, R and YOUNG, J. eds. Contemporary Social Problems in Britain. Farnborough: Saxon House.

AVES, G. (1969) The Voluntary Worker in the Social Services. Report of a Committee jointly set up by the National Council of Social Service and the National Institute for Social Work Training. London: George Allen and Unwin.

BAILEY, M. (1994) Rural Society. IN: HORROX, R. ed. Fifteenth Century Attitudes. Perceptions of Society in late Medieval England. Cambridge: Cambridge University Press.

BAILEY, R. and YOUNG, J. eds. (1973) Contemporary Social Problems in Britain. Farnborough: Saxon House.

BAILEY, V. ed. (1981) Policing and Punishment in Nineteenth Century Britain. London: Croom Helm.

BAINHAM, A. and CRETNEY, S. (1993) Children: the modern law. Bristol: Family Law.

BAKAL, Y. ed. (1973) Closing Correctional Institutions. New Strategies for Youth Services. Lexington: Lexington Books.

BALL, C. and BALL, M. (1973) Education for a Change. Community Action and School. Middlesex: Penguin.

BARR, H. and O'LEARY, E. (1966) Trends and Regional Comparisons in Probation (England and Wales). London: H.M.S.O.

BARR, H. (1972) The Role of the Volunteer: a reappraisal. London: NACRO (Nacro Papers and Reprints).

BARRY, J. (1960) Alexander Machonochie, 1787-1860. IN: MANNHEIM, H. ed. Pioneers in Criminology. London: Longman;
(1985) Popular Culture in Seventeenth-Century Bristol. IN: REAY, B. ed. Popular Culture in Seventeenth Century England. London: Croom Helm.

BARTRIP, P.W.J. and BURMAN, S.B. (1983) The Wounded Soldiers of Industry: industrial compensation policy, 1833-1897. Oxford: Oxford University Press.

BARTY-KING, H. (1991) The Worst Poverty: a history of debt and debtors. London: Stroud.

BATES, T. (1975) Gramsci and the Theory of Hegemony. Journal of the History of Ideas Vol. XXXVI, No. 2, pp. 351-366.

BAUDRILLARD, J. (1998 repr) The Consumer Society: myths and structures. London: Sage

BAUGH, D.A. ed. (1977) Naval Administration, 1715-1750. London: Navy Records Society;
(1995) The Eighteenth Century Navy as a National Institution. IN: HILL, J.R. ed. The Oxford Illustrated History of the Royal Navy. Oxford: Oxford University Press.

BAUMANN, J. *et al* (1966) Alternativ-Entwurf eines Strafgesetz-buches Allgemeiner Teil. Tübingen: JCB Mohr.

BEAN, P. (1974) The Social Control of Drugs. London: Martin Robertson;
(1976) Rehabilitation and Deviance. London: Routledge and Kegan Paul.

BEARD, C. (1934) Written History as an Act of Faith. The American Historical Review Vol. XXXIX, pp. 219-229.

BEATTIE, J.M. (1986) Crime and the Courts in England, 1660-1800. Princeton: Princeton University Press.

BECCARIA, C. (1963) On Crimes and Punishment. IN: HEATH, J. ed. Eighteenth Century Penal Theory. Oxford: Oxford University Press.

BECHER, T. and KOGAN, M. (1991) Process and Structure in Higher Education. (2nd edn.) London: Routledge.

BECK, B. (1979) The Limits of Deinstitutionalisation. IN: LEWIS, M ed. Research in Social Problems and Public Policy. Connecticut: JAI Press. Vol. I.

BECKER, C. (1932) Everyman his own Historian. The American Historical Review Vol. XXXVII, pp. 221-236.

BEHA, J. *et al* (1977) Sentencing to Community Service. Washington: U.S. Printing Office.

BEIER, A.L. (1985) Masterless Men: the vagrancy problem in England, 1560-1640. London: Methuen;
and FINLAY, R. ed. (1986) London, 1500-1700: the Making of the Metropolis. London: Methuen;
et al eds. (1989) The First Modern Society: essays in English history in honour of Lawrence Stone. Cambridge: Cambridge University Press.

BENTHAM, J. (1962) The Works of Jeremy Bentham. New York: Russell and Russell (ed. by John Bowring);
(1970) An Introduction to the Principles of Morals and Legislation. University of London: Athlone Press (ed. by J.H. Burns and H.L.A. Hart).

BERMANN, G.A. *et al* (1994) French Law: constitution and selective legislation. (11th ed.) 1994. New York: Transnational Juris Publications.

BEVAN, C. ed. (1983) Community Service Orders in Australia and New Zealand. Canberra: Australian Institute of Criminology.

BEVERIDGE, L. (1948) Voluntary Action: a report on methods of social advance. London: George Allen and Unwin.

BIENEFELD, M.A. (1972) Working hours in British industry: an economic history. London: Weidenfeld and Nicolson.

BION, W.R. (1961) Experiences in Groups and Other Papers. London: Tavistock.

BIRCH, A.H. (1993) The Concepts and Theories of Modern Democracy. London: Routledge.

BIRLEY, D. (1993) Sport and the Making of Britain. Manchester: Manchester University Press.

BISHOP, N. (1960) Group Work at Pollington Borstal. The Howard Journal Vol. X. No. 3. 185-193;
    (1988) Non-Custodial Alternatives in Europe. Helsinki: Institute for Crime Prevention Control.

BITTER, W. ed. (1960) Zur Rettung des Menschlichen in unserer Zeit. Ein Tagunsbericht. Stuttgart: Ernst Klegg Verlag.

BLACK, J. and WOODFINE, P. eds. (1988) The British Navy and the Use of Naval Power in the Eighteenth Century. Leicester: Leicester University Press.

BLANE, G. (1965) Observations of the Diseases of Men. IN: LLOYD, C. ed. The Health of Seamen: Selections from the works of Dr. James Lind, Sir Gilbert Blane and Dr. Thomas Trotter. London: Navy Records Society.

BLOCH, M. (1978) Feudal Society. The Growth of Ties of Dependence. (2nd edn.) London: Routledge and Kegan Paul. Vol.I.

BLOMBERG, T. and COHEN, S. eds. (1995) Punishment and Social Control: essays in honor of Sheldon L. Messinger. New York: Aldine de Gruyter.

BLOMBERG, T. (1995) Beyond Metaphors: penal reform as net widening. IN: BLOMBERG, T. and COHEN, S. eds. Punishment as Social Control: essays in honour of Sheldon L. Messinger. New York: Aldine de Gruyter.

BLOM-COOPER, L.J. (1974) Progress in Penal Reform. Oxford: Clarendon Press;

(1978) The Centralisation of Government Control of National Prison Services with special reference to the Prison Act, 1877. IN: FREEMAN, J. C. ed. Prisons Past and Future. London: Heinemann Educational Books.

BOCHEL, D. (1976) Probation and After-Care: its development in England and Wales. Edinburgh: Scottish Academic Press.

BORDUA, D. ed. (1967) The Police: six sociological essays. London: John Wiley and Sons.

BOS, M. ed. (1973) The Present State of International Law and other Essays. Deventer: Kluwer.

BOTTOMLEY, K.A. (1984) Dilemmas of parole in a penal crisis. The Howard Journal XXIII, no. 1, pp. 24-40;

and PEASE, K. (1986) Crime and Punishment: interpreting the data. Milton Keynes: Open University Press.

BOTTOMS, A.E. and McCLINTOCK, F.H. (1973) Criminals coming of Age: a study of institutional adaptation in the treatment of adolescent offenders. London: Heinemann.

BOTTOMS, A.E. (1981) The suspended sentence in England, 1967-1978. British Journal of Criminology XXI, no, 1, pp. 1-26;

(1983) Neglected Features of Contemporary Penal Systems. IN: GARLAND, D and YOUNG, P. eds. (1983) The Power to Punish: contemporary penality and social analysis. London: Heinemann Educational;

(1987) Limiting Prison Use: experience in England and Wales. The Howard Journal Vol. XXVI. No. 3, pp 171-202;

and STEVENSON, S. (1992) What Went Wrong? Criminal Justice Policy in England and Wales, 1945-1970. IN: DOWNES, David. ed. Unravelling Criminal Justice: eleven British studies. Hampshire: The Macmillan Press.

BOWMAN, M.J. and HARRIS, D.J. (1984) Multilateral Treaties: index and current status. London: Butterworths.

BOYCE, G. *et al* eds. (1978) Newspaper History: from the seventeenth century to the present day. London: Constable.

BOYLE, J. (1977) A Sense of Freedom. London: Pan Books.

BOYSON, R. (1971) Down with the Poor. London: Churchill Press.

BRAKE, M. (1980) The Sociology of Youth Culture and Youth Subcultures: sex and drugs and rock n' roll. London: Routledge and Kegan Paul.

BRANCH-JOHNSON, W. (1957) The English Prison Hulks. London: Christopher Johnson.

BRASNET, M. (1969) Voluntary Social Action: a history of the National Council of Social Service, 1919-1969. London: National Council of Social Service.

BRAUDEL, F. (1980) On History. London: Weidenfeld and Nicolson.

BRENTON, M. (1985) The Voluntary Sector in British Social Services. London: Longman.

BREWER, J. and STYLES, J. eds. (1980) An Ungovernable People: the English and their law in the seventeenth and eighteenth centuries. London: Hutchinson.

BRIGGS, A. (1979) The Age of Improvement, 1783-1867. London: Longman.

BRITTAN, S. (1973) Capitalism and the Permissive Society. London: Macmillan.

BROCKAWAY, A.F. (1919) Prisons as Crime Factories. London: I.L.O.

BRODY, S.R. (1978) The Effectiveness of Sentencing: a review of the literature. London: H.M.S.O.

BROMLEY, J.S. ed. (1974) The Manning of the Royal Navy: selected public pamphlets, 1693-1873. London: Navy Records Office.
BRUCE, M. (1972) The Coming of the Welfare State. (4th edn.) London: Batsford.
BUGLER, J. (1965) The Voluntary Upsurge. New Society No. 159, pp. 18-19.
BURCHELL, G. *et al* eds. (1991) The Foucault Effect: studies in governmentality with two lectures by and an interview with Michel Foucault. Chicago: Chicago University Press.
BURLEY, D. (1980) Issues in Community Service. Leicester: National Youth Bureau.
BUTLER, D.E. and KING, A. (1966) The British General Election of 1966. London: Macmillan;
and PINTO-DUCHINSKY, M.(1971) The British General Election of 1970. London: Macmillan.
BUTTERFIELD, H. (1963) The Whig Interpretation of History. London: G. Bell and Sons.

CAPON, J. (1972) And There Was Light: the story of the nationwide Festival of Light. London: Lutterworth Press.
CAPP, B. (1989) Cromwell's Navy. The Fleet and the English Revolution, 1648-1880. Clarendon Press: Oxford.
CARDWELL, P.S.L. (1972) The Organisation of Science in England. London: Heinemann.
CARR, E.H. (1986) What is History? (2nd edn.) Basingstoke: Macmillan.
CARSON, W.G. and WILES, P. eds. (1971) Crime and Delinquency in Britain: sociological readings. London: Martin Robertson and Co.
CARTER, R.M. *et al* (1987) Community Service: a review of basic issues. Federal Probation pp. 4-10.

CARY, J. (1700) An account of the Proceedings of the Corporation of Bristol, in execution of the Act of Parliament for the better employing and maintaining the Poor of that city. London: F Collins.

CASSESE, A. (1986) International Law in a Divided World. Oxford: Clarendon Press.

CENTRAL STATISTICAL OFFICE (1938-1949) Annual Abstract of Statistics. No. 87. London: H.M.S.O.

CENTRAL STATISTICAL OFFICE (1954) Annual Abstract of Statistics. No. 91. London: H.M.S.O.

CENTRAL STATISTICAL OFFICE (1958) Annual Abstract of Statistics. No. 95. London: H.M.S.O.

CENTRAL STATISTICAL OFFICE (1962) Annual Abstract of Statistics. No. 99. London: H.M.S.O.

CENTRAL STATISTICAL OFFICE (1964) Annual Abstract of Statistics. No. 101. London: H.M.S.O.

CENTRAL STATISTICAL OFFICE (1967) Annual Abstract of Statistics. No. 104. London: H.M.S.O.

CENTRAL STATISTICAL OFFICE (1968) Annual Abstract of Statistics. No. 105. London: H.M.S.O.

CENTRAL STATISTICAL OFFICE (1973) Annual Abstract of Statistics. No. 110. London: H.M.S.O.

CHAPEL, V. ed. (1994) The Cambridge Companion to Locke. 1994. Cambridge: Cambridge University Press.

CHESNEY, K. (1970) The Victorian Underworld. London: Maurice Temple Smith Ltd.

CHIBNALL, S. (1977) Law and Order News: an analysis of crime reporting in the British Press. London: Tavistock Publications.

CHRISTIE, N. (1977) Conflicts as Property. The British Journal of Criminology Vol. 17. No. 1, pp. 1-15.

CIPOLLA, C.M. ed. (1974) The Sixteenth and Seventeenth Centuries. London: Fontana.

CLAY, W.L. (1861) The Prison Chaplain: a memoir of the Rev. John Clay, late chaplain of the Preston Gaol, with selections from his reports and correspondence, and a sketch of prison discipline in England. Cambridge: Macmillan.

CLAYRE, A. (1974) Work and Play: ideas and experiences of work and leisure. London: Weidenfeld and Nicholson.

COBBETTS Parliamentary Debates during the sixth session of the fourth Parliament of the United Kingdom of Great Britain and Ireland. Vol. XXI. 7 January, 1812 to 16 March, 1812.

COBBETTS Parliamentary History of England: From the Norman Conquest in 1066 to the Year 1803. Vol. XII. Session 1741 to 1743, 1812.

COHEN, J. (1982) The History of Imprisonment for Debt and its relation to the development of Discharge in Bankruptcy. The Journal of Legal History Vol. 3, pp. 153-171.

COHEN, S. (1971) Mods, Rockers and the Rest: reactions to Juvenile Delinquency in Britain. IN: CARSON, W.G. and WILES, P. eds. Crime and Delinquency in Britain: sociological readings. London: Martin Robertson and Co;

(1973) Folk Devils and Moral Panics: the creation of the Mods and Rockers. Paladin: St. Albans;

and YOUNG, Jock eds. (1973) The Manufacture of News: social problems, deviance and the mass media. London: Constable;

(1974) "Human Warehouses: the future of our prisons". New Society XXX: No. 632, pp. 407-411;

(1979a) Community Control - a new utopia. New Society Vol. 47, No. 858, pp. 609-611;

(1979b) "The Punitive City: notes on the dispersal of social control". Contemporary Crises Vol III, pp. 339-363;

(1983) Social Control Talk: telling stories about correctional change. IN: GARLAND, D and YOUNG, P. eds. The Power to Punish: contemporary penality and social analysis. London: Heinemann Educational;

and SCULL, A. eds. (1983) Social Control and the State: historical and comparative essays. Oxford: Basil Blackwell;
(1994) Visions of Social Control: crime, punishment and classification. Cambridge: Polity.

COKE, E. (1797) The Second Part of the Institutes of the Laws of England: containing the exposition of many ancient and other statutes. London: C. and R. Brooke.

COLEMAN, W. (1977) Biology in the Nineteenth Century: problems of form, function, and transformation. Cambridge: Cambridge University Press.

COMMITTEE ON VOLUNTARY ORGANISATIONS (1978) The future of voluntary organisations: report of the Wolfenden Committee. London: Croom Helm.

CONLEY, F. (1994) General Elections Today. (2nd edn.) Manchester: Manchester University Press.

CONNOLLY, M. (1974) Remarks on Manning the Navy. IN: BROMLEY, J.S. ed. The Manning of the Royal Navy: selected public pamphlets, 1693-1873. London: Navy Records Office.

CONRAD, J.P. (1967) The Evaluation of the Correctional Community. IN: FENTON, N. *et al* eds. The Correctional Community: an introduction and guide. London: Cambridge University Press.

CONSERVATIVE PARTY (1966) Crime Knows No Boundaries. London: Conservative Political Centre;
(1971) Crisis in Crime and Punishment. London: Conservative Political Centre.

COOGAN, T.P. (1995) The Troubles: Ireland's Ordeal, 1966-1995, and the search for peace. London: Hutchinson.

COOPER, J. (1970) Social Care and Social Control. Probation Vol. 15. pp. 22-25.

CORNISH, W. R. (1978) Crime and Law in Nineteenth Century Britain. Dublin: Irish University Press.

CORNISH, W.R. and De N. CLARK, G. (1989) Law and Society in England, 1750-1950. London: Sweet and Maxwell.

CORRY McDONALD, D. (1986) Punishment without Walls: Community Service sentences in New York City. New Brunswick: Rutgers University Press.

COUNCIL'S WORKING GROUP FOR CRIMINAL POLICY (1978) A New Penal System. Ideas and Proposals. (English Summary of the Report.) Stockholm: National Swedish Council for Crime Prevention. No. 5.

CRAWFORD, J. ed. (1988) The Rights of People. Oxford: Clarendon Press.

CRICK, B. (1974) Crime, Rape, and Gin: reflections on contemporary attitudes to violence, pornography and addiction. London: Elek Books.

CRITCHLEY, T.A. (1967) A History of Police in England and Wales, 900-1966. London: Constable.

CROSS, R. (1971) Punishment, Prison and the Public. 1971. London: Stevens and Sons.

CROSSMAN, R.H.S. (1973) The Role of the Volunteer in the Modern Social Service. IN: HALSEY, A.H. ed., Traditions of Social Policy: essays in honour of Violet Butler. Oxford: Basil Blackwell.

CROWTHER, M.A. (1981) The Workhouse System, 1834-1929: the history of an English Social Institution. London: Methuen.

CUNNINGHAM, H. (1980) Leisure in the Industrial Revolution, c.1780-c.1880. London: Croom Helm.

CURRAN, J. (1978) The Press as an Agency of Social Control: an historical perspective. IN: BOYCE, G. *et al* eds. Newspaper History: from the seventeenth century to the present day. London: Constable.

DARTINGTON, T. (1971) Task Force. London: Michael Beazley Ltd.

DARWIN, C. (1871) The Descent of Man, and Selection in Relation to Sex. New York: Appleton and Co. Vol. I.

DAVIES, C. (1975) Permissive Britain: social change in the sixties and seventies. London: Pitman.

DAVIES, J.D. (1991) Gentlemen and Tarpaulins. The Officers and Men of the Restoration Navy. Oxford: Clarendon Press.

DAVIS, J. (1980) The London Garrotting Panic of 1862: a moral panic and the creation of a criminal class in Mid-Victorian England. IN: GATRELL, V.A.C. *et al* eds. Crime and the Law: the social history of crime in Western Europe since 1500. London: Europa.

DAVITT, M. (1885) Leaves from a Prison Diary, or Lectures to a "Solitary Audience". London: Chapman and Hall. Vol. I.

DEANE, P. (1979) The First Industrial Revolution. (2nd edn.) Cambridge: Cambridge University Press;
(1988) The First Industrial Revolution (2nd edn.) Cambridge: Cambridge University Press.

DEEM, R. (1982) Women, Leisure and Inequality. Leisure Studies I, pp. 29-46;
(1986) All Work and No Play. Milton Keynes: Open University Press.

DE GRAZIA, S. (1974) Of Time, Work and Leisure. IN: MARRUS, Michael R. ed. The Emergence of Leisure. London: Harper and Row.

DE LACY, M. (1986) Prison Reform in Lancashire, 1750-1850: a study in local administration. Manchester: Manchester University Press.

DEL VECCHIO, G. (1969) The Struggle against Crime. IN: ACTON, H.B. ed. The Philosophy of Punishment: a collection of papers. London: Macmillan.

DEPT OF EDUCATION AND SCIENCE (1969) Youth and Community Work in the 70s. Proposals by the Youth Service Development Council. London: H.M.S.O.

DEPT OF EMPLOYMENT (1971) British Labour Statistics: historical abstract, 1886-1968. London: H.M.S.O.

DEPT OF EMPLOYMENT (1973) Unemployment, Great Britain, Males and Females. Department of Employment Gazette p. 194.

DEPT OF HEALTH (1972) Intermediate Treatment: a guide for the regional planning of new forms of treatment for children in trouble. London: H.M.S.O.

DEPT OF HEALTH (1973) Intermediate Treatment Project: an account of a project set up to demonstrate some ways of providing intermediate treatment. London: H.M.S.O.

DEPT OF HEALTH (1976) Intermediate Treatment: report of a residential conference held at Birmingham, 2-5 December 1974. London: H.M.S.O.

DEPT OF LABOUR (1938) Report of the Committee on Holidays with Pay. Cmd. 5724. London: H.M.S.O.

DICEY, A.V. (1914) Lectures on the Relation between Law and Public Opinion in England during the Nineteenth Century. (2nd edn.) London: Macmillan.

DICKENS, C. (1865) Our Mutual Friend. London: Chapman and Hall.

DICKSON, A. (1976) A Chance to Serve. London: Dobson.

DOBASH, R. *et al* (1986) The Imprisonment of Women. Oxford: Basil Blackwell.

DOBBIE, F. (1972) Land Aflame. London: Hodder and Stoughton.

DOBSON, M.J.A. (1987) A chronology of epidemic disease and mortality in South East England, 1601-1800. London: Historical Geography Research Series. (No. 19).

DORR, N. (1994) Introduction: developments since 1945. IN: HEFFERNAN, L. ed. Human Rights: a European Perspective. Dublin: Round Hall.

DOWNES, D. (1992) Unravelling Criminal Justice: eleven British studies. Hampshire: The Macmillan Press;
(1993) Contrasts in Tolerance: post-war penal policy in the Netherlands and England and Wales. Oxford: Clarendon Press;

and MORGAN, R. (1994) Hostages to Fortune? The Politics of Law and Order in Post War Britain. IN: MAGUIRE, M. *et al* eds. The Oxford Handbook of Criminology. Oxford: Clarendon Press.

DRIVER, F. (1993) Power and Pauperism: the workhouse system, 1834-1884. Cambridge: Cambridge University Press.

DROST, P.N. (1965) Human Rights as Legal Rights: the realisation of individual human rights in positive international law. Leyden: Sitjhoff.

DU CANE, E.F. (1872) An account of the manner in which sentences of penal servitude are carried out in England (printed at Her Majesty's Convict Prison, Millbank).

DUNKEL, F. and MEYER, K. eds. (1985) Jugendstrafe und Jugendstrafvollzug. Stationare Massnahmen der Jugend-kriminalrechtspflege im Internationalen Vergleich. Freiburg: C.F. Dreyspring GmbH. Vol. I.

DUNN, J. (1968) The identity of the history of ideas. The Journal of the Royal Institute of Philosophy XIII no. 164, pp. 85-104.

EHRMAN, J. (1953) The Navy in the War of William III, 1689-1697: its state and direction. Cambridge: Cambridge University Press.

EKIRCH, R.A. (1987) Bound for America: the transportation of British convicts to the colonies, 1718-1775. Oxford: Clarendon Press.

ELKIN, W. (1957) The English Prison System. Harmondsworth: Penguin.

ELLIS, H. (1910) The Criminal. London: Walter Scott.

ELTON, G.R. (1984) Herbert Butterfield and the Study of History. The Historical Journal Vol. 27. No. 3, pp. 729-743.

EMERSON SMITH, A. (1934) The Transportation of Convicts to the American Colonies in the Seventeenth Century. American Historical Journal Vol. 39. No. 2, pp. 232-249.

EMSLEY, C. (1980) The Recruitment of Petty offenders during the French Wars, 1793-1815. The Mariner's Mirror Vol. 66, pp. 200-205;

(1987) Crime and Society in England, 1750-1900. London: Longman;

(1991) The English Police: a political and social history. Hertfordshire: Harvester Wheatsheaf;

(1996) Crime and Society in England, 1750-1900. (2nd edn.) London: Longman;

ERICSON, R.V. ed. (1995) Crime and the Media. 1995. Aldershot: Dartmouth Publishing Co;

and HEGGARTY, K.D. (1997) Policing the Risk Society. Oxford: Clarendon Press.

EUROPEAN COMMITTEE ON CRIME PROBLEMS (1974) Group and Community Work with Offenders. Strasbourg: Council of Europe;

(1976) Alternative Penal Measures to Imprisonment. Strasbourg: Council of Europe.

EVANS, P. (1980) Penal Crisis. London: George Allen and Unwin.

EVANS, R. (1982) The Fabrication of Virtue: English prison architecture, 1750-1840. Cambridge: Cambridge University Press.

FEELEY, M. (1992) Between Two Extremes: an examination of the efficiency and effectiveness of community service orders and their implications for the U.S. sentencing guidelines. Southern California Law Review Vol. 66, pp. 155-207.

FENNELL, P. *et al* eds. (1996) Criminal Justice in Europe: a comparative study. Oxford: Clarendon Press.

FENTON, Norman *et al* eds. (1967) The Correctional Community: an introduction and guide. London: Cambridge University Press.

FINE, B. *et al* eds. (1979) Capitalism and the Rule of Law: From Deviancy Theory to Marxism. London: Hutchinson and Co.

FINLAYSON, G. (1994) Citizen, State and Social Welfare in Britain, 1830-1900. Oxford: Clarendon Press.

FITTON, R.S. and WADSWORTH, A.P. (1958) The Strutts and The Arkwrights, 1758-1830: a study of the early factory system. Manchester: Manchester University Press.

FITZGERALD, M. (1977) Prisoners in Revolt. Harmondsworth: Penguin;
and SIM, J. (1979) Britain's Prisons. Oxford: Basil Blackwell.

FLEMING, J.G. (1985) An Introduction to the Law of Torts. (2nd edn.) Oxford: Clarendon Press.

FLETCHER, A. and STEVENSON, J. eds. (1985) Order and Disorder in Early Modern England. Cambridge: Cambridge University Press.

FORSYTHE, W.J. (1987) The Reform of Prisoners, 1830-1900. New York: St. Martin's Press;
(1991) Penal Discipline, Reformatory Projects and the English Prison Commission, 1895-1939. Exeter: Exeter University Press.

FOUCAULT, M. (1970) The Order of Things: an archeology of the Human Sciences. London: Tavistock;
(1972) The Archaeology of Knowledge. London: Tavistock Publications (translated from the French by Alan Sheridan);
(1980a) Prison Talk. IN: GORDON, C. ed. (1980) Power of Knowledge: selected interviews and other writings, 1972-1977. London: The Harvester Press;
(1980b) The Eye of Power: an interview with Jean-Pierre Barrou and Michelle Perrot. IN: GORDON, C. ed. Power of Knowledge: selected interviews and other writings 1972-1977. London: The Harvester Press;
(1986) Discipline and Punish: the birth of the prison. Harmondsworth: Penguin Books;
(1991a) Truth and Power. IN: RAINBOW, P. ed. The Foucault Reader. Harmondsworth: Penguin Books;
(1991b) Discipline and Punish: the birth of the prison. London: Penguin Books;

(1997) Madness and Civilisation: a history of insanity in the Age of Reason. London: Routledge.

FOULKES, S.H. (1964) Therapeutic Group Analysis. London: Allen and Unwin.

FOX, L.W. (1952) The English Prison and Borstal Systems. London: Routledge and Kegan Paul.

FRANCES, S. and WEATHERRIT, M. (1974) The Use of Bail and Custody by London Magistrates' Courts before and after the Criminal Justice Act, 1967. London: H.M.S.O.

FRAYNE, L. (1993) The History of Change. IN: WHITFIELD, D. and SCOTT, D. eds. Paying Back: twenty years of community service. Winchester: Waterside Press.

FREEDEN, M. (1978) The New Liberalism: an ideology of social reform. Oxford: Clarendon Press.

FREEMAN, J.C. ed. (1978) Prisons Past and Future. London: Heinemann Educational.

FRIEDMAN, W. (1964) The Changing Structure of International Law. London: Stevens.

FUCHS, C. (1985) Der Community Service Order als Alternative zur Freiheitsstrafe. Pfaffenweiler: Centauus Verlagsgesellschaft.

GALAWAY, B. *et al* (1983) Restitution and Community Service: an annotated bibliography. Massachusetts: National Institute for Sentencing Alternatives.

GALENSON, D.W. (1981) White Servitude in Colonial America: an economic analysis. New York: Cambridge University Press.

GALTON, F. (1962) Hereditary Genius: an inquiry into its laws and consequences. London: Fontana.

GAMBLE, A. (1974) The Conservative Nation. London: Routledge and Kegan Paul.

GARLAND, D. (1981) The Birth of the Welfare Sanction. British Journal of Law and Society Vol. 8. No. 1, pp. 29-45;

and YOUNG, Peter eds. (1983) The Power to Punish: contemporary penality and social analysis. London: Heinemann Educational;

(1985) Punishment and Welfare: a history of penal strategies. Aldershot: Gower;

(1990) Punishment and Modern Society: a study in social theory. Chicago: University of Chicago;

(1994) Of Crimes and Criminals: the development of criminology in Britain. IN: MAGUIRE, M. *et al* eds. The Oxford Handbook of Criminology. Oxford: Clarendon Press;

(1994b) The Criminal and his Science. IN: ROCK, Paul ed. History of Criminology. Aldershot: Dartmouth;

(1995) Penal Modernism and Postmodernism. IN: BLOMBERG, Thomas G. and COHEN, Stanley eds. Punishment and Social Control: essays in honor of Sheldon L. Messinger. New York: Aldine de Gruyter;

(1996) The Limits of the Sovereign State: strategies of crime control in contemporary society. British Journal of Criminology Vol. 36. No. 4, pp. 445-471;

(1997) The Punitive Society: penology, criminology and the history of the present. Edinburgh Law Review Vol. I, pp. 180-199.

GAROFALO, R. (1914) Criminology. London: Heinemann.

GATRELL, V.A.C. (1980) The Decline of Theft and Violence in Edwardian England. IN: GATRELL, V.A.C. *et al* eds. Crime and the Law: the social history of crime in Western Europe since 1500. London: Europa;

et al eds. (1980) Crime and the Law: the social history of crime in Western Europe since 1500. London: Europa;

(1990) Crime, Authority and the Policeman State. IN: THOMPSON, F.L. ed. The Cambridge Social History of Britain, 1750-1900. Cambridge: Cambridge University Press.

GENDERS, E. and PLAYER, E. (1995) Grendon: a study of a therapeutic prison. Oxford: Clarendon Press.

GERARD, D. (1985) Values and Voluntary Work. IN: ABRAMS, M. *et al* eds. Values and Social Change in Britain. London: Macmillan.

GIDDENS, A. (1991) Modernity and Self-Identity: self and society in the late modern age. London: Polity;
(1996) The Consequences of Modernity. London: Polity (repr).

GILL, C. (1913) The Naval Mutinies of 1797. Manchester: Manchester University Press.

GILL, M.L. and MAWBY, R.I. (1990) Volunteers in the Criminal Justice System: a comparative study of probation, police and victim support. Milton Keynes: Open University Press.

GLASS, D.V. ed. (1973) The Population Controversy. 1973. Farnborough: Gregg.

GODBEY, G. (1978) Recreation, Park and Leisure Services. Philadelphia: W.B. Saunders.

GOFFMAN, E. (1974) Asylums: essays on the social situation of mental patients and other inmates. Harmondsworth: Penguin Books.

GOLDBY, J.M. and PURDUE, A.W. (1984) The Civilisation of the Crowd: popular culture in England, 1750-1900. New York: Schocken Books.

GOLDMAN, R. (1969) Angry Adolescents. London: Routledge and Kegan Paul.

GORDON, C. ed. (1980) Power of Knowledge: selected interviews and other writings, 1972-1977. London: The Harvester Press;
(1991) Government Rationality: an introduction. IN: BURCHELL, G. *et al* eds. The Foucault Effect: studies in governmentality with two lectures by and an interview with Michel Foucault. Chicago: Chicago University Press.

GORING, C. (1913) The English Convict: a statistical study. London: H.M.S.O.

GOUGH, I. (1975) State Expenditure in Advanced Capitalism. New Left Review No. 92, pp. 53-92.

GRADISH, S.F. (1980) The Manning of the British Navy During the Seven Years War. London: Royal Historical Society.

GRAMSCI, A. (1971) Selections from the Prison Notebooks. London: Lawrence and Wishart.

GREEN, E. *et al* (1990) Women's Leisure: What Leisure? London: Macmillan.

GREEN, V.H.H. (1971) Medieval Civilisation in Western Europe. London: Edward Arnold.

GRIFFITHS, A. (1875) Memorials of Millbank and Chapters in Prison History. London: Henry S. King and Co. Vol. I.

GRUNHUT, M. (1948) Penal Reform: a comparative study. Oxford: Oxford University Press.

HABERMAS, J. (1987) The Philosophical Discourse of Modernity: twelve lectures. Massachussets: M.I.T.

HADLEY, R. *et al* (1975) Across the Generations: old people and young volunteers. London: George Allen and Unwin.

HALE, M. (1971) The History of the Pleas of the Crown. Abingdon: Professional Books.

HALL, R. (1983) On Whiggism. History of Science Vol. 21: No. 51, pp. 45-59.

HALL, S. (1972) The Hippies: dissent in America. IN WORSLEY, P. ed. Problems of Modern Society. London: Penguin;
(1980) Reformism and the Legislation of Consent. IN: NATIONAL DEVIANCY COUNCIL ed. Permissiveness and Control: the fate of the sixties legislation. London: Macmillan;
et al (1981) Policing the Crisis: mugging, the state, and law and order. London: Macmillan

HALLORAN, J.D. *et al* (1970) Demonstrations and Communications: a case study. Harmondsworth: Penguin.

HALL WILLIAMS, J.E. (1970) The English Penal System in Transition. London: Butterworths.

HALSEY, A.H. ed. (1976) Traditions of Social Policy: essays in honour of Violet Butler. Oxford: Basil Blackwell.

HANSARD. House of Commons Parliamentary Debates. (3rd Series) Vol. CXII. Session 19 July, 1850 to 15 August, 1850.

HANSARD. House of Commons Parliamentary Debates. (3rd Series) Vol. CLXXV. Session 4 May, 1864 to 20 June, 1864.

HANSARD. House of Commons Parliamentary Debates. (3rd Series) Vol. CCX. Session 15 March, 1872 to 30 April, 1872.

HANSARD. House of Commons Parliamentary Debates. (3rd Series) Vol. CCXXIX. Session 3 May, 1876 to 16 June, 1876.

HANSARD. House of Commons Parliamentary Debates. (5th Series) Vol. 630. Session 14 November, 1960 to 25 November, 1960.

HANSARD. House of Commons Parliamentary Debates. (5th Series) Vol. 697. Session 22 June, 1964 to 3 July, 1964.

HANSARD. House of Commons Parliamentary Debates. (5th Series) Vol. 738. Session 12 December, 1966 to 21 December, 1966.

HANSARD. House of Commons Parliamentary Debates. (5th Series) Vol. 745. Session 17 April, 1967 to 28 April, 1967.

HANSARD. House of Commons Parliamentary Debates. (5th Series) Vol. 826. Session 15 November, 1971 to 26 November, 1971.

HANSARD. House of Commons Parliamentary Debates. (5th Series) Vol. 909. Session 5 April, 1976 to 14 April, 1976.

HANSARD. House of Lords Parliamentary Debates. (5th Series) Vol. 283. Session 17 April, 1967 to 28 April, 1967.

HANSARD. House of Lords Parliamentary Debates. (5th Series) Vol. 332. Session 19 June to 6 July, 1972

HARDING, C. *et al* eds. (1985) Imprisonment in England and Wales: a concise history. London: Croom Helm;

and WILKIN, L. (1988a) "The Dream of a Benevolent Mind": the Victorian response to the problem of inebriety. Criminal Justice History Vol. IX, pp. 189-208;

(1988b) The Inevitable end of a Discredited System? The Origins of the Gladstone Committee Report on Prisons, 1895. The Historical Journal. Vol. 31. No. 3, pp. 591-608;

and IRELAND, R.W. (1989) Punishment: rhetoric, rule, and practice. London: Routledge.

HARLAND, A.T. (1980) Court-Ordered Community Service in Criminal Law: the continuing tyranny of benevolence? Buffalo Law Review Vol. 29, pp. 425-486

HARRIS, M. (1979) Community Service by Offenders. Washington: National Council on Crime and Delinquency.

HARVARD, J.D. (1961) The Mental Health Act and the Criminal Offender. The Criminal Law Review pp. 296-308.

HATCH, S. (1980) Outside the State: Voluntary Organisations in Three English Towns. London: Croom Helm.

HATTENDORF, John B. *et al* eds. (1993) Publications of the Navy Records Society: British Naval Documents, 1204-1960. London: Navy Records Society.

HAUSER, R. (1963) Prison Reform and Society. Prison Service Journal Vol. 3 No. 9, pp. 2-18.

HAWKINGS, D. (1992) Criminal Ancestors: a guide to historical criminal records in England and Wales. Sutton: Stroud.

HAWKINS, K. (1975) Alternatives to Imprisonment. IN: McCONVILLE, S. ed. The Use of Imprisonment: essays in the changing state of English penal policy. London: Routledge and Kegan Paul.

HAXBY, D. (1972) Intermediate Treatment. IN: JONES, K. ed. The Year Book of Social Policy in Britain. London: Routledge;

(1978) Probation: a changing service. London: Constable.

HAY, D. (1975) Property, Authority and the Criminal Law. IN: HAY, D. *et al* eds. Albion's Fatal Tree: crime and society in eighteenth century England. London: Allen and Unwin.

HAYWOOD, L. *et al* (1995) Understanding Leisure. (2nd edn.) Cheltenham: Stanley Thorpes.

HEATH, C. (1913) On Punishment: a modern view of the rational treatment of crime. London: Longman.

HEDLEY, R. and DAVIS SMITH, J. (1992) Volunteering and Society: principles and practice. London: N.V.C.O.

HEFFERNAN, L. ed. (1994) Human Rights: a European Perspective. Dublin: Round Hall.

HENRIQUES, U.R.Q. (1972) The Rise and Decline of the Separate System of Prison Discipline. Past and Present No. 54, pp. 61-93; (1979) Before the Welfare State: social administration in early industrial Britain. London: Longman.

HENRY, I.P. (1993) The Politics of Leisure Policy. London: Macmillan.

HERRUP, C.B. (1987) The Common Peace: participation and the criminal law in seventeenth century England. Cambridge: Cambridge University Press.

HEWITT, P.B. (1993) About Time: the revolution in work and family life. London: Oram Press.

HILL, A.M. and ASHCROFT, M.Y. (1978) North Riding Naval Recruits. The Quota Acts and Quota Men, 1795-1797. Northallerton: North Yorkshire County Council.

HILL, C. (1986) Society and Puritanism in Pre-revolutionary England. Harmonsworth: Penguin.

HILL, J.R. ed. (1995) The Oxford Illustrated History of the Royal Navy. Oxford: Oxford University Press.

HILL, M. (1993) The Welfare State in Britain: a political history since 1945. London: Edward Elgar.

HIMMLEWEIT, H.T. *et al* (1981) How Votes Decide. A longitudinal study of political attitudes and voting over fifteen years. London: Academic Press.

HINDE, R.S.E. (1977a) Sir Walter Crofton and the Reform of the Irish Convict System, 1854-1861. The Irish Jurist Vol. XII. Part I, pp. 115-147; (1977b) Sir Walter Crofton and the Reform of the Irish Convict System, 1854-1861. The Irish Jurist Vol. XII. Part II, pp. 295-337.

HINE, J. (1993) Access for Women: friendly and flexible. IN: WHITFIELD, D and SCOTT, D. eds. Paying Back: twenty years of community service. Winchester: Waterside Press.

HINES, W.D. *et al* eds. (1990) English Legal History. A Bibliography and Guide to the Literature. New York: Garland Publishing.

HOBBS, D. (1992) Doing the Business: entrepreneurship, the working class, and detectives in the East End of London. Oxford: Clarendon Press.

HOBHOUSE, S. and BROCKWAY, F. (1922) English Prisons Today. London: Labour Research Department.

HOBMAN, D.L. (1953) The Welfare State. London: John Murray.

HOBSBAWN, E.J. (1952) The Machine Breakers. Past and Present no. 1, pp. 57-70;

(1968) Industry and Empire: an economic history of Britain since 1750. London: Weidenfeld and Nicolson;

(1974) Labour's Turning Point: 1880-1900. (2nd edn.) Brighton: Harvester Press.

HOGGARTH, E. (1991) Selection for Community Service Orders. Aldershot: Avebury.

HOLDSWORTH, W. (1908) A History of English Criminal Law. Vol. 3. London: Methuen.

HOLLINGDALE, R.J. ed. (1983) Untimely Mediations. Cambridge: Cambridge University Press.

HOLZSCHUH, K. (1960) Gefährdete Jugend vor dem Richter. IN: BITTER, W. ed. Zur Rettung des Menschlichen in unserer Zeit. Ein Tagungsbericht. Stuggart: Ernst Klett Verlag.

HOME OFFICE (1925) Report of the Prison Commissioners for 1923-24. Cmnd. 2307. London: H.M.S.O.

HOME OFFICE (1945) Prisons and Borstals. A Statement of Policy and Practice in the Administration of Prisons and Borstal Institutions in England and Wales. London: H.M.S.O.

HOME OFFICE (1945) Report of the Commissioners of Prisons and Directors of Convict Prisons for the Years, 1942-1944. Cmnd. 7010. London: H.M.S.O.

HOME OFFICE (1946) Report of the Commissioners of Prisons and Directors of Convict Prisons for the Years 1939-1941.Cmnd. 6820. London: H.M.S.O.

HOME OFFICE (1947) Report of the Commissioners of Prisons and Directors of Convict Prisons for the Year, 1946. Cmnd. 7271. London: H.M.S.O.

HOME OFFICE (1948) Report of the Commissioners of Prisons and Directors of Convict Prisons for the Year 1947. Cmnd. 7475. London: H.M.S.O.

HOME OFFICE (1950) Prisons and Borstals. A Statement of Policy and Practice in the Administration of Prisons and Borstal Institutions in England and Wales. London: H.M.S.O.

HOME OFFICE (1950) Report of the Commissioners of Prisons and Directors of Convict Prisons for the Year 1949. Cmd. 8088. London: H.M.S.O.

HOME OFFICE (1954) Report of the Commissioners of Prisons for the Year 1953. Cmnd. 9259. London: H.M.S.O.

HOME OFFICE (1956) Report of the Commissioners of Prisons for the Year 1955. Cmnd. 10. London: H.M.S.O.

HOME OFFICE (1957) Alternatives to Short Terms of Imprisonment. Report of the Advisory Council on the Treatment of Offenders. London: H.M.S.O.

HOME OFFICE (1957) Report of the Commissioners of Prisons for the Year 1956. Cmnd. 322. London: H.M.S.O.

HOME OFFICE (1958) Report of the Commissioners of Prisons for the Year 1957. Cmnd. 496. London: H.M.S.O.

HOME OFFICE (1959) Penal Practice in a Changing Society: aspects of future development (England and Wales). Cmnd. 645. London: H.M.S.O.

HOME OFFICE (1960) Report of the Commissioners of Prisons for the Year 1959. Cmnd. 1117. London: H.M.S.O.

HOME OFFICE (1961) Report of the Commissioners of Prisons for the Year 1960. Cmnd. 1467. London: H.M.S.O.

HOME OFFICE (1962) Work and Vocational Training in Borstals (England and Wales). Report of the Advisory Council on the Employment of Prisoners. London: H.M.S.O.

HOME OFFICE (1963) The Organisation of After-Care. Report of the Advisory Council on the Treatment of Offenders. London: H.M.S.O.

HOME OFFICE (1964) Prisons and Borstals. Report on the work of the Prison Department for the Year 1963. Cmnd. 2381. London: H.M.S.O.

HOME OFFICE (1964) The Organisation of Work for Prisoners. Report of the Advisory Council on the Employment of Prisoners. London: H.M.S.O.

HOME OFFICE (1965) Prisons and Borstals. Report on the work of the Prison Department for the Year 1964. Cmnd. 2708. London: H.M.S.O.

HOME OFFICE (1965) The Adult Offender. Cmnd. 2852. London: H.M.S.O.

HOME OFFICE (1965) The Child, the Family and the Young Offender. Cmnd. 2742. London: H.M.S.O.

HOME OFFICE (1966) Report of the Inquiry into Prison Escapes and Security. Cmnd. 3175. London: H.M.S.O.

HOME OFFICE (1966) Report on the Work of the Prison Department for the Year 1965. Cmnd. 3088. London: H.M.S.O.

HOME OFFICE (1966) Report on the Work of the Probation and After-Care Department, 1962 to 1965. Cmnd. 3107. London: H.M.S.O.

HOME OFFICE (1966) Report on the Work of the Prison Department for the Year 1965. Cmnd. 3408. London: H.M.S.O.

HOME OFFICE (1967) Report on the Work of the Children's Department, 1964-66. London: H.M.S.O.

HOME OFFICE (1967) Report on the Work of the Prison Department for the Year 1966. Cmnd. 3048. London: H.M.S.O.

HOME OFFICE (1968) Children in Trouble. Cmnd. 3601. London: H.M.S.O.

HOME OFFICE (1968) Report on the Work of the Prison Department for the Year 1967. Cmnd. 3774. London: H.M.S.O.

HOME OFFICE (1968) The Regime for Long-Term Prisoners on Conditions of Maximum Security. Report of the Advisory Council on the Penal System. London: H.M.S.O.

HOME OFFICE (1969) People in Prison (England and Wales). Cmnd. 4214. London: H.M.S.O.

HOME OFFICE (1969) Report on the Work of the Probation and After-Care Department, 1966 to 1968. Cmnd. 4233. London: H.M.S.O.

HOME OFFICE (1969) The Sentence of the Court: a handbook for the courts on the treatment of offenders. (2nd edn.) London: H.M.S.O.

HOME OFFICE (1970) Non-Custodial and Semi-Custodial Penalties. Report of the Advisory Council on the Penal System. London: H.M.S.O.

HOME OFFICE (1970) Report on the Work of the Children's Department, 1967-69. London: H.M.S.O.

HOME OFFICE (1970) Report on the Work of the Prison Department for the Year 1969. Cmnd. 4486. London: H.M.S.O.

HOME OFFICE (1970b) Report of the Advisory Council on the Penal System. Reparation by the Offender. London: H.M.S.O.

HOME OFFICE (1970c) Detention Centres. Report of the Advisory Council on the Penal System. London: H.M.S.O.

HOME OFFICE (1971) Report on the Work of the Prison Department for the Year 1970. Cmnd. 4724. London: H.M.S.O.

HOME OFFICE (1971) The Sentence of the Court. A Handbook for the Courts on the Treatment of Offenders. London: H.M.S.O.

HOME OFFICE (1972) Report on the Work of the Prison Department for the Year 1971. Cmnd. 5037. London: H.M.S.O.

HOME OFFICE (1974) Young Adult Offenders. Report of the Advisory Council on the Penal System. London: H.M.S.O.

HOME OFFICE (1977) Prisons and the Prisoner. The Work of the Prison Service in England and Wales. London: H.M.S.O.

HOME OFFICE (1978) Report on the Work of the Prison Department for the Year 1977. Cmnd. 7290. London: H.M.S.O.

HOME OFFICE and SCOTTISH HOME DEPARTMENT (1961) Work for Prisoners. Report of the Advisory Council on the Employment of Prisoners. London: H.M.S.O.

HOOD, R. (1965) Borstal Reassessed. London: Heinemann;
(1974) Criminology and Penal Change: a case study of the nature and impact of some recent advice to governments. IN: HOOD, R. ed. Criminology and Public Policy. Essays in Honour of Sir Leon Radzinowicz. London: Heinemann;
ed. (1974) Criminology and Public Policy. Essays in Honour of Sir Leon Radzinowicz. London: Heinemann;
and SPARKS, R. (1978) Key Issues in Criminology. London: Weidenfeld and Nicolson.

HORROX, R. ed. (1994) Fifteenth-Century Attitudes. Perceptions of Society in late Medieval England. Cambridge: Cambridge University Press.

HOULDING, J.A. (1981) Fit for Service: the training of the British Army, 1715-1795. Oxford: Oxford University Press.

HOWARD, J. (1977) The State of the Prisons. Abingdon: Professional Books (preface by Martin Wright).

HOWE, G. (1972) Man, Environment and Disease in Britain: a medical geography of Britain through the ages. New York: Bases and Noble.

HOWKINS, A. (1981) The Taming of Whitsun: the changing face of a nineteenth century rural holiday. IN: YEO, E and YEO, S. eds. Popular Culture and Class Conflict, 1590-1914: explorations in the history of labour and leisure. Hassocks: Harvester Press.

HUGHES, R. (1987) The Fatal Shore: a history of the transportation of convicts to Australia, 1787-1868. London: Collins Harvill;
(1996) The Fatal Shore: a history of the transportation of convicts to Australia, 1787-1868. (2nd edn.) London: Harvill.

HUMPHREY, J.P. (1973) The International Law of Human Rights in the Middle Twentieth Century. IN: BOS, M. ed. The Present State of International Law and other Essays. Deventer: Kluwer.

HUNT, E.H. (1981) British Labour History, 1815-1914. London: Weidenfeld and Nicolson.

HUTCHINSON, J.R. (1913) The Press Gang: afloat and ashore. London: Evaleigh Nash.

IGNATIEFF, M. (1978) A Just Measure of Pain. The Penitentiary in the Industrial Revolution, 1750-1850. London: Macmillan;
(1981) The Ideological Origins of the Penitentiary. IN: M. FITZGERALD *et al* eds. Crime and Society: readings in history and theory. London: Routledge and Kegan Paul;
(1983) State, Civil Society, and Total Institutions: a critique of recent social histories of punishment. IN: COHEN, S. and SCULL, A. eds. Social control and the State: historical and comparative essays. Oxford: Basil Blackwell.

INNES, J. (1980) The King's Bench Prison in the later Eighteenth Century: law, authority and order in a London debtors' prison. IN: BREWER, J. and STYLES, J. eds. An Ungovernable People: the English and their law in the seventeenth and eighteenth centuries. London: Hutchinson;
(1987) Prisons for the Poor: English Bridewells, 1555-1800. IN: SNYDER, F and HAY, D. eds. Law, Labour and Crime: an historical perspective. London: Tavistock.

INTERNATIONAL LABOUR OFFICE (1931) The International Labour Organisation: a first decade. London: G Allen and Unwin.

IRELAND, R.W. (1987) Theory and Practice within the Medieval Prison. American Journal of Legal History Vol. 31. No. 1, pp. 56-67;
(forthcoming) The Felon and the Angel Copier: criminal identity and the promise of photography in England. Criminal Justice History.

IVES, G. (1914) A History of Penal Methods: criminals, witches, lunatics. London: St. Paul and Co.

JEFFERSON, T. and GRIMSHAW, R. (1984) Controlling the Constable: police accountability in England and Wales. London: Frederick Muller.

JEPSON, N. (1971) The Value of Prison. The Howard Journal of Penology and Crime Prevention XIII, No. 2, pp. 234-245.

JONES, H. (1962a) The Group Approach to Treatment. The Howard Journal Vol. XI, 58-63;
(1962b) Crime and the Penal System. (2nd edn.) London: University Tutorial Press.

JONES, K. ed. (1972) The Year Book of Social Policy in Britain. 1971. London: Routledge and Kegan Paul;
(1993) Asylums and After. A revised history of the mental health services from the early 18th century to the 1990s. London: Athlone Press.

JONES, M. and TANNER, J.M. (1948) Clinical Characteristics, Treatment and Rehabilitation of Repatriated Prisoners of War with Neurosis. Journal of Neurosurgery and Psychiatry Vol. 11, 42-61.

JONES, M. (1968) Social Psychiatry in Practice: the idea of a therapeutic community. Harmondsworth: Penguin.
(1976) Maturation of the Therapeutic Community: an organic approach to health and mental health. New York: Human Sciences Press;
(1982) The Process of Change. London: Routledge and Kegan Paul.

JONES, V.J. (1983) Community Service Orders in Western Australia. IN: BEVAN, C. ed. Community Service Orders in Australia and New Zealand. Canberra: Australian Institute of Criminology.

JORG-ALBRECHT, H. and SCHADLER, W. (1986) Gemeinnutzige Arbeit: Current Trends in Implementing Community Service as an additional Option for Fine Defaulters in the Federal Republic of Germany. IN: JORG-ALBRECHT, H and SCHADLER, W. eds. Community Service: a new option for punishing offenders in Europe. Freiburg: Max Planck Institute.

JOURNALS of the House of Commons, 1778-1780. Vol. 37. Session 26 November, 1778 to 24 August, 1780.

JOURNALS of the House of Commons, 1784-1785. Vol. 40. Session 18 May, 1784 to 1 December, 1785.

JUDD, M. (1983) The Oddest Combination of Town and Country: popular culture and the London fairs, 1800-60. IN: WALTON, J.K. and WALVIN, J. eds. Leisure in Britain, 1780-1939. Manchester: Manchester University Press.

KAMENKA, E. (1988) Human Rights, People's Rights. IN: CRAWFORD, J. ed. The Rights of People. Oxford: Clarendon Press.

KELK, C. (1995) Criminal Justice in the Netherlands. IN: FENNELL, P. *et al* eds. Criminal Justice in Europe: a comparative study. Oxford: Clarendon Press.

KENNARD, D. and ROBERTS, J. (1983) An Introduction to Therapeutic Communities. London: Routledge.

KENNEDY, P.M. (1983) The Rise and Fall of British Naval Mastery. London: Macmillan.

KENT PROBATION AND AFTER CARE SERVICE (1975) Community Service Orders. IN: PEASE, K. *et al* eds. Community Service Orders. London: H.M.S.O. (Home Office Research Study No. 29).

KILCOMMINS, S. (1999) Impressment and its genealogical claims in respect of community service orders in England and Wales. The Irish Jurist XXXIV 223-255;

(2000) Context and Contingency in the Historical Penal Process: the revision of revisionist analysis using the Twelve Judges' Notebooks as one tool of analysis. The Holdsworth Law Review XIX. No. 1, pp.1-54.

KING, A. (1975) Overload: problems of governing in the 1970s. Political Studies XXIII, 284-296.

KINGSMILL, J. (1854) Chapters on Prison and Prisoners, and the Prevention of Crime. (3rd edn.) London: Longmans.

KNIGHT, D. (1986) The Age of Science: the scientific world view in the nineteenth century. Oxford: Basil Blackwell.

KOENIGSBERGER, H.G. (1987) Medieval Europe, 400-1500. London: Longman.

KRAMER, R. and SPECHT, H. eds. (1969) Readings in Community Organisation Practice. Englewood Cliffs: Prentice Hall.

KRITZMAN, L. (1990) Michel Foucault: Politics, Philosophy, Culture: interviews and other writings, 1977-1984. London: Routledge.

KUHN, T.S. (1970) The Structure of Scientific Revolutions. 2nd edn. Chicago: University of Chicago Press.

KUMAR, K. (1988) From Work to Employment and Unemployment: the English Experience. IN: PAHL, R.E. ed. On Work: historical, comparative and theoretical approaches. London: Basil Blackwell.

LABOUR PARTY (1964) Crime - a challenge to us all. Sussex: Labour Party.

LANDES, D.S. (1983) Revolution in Time: clocks and the making of the modern world. Cambridge: The Belknap Press.

LAQUER, T.W. (1989) Crowds, Carnival and the State in English Executions, 1604-1868. IN: BEIER, A.L. *et al* eds. The First Modern Society: Essays in English history in honour of Lawrence Stone. Cambridge: Cambridge University Press.

LAVERY, B. (1989) Nelson's Navy. The Ships, Men and Organisation, 1793-1815. London: Conway Maritime.

LEA, J. and YOUNG, J. (1984) What is to be Done about Law and Order? Harmondsworth: Penguin Books.

LE GOFF, J. (1980) Time, Work and Culture in the Middle Ages. Chicago: University of Chicago Press. (Translated by Arthur Goldhammer.)

LEIBRICH, J. *et al* (1984) Community Service Orders in New Zealand: three research reports. Wellington: Dept. of Justice; (1985) Use of Community Service in New Zealand. Australia and New Zealand Journal of Criminology Vol. 18, pp 85-94.

LEMAINE, G. *et al* (1976) Perspectives on the Emergence of Scientific Disciplines. The Hague: Mouton.

LEONARD, E.M. (1900) The Early History of English Poor Relief. London: Cass.

LEVI, L. (1880) The History of British Commerce and of the Economic Progress of the British Nation, 1763-1878 (2nd edn.) London: J Murray (2nd edn.).

LEWIS, M. (1960) A Social History of the Navy, 1793-1815. London: Allen and Unwin.

LEWIS, M. ed. (1960) Research in Social Problems and Public Policy. Col. I. Connecticut: JAI Press.

LIND, J. (1965) An essay on the most effectual means of preserving the health of seamen in the Royal Navy and a dissertation on fevers and infections. IN: LLOYD, C. ed. The Health of Seamen: selections from the works of Dr. James Lind, Sir Gilbert Blane, and Dr Thomas Trotter. London: Navy Records.

LITTLE, A. (1962) Borstal success and the quality of inmates. British Journal of Criminology Vol. 2, pp. 6-19.

LITTLE, R. (1957) Let Reparation Fit the Crime. The Reader's Digest. September, pp. 27-31.

LLOYD, C. ed. (1965) The Health of Seamen: Selections from the Works of Dr. James Lind, Sir Gilbert Blane and Dr. Thomas Trotter. London: Navy Records; (1968) The British Seaman, 1200-1860: a social survey. London: Collins.

LOCKE, J. (1989) Two Treatises of Government. London: Everyman's Library (introduction by W.S. Carpenter).

LOMBROSO, C. (1911) Crime: its causes and remedies. London: Heinemann.

LOMBROSO FERRERO, G. (1911) Criminal Man According to the Classification of Cesare Lombroso. New York: Putnam.

LOW, D. (1982) Thieves Kitchen: the regency underworld. London: J.H. Dent and Sons.

LOWENTHAL, D. (1985) The Past is a Foreign Country. Cambridge: Cambridge University Press.

LOWMAN, J. (1987) Transcarceration: essays in the sociology of social control. Aldershot: Gower.

LUCKEN, K. (1998) Contemporary Penal Trends: Modern or Post-modern. British Journal of Criminology Vol. 38. pp. 106-123.

LYND, H. (1968) England in the Eighteen-Eighties: toward a social basis for freedom. London: F Cass.

LYON, D. (1994) Postmodernity. Buckingham: Open University Press.

LYOTARD, J.F. (1984) The Postmodern Condition: a report on knowledge. Manchester: Manchester University Press.

MACAULAY, T. (1858-1862) The History of England from the accession of James the Second. London: Longman.

MacDONAGH, O. (1960) The Nineteenth Century Revolution in Government: a reappraisal reappraised. The Historical Journal Vol. III. No. I, pp. 17-37.

MacFARLANE, S. (1986) Social Policy and the Poor in the late Seventeenth Century. IN: BEIER, A.L. and FINLAY, R. eds. London, 1500-1700: the making of the metropolis. London: Longman.

MAGEE, B. (1973) Popper. London: Fontana.

MAGUIRE, Mike *et al* eds. (1994) The Oxford Handbook of Criminology. Oxford: Clarendon Press.

MAHAN, A.T. (1890) The Rise and Fall of British Naval Mastery. Boston: Little, Brown.

MAHER, R.J. and DUFOUR, H.E. (1987) Experimenting with community service: a punitive alternative to imprisonment. Federal Probation pp. 22-27.

MANCHESTER, A.H. (1980) A Modern Legal History of England and Wales, 1750-1950. London: Butterworths.

MANNHEIM, H. and WILKINS, L.T. (1955) Prediction Methods in Relation to Borstal Training. London: H.M.S.O.

MANNHEIM, H. ed. (1960) Pioneers in Criminology. London: Stevens.

MANNING, N. (1989) The Therapeutic Community Movement: charisma and routinisation. London: Routledge.

MANWARING-WHITE, S. (1983) The Policing Revolution: police, technology, democracy and liberty in Britain. Brighton: The Harvester Press.

MARC, G. (1985) Le Travail D'înteret Général en Droit Compare Revue Penitentiaire et de Droit Penal Vol. 109, pp. 111-125.

MARCUS, G.J. ed. (1975) Heart of Oak: a survey of British sea power in the Georgian era. London: Oxford University Press.

MARRUS, M.R. ed. (1974) The Emergence of Leisure. London: Harper and Row.

MARSHALL, D. (1982) Industrial England, 1776-1851. London: Routledge.

MARTIN, B. and MASON, S. (1992) Current Trends in Leisure: the changing face of leisure provision. Leisure Studies XI, pp. 81-86.

MARTINSON, R. (1974) What works? Questions and Answers about Prison Reform. The Public Interest XXXV: pp. 22-54.

MARWICK, A. (1989) The Nature of History. London: Macmillan; (1990) British Society since 1945. (2nd edn.) Harmondsworth: Penguin; (1996) British Society since 1945. (3rd edn.) Harmondsworth: Penguin Books;

(1998) The Sixties: cultural revolution in Britain, France, Italy and the United States. Oxford: Oxford University Press.

MARYAN GREEN, N.A. (1987) International Law. (3rd edn.) London: Pitman.

MATHIAS, P. (1979) The Transformation of England: essays in the economic and social history of England in the eighteenth century. London: Methuen;
(1983) The First Industrial Nation: an economic history of Britain, 1700-1914. London: Methuen.

MATHIESEN, T. (1983) The Future of Control Systems - the case of Norway. IN: GARLAND, D. and YOUNG, P. eds. The Power to Punish: contemporary penality and social analysis. London: Heinemann Educational;
(1995) The Eagle and the Sun: on panoptical systems and mass media in modern society. IN: ERICSON, R.V. ed. Crime and the Mass Media. Aldershot: Dartmouth Publishing.

MATTHEWS, R. (1979) Decarceration and the Fiscal Crisis. IN: FINE, B. *et al* eds. Capitalism and the Rule of Law: from deviancy theory to Marxism. London: Hutchinson and Co;
(1987) Decarceration and Social Control: fantasies and realities. IN: LOWMAN, J. *et al* eds. Transcarcertation: essays in the sociology of social control. Aldershot: Gower.

MATTICK, H.W. (1967) The Future of Imprisonment in a Free Society. The British Journal of Criminology Vol. VII, pp. 450-453.

MAUDSLEY, H. (1874) Responsibility in Mental Disease. London: King.

MAYHEW, H. and BINNY, J. (1862) The Criminal Prisons of London and Scenes of Prison Life. London: Griffin, Bohn and Co;
(1971) The Unknown Mayhew: selections from the *Morning Chronicle*, 1849-1850. London: Merlin Press (ed. by E.P. Thompson and Eileen Yeo).

MAYS, J.B. (1975) Crime and its Treatment. London: Longman.

McCLEAN, J.D. and WOOD, J.C. (1969) Criminal Justice and the Treatment of Offenders. London: Sweet and Maxwell.

McCLINTOCK, F.H. and AVISON, H.N. (1968) Crime in England and Wales. London: Heinemann.

McCONVILLE, S. ed. (1975) The Use of Imprisonment: essays in the changing state of English penal policy. London: Routledge and Kegan Paul;

(1981) A history of English Prison Administration, 1750-1877. London: Routledge and Kegan Paul. Vol. I;

(1995) English Local Prisons, 1860-1900: Next Only to Death. London: Routledge.

McGOWEN, J. (1978) Nineteenth Century Developments in Irish Prison Administration. Journal of Administration Vol. 26, pp. 496-508.

McGOWEN, R. (1981) The Changing Face of God's Justice. The Debates over Divine and Human Punishment in eighteenth century England. Criminal Justice History Vol. IX, pp. 63-98;

(1986) A Powerful Sympathy: terror, the prison and humanitarian reform in early nineteenth century Britain. Journal of British Studies Vol. 25, pp. 312-334;

(1995) The Well Ordered Prison, England: 1780-1865. IN: MORRIS, N. and ROTHMAN, D. eds. The Oxford History of the Prison: the practice of punishment in Western Society. New York: Oxford University Press.

McGRATH, A. (1990) A Life of John Calvin. A Study in the shaping of Western Culture. Oxford: Basil Blackwell.

McIVOR, G. (1992) Sentenced to Serve. The Operation and Impact of Community Service by Offenders. Aldershot: Avebury;

(1995) Working with Offenders: research highlights in social work. London: Jessica Kingsley;

(1998) Jobs for the Boys: gender differences in referral to community service. The Howard Journal of Criminal Justice Vol. 37. No. 3, pp. 280-290.

McKENDRICK, N. (1961) Josiah Wedgwood and Factory Discipline. The Historical Journal IV. No. 1, pp. 30-55.

McKIE, D. and COOK, C. (1970) Election 70. London: Panther Books.

McLAUGHLIN, E. and MUNCIE, J. eds. (1996) Controlling Crime. London: Sage.

McLYNN, F. (1989) Crime and Punishment in Eighteenth Century England. London: Routledge.

McMAHON, M.W. (1991) "Net Widening": vagaries in the use of a concept. The British Journal of Criminology Vol. 30. No. 2, pp 121-149;

(1992) The Persistent Prison: rethinking decarceration. Toronto: Toronto University Press.

MEDHURST, A. (1997) Negotiating the Gnome Zone: versions of suburbia in British popular culture. IN: SILVERSTONE, R. ed. Visions of Suburbia. London: Routledge.

MELOSSI, D. and PAVARINI, M. (1981) The prison and the factory: origins of the penitentiary system. London: Macmillan.

MENZIES, K. (1986) The Rapid Spread of Community Service Orders in Ontario. Canadian Journal of Criminology Vol. 28. No. 2, 157-169;

and VASS, A. (1989) The Impact of Historical, Legal and Administrative Differences on a Sanction: community service orders in England and Ontario. The Howard Journal Vol. 28. No. 3 pp. 204-217.

MILES, A.E. (1969) The Effects of a Therapeutic Community on the interpersonal relationships of a group of psychopaths. British Journal of Criminology Jan 1969, Vol. 9 No. 1, 22-38.

MILL, J.S. (1878) Political Economy with Some of their Applications to Social Philosophy. London: Routledge.

MILSON, F. (1974) An Introduction to Community Work. London: Routledge.

MINCHINTON, W. (1974) Patterns and Structures of Demand, 1500-1750. IN: CIPOLLA, C.M. ed. The Fontana Economic History of Europe. The Sixteenth and Seventeenth Centuries. London: Fontana.

MINISTRY OF EDUCATION (1960) The Youth Services in England and Wales. Report of a Committee appointed by the Minister of Education in November, 1958. Cmnd. 929. London: H.M.S.O.

MINISTRY OF EDUCATION (1963) Half our Future. A Report of the Central Advisory Council for Education (England). London: H.M.S.O.

MISHRA, R. (1989) The Welfare State in Crisis: social thought and social change. Brighton: Wheatsheaf.

MORE, T. (1967 repr.) Utopia. Harmondsworth: Penguin.

MORRIS, A. and McISAAC, M. (1978) Juvenile Justice: the practice of social welfare. London: Macmillan.

MORRIS, A. *et al* (1980) Justice for Children. London: Macmillan.

MORRIS, A. and GILLER, H. (1987) Understanding Juvenile Justice. London: Croom Helm.

MORRIS, N. and ROTHMAN, D. eds. (1995) The Oxford History of the Prison: the practice of punishment in Western Society. New York: Oxford University Press.

MORRIS, T. and MORRIS, P. (1962) The Experience of Imprisonment. The British Journal of Criminology Vol. II: No. 4, pp. 337-360; and

(1963) Pentonville: a sociological study of an English prison. London: Routledge and Kegan Paul;

(1989) Crime and Criminal Justice since 1945. Oxford: Basil Blackwell.

MORRISON, R.L. (1961) Group Counselling in Penal Institutions. The Howard Journal Vol. X, No. 4. 279-297.

MOWERY ANDREWS, R. (1994) Law, Magistracy and Crime in Old Regime Paris. Vol. I. The System of Criminal Justice. Cambridge: Cambridge University Press.

MUDIE, J. (1965) The Felonry of New South Wales. London: Angus and Robertson (ed. by Walter Stone).

MUELLER, O.W. (1961) The German Penal Code of 1871. London: Sweet and Maxwell (translated by O.W. Mueller and Thomas Burgenthal);

ed. (1977) Alternative Draft of a Penal Code for the Federal Republic of Germany. London: Sweet and Maxwell (translated by Joseph J Darby).

MUNCIE, J. and SPARKS, R. eds. (1991) Imprisonment: European Perspectives. Hemel Hempstead: Harvester Wheatsheaf.

MURDOCK, G. (1973) Political deviance: the press presentation of a militant mass demonstration. IN: COHEN, S. and YOUNG, J. eds. The Manufacture of News: social problems, deviance and the mass media. London: Constable.

MURPHY, J.G. ed. (1973) Punishment and Rehabilitation. California: Wadsworth Publishing.

NATIONAL DEVIANCY COUNCIL (1980) Permissiveness and Control: the fate of the sixties legislation. London: Macmillan.

NELKEN, D. (1994) The Futures of Criminology. London: Sage.

NEWBURN, T. (1995) Crime and Criminal Justice Policy. London: Longman Group.

NEWLAKE, H. (1858) The Convict Converted. London: Partridge.

NICHOLAS, S. ed. (1988) Convict Workers: reinterpreting Australia's past. Cambridge: Cambridge University Press.

NICHOLAS, S. and SHERGOLD, P. (1988) Convicts as Migrants. IN: NICHOLAS, S. ed. Convict Worker's: reinterpreting Australia's past. Cambridge: Cambridge University Press.

NIETZSCHE, F. (1874) On the Uses and Disadvantages of History for Life. IN: HOLLINGDALE, R.J. ed. (1983) Untimely Mediations. Cambridge: Cambridge University Press;

(1956) The Genealogy of Morals: an attack. New York: Anchor Books;

(1969) Thus Spoke Zarathustra. Harmondsworth: Penguin Books.

NORTON, P. ed. (1984) Law and Order in British Politics. Gower: Aldershot.

O'BRIEN, P. (1982) The Promise of Punishment: prisons in nineteenth century France. Princeton: Princeton University Press.

O'DONOGHUE, E.G. (1923) Bridewell Hospital: Palace, Prison and Schools. London: Bodley Head (Vol. I).

O'DONOVAN, D. (1990) Committals to Custody - What Impact have Community Service Orders Made? Dublin: Research and Statistics Unit.

OLDROYD, D.R. (1980) Darwinian Impacts: an introduction to the Darwinian Revolution. Milton Keynes: Open University Press.

O'NEILL, J. (1977) Transported to Van Diemen's Land: the story of two convicts. Cambridge: Cambridge University Press.

OSBOROUGH, N. (1969) The Emergence of the Suspended Sentence in England. The Irish Jurist Vol. IV. New Series: Part I; (1975) Borstal in Ireland: custodial provision for young adult offenders, 1906-1974. Dublin: Institute of Public Administration.

OWEN, D. (1964) English Philanthropy: 1660-1960. Cambridge: Belknap Press of Harvard University Press.

OWEN, D. (1994) Maturity and Modernity: Nietzsche, Weber, Foucault and the ambivalence of reason. London: Routledge.

OXLEY, G. W. (1974) Poor Relief in England and Wales, 1601-1834. Newton Abbot: David and Charles.

PALEY, W. (1787) The Principles of Moral and Political Philosophy. London: Collins.

PALMER, T.B. (1971) California's Community Treatment Programme for Delinquent Adolescents. Journal of Research in Crime and Delinquency Vol 8. No. 1, 74-92.

PARKER, H. et al (1981) Receiving Juvenile Justice: adolescents and state care and control. Oxford: Blackwell.

PARKER, S. (1976) The Sociology of Leisure. London: Allen and Unwin.

PARRIS, H. (1960) The Nineteenth Century Revolution in Government: a reappraisal reappraised. The Historical Journal Vol. II. No. I, pp 74-92.

PASQUINO, P. (1991) Criminology: the birth of a special knowledge. IN: BURCHELL, G. *et al* eds. The Foucault Effect: studies in governmentality with two lectures by and an interview with Michel Foucault. Chicago: Chicago University Press.

PEARL, V. (1978) Puritans and Poor Relief. The London Workhouse, 1649-1660. IN: PENNINGTON, D. and THOMAS, K. eds. Puritans and Revolutionaries. Essays in Seventeenth Century History presented to Christopher Hill. Oxford: Clarendon Press.

PEARSON, G. (1983) Hooligan: a history of respectable fears. London: Macmillan Press.

PEARSON, K. (1912) Eugenics and Public Health: an address to public health officers. London: Constable.

PEASE, K. *et al* (1975) Community Service Orders. London: H.M.S.O. (Home Office Research Study. No. 29);
(1980) A brief history of Community Service. IN: PEASE, K. and McWILLIAMS, W. eds. Community Service by Order. Edinburgh: Scottish Academic Press;
and McWILLIAMS, W. eds. (1980) Community Service by Order. Edinburgh: Scottish Academic Press.

PECK, M. (1987) The Different Drum: community making and peace. New York: Simon and Schuster.

PELLEW, J. (1982) The Home Office, 1848-1914: from clerks to bureaucrats. London: Heinemann.

PENNINGTON, D. and THOMAS, K. eds. (1978) Puritans and Revolutionaries. Essays in Seventeenth Century History presented to Christopher Hill. Oxford: Clarendon Press.

PERKIN, H. (1989) The Rise of Professionalised Society: England since 1880. London: Routledge.

PFOHL, M. (1983) Gemeinnutzige Arbeit als strafrechtliche Sanktion: eine rechtsvergleichende Untersuchung unter Beruchsichtigung der Britischen Community Service Order. Berlin: Duncker and Humblot.

PHILIPS, D. (1983) A Just Measure of Crime, Authority, Hunters and Blue Locusts: The "Revisionist" Social History of Crime and Law in Britain, 1780-1850 IN: COHEN, S. and SCULL, A. eds. Social Control and the State: historical and comparative essays. Oxford: Blackwell.

PIERSON, C. (1981) Beyond the Welfare State: the new political economy of welfare. Cambridge: Polity Press.

PISCIOTTA, A. (1981) Corrections, Society and Social Control in America: a metahistorical review of the literature. Criminal Justice History Vol. II, pp. 109-130.

PITTS, J. (1981) The Politics of Juvenile Crime. London: Sage Publications;
(1996) The Politics and Practice of Youth Justice. IN: McLAUGHLIN, E. and MUNCIE, J. eds. Controlling Crime. London: Sage.

PIVEN, F. and CLOWARD, R. (1972) Regulating the Poor. The Functioning of Public Welfare. London: Tavistock.

PLAYFAIR, G. (1971) The Punitive Obsession: an unvarnished history of the English Prison System. London: Gollanz.

PLUMB, J.H. (1971) England in the Eighteenth Century. Harmondsworth: Penguin.

POCOCK, J.G.A. (1957) The Ancient Constitution and the Feudal Law. Cambridge: Cambridge University Press;
(1971) Politics, Language and Time: essays on political thought and history. London: Methuen.

PORTER, R. (1982) English Society in the Eighteenth Century. London: Allen and Unwin.

PORTER, R. (1987) Disease, Medicine and Society in England, 1550-1860. Basingstoke: Macmillan.

POTTER, H. (1993) Hanging in Judgment: religion and the death penalty from the bloody code to abolition. London: SCM Press.

POYNTER, J.R. (1969) Society and Pauperism: English ideas on poor relief, 1775-1834. London: Routledge and Kegan Paul.

PRICE, R. (1973) Observations in the expectations of Lives. IN: GLASS, D.V. ed. The Population Controversy. Farnborough: Gregg.

PRIESTLEY, P. (1985) Victorian Prison Lives, 1830-1914. London: Methuen;

(1989) Jail Journeys: the English prison experience since 1918. London: Routledge.

PRIME, T. (1971) Reparation from the Offender. The Solicitors Journal Vol. 115. No. 48, pp. 880-882.

PRISON REFORM COUNCIL (1962) Inside Story. A Report submitted by a group of ex-prisoners to the prison commission, drawing attention to discrepancies between policy and practice in prison administration. London: Prison Reform Council.

PYM, B. (1974) Pressure Groups and the Permissive Society. Newton Abbot: David and Charles.

RADZINOWICZ, L. (1944) Some Sources of Modern English Criminal Legislation. The Cambridge Law Journal Vol. 8, pp. 180-194;

(1948) A History of English Criminal Law and its Administration from 1750: the movement for reform. London: Stevens. Vol. I;

(1961) In Search of Criminology. London: Heinemann;

(1966) Ideology and Crime: a study of crime in its social and historical context. London: Heinemann;

(1968) A history of English Criminal Law and its Administration from 1750: grappling for control. London: Stevens. Vol. 4;

(1968b) Impressment into the Army and Navy - a rough and ready instrument of preventive police and criminal justice. IN: WOLFGANG, M.E. ed. Crime and Culture: essays in honor of Thorsten Sellin. New York: Wiley.

RADZINOWICZ, L. and HOOD, R. (1986) A History of English Criminal Law and its Administration: the emergence of penal policy. London: Stevens. Vol. 5.

RAINBOW, P. ed. (1991) The Foucault Reader. Harmondsworth: Penguin Books.

RAPOPORT, R.W. (1960) Community as doctor: new perspectives on a therapeutic community. London: Tavistock.

RAWLINGS, P. (1990) Recent Writing on Crime, Criminal Law, Criminal Justice, and Punishment in the Early Modern Period. IN: HINES, W.D. *et al* eds. English Legal History: a bibliography and guide to the literature. New York: Garland Publishing;;
(1992) Drunks, Whores and Idle Apprentices: criminal biographies of the eighteenth century. London: Routledge.

REAY, B. ed. (1985) Popular Culture in Seventeenth-century England. London: Croom Helm.

REINER, R. (1992) The Politics of the Police. (2nd edn.) Hertfordshire: Harvester Wheatsheaf;
(1994) Policing the Crisis. IN: MAGUIRE, M *et al* eds. The Oxford Handbook of Criminology. Oxford: Clarendon Press.

RENTZMANN, W. and ROBERT, J.P. (1986) Alternative Measures to Imprisonment. 7th Conference of the Directors of Prison Administration. Strasbourg: Council of Europe.

REPORT (1810-1811) from the Select Committee on the laws relating to Penitentiary Houses. (199) Vol. III. IN: Irish University Press Series of British Parliamentary Papers. Crime and Punishment. Transportation. Session 1810-1832. Vol. I.

REPORT (1811) Second Report from the Committee on the laws relating to Penitentiary Houses. (217) Vol. III. IN: Irish University Press Series of British Parliamentary Papers. Crime and Punishment. Transportation. Session 1810-1832. Vol. I.

REPORT (1812) Third Report from the Committee on the laws relating to Penitentiary Houses. (306) Vol. II. IN: Irish University Press Series of British Parliamentary Papers. Crime and Punishment. Transportation. Session 1810-1832. Vol. I.

REPORT (1822) from the Select Committee on the Police of the Metropolis. (440) Vol. IV. IN: Irish University Press Series of British Parliamentary Debates. Crime and Punishment. Police. Session 1828. Vol. 3.

REPORT (1823) from the Select Committee on the State of the Penitentiary at Millbank. (533) Vol. V. IN: Irish University Press Series of British Parliamentary Papers. Crime and Punishment. Prisons. Vol. 10. Sessions 1823-1824.

REPORT (1828) from the Select Committee on the Police of the Metropolis. (533) Vol. VI. IN: Irish University Press Series of British Parliamentary Debates. Crime and Punishment. Police. Session 1828. Vol. 3.

REPORT (1835) from the Select Committee of the House of Lords on the Present State of the Several Gaols and Houses of Correction in England and Wales. (438) Vol. XI. IN: Irish University Press Series of British Parliamentary Papers. Crime and Punishment. Prisons. Session. 1835. Vol. 3.

REPORT (1835) First Report of the Select Committee of the House of Lords appointed to enquire into the present state of several Gaols and Houses of Correction in England and Wales. (439) Vol. XI. IN: Irish University Press Series of British Parliamentary Papers. Crime and Punishment. Prisons. Session 1835. Vol. 3.

REPORT (1835) First Annual Report of the Poor Law Commissioners for England and Wales. 1835. London: H.M.S.O.

REPORT (1837-1838) from the Select Committee on Transportation. (669) Vol. XXII. IN: Irish University Press Series of British Parliamentary Papers. Crime and Punishment. Transportation. Sessions 1837-1861. Vol. 3.

REPORT (1847) of the General Treatment and Condition of Convicts in the Hulks at Woolwich. (831) Vol. XVIII. IN: Irish University Press Series of British Parliamentary Papers. Crime and Punishment. Prisons. Session. 1847. Vol. 12.

REPORT (1850) from the Select Committee on Prison Discipline. (632) Vol. XVII. IN: Irish University Press Series of British Parliamentary Papers. Crime and Punishment. Prisons. Session 1850. Vol. 5.

REPORT (1863) of the Commissioners on Acts relating to Transportation and Penal Servitude. [3190] Vol. XXI. IN: Irish University Press Series of British Parliamentary Papers. Crime and Punishment. Transportation. Session 1863. Vol. 5.

REPORT (1863) from the Select Committee on the House of Lords on the present state of discipline in Gaols and Houses of Correction. (499) Vol. IX. IN: Irish University Press Series of British Parliamentary Papers. Crime and Punishment. Prisons. Session 1863. Vol. 6.

REPORT (1874) Thirty Eighth Report of the Inspectors of Prisons appointed under the provision of the Act 5 and 6 Gul. IV. c. 38. to view the different prisons of Great Britain. [c.1020] Vol. XXIX.

REPORT (1895) from the Departmental Committee on Prisons. 1895. [c.7702] Vol. LVI. IN: Irish University Press Series of British Parliamentary Papers. Crime and Punishment. Prisons. Session 1895-1898. Vol. 19.

REPORT (1905) Copy of the Report made in 1834 by the Commissioners of Inquiry into the administration and practical operation of the Poor Laws. London: H.M.S.O.

REPORT (1909) from the Royal Commission on the Poor Laws and Relief of Distress. London: H.M.S.O.

REPORT (1922) of the Departmental Committee on the Training, Appointment and Payment of Probation Officers. Cmnd. 1610. London: H.M.S.O.

REPORT (1932) from the Departmental Committee on Persistent Offenders. Cmnd. 4090. London: H.M.S.O.

REPORT (1933) of the Departmental Committee on the Employment of Prisoners. Part I. Employment of Prisoners. Cmnd. 4462. London: H.M.S.O.

REPORT (1951-52) Seventh Report from the Select Committee on Estimates together with Minutes of Evidence taken before Sub Committees E and appendices. IN: Report from Committees. Vol. VI. 1951-52. Session 31 Oct. 1951-30 Oct, 1952.

REPORT (1957) The Royal Commission on the Law relating to Mental Illness and Mental Deficiency, 1954-1957. Cmnd. 1969. London: H.M.S.O.

REPORT (1958) of the Cambridge Department of Criminal Science: the results of probation. London: Macmillan.

REPORT (1961) of the Interdepartmental Committee on the Business of the Criminal Courts. Cmnd. 1289. London: H.M.S.O.

REPORT (1962) of the Departmental Committee on the Probation Service. Cmnd. 1650. London: H.M.S.O.

REPORT (1968) of the Committee on Local Authority and Allied Personal Social Services. Cmnd. 3703. London: H.M.S.O.

REPORT (1969) of the Committee on the Enforcement of Judgment Debts. Cmnd. 3909. London: H.M.S.O.

REPORT (1972) The Longford Report. London: Coronet.

REPORT (1979) of the Committee of Inquiry into the United Kingdom Prison Services. Cmnd. 7673. London: H.M.S.O.

REPORT (1985) of the Committee of Inquiry into the Penal System. Dublin: Stationery Office.

RICHARDSON, A. (1983) Participation. London: Routledge and Kegan Paul.

ROBERTS, D. (1969) Victorian Origins of the Welfare State. Hamden: Archon Books.

ROBERTS, K. (1970) Leisure. London: Longman; (1983) Youth and Leisure. London: George Allen and Unwin; (1999) Leisure in Contemporary Society. London: CABI Publishing.

ROBERTS, R.A. ed. (1879) Calendar of the Home Office: papers of the reign of George III, 1766-1769. London: Longman. Vol. II; ed. (1881) Calendar of the Home Office: papers of the reign of George III, 1770-1772. London: Longman. Vol. III.

ROBERTSON, A.H. and MERRILS, J.G. (1989) Human Rights in the World: an introduction to the study of the international protection of human rights. Manchester: Manchester University Press.

ROBERTSON, G. (1993) Freedom, the Individual and the Law. (7th edn.) London: Penguin.

ROBERTSON, J. (1985) Future Works: Jobs, self-employment and leisure after an Industrial Age. London: Gower.

ROBSON, L.L. (1965) The Convict Settlers of Australia: an inquiry into the origin and character of the convicts transported to New South Wales and Van Diemen's Land, 1787-1852. Victoria: Melbourne University Press.

ROCK, P. (1983) Law, Order and Power in late Seventeenth and early Eighteenth Century England. IN: COHEN, S. and SCULL, A. eds. Social Control and the State: historical and comparative essays. Oxford: Blackwell;

(1990) Helping Victims of Crime: the Home Office and the rise of victim support in England and Wales. Oxford: Clarendon Press;

ed. (1994) History of Criminology. Aldershot: Dartmouth.

RODGER, N.A.M. (1986) The Wooden World: an anatomy of the Georgian navy. London: Collins.

RORTY, R. (1993) Human Rights, Rationality and Sentimentality. IN: SHUTE, S. and HURLEY, S. eds. "On Human Rights": the Oxford Amnesty Lectures. New York: Basic Books.

ROSE, G. (1961) The Struggle for Penal Reform. The Howard League and its Predecessors. London: Stevens.

ROSHIER, B. (1973) The Selection of Crime News by the Press. IN: COHEN, S. and YOUNG, J. eds. The Manufacture of News: social problems, deviance and the mass media. London: Constable.

ROSS, M.G. and LEPPIN, B.W. (1955) Community Organisation: theory and principles. London: Harper.

ROTHMAN, D. (1995) Perfecting the Prison: United States, 1789-1865. IN: MORRIS, N. and ROTHMAN, D.J. eds. The Oxford History of the Prison: the practice of punishment in Western Society. New York: Oxford University Press.

RUGGLES-BRISE, E. (1921) The English Prison System. London: Longman;

(1924), Prison Reform: at home and abroad. London: Longman.

RULE, J. (1986) The labouring classes in early industrial England, 1750-1850. London: Longman;

(1992) Albion's People: English Society, 1714-1815. London: Longman.

RUSCHE, G. and KIRCHHEIMER, O. (1968) Punishment and Social Structure. New York: Russell and Russell.

RUTHERFORD, A. (1984) Prisoners and the Process of Justice: the reductionist challenge. London: Heinemann;

(1993) Time for another Big Idea. IN: WHITFIELD, D. and SCOTT, D. eds. Paying Back: twenty years of community service. Winchester: Waterside Press.

RYAN, M. (1983) The Politics of Penal Reform. London: Longman.

SABINE, G. (1963) A History of Political Theory. (3rd edn.) London: Harrap.

SABOL, W.J. (1990) Imprisonment, fines and diverting offenders from custody implications of sentencing discretion from penal policy. The Howard Journal Vol. 23. No. I, pp. 25-41.

SASSOON, A. (1980) Gramsci's Politics. London: Croom Helm.

SAYERS, S. (1989) Work, Leisure and Human Needs. IN: WINNIFRITH, T. and BARRETT, C. eds. The Philosophy of Leisure. Basingstoke: Macmillan.

SCHAFER, S. (1960) Restitution to Victims of Crime. London: Stevens and Sons.

SCHOOLS' COUNCIL (1968) Community Service and the Curriculum. London: H.M.S.O. (Working Paper No. 17.)

SCOTT, M. (1993) Leisure Services Law. (2nd edn.) London: Sweet and Maxwell.

SCULL, A. (1977) Decarceration. Community treatment and the deviant: a radical view. Englewood Cliffs: Prentice Hall;

(1983) Community Corrections: panacea, progress or pretence. IN: GARLAND, D. and YOUNG, P. eds. The Power to Punish: contemporary penality and social analysis. London: Heinemann;

(1984) Decarceration. Community treatment and the deviant: a radical view. 2nd edn. Cambridge: Polity Press;

(1987) Decarceration reconsidered. IN: LOWMAN, J. *et al* eds. Transcarceration: essays in the sociology of social control. Aldershot: Gower.

SEAL, V. and BEAN, P. eds. (1992) Barbara Wootton: selected writings. London: Macmillan. Vol. 2.

SEYMOUR-URE, C. (1996) The British Press and Broadcasting since 1945. (2nd edn.) Oxford: Blackwell Publishers.

SHAPLAND, J. *et al* (1988) Victims in the Criminal Justice System. Aldershot: Gower.

SHARPE, J.A. (1990) Judicial Punishment in England. London: Faber.

SHAW, A.G.L. (1966) Convicts and the Colonies: a study of penal transportation from Great Britain and Ireland to Australia and other parts of the British Empire. London: Faber.

SHAW, S. (1980) Paying the Penalty: an analysis of the cost of penal sanctions. London: Nacro.

SHEARD, J. (1992) Volunteering and Society, 1960 to 1990. IN: HEDLEY, R. and DAVIS SMITH, J. eds. Volunteering and Society: principles and practice. London: N.V.C.O.

SHUTE, S. and HURLEY, S. eds. (1993) On Human Rights: the Oxford Amnesty Lectures. New York: Basic Books.

SIEGHART, P. (1983) The International Law of Human Rights. Oxford: Clarendon Press;

(1985) The Lawful Rights of Mankind: an introduction to the international legal code of human rights. Oxford: Oxford University Press.

SILBERMAN, S. (1986) Community Service as an Alternative Sentence for Juveniles. New England Law Journal on Criminal Law and Civil Confinement Vol. XII, 123-150.

SILVER, A. (1967) The Demand for Order in Civil Society: a review of some themes in the history of urban crime, police, and riot. IN: BORDUA, D. ed. The Police: six sociological essays. London: John Wiley and Sons.

SILVERSONE, R. ed. (1997) Visions of Suburbia. London: Routledge.

SIM, J. (1990) Medical Power in Prisons: the prison medical service in England, 1774-1989. Milton Keynes: Open University Press

SIMON, J. and FEELEY, M. (1995) True Crime: the new penology and public discourse on crime. IN: BLOMBERG, T. and COHEN, S. eds. Social Control: essays in honour of Sheldon L. Messinger. New York: Aldine de Gruyter.

SKINNER, Q. (1969) Meaning and Understanding in the History of Ideas. History and Theory Vol. VIII, pp. 3-53;
(1974) Some Problems in the Analysis of Political Thought and Action. Political Theory Vol. 2. No. 3, pp. 277-303.

SLACK, P. (1988) Poverty and Policy in Tudor and Stuart England. London: Longman.

SMITH, B. (1981) The Irish Prison System, 1885-1914: Land War to World War. The Irish Jurist. Vol. XVI. Part II, pp. 316-349.

SMITH, J. (1974) The Community Service Order. IN: BLOM COOPER, L. ed. Progress in Penal Reform. Oxford: Clarendon Press.

SPARKS, R.F. (1971) Local Prisons: the crisis in the English penal system. London: Heinemann;
(1971b) The Use of Suspended Sentences. Criminal Law Review pp. 384-401;

(1996) Prisons, Punishment and Penality. IN: McLAUGHLIN, E. and MUNCIE, J. eds. Controlling Crime. London: Sage Publications.

SPIERENBURG, P. (1984) The Spectacle of Suffering: executions and the evolution of repression - from a preindustrial metropolis to the European experience. Cambridge: Cambridge University Press.

STEDMAN JONES, G. (1971). Outcast London: a study in the relationship between classes in Victorian Society. Oxford: Clarendon Press;

(1985) Class Expression versus Social Control? A Critique of Recent Trends in the Social History of 'Leisure'. IN: COHEN, S. and SCULL, A. eds. Social Control and the State: historical and comparative essays. Oxford: Basil Blackwell.

STEEL, A. (1957) Diana versus Caravan and Topaz. The Mariner's Mirror Vol. 43, pp. 46-58.

STEINBERG, R. (1981) Wages and Hours: labor and reform in twentieth-century America. New Brunswick: Rutgers University Press.

STERN, V. (1993) Bricks of Shame: Britain's prisons. (3rd edn.) Harmondsworth: Penguin.

STORCH, R.D. (1975) The Plague of Blue Locusts: police reforms and popular resistance in Northern England, 1840-1857. International Review of Social History Vol. XX, pp. 61-90.

SUMNER, C. ed. (1982) Crime, Justice and the Mass Media. Cambridge: Cropwood Conference Series. No. 14.

SUSSEX, J. (1976) Community Service by Offenders: Year One in Kent. Chichester: Rose.

SYKES, G.M. (1958) The Society of Captives: a study of a maximum security prison. Princeton: Princeton University Press.

SYNDER, F. and HAY, D. eds. (1987) Law, Labour and Crime: an historical perspective. London: Tavistock.

SZABO, I. (1982) Historical Foundations of Human Rights and Subsequent Developments. IN: VASAK, K. ed. The International Dimensions of Human Rights. Connecticut: Greenwood Press. (edited for the English version by Philip Alston) Vol. I.

TAYLOR, I. (1981) Law and Order: arguments for socialism. London: Macmillan.

TAYLOR, M. (1991) Community Service is not just a cut-price alternative to Jail. Irish Independent Jan 6.

TAWNEY, R.H. and POWER, E. eds. (1924) Tudor Economic Documents: being select documents illustrating the economic and social history of Tudor England. London: Longmans Green. Vol. II

TAWNEY, R.H. (1966) The Acquisitive Society. London: Collins; (1987) Religion and the Rise Of Capitalism. Harmondsworth: Penguin.

TEFF, H. (1975) Drugs, Society and the Law. Saxon: Lexington Books.

THANE, P. (1982) Foundations of the Welfare State. London: Longman.

THOMAS, D. ed. (1972) State Trials: the public conscience. London: Longman.

THOMAS, J.E. (1972) English Prison Officers since 1850: a study in conflict. London: Routledge and Kegan Paul; and POOLEY, R. (1980) The Exploding Prison: prison riots and the case of Hull. London: Junction Books.

THOMAS, K. (1964) Work and Leisure in Pre-industrial Society. Past and Present No. 29, pp. 50-63.

THOMAS, M. (1971) Work Camps and Volunteers. The P.E.P. study of International Work-Camp Volunteers. London: Political and Economic Planning.

THOMIS, M. (1976) Responses to Industrialisation. The British Experience, 1780-1850. Newton Abbot: David and Charles.

THOMPSON, E.P. (1967) Time, work-discipline and industrial capitalism. Past and Present No. 38, pp. 56-97;
(1971) The Moral Economy of the English Crowd in the Eighteenth Century. Past and Present Vol. 50;
(1988 repr.) The Making of the English Working Class. Harmondsworth: Penguin.

THOMPSON, F.M.L. (1981) Social Control in Victorian Britain. The Economic History Review Vol. XXXIV, No. 2, pp. 189-208;
ed. (1990) The Cambridge Social History of Britain, 1750-1900. Cambridge: Cambridge University Press.

THORPE, D.H. *et al* (1980) The Community Support of Juvenile Offenders. London: George Allen and Unwin.

TOMLINSON, M. (1981) Penal Servitude, 1846-1865: a system in evolution. IN: BAILEY, V. ed. Policing and Punishment in Nineteenth Century Britain. London: Croom Helm.

TOSH, J. (1991) The Pursuit of History: aims, methods and new directions in the study of modern history. (2nd edn.) London: Longman.

TOWNSEND, P. (1962) The Last Refuge: a survey of residential institutions and homes for the aged in England and Wales. London: Routledge and Kegan Paul.

TOYNBEE, A. (1908) Lectures on the Industrial Revolution. London: Longman.

TRASLER, G. (1974) The Role of Psychologists in the Penal System. IN: BLOM-COOPER, L. ed. Progress in Penal Reform. Oxford: Clarendon Press.

UGLOW, S. (1988) Policing Liberal Society. Oxford: Oxford University Press.

USHER, R. (1950-51) Royal Naval Impressment during the American Revolution. The Mississippi Valley Historical Review Vol. XXXVII, pp. 686-694.

VALIER, C. (1998) True Crime Stories: scientific methods of criminal investigation, criminology and historiography. British Journal of Criminology. Vol. 38. No. 1, pp. 88-105.

VAN ASBECK, F. (1962) Growth and Movement of International Law. The International and Comparative Law Quarterly Vol. 11, 1054-1072.

VAN DER SLICE, A. (1991) Elizabethan houses of correction. IN: MUNCIE, J. and SPARKS, R. eds. Imprisonment: European Perspectives. Hemel Hempstead: Harvester Wheatsheaf.

VAN KALMTHOUT, A. and TAK, P. (1988) Sanction Systems in the Member States of the Council of Europe: deprivation of liberty, community service and other substitutes. Arnhem: Kluwer. Part I;

(1992) Sanction Systems in the Member States of the Council of Europe: deprivation of liberty, community service and other substitutes. Arnhem: Kluwer. Part II.

VASAK, K. ed. (1982) The International Dimensions of Human Rights. 1982. Connecticut: Greenwood Press. (ed. by Philip Alston) Vol. I.

VASS, A. (1984) Sentenced to Labour: close encounters with a prison substitute. St. Ives: Venus Academica;

(1990) Alternatives to Prison: punishment, custody and the community. London: Sage.

VOLD, G.B. (1958) Theoretical Criminology. New York: Oxford University Press.

WALKER, N. and McCABE, S. (1973) Crime and Insanity in England: new solutions and new problems. Edinburgh: University Press. Vol. 2.

WALSH, D. and SEXTON, D. (2000) An Empirical Study of Community Service Orders in Ireland. Limerick: University of Limerick.

WALTON, J.K. and WALVIN, J. eds. (1983) Leisure in Britain, 1780-1939. Manchester: Manchester University Press.

WALVIN, J. (1978) Leisure and Society, 1830-1950. London: Longman.

WEBB, A. *et al* (1976) Voluntary Social Services. London: Personal Social Services.

WEBB, P. (1988) Construction, repair and maintenance in the battle fleet of the Royal Navy, 1793-1815. IN: BLACK, J. and WOODFINE, P. eds. The British Navy and the Use of Naval Power in the Eighteenth Century. Leicester: Leicester University Press.

WEBB, S. and WEBB, B. (1922) English Prisons under Local Government. London: Longman;
and (1927) English Local Government: English Poor Law History. London: Longmans. Vol. I.

WEBER, M. (1976) The Protestant Ethic and the Spirit of Capitalism. (2nd edn.) London: Allen and Unwin.

WEGG-PROSSER, C. (1986) The Police and the Law. (3rd edn.) London: Longman.

WEIDENHOFER, M. (1981) Port Arthur: a place of misery. Oxford: Oxford University Press.

WEST, D.J. (1980) Sex Offenders in the Criminal Justice System: papers presented to the 12th Cropwood Round-Table Conference. Cambridge: University of Cambridge Institute of Criminology.

WHITFIELD, D (1993) Extending the Boundaries. IN: WHITFIELD, D. and SCOTT, D. eds. Paying Back: twenty years of community service. Winchester: Waterside Press;
and SCOTT, D. eds. (1993) Paying Back: twenty years of community service. Winchester: Waterside Press.

WHITLEY, J. (1970) The Therapeutic Communities. The Howard Journal Vol. XIII. No. 1, 60-64.

WHITROW, G. J. (1988) Time in History: the evolution of our general awareness of time and temporal perspective. Oxford: Oxford University Press.

WIENER, M. (1990) Reconstructing the Criminal. Culture, Law and Policy in England, 1830-1914. Cambridge: Cambridge University Press.

WIGMORE, J.H. *et al* (1911) General Introduction to the Modern Criminal Science Series. IN: LOMBROSO, C. Crime: its causes and remedies. London: Heinemann.

WILKINSON, G.T. ed. (1963) The Newgate Calendar. London: Routledge.

WILLIAMS, G. (1960) The Concept of Egemonia in the Thought of Antonio Gramsci: some notes on interpretation. Journal of the History of Ideas Vol. XXI. No. 4.

WINDELSHAM, L. (1993) Responses to Crime. Oxford: Clarendon Press. Vol. II.

WINIFIELD, S. (1977) What has the Probation Service done to Community Service? Probation Journal Vol. 24. No. 4.

WINNIFITH, T. and BARRETT, C. eds. (1989) The Philosophy of Leisure. Basingstoke: Macmillan.

WOLFF, M. (1967) Prison. The Penal Institutions of Britain: prisons, borstals, detention centres, attendance centres, approved schools and remand homes. London: Eyre and Spottiswoode.

WOLFGANG, M.E. ed. (1968) Crime and Culture: essays in honor of Thorsten Sellin. New York: Wiley.

WOODWARD, J. (1974) To do the Sick no Harm: a study of the British voluntary hospital system to 1875. London: Routledge and Kegan Paul.

WOOTTON, B. (1968) The White Paper on Children in Trouble. The Criminal Law Review pp. 465-473;
(1973) Community Service. The Criminal Law Review pp. 16-20;
(1978). Crime and Penal Policy: reflections on fifty years experience. London: Allen and Unwin.

WORRALL, A. (1995) Gender, Criminal Justice and Probation. IN: McIVOR, G ed. Working with Offenders: research highlights in social work. London: Jessica Kinsley.

WORSLEY, P. ed. (1972) Problems of Modern Society. London: Penguin.

WRIGHTSON, K. (1981) Alehouses, Order and Reformation, 1590-1600. IN: YEO, E. and YEO, S. eds. Popular Culture and Class Conflict, 1590-1914: explorations in the history of labour and leisure. Hassocks: Harvester Press.

YEO, E. and YEO, S. eds. (1981) Popular Culture and Class Conflict, 1590-1914: explorations in the history of labour and leisure. Hassocks: Harvester Press.

YOUNG, J. (1973) The Myth of Drug Taker in the Mass Media. IN: COHEN, S. and YOUNG, J. eds. The Manufacture of News: social problems, deviance and the mass media. London: Constable.

YOUNG, P. (1983) Sociology, the State and Penal Relations. IN: GARLAND, D. and YOUNG, P. eds. The Power to Punish: contemporary penality and social analysis. London: Heinemann Educational Books.

YOUNG, W. (1979) Community Service Orders: the development and use of a new penal measure. London: Heinemann.

YOUNGHUSBAND, E. (1978) Social Work in Britain, 1950-1975. London: George Allen and Unwin. Vol. I.

YOUNGS, R. (1994) Sourcebook on German Law. London: Cavendish.

ZEITLYN, B.B. (1967) The Therapeutic Community - Fact or Fantasy. British Journal of Psychiatry Vol.113, No.503, 1083-1086.

INDEX

Lincolnshire 91, 342
Lind, Dr James 164
Lisbon 336
Liverpool 319
local authorities 131, 139, 145-6,
  217
  community ideology 252, 261
  employment of prisoners 320
  intermediate treatment 407,
    411-12, 415
  police 81, 83-4, 86
  prisons 77-80, 85-6, 88-90, 94,
    188
  probation 102, 127, 141
  rehabilitation 506
  rise in State control 64-5, 77-
    81, 83-6, 88-90, 94, 102-3
  transformations in penal
    labour 293, 297, 299, 303
  transportation 161
  voluntary sector 362
London 14, 26, 175-6, 375, 496
  garrotting panic 188-9, 295,
    445
  police 81-3, 83, 457
Lopes, Sir Massey 90
Luxembourg 434

Macaulay, Lord 345
Machonochie, Captain
  Alexander 65, 182-3, 227-8,
    292
Mackworth, Sir Herbert 287
Madeira 336
Maison de Force (Ghent) 162
malicious damage 144
Malthus 62, 166

Manchester 319
Mansfield, Lord 539
marks system 65, 182-3, 184,
  196, 292
Married Women's Association
  460
Marxism 60, 209, 278-9, 281,
  297, 301-3
  transportation 283, 285
Maudling, Reginald 517-19
Maudsley, Henry 119
Maudsley Hospital 248-9
maximum security prisoners
  488, 489-90, 491
Maxwell, Mr William 310,
  351
May Committee 483
Mayhew, Henry 118-19
medium security prisons 465,
  467
Medway 336
Melossi and Pavarini 60, 278,
  281, 297-8, 302-3
mental health 96, 98-102, 132-3,
  282
  community ideology 247-54,
    256
  distinguishing offenders 106-
    7, 110, 115, 118-27, 130-4,
    141, 146
  human rights 240
  reformative practices 170, 198
merchant seamen 334, 336, 343,
  357
Merry, William 295
Methodism 29, 32
Metropolitan Police 83

629

voluntary sector 373
Radzinowicz Report (1968) 488-
9, 496-7
impressment 331, 333, 344-6,
355
rape 331
rates 80, 89-90, 92, 281
rational recreation 30-1, 32, 33
rationalisation 2, 149-218, 272,
453
prisons 86-7, 89, 91, 94-5, 103
transformations in penal
labour 288-9, 291-4, 299,
302-3, 327
recidivism 58, 195-6, 256, 260,
405, 486
distinguishing offenders 123,
125, 140
rehabilitation 487, 490, 493-7,
504-7, 510
see also habitual offenders;
persistent offenders
reformative practices 58, 60,
149-218, 220, 328, 394-5, 546-7
community ideology 266,
267-8
distinguishing offenders 107,
124-5, 127, 129, 136
forced labour 227
impressment 333, 354, 356
rehabilitation 160, 205, 207,
211-13, 218, 489, 495
rise of State control 100-1
transformations in penal
labour 277, 290-1, 295,
299, 302-6, 310-11, 324, 327
young offenders 125, 129-30

reformatory school 97, 101, 109-
10, 130
rehabilitation 487-510
community ideology 248,
250, 262, 275
declining influence 441, 453,
462, 487-510, 537, 542, 551,
555
forced labour 222, 239
impressment 333, 346,
354
individualisation 101,
104
parole 512
penal crisis 463, 470, 473, 478,
487-510
prisoners of war 248
reformative practices 160,
205, 207, 211-13, 218,
489, 495
transformation in penal
labour 309, 322
reintegration 306, 311, 322, 329,
506
community ideology 256,
258, 263, 265
intermediate treatment 413,
438
release on licence 244, 258, 260,
494
religion 147, 290, 393, 460
1500-1750 8-11, 17-19
1750-1850 29, 31
1850-1970 44, 46
Darwinism 115
human rights 241
Middle Ages 7